EVERY STEP OF THE WAY

The journey to freedom
in South Africa

EVERY STEP OF THE WAY

The journey to freedom
in South Africa

MINISTRY OF EDUCATION

HSRC PRESS

Commissioned and funded by the Ministry of Education

Compiled by the Social Integration and Cohesion Research Programme of the Human Sciences
Research Council

Published by HSRC Press
Private Bag X9182, Cape Town, 8000, South Africa
www.hsrcpublishers.ac.za

ISBN 0 7969 2061 3

Written by Michael Morris
Historical advisor: Professor Bill Nasson
Cover and text design by Jenny Young
Edited by John Linnegar
Photo research by Elsie Joubert
Cover photograph by Benny Gool
Printed by Paarl Printers

Distributed in Africa by Blue Weaver Marketing and Distribution,
PO Box 30370, Tokai, Cape Town, 7966, South Africa.
Tel: +27 +21-701-4477
Fax: +27 +21-701-7302
email: booksales@hsrc.ac.za

Distributed worldwide, except Africa, by Independent Publishers Group,
814 North Franklin Street, Chicago, IL 60610, USA.
www.ipgbook.com
To order, call toll-free: 1-800-888-4741
All other inquiries, Tel: +1 +312-337-0747
Fax: +1 +312-337-5985
email: Frontdesk@ipgbook.com

[contents]

[foreword]

On the tenth anniversary of our transition to democracy, it is appropriate that we give some thought to what South Africa has become. Obviously, after abandoning apartheid and the oppression on which it rested, South Africa is now a free country. The fruits of that freedom may still be rather slow in reaching some of our people, but all the same those fruits are ripening and more and more people are enjoying the flavour of freedom.

As a result of our freedom, South Africa is now a single country in the normal sense of that term. Of course, previous governments did their best to deny our unity, using the policies of apartheid to divide South Africans and distort the growth of a common nationhood. Even today, it might be said, some South African citizens themselves have not yet recognised the historical reality of their present, that they are an interdependent part of a single and increasingly normal country. After all, a sceptical observer could say, given the depth of its historical divisions, that South Africa can hardly be seen as a uniform country or a national unity. South Africa has a burdensome past, huge economic inequalities, continuing racial divisions and sharp gender inequalities. On top of all this, it is faced with the cultural and political consequences of having almost a dozen official languages. Certainly, these factors challenge any simple notion of South Africa being a single, unified country.

Yet we would do well to take stock of what history has to teach us about the creation of states and nations, and where South Africa stands in relation to these other places. All recognised countries, even those with the strongest kind of patriotic nationhood, live with their divisions. Moreover, these divisions are of a familiar kind. Thus, they would include cultural differences – which may in places be defined as racial or ethnic divisions – economic inequalities, gender discrimination, urban and rural disparities, and differing kinds of religion. It is certainly true that these divisions may be more acute in South Africa than they are in some other countries, but they are not peculiarly South African in any way. And the extent to which a democratic South Africa is committed to the removal of the inequalities of the past and to the construction of a more just social order merely confirms that it has become a normal, progressive and forward-looking country.

Nor is this the only reality to consider when contemplating how South Africa has at last matured into a single country. South Africans have a national imagination which encourages them to think that they continue to live in an entirely special or distinctive place, whereas their national experience may actually have things in common with the histories of Europe, the United States of America, Asia, and, by no means least, the rest of Africa.

Other countries have had to forge unity out of diversity. To cite only a few examples: when Italy was united as a country in 1860, there was no shared past, no culture of common patriotism, and no more than about five percent of its people actually spoke Italian; present-day Belgium still consists of two cultural and linguistic halves that are not always all for one and one for all; in the 1960s, which was the great freedom decade for most of colonial Africa, that part of the American population which was black still seemed hardly to be recognised as American at all within the 'national unity' of the United States.

And so it has been on our own continent, too. The achievement of a meaningful nationhood – the common recognition of fellow citizens – has been the product of various struggles, often bitter. Indeed, as we have seen all too tragically in our own time, several states to our north that came to nationhood as single countries have fragmented or almost dissolved, while some who once combined as citizens have become hostile rebels or regional factions in societies that have found themselves no longer able to resolve decisive national issues through negotiation and compromise.

If we accept the historical truth that nations everywhere have to be made through both conflict and compromise, then contemporary South Africa is probably not very different from other single, sovereign states, whether in Africa, Europe, or elsewhere. In Africa, South Africa is a particularly powerful and advanced state, but in some aspects of its historical past, its achievement of a unified nationhood resembles that of many other peoples of the continent.

Imagine an African land with a deep and rich pre-colonial past and a heritage of pre-colonial African customs and practices which continue to influence its present. For many years it was governed and exploited on the basis of white supremacy. Over a long period there were political protests and civil struggles against the injustices and oppression of undemocratic minority rule. Different sorts of people were involved, often disputing among themselves how resistance might be conducted most effectively. Towards the end, a militant minority took up arms and confronted repression with bloody consequences. Inevitably, white minority domination grew too costly to maintain, even though those who opposed it were a long way from actually toppling the state.

When the shooting was effectively over, a new and more inclusive politics started. Politicians of various ideological colours, as well as skin colours, entered a tricky and by no means predictable terrain of negotiations to settle on a new order of freedom and democratic rights for all. Negotiations produced a unitary country with a new political culture rooted in universal rights, committed to the franchise, to the dignity of equal treatment, to freedom from gender discrimination, and other rights. Out of this grew the civilised conditions for shared citizenship in a single yet healthily plural nation, with a great assortment of peoples, communities, customs, cultures, religions, traditions and life chances. Perhaps, more than anything, inclusion was what people most wanted from their new statehood.

When freedom finally came to this land, it did not come altogether quietly and calmly. In fact, its birth was accompanied by considerable public argument over how it should be recognised. In part, this argument was about who had done most to bring about freedom, and who had sacrificed most. At the same time, the argument was about remembrance and forgetting, and reconciliation and forgiving, about whose contribution to freedom was perhaps being unjustly ignored or forgotten, or whose was being exaggerated, or about what the fate should be of those who had gone to the wire in their struggle to prevent the emergence of a new country. And yet another aspect of the argument was about who had gained most from the flowering of freedom, and who, it seemed, was still being left behind, and at what cost, in the country's advance.

This is, self-evidently, not the description of an imaginary country. It is a description of South Africa at the turn of the 20th century. It could also be a fair description of the nation of Kenya, which emerged in the 1960s. There, also, a nation was born out of historical processes of conflict, negotiation and compromise that would later characterise South Africa's transition to freedom. For our purposes, what matters is the historical point: South Africans are like others in the ways in which they have come to the challenge of hammering together a nation. If building a nation has involved robust arguments, principled disputes, the resolution of conflict through compromise, or mediation between the haves and the have-nots, that is how nations all over the world have come to be made.

Nationhood has also always come about when people have faced up squarely to the nature of their past, and to the questions it has raised, even when these have not been easy questions.

Equally, it is present history which moves them forward, always into unknown territory. With the past behind and the future ahead, all of us face futures we can only but imagine, carried by the hope that through the right choices and influence, things will go our way rather than come to get us. As *Every Step of the Way* so rightly concludes, 'looking ahead, collectively as much as privately, we are drawn to what happened in the last decade, the last century, the last millennium. It is part and parcel of what it is to be human, to be conscious, to remember and, ultimately, to be hopeful'.

This book is a vigorous, sweeping historical narrative which shows how South Africa has at last become a single democratic country. Constantly picking out why people in their own time took the actions which they did, in the face of uncertain futures and unforeseen outcomes, it tells the story of the distant past, recent times and the present in a particularly reflective way. Amidst its impressive flow of description, explanation and illustration, *Every Step of the Way* repeatedly reminds us that our histories – there is always more than one – are the product of many wills, many visions, many choices. Futures were not inevitable, whether in 1497, 1837, 1948 or in 1994. Nor were consequences always predictable.

This, then, is a history which does not provide simplistic answers or heroic myths, as if it were a ready guidebook to the saints and sinners through the centuries who have made South Africa. More valuably, *Every Step of the Way* asks its readers to confront the tangled stories, records and other fragments which make up our history, and to be aware that the past is always another country, even if, as the text suggests, it is 'always crowding into the present, making us think like this or like that'. It is also a strikingly humane history, aware of the ease with which hindsight can lead us into harsh judgements of our past. In other words, here is a story which is mindful not only of the price of South Africa's history, with its racial cruelties, economic waste and political deceptions, but also of the implications of a long and lighter history of moral consciousness, of South African people embracing one another's common humanity and choosing the politics of healing.

This humane and humanising sense of history is clear in one of this book's early declarations, that while 'there is no guarantee – humanness being what it is – that we will not ever repeat some of the tragic errors of the past decades and centuries … the triumph of kinder ideas in the long human story of southern Africa does remind us how it is possible to make better choices, today and tomorrow'. This emphasis on the triumph of humanity, rising out of our troubled history, recalls the promise of the great Irish poet Seamus Heaney, who was inspired by Nelson Mandela's release from prison in 1992 to write:

History says, Don't hope
On this side of the grave,
But then, once in a lifetime
The longed-for tidal wave
Of justice can rise up
And hope and history rhyme

Every Step of the Way is part of the larger effort by the Ministry of Education to revitalise the study of history. We have many people to thank. The South African History Project, which has been driving this initiative, under the direction of Dr June Bam, and the Social Cohesion and Integration Research Programme of the Human Sciences Research Council, under the leadership of its executive director, Professor Wilmot James, undertook this book as a collaborative project. We gratefully acknowledge the work of Professor Bill Nasson, one of our most distinguished professors of history, and Michael Morris, one of our most seasoned Press journalists. Morris, in particular, brought his gift of clear exposition to the book, picking out the essential facts in a historical situation and drawing thoughtful conclusions. He writes with zest, in sentences that tingle with life and meaning. And, by no means least, he bites at ideas and issues and worries at them, as a dog does a bone. All of this makes the volume a compelling read. Finally, we thank the members of the Ministerial History and Archaeology Panel for their consultation and HSRC Press for bringing this endeavour to fruition.

Professor Kader Asmal, MP
Minister of Education

[prologue]

Fires

Fires

It was going to be a long night, but the five men sitting around the braai, talking and drinking beer, had the patience for it. If it took the whole night, well, they would just have to sit it out.

So they kept feeding the flames, and drinking, and talking. There was a lot to talk about, though to be honest, we don't know much about what they did talk about. We can imagine, privately, what went through their minds, and which of those thoughts they expressed, and which they kept to themselves.

We know some of the stark facts of this braai in the bush near Komatipoort on the Mozambican border in the winter of 1981.

We know that the five men were policemen. We know that three of them had travelled to this spot from the Eastern Cape that day. We surmise that they were convinced, then, that what they were doing was somehow permitted, or even that it was expected of them, that it was, as they saw it perhaps, their duty.

And we know that when they packed up to go, as the lowveld sky began to pale in the east, they left behind in the burnt-out coals of a second fire the ashes of a young man they had drugged and murdered early on the previous evening. Sizwe Kondile had been kidnapped on the outskirts of the seaside hamlet of Jeffreys Bay, bundled into a car and driven to his end.

The question is, what do we do with these facts in 2004, and in the years to come? The events of the early 1980s seem so far off, and so foreign in a way, that we may be tempted to just leave it all there: yesterday's stuff, of a world that is not ours, that we are not responsible for, and that, ultimately, we cannot change.

But the story of the five men drinking beer under the stars while they fed the fire they hoped would burn their victim to oblivion doesn't ever go away. At the time they thought it would. But, like so many other South African stories, it all came back.

Stories, records, memories, the fractions of history, are like that: demanding, complicated, always crowding into the present, making us think like this or like that. And so, bit by bit, our pasts make us what we are, and how we are to one another.

Things have changed since 1981, but the events of that year, just as much as those of all the years before and since, linger in our histories, histories that are often different, and about which there may never really be agreement.

There is no truth available to produce a single, believable history of – or for – everyone.

But to be conscious of that difficulty, the difficulty of knowing the past that has made us, is to be conscious of the difficulty of fashioning the future we wish or hope to make.

It is probably no guarantee – humanness being what it is – that we will not ever repeat some of the tragic errors of past decades and centuries; but the triumph of kinder ideas in the long human story of southern Africa does remind us how it is possible to make better choices, today and tomorrow.

It is, ultimately, the triumph of memory over forgetting.

———— ❖ ————

Fire runs like a metaphor through southern Africa's centuries. It illuminates events and casts shadows we recognise only too well. The two fires near Komatipoort in 1981, the braai and the fire of intended oblivion, have countless precedents.

The sparks, blazes and cinders have left traces of our predecessors' wants, anger and compassion, their greed, ingenuity and hatred, their courage and love.

Control of fire changed human life.

It began at a distant, imprecise date. At least a thousand centuries ago, and possibly even earlier, human beings learned to control nature's most frightening force. It was revolutionary. Like the wheel, or flight, it changed the way they lived, and how they viewed the world. It lit the dark and it warmed them; it warded off dangerous animals, and it altered their diet. It became essential in making tools and weapons that, in turn, transformed the patterns of living.

We are unable to date the first fire-making with certainty.

> *The evidence for using fire is not as incontrovertible as that of the numerous hearths to be seen in sites dating to the last 100 000 years. At these younger sites, the ability to make fire at will, presumably using fire sticks, is not in doubt. There are archaeological sites that may be as old as half a million years at which evidence for hearths has been claimed, and purposeful fire-making may have antiquity. However, scientists are reluctant to interpret the occurrence of some dispersed million-year-old burnt bones at Swartkrans as more than fire-tending. This would mean getting and keeping alight burning wood from veld fires.*
>
> From *Human Beginnings in South Africa – Uncovering the Secrets of the Stone Age* (1999) by HJ Deacon and Janette Deacon

What is certain, though, is that, as John Reader describes it in *Africa, A Biography of the Continent* (1997), the harnessing of fire was 'a technological development which, perhaps more than any other, opened new worlds of opportunity …'.

In the ages that have since elapsed, societies and individuals have used fire in increasingly sophisticated ways to transform or influence their environment according to their needs. The traces are evident in the life and times of the hunter-gatherers of past millennia, the farmers, colonisers and industrialists of the last few hundred years, and the scientists, military strategists, engineers and even brutish individuals of more recent times. The modifying and transforming use of fire is true of advances in agriculture and refinements in technology and domestic convenience as much as of political repression and revolt or national defence.

The earliest records of European observers reveal evidence of the skilled use of fire among the people they met for first time at the southern tip of Africa. On the day that Portuguese explorer Vasco da Gama first stepped ashore in southern Africa – at Stompneus Bay, on 8 November, 1497 – his anonymous diarist made a note of the people they encountered, and their use of fire in producing weapons. 'In this land the men are swarthy,' he wrote. '… Their arms are staffs of wild olive trees tipped with fire-treated horns' (*Vasco da Gama, The Diary of his Travels through African Waters* (1998) by Eric Axelson).

Some hundred years later, in 1595, a Dutch sailor visiting the Cape noted a dusk routine that was or had been universal to early human communities throughout the world.

> *'We saw most of them make fires under bushes,' Willem Lodewijckz recorded, 'which they did very quickly by twisting one piece of wood against another. Thus they passed the night, and such*

fires we saw every night in various places.'
From *Before Van Riebeeck* (1967) by R Raven-Hart

———— ❖ ————

In human hands, fire is an agent of extremes – of disfigurement and destruction, but also of fusion, refinement and energy.

Through time, it has been at the heart of the comforting routine of daily life, of cooking, of light and warmth, of braais and campfires and feasts. It is a part of rituals, from cremations to festivals of light, the burning of incense and the lighting of candles to celebrate and memorialise people and past events and mark turning points in national life.

In today's world of light bulbs and electric geysers, fire remains the only source of heat and light for people living, not necessarily by choice, in an 'older', harder world.

The domestic hearth represents fire at its most basic and comforting, the nucleus of the home, and of the homely routines of cooking and gathering around the light and warmth it provides. It is captured with striking simplicity by Nelson Mandela's affectionate memory of his rural childhood in Transkei, when he recalls that '[m]y mother cooked food in a three-legged iron pot over an open fire in the centre of the hut or outside' (*Long Walk to Freedom* (1994)).

———— ❖ ————

As society changed in the emerging South Africa, African women especially found themselves cast increasingly in a role of service to households that were not their own, cooking and cleaning and, before electricity, tending the hearth fire.

Equally, with quickening population growth and shifts in settlement, the energy needs of domestic fires, for feeding and warming households, had sometimes devastating consequences for the countryside and, often, for those who occupied it.

This was starkly true after the discovery of diamonds in the Northern Cape in the late 1860s, which drew thousands upon thousands of new settlers to a stretch of veld that could not in itself sustain such a large population.

> *It is difficult to tell how many hundred head of oxen are here inspanned into wagons used solely for drawing wood for the cooks and housekeepers of the New Rush. A person visiting this country for the first time would ask where it comes from, for there are not ten trees of ten feet high to be seen all along the road leading to this camp for miles and miles, travel which way you will; and yet morning after morning long trains of wagons come loaded to market, for there are customers more than sufficient for every branch of firewood that comes to the market-master.*
>
> From *The Diamond-Field Keepsake* (1873) by Richard William Murray

The industrial capitalism that evolved after the discovery of precious gems and ore in the last quarter of the 19th century brought with it telling refinements in the technologies of combustion. Yet, well before European industrialism made itself felt, Africans were familiar with the transforming qualities of heat.

When he visited the Tlhaping capital of Dithakong in 1812, explorer William Burchell was fascinated by the ingenuity of a blacksmith, or *moturi*, and the technology he employed to forge iron into tools or weapons.

> *By taking a bag [bellows made from goat skins] in each hand, and continuing this action of raising and depressing them alternately, a strong and constant stream of wind was produced, which presently raised a very small fire to a degree of heat equal to rendering a hatchet red-hot in two minutes.*
>
> From *Travels in the interior of Southern Africa* (facsimile, 1967) by William John Burchell

Much later, the national wealth of the country was determined by the successful extraction of gold, the smelting of which was, in principle, well understood by that Dithakong *moturi.*

> *[The Rand Refinery in Germiston] is easily the largest gold refinery in the world.*
> *Nevertheless, the visitor is struck by the smallness of the building and the matter of fact way in which the glorious, golden stream of molten metal is poured from the crucibles almost as though it were soup.*
> From *The Gold Miners* (1962) by AP Cartwright

———— ❖ ————

But the metaphor of flame is harsher, too.

In South Africa's history of flashpoints, the fire-making of past wars has shaped the borders and the politics in which we live today.

In recent times, our memories are shaded by smoke – or images of it, in photographs and television footage – billowing from scorched fields or burning farms, darkly obscuring barricades of burning tyres or hovering noxiously over a bomb's devastation.

Hundreds of years ago, the sight of smoke rising from a hill top in the clear morning air was immediately recognisable: it meant people were living there. For many of us, these are ancestors, the hill-top dwellers, but also the outsiders looking on, scheming intruders or apprehensive newcomers. Smoke is a fleeting vestige, but the leftovers of fire itself are more lasting – tempered steel, blackened rocks, charred wood, refined gold, memories of intimacy, memories of pain, scars, wealth, industry, monuments, ash.

———— ❖ ————

Fire is a ready companion to human combat, to hatred and anger, desperation and revenge, and to acts of war that some regard as bravery, others as brutality.

> In November 1900, Captain March Phillipps of the Rimington Rifles described the burning of Boer farms in the Free State during the South African War with the perhaps unconsciously callous tone one might expect from someone who believed it was the right thing to do.
>
> *We usually burn from six to a dozen farms a day; those being about all that in this sparsely inhabited country we encounter. I do not gather that any special reason or cause is alleged or proved against the farms burnt. Anyway, we find that one reason or another generally covers pretty nearly every farm we come to, and so to save trouble we burn the lot without inquiry.*
>
> From *Methods of Barbarism?* (2001) by SB Spies

Thirty years later, during the Second World War, a former delivery man from Springs was awarded the

Military Medal for setting off an explosion that was taken as an act of selfless valour.

Job Maseko had volunteered to serve with the 2nd South African Division in North Africa, and was one of 1 200 members of the Native Military Corps among the 10 722 South Africans who became prisoners-of-war at the surrender of Tobruk on 21 June, 1942. The citation that accompanied his medal describes his feat:

The King has been graciously pleased to approve the following award in recognition of gallant and distinguished service in the Middle East: MILITARY MEDAL, No N 4448 L/Cpl Job Masego [sic] – Native Military Corps. For meritorious and courageous action in that on or about the 21st July [1942], while a Prisoner of War, he, Job Masego, sank a fully laden enemy steamer – probably an 'F' boat – while moored in Tobruk Harbour. This he did by placing a small tin filled with gunpowder in among drums of petrol in the hold, leading a fuse from there to the hatch and lighting the fuse upon closing the hatch. In carrying out this deliberately planned action, Job Masego displayed ingenuity, determination and complete disregard of personal safety from punishment by the enemy or from the ensuing explosion which set the vessel alight.

From the *Military History Journal* of the South African Military History Society Vol 10 No 1 (June, 1995) by JS Mohlamme

Job Maseko's pluck and resourcefulness was, in one sense, ironic: he, like all Native volunteers, was not permitted to carry arms, and his part in the Allies' avowed war of freedom from fascism was not matched by liberation for his people at home. Though he was remembered by the community of KwaThema near Springs when it named a primary school and a road after him, it was only in 1997 that this unassuming hero was given national recognition when the SA Navy strike craft SAS *Kobie Coetsee* was renamed SAS *Job Masego*.

——— ❖ ———

While the repression of black South Africans became increasingly inflammatory in the ensuing decades, the collective yearning to freedom could not be extinguished.

This was powerfully demonstrated by the protest campaigns of the Fifties and Sixties which included the symbolic burning of pass books – tokens of a deeply resented system of racist authority.

Brian Lapping records how, in March 1960, African National Congress (ANC) leader Albert Luthuli himself was 'sentenced to a year's imprisonment or a £100 fine … after he had publicly burned his pass book as an act of sympathy with those killed at Sharpeville and Langa'. The fine was paid by friends (*Apartheid, A History* (1986)).

In the mid-1970s, the spirit of revolt burned more fiercely.

Phydian Matsepe recalled Soweto aflame on Wednesday, 16 June, 1976.

In Orlando the municipal office was burnt down. In Orlando East the rent office was burnt down. At the first office there was a fruit market which also fell under the municipality, it was also burnt down. I remember there were also shops that were burnt down because the owners refused to give us paraffin when we asked for it. We used paraffin to burn down these government buildings.

From *Recollected 25 years later: Soweto 16 June 1976* (2001) by Elsabé Brink, Gandhi Malungane, Steve Lebelo, Dumisani Ntshangase and Sue Krige

Greater sophistication in planning attacks and deploying operatives marked Umkhonto we'Sizwe (MK) operations in the Eighties.

Guerrilla David Motshwane Moisi played a leading role in the attack on the Sasol 2 plant at Secunda on 31 May – Republic Day – 1981 which resulted in a huge blaze. He noted that MK had also planned an attack on the Caltex oil refinery in Cape Town 'so that ANC leaders imprisoned on Robben Island could see the flames'. Moisi was arrested after entering South Africa on a reconnaissance trip to the refinery. He was convicted and sentenced to death for treason, but his sentence was later commuted and he was released in 1991 in terms of the Pretoria Minute.

> The timing of the Secunda attack was deliber-ately symbolic, as David Moisi explained:
>
> *We could have attacked the target much earlier but Republic Day was decided on because the old regime normally displayed their military might and we decided to send a clear message to the masses that the racist regime was not invincible.*
>
> From a South African Press Association report 12 May, 1998

It was not long after the attack on the Sasol plant that Sizwe Kondile was detained, murdered and burned to ash. This atrocity was described to the Truth and Reconciliation Commission in 1996 by former policeman Dirk Coetzee:

> *The four junior officers ... each grabbed a hand and a foot, put it on to the pyre of tyres and wood, poured petrol on it and set it alight. Now ... the burning of a body to ashes takes about seven hours, and whilst that happened we were drinking and even having a braai next to the fire. Now, I don't say that to show our braveness, I just tell it to the Commission to show our callousness and to what extremes we have gone to in those days ... the chunks of meat and especially the buttocks and the upper part of the legs had to be turned frequently during the night to make sure that everything burned to ashes. And the next morning, after raking through the rubble to make sure there were no pieces of meat or bone left at all, we departed and all went on our own way.*
>
> From *Truth and Lies* (2001) by Jillian Edelstein

Many South Africans claimed they were unaware of the truer nature of apartheid repression, and without doubt much of the horrific detail of actions taken – in the 1980s especially – was deviously concealed. For most black South Africans, however, the repression was a raw, daily experience, and there was no mistaking it for anything less than systematic brutality. It was a reality that bred seething anger and spurred communities and individuals to harsh measures and excesses.

> A sense of the rage that gave potency to the 'necklace' is evident in this controversial passage from a speech by Winnie Mandela on 13 April, 1986 at a rally at Munsieville:
>
> *We have no guns – we have only stones, boxes of matches, and petrol. Together, hand in hand, with our boxes of matches and our necklaces we shall liberate this country.*
>
> From *The Lady, The Life and Times of Winnie Mandela* (1993) by Emma Gilbey

❖

Within less than a decade, the political trajectory of South Africa was utterly different. Hopelessness and fury had given way to optimism and a conviction that reconciliation was both desirable and possible. Yet the embers of racial animosity, fear and dissent still smouldered here and there. And so, just as millions of people prepared to vote for the first time in the country's inaugural democratic elections, disaffected right-wing elements detonated a series of bombs they evidently hoped would undermine, or at least delay, the historic poll.

One of the blasts was in central Johannesburg on 24 April, 1994. Nine people were killed and 92 injured. The target appeared to be Shell House, later renamed Luthuli House. It was the headquarters of the ANC, which, within days, formed the new government.

> Glass carpeted the street. The explosion had punctured the tarmac, hurled a car through the burglar bars of a shop, and shattered windows right the way up Shell House tower.
>
> From a *Cape Argus* news report 25 April, 1994

The chilling practice of 'necklacing' – ramming a tyre over the head and shoulders of a victim, filling it with petrol and setting it alight – became a common method of killing people accused or suspected of being police informers or collaborators.

The 'necklace' became a powerful political tool, and a gut-wrenching image.

The elections were neither delayed nor undermined. And with the socio-political enlightenment that followed the first steps to democracy in 1994 the metaphor of flame and fire assumed connotations of affirmation and celebration.

At the adoption of the new Constitution on 8 May, 1996, Deputy President Thabo Mbeki used the analogy of fire, or its consequences, to convey the idea of renewal:

This thing that we have done today, in this small corner of a great continent that has contributed so decisively to the evolution of humanity says that Africa reaffirms that she is continuing her rise from the ashes.

It was flame as a symbol of hope and conviction that was at the centre of the lighting of a symbolic candle by Nelson Mandela in his former Robben Island cell on 1 January, 2000. On that occasion he addressed his successor, Thabo Mbeki, with the following words:

Mr President, I hand over the flame of freedom to you. You are the only person in this country who should receive this flame and keep it burning and pass it to younger generations.

Control of fire, its multiplicity of forms and associations suggests, has brought out the best and the worst in us over the centuries. It is one thing to affirm the good things, but what of the bad?

South Africa, it is sometimes said, is a country that has much to forget and little to gain from dwelling on its past. Yet it is, perhaps, to illuminate the future that we are drawn to the vivid lights of history.

To test how much heat it takes to harden an arrow point is to explore an ancient technology that, however remotely, helped to shape South African life.

Then again, to ask how much fire – and for how long – to burn a fellow human being to ash is a terrible, unavoidable question of our own time. We cannot afford to flinch from it. If we did, we'd be turning back to the dark.

[chapter one]

First
steps

First steps

How had it come to this, //Kabbo might have wondered as the train rattled and hissed through the night, drawing him and his companions further and further away from all they knew?

Gradually, the dim landscape altered. The air cooled, mountains blacked out whole clusters of familiar stars. There were new smells.

By dawn it was the foreign scent of the sea that struck them, and the piercing gulls' calls, the metallic clanking and screeching of steel and whistles, and the racket of voices, of inquisitive men, all in hats. At the harbour, a strange forest of ships' masts and, here and there, smoke rising into the sky from hidden fires.

How could one survive this, this civilisation?

So it is that //Kabbo may have wondered about his fate. The clanking of steel, of chains, of forbidding prison gates, is one part of the story of //Kabbo the /Xam prisoner, arrested in the Vanwyksvlei district in 1870 for stealing sheep to feed his family and sent to jail at the Breakwater

Prison (now at the centre of Cape Town's popular Waterfront).

But the other story, the other stories, of prisoner 4628 and his companions are those that reach far back and far forward from the moment they were written down by two remarkable people.

Whatever their faults – and they have been judged harshly since, in some quarters – German philologist Wilhelm Bleek and his sister-in-law Lucy Lloyd took enough of an interest in the culture of South Africa's indigenous people to sit down with these prisoners, learn their language and listen to, and record, what they had to say.

They left a vast 12 000-page collection of /Xam San beliefs and histories that has been central to understanding the San worldview.

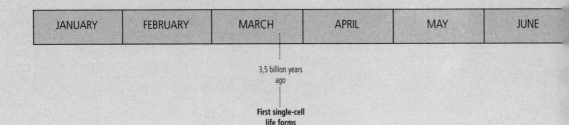

| JANUARY | FEBRUARY | MARCH | APRIL | MAY | JUNE |

3,5 billion years ago

First single-cell life forms

Compressed into a single year, from the first second of January to the last second of December, the emergence of life in the 4,6 billion year history of planet Earth can be seen at a glance as a calendar of highlights. It is deceptive, as all simplifications are, but useful for simplifying an immense complexity.

It is only in late March (3,5 billion years ago) that the first single-cell bacteria-like life forms appear. While nowhere near as complex as a flea, these forms are the building blocks of every living thing

that will eventually grow on Earth, from germs, algae, shrimps and bees to whales, trees, eagles, elephants and human beings.

It is not until the second week of August (1,8 billion years ago) that cells with a nucleus emerge, and mid-November (600 million years ago) before the first multi-celled organisms appear. Within the next 300 million years, the first animals with backbones appear, and the first fish, land plants, insects, amphibians and reptiles.

By special arrangement, //Kabbo or 'Dream' – also known as Oud Jantje Tooren – and a number of other informants from the prison actually spent long periods – up to two years and more – living at the Bleeks' home in Mowbray.

Of course, we don't know much about what went through //Kabbo's mind or what he noticed and what he missed in the urban landscape of Cape Town from his arrival at the end of 1870 or early in 1871 until he left for home towards the end of 1873.

It's a token of loss that there is much that we do not know of this /Xam man's thinking.

But he was – then, and now – an extraordinary link, through Bleek and Lloyd, between the modern world of steam trains and linguists, books and photographs, and the ancient universe of human beginnings in Africa.

There is a movingly fatalistic, but also prophetic, quality to much of the belief and history that //Kabbo and his companions revealed in the late 1800s. This is perhaps especially true of //Kabbo's poetic conception of heritage and memory, and of the human presence in the landscape.

'I feel that a story is the wind,' he told Bleek and Lloyd, 'the story is wont to float along to people in another place. Then our names, passing behind the mountain's back, pass through those people, while we ourselves are invisible to them.'

Where did //Kabbo's journey to jail really begin?

//Kabbo

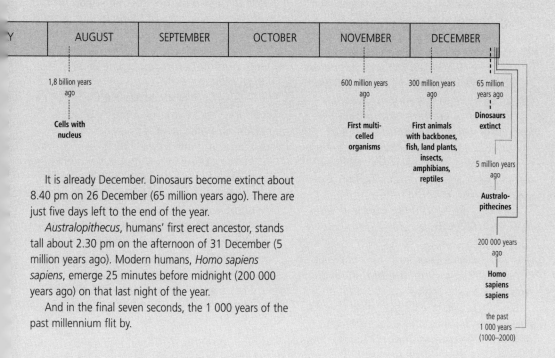

Y	AUGUST	SEPTEMBER	OCTOBER	NOVEMBER	DECEMBER

1,8 billion years ago

Cells with nucleus

600 million years ago

First multi-celled organisms

300 million years ago

First animals with backbones, fish, land plants, insects, amphibians, reptiles

65 million years ago

Dinosaurs extinct

5 million years ago

Australo-pithecines

200 000 years ago

Homo sapiens sapiens

the past
1 000 years
(1000–2000)

It is already December. Dinosaurs become extinct about 8.40 pm on 26 December (65 million years ago). There are just five days left to the end of the year.

Australopithecus, humans' first erect ancestor, stands tall about 2.30 pm on the afternoon of 31 December (5 million years ago). Modern humans, *Homo sapiens sapiens*, emerge 25 minutes before midnight (200 000 years ago) on that last night of the year.

And in the final seven seconds, the 1 000 years of the past millennium flit by.

———— ❖ ————

By many routes, South Africans have come a long way. It is such a great distance that it is often hard to make out the paths they have followed.

//Kabbo's unchosen journey from the Karoo to Cape Town in 1870 – even where it links Africa's antiquity with its emerging modernity – represents a mere few paces of the longer travels of humanity.

The terrain is so old, and the span of time so great, that it's difficult to grasp the scale of the human journeys that converge in the present. But if the long history of life and landscape is scaled down to a manageable dimension, a clearer picture emerges (see the timeline on pages 10 and 11).

The last thousand years is the millennium that most people believe best defines who they are. At first glance, it is the period in which everything that is the essence of the modern world occurred, was invented, was discovered, was made.

It's an extraordinary range of achievement encompassing ships, trains, cars, aeroplanes, printing and photography, electricity and telephones, nuclear power, many of the national boundaries and the contemporary institutions of state, much of the law, most of the conventions of dress and fashion, the modern forms of speech and writing, most of the musical instruments as they are known today and most of the music that's played on them, the bulk of what might be considered the great architecture of the world, most of the art that is most admired, most of the science that explains or suggests how the world works, and almost all medicine on which people depend when they are ill or injured.

Yet the sum of earthly existence and what it means to be human is not reducible to a list of modern accomplishments and conveniences. It goes beyond cellphones and books, nylon, microchips, space travel, hamburgers, organ transplants and cooldrink in tins.

Before the year 1000, before the age of exploration when Europeans made the journeys that are often mistaken as voyages of 'discovery', there were ships and seafaring elsewhere. In Europe, as much as on other continents, music, language, art, architecture, politics and engineering flourished.

But even before these things – before pyramids, Chinese science, African mythology, Indian art, Arabian mathematics and Greek philosophy – the

recognisable impulses of human beings can be traced much further back.

In various ways, today's objects, ideas and ways of doing things all have early origins in an almost entirely unrecorded past that often seems mysterious and is largely hidden from view. People have changed, and adapted to a changing environment. The more sophisticated the study of the long history of the world becomes, the clearer it is that the essentials – surviving, moving from place to place, expressing beliefs and emotion, thinking, keeping in touch with others, and being part of the community of people – stem from the gradual development of humanity over millions of years. And it's in Africa, all the evidence suggests, that modern humans first emerged.

It is, of course, misleading to think of humanity's 'first steps' as if it were an event, a date on a calendar.

In the limited span of our own lives, memorable dates and their anniversaries are appealing, and important. This book itself marks a memorable date, the anniversary of the first democratic elections in South Africa on 27 April, 1994. With the benefit of detailed records, it is possible, for example, to identify and attach dates to the first slave ship to arrive in the Cape, or the first heart transplant, and the first sitting of South Africa's Constitutional Court.

But it becomes more difficult to pinpoint the origin and development of the ideas without which these events could not have happened. By their nature, they developed over time. The use of slaves had ancient precedents, much refined by the late 1600s when the Dutch adopted slave labour at their African outpost.

Chris Barnard's heart transplant at Groote Schuur hospital in Cape Town in 1967 was a culmination of medical research as much as a new departure. And who could point with any certainty to the moment at which the gathering force of constitutionalism in South Africa was born? So it is false to think that there really was a moment in the past when a being we would recognise as human stood up and took her first steps. There was no such stark and simple event. It would be deceiving to reduce the complexity of the emergence of human beings to a few key events and highlighted dates.

What, then, is known, and how has it been established?

———— ❖ ————

Fragments of glass, shredded plastic, twists of paper and buckled tins, used teabags, cigarette butts, orange peel and egg shells, used batteries, fish bones, mouldy bread crusts and beer bottles, out-of-date telephone directories … the possible contents of a modern rubbish dump seem inexhaustible.

People produce a lot of rubbish. Paul Harrison writes in *The Third Revolution: Population, Environment and a Sustainable World* (1992) that in an average lifetime a typical Third World city dweller will generate 149 times his body weight in municipal and industrial waste. The figure for a typical European is 971 times his body weight, and the average American will leave a vast mound 3 900 times his own weight. Waste leaves a telling trace: the rubbish tips of towns and cities provide rich evidence about the people who live in them, and how they live. Analyse it carefully and the refuse will reveal clues to everything from computer technology, satellite communication and fast foods to fashion trends, wealth and Aids.

It might not seem necessary to pick through the contents of the bin, since there is such an extensive written and pictorial record of modern life in books, magazines, letters, on CD-ROM, in movies, on DVD and in television archives. We can even look at our world in high-resolution pictures taken from space. These things would make it easier for the contemporary world to be understood by a stranger to it.

But if there were no deliberate record, in libraries, film archives or databases, and there were just the accidental, unintended record of ruins, leftovers and discarded waste – and the skeletal and other remains of people themselves, in graveyards and elsewhere – that would be where the archaeologists, palaeoanthropologists and genetic scientists of the future would examine modern society and attempt to make sense of it.

The science of leftovers has yielded immense knowledge.

'When true humans appeared on the earth,' archaeologist Hilary Deacon writes, 'they left a trail of artefacts for archaeologists to follow. It is through the study of artefacts and their context that peoples of the past live again.'

This trail of artefacts and their contexts – where they are found and what is found with them – is especially rich in southern Africa, but it has taken decades of methodical research to order and assign meaning to the evidence.

The evidence is a revealing assemblage.

There are masses of stone tools of various sizes, chipped into neat shapes, some vaguely resembling ancient, fossilised teeth. There are engravings on rocks, 'pictures' or patterns chipped into the faces of exposed boulders. There are paintings, mostly in caves, of human and animal forms, and of mythical or spiritual figures. There are bones, skulls, fragments of jaws, femurs so old they have turned to rock, bones shaped and turned into tools. There are fragments of shell, wood, plant fibre, animal skin, and evidence of fire – ash, burnt bones and charred wood.

On their own, individual items of this body of

Stone artefacts are telling traces of the technology of the early inhabitants of southern Africa.

evidence probably have limited meaning. But through careful study of the objects in the context of where they are found, geographically, but also at what levels or strata in the ground, and what is found with them, a deepening understanding of the past and the people of the past emerges.

It is in this way, at its simplest, that answers have been and are being sought to some of the most significant questions about southern Africa's – humanity's – past: For how long have people been living here? Who were they? How did they survive? What did they know?

——— ❖ ———

People, human beings, have evolved over millennia.

The emergence of the modern human being, *Homo sapiens sapiens*, about 200 000 years ago, followed a succession of biological developments going back to the first single-cell bacteria-like organisms that appeared a little more than one billion years after the Earth's formation. These simple life forms carried the makings of all living things.

The idea of a common ancestry from the very distant past is supported by the fact that the same 20 amino acids are the building blocks of the proteins found in the cells of bacteria, mice and humans.

Central to understanding this process – and to the biological sciences generally, the development of other animals and plants – is the theory of evolution by natural selection advanced by Charles Darwin in his book *On the Origin of Species*, published in 1859.

Darwin sought to explain how simpler life forms changed or evolved into more complex ones. His concept of 'natural selection' suggested that in nature those individuals best suited to the total environment would survive and produce the most offspring at the expense of the less fit.

In the nearly 150 years since Darwin's book was published, his theory has been constantly updated as new evidence of how life has changed and evolved has become available.

——— ❖ ———

Human evolution was not the straightforward progression suggested by this classic illustration, yet bipedalism – the change to walking on two feet – was a vital step.

Greater understanding of the shared biological roots of the human species has been gained through more recent refinements in the study of genes.

Because our genetic imprints are transmitted to succeeding generations through the nuclear DNA of both parents and the mitochondrial DNA of mothers, the modern human genome contains an indelible record of our evolutionary past.

Dr Himla Soodyall, director of the Medical Research Council/National Health Laboratory Service/University of the Witwatersrand Human Genomic Diversity and Disease Research Unit

Even so, scientists point out that genetic research does not replace the investigation of other evidence:

More and more, our understanding of human evolution – and particularly modern human origins – has been influenced by genetic data, in addition to, and in the minds of some researchers, in place of, paleoanthropological data. Genetic data is not more accurate or meaningful than fossil data, or vice versa. Both are just tools for understanding human evolution. Importantly ... paleontological data can uniquely provide information on evolutionary process, on the tempo and mode of evolution. Paleontological data also has one obvious advantage over molecular data: more than 85% of mammalian genera – no doubt including many, if not most, human ancestors – are extinct, and are studied from fossils in which bones and teeth – and not genes – are the only structures left.

Dr Becky Rogers Ackermann of the Department of Archaeology at the University of Cape Town

New knowledge has been central to thinking differently about what it is to be human.

Genetics means that now, at last, perceptions of human quality need not depend on what is on the surface. For the first time, it is possible to form an impartial view of just how different races might be. The answer is clear. The biological differences among them are small and the evidence for the mental superiority of one or the other so flimsy, confused and full of intellectual dishonesty as to be scarcely worth considering.

From *In the Blood: God, Genes and Destiny* (1996) by Steve Jones

Difference, genetically, between continents and races – which correspond – are really a small part of human variation because they are very recent and are adaptations to local climate, and thus also to local flora and fauna, or diet. It is ridiculous that we are racist because we are merely different for having adapted to different climates.

Dr Luca Cavalli-Sforza, Stanford University

After losing their hair as an adaptation to keeping cool, early hominids gained pigmented skins. Scientists initially thought that such pigmentation arose to protect against skin-cancer-causing ultraviolet radiation. ... An alternative theory suggests that dark skin might have evolved primarily to protect against the breakdown of folate, a nutrient essential for fertility [and the development of the foetus in pregnant women]. Skin that is too dark blocks the sunlight necessary for [producing] vitamin D, which is crucial for maternal and foetal bones. Accordingly, humans have evolved to be light enough to make sufficient vitamin D yet dark enough to protect their stores of folate. As a result of more recent human migrations, many people now live in areas that receive more – or less – ultraviolet radiation than is appropriate for their skin colour.

Nina G Jablonski and George Chaplin, *Scientific American* (October 2002)

[In the debate about] the most fundamental value: what it means to be human ... [there is on the one side] the view that we have become what we are because our technological capacities made us the most successful killers in the animal kingdom. On the other, there is the argument that we evolved so successfully because of our unique capacity to care and to share.

Historian Professor Jeff Guy, University of KwaZulu-Natal, Pietermaritzburg

Chimpanzees, gorillas and humans have a common African ancestor.

the freeing of the arms for carrying infants or food, and the freeing of the hands for using objects and eventually making and using tools.

From one of the various lineages of australopithecines – which became extinct about 1,4 million years ago – there emerged in Africa the first ancestors of the genus *Homo*, about 2,5 million years ago.

The essence of human evolution is ever-increasing control over the environment, and evidence suggests that environmental challenges of various kinds prompted or made evolutionary changes necessary. The genus *Homo* may have emerged as a result of a global cooling and drying trend, which turned woodlands into more open savannas over much of Africa after about 2,8 million years ago. This harsher African environment, it is argued, created challenges that spurred evolutionary refinements.

Skills steadily increased, enabling humans to survive better in open veld they shared with fierce meat-eating mammals, to hunt and gather food, to make shelter, to care for their young, and ultimately to make better sense of their world, and to express it.

❖

If modern humans – *Homo sapiens sapiens* – emerged 200 000 years ago, what came before?

A turning point for eventual human development was the mass extinction of dinosaurs 65 million years ago. Mammals flourished after the dinosaurs disappeared. And one consequence of the steady diversification or evolution of mammals was the emergence of humans over tens of millions of years.

About 30 million years ago, humans and monkeys shared a common ancestor, and possibly as recently as six million years ago, chimpanzees and humans shared a common ancestor. Humankind's first erect or bipedal ancestors – the first to stand on two feet – were the australopithecines, which emerged between four and five million years ago.

Social creatures with small brains, long arms and short legs, they still lived partly in the trees, like the apes, and lived mainly off plant foods such as berries and bulbs.

Bipedalism was a vital step that led to significant evolutionary changes such as increased brain size and stature (tallness), hair loss,

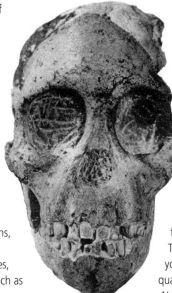

The Taung child.

It was once thought that modern human beings evolved in Europe and spread around the world from there. This was partly because of the 'discovery' of the so-called Piltdown Man in southern England in 1912. This fossilised, fragmentary skull was long believed to represent the oldest human species. In 1953, however, it was found to be a hoax: the skull had human cranial bones, but the jaw of an orang-utan.

An altogether different – genuine, and also far-reaching – find was made in South Africa in 1924. This was the Taung skull, the skull of a young hominid, found in a limestone quarry near the town of Taung in the Northern Cape. It was given the name *Australopithecus africanus* by anatomy professor Raymond Dart.

When Dart published a paper on his find in 1925,

it did not stir much interest, partly because the features of the Taung skull were contradicted by the Piltdown Man fossil which, at that time, was still regarded as marking the beginning of humankind. But in time the Taung skull came to be seen as probably the most important hominid fossil find because it set the direction of the study of human origins that is still being followed.

Later excavations at Klasies River near Plettenberg Bay and various other sites became the basis for claims that modern humans were living in southern Africa (between 90 000 and 120 000 years ago) at a time when Neanderthals, an older, less advanced strain of humankind, were living in Europe.

Advances in genetic science offer the prospect of a more refined view of how modern humans evolved and moved about the globe. Genetic scientist Dr Himla Soodyall notes:

> By examining the DNA in living people, we have been able to trace the origin of our species to between 100 000 and 150 000 years ago.
>
> Moreover, our genetic studies have shown that living Khoe-San (indigenous South African) populations have retained some of the ancestral DNA signatures found in modern humans, making southern Africa the most likely region for the origin of Homo sapiens sapiens.

The origin of the species of *Homo* and how they spread throughout the world are among the preoccupations of archaeologists, palaeontologists and others, and, as new finds are made, so the dates and other details of key developments change, too.

Evidence suggests there could have been three main migrations out of Africa between about 1,9 million years ago and 70 000 years ago. In earlier dispersals, older forms of humans spread out of Africa into Europe and to the Far East. The emergence in Africa of *Homo sapiens* (which means 'wise man') – the only surviving hominid species to which all living people belong – was the precursor to more recent population movements.

The predominant theory points to an all-important dispersal from Africa after about 70 000 years ago.

The initial spread was eastwards, where dating shows that they crossed about 50 kilometres of sea to reach previously uninhabited Australia by 50 000 years ago. Another movement of early modern people entered western Europe after 42 000 years

ago to replace the indigenous Neanderthals, who continued to live in remote regions there for another 10 000 years.

———— ❖ ————

From the emergence of *Homo sapiens* up to 2 000 centuries ago, the skills, behaviour and patterns of living that define what it is to be human occurred in part under the pressure of environmental influences on people, and their need to influence, as far as they could, the environment in which they lived.

Over time, the quest for food, the most basic human activity, shaped economic, social and political patterns, as well as culture and religion.

And it is the stone tools used for hunting and foraging, the left-over bones and plant fibre, and the evidence of fire, that are vital clues to where and how people lived.

Early humans became reliant on stone artefacts for getting and processing food to an extent not approached by the australopithecines. And since stone artefacts are virtually indestructible, they are the most important means of tracking early human activities. Stone tools were easy to make and were as quickly discarded, and so, as artefacts, left a trail of sites across the landscape.

Archaeologist Garth Sampson notes that the

> South African central plateau is unique in the world … in that it supported large numbers of non-farming people who were also prolific makers of stone tools until very recent times. A brief comparison of surveys conducted elsewhere in the world reveals promptly and unambiguously that South Africa is richer in Stone Age remains than any other place on earth.
> Seekoei Valley survey (1985)

In Later Stone Age times (from about 22 000 years ago until the Iron Age, about 2 000 years ago) – and particularly in the last 10 000 years in southern Africa – more sophisticated tool-making, including, for instance, bows and arrows, fishing equipment, better ways of gathering and containing food and processing it, enabled more diversified hunting and gathering.

But there is more to being human than just finding the next meal.

With technological developments throughout the

Stone Age came changes in social relations that brought greater complexity to what it meant to be human – in language and thinking, belief and art. Well before the earliest written records, dating to about 5 300 years ago, the use of symbols to express thought, to communicate ideas, was a telling step in the development of modern behaviour.

The arched cranial base of the Kabwe (Homo heidelbergensis) skull suggests this ancestor was capable of fully modern speech.

❖

The ability to share meaning was linked to the development of language. However, speech requires not merely mental ability but having the right physical 'equipment' – a suitable voice box, an arched skull base and a pharynx long enough to produce the range of sounds needed for language. In typical mammals the voice box is high in the neck and the base of the skull is flat, resulting in a short pharynx that can only produce a rather limited range of sounds. Research suggests that a fully modern vocal tract first arose in Africa about one million years ago. The *Homo heidelbergensis* skull from Kabwe in Zambia, for instance, has an arched cranial base, suggesting that this ancestor was capable of fully modern speech. In modern human adults, the voice box is further down the neck and the skull base is arched, resulting in a longer pharynx that can produce the much wider range of sounds needed for language.

On 21 July, 1969, the American astronaut Neil Armstrong became the first human to step onto the surface of the moon at 10.56 pm Eastern Daylight Time. His first words were: 'That's one small step for a man, one giant leap for mankind.' He reported sinking approximately one-eighth of an inch into the fine powdery surface material, which adhered to his lunar boots in a thin layer.

These dramatic events were being followed round the globe by millions of people who formed the biggest collective news audience of any single event in history. Among them was a man in a cave in southern Africa.

He was German research archaeologist Erich Wendt, then excavating a cave in southern Namibia. Fittingly, he named the site Apollo 11 to mark the momentous step in human history being played out in space as he worked his way through ancient deposits.

Wendt's work, it emerged well after the astronauts returned to planet Earth, was a historic milestone, too: seven painted stones extracted from the deposits at Apollo 11 over four years were found in a layer dating to 27 500 years ago. Until then, it had been considered inconceivable that the southern African rock art tradition was that old.

Here, you could say, was a leap for mankind, too.

More recently, another cave – in a cliff overlooking the Indian Ocean at Blombos near Stilbaai on the southern Cape coast – yielded dramatic evidence about early human development, eclipsing Wendt's finds. Over a period of two years, from 1999 to 2002, archaeologists Christopher Henshilwood and Royden Yates discovered abstract representations engraved on pieces of red ochre, and a large set of specialised bone tools, dating from about 77 000 years ago. These were remarkable finds.

Attention focused in particular on two pieces of ochre found in the Middle Stone Age layer of the cave. Both were engraved with complex and apparently symbolic cross-hatched and horizontal lines, indicating what Henshilwood described as 'a deliberate sequence of choices'.

The finds demonstrated, Henshilwood said, 'that ochre use in the Middle Stone Age was not exclusively utilitarian and, arguably, the transmission and sharing of the meaning of the engravings relied on fully syntactical [ordered, grammatical] language'.

A revolutionary change in human society occurred with the shift from hunting and gathering to food production – farming. But it did not occur universally, or at once.

With a change of climate between 10 000 and 15 000 years ago, people were forced to live near permanent water sources in some areas. Wild plants and animals, also under climatic stress, were exploited more intensively, and, through increasing control, domestication of some plant and animal species began to take place.

In Africa this began about 7 000 years ago. Plants such as yam, sorghum and millet were domesticated in Africa, while wheat – and various animal species, including cattle and sheep – were introduced from outside the continent.

Farmers with domesticated animals and crops migrated southwards from East Africa more than 2 000 years ago.

A pastoralist lifestyle based on the herding of sheep and cattle arose among ancestors of the Khoekhoe. Traces of sheep farming, from a period a little earlier than 2 000 years ago, have been found at a site at Spoeg River on the Namaqualand coast, with numerous later sites known from the western half of South Africa. Practising a stone tool-making technology, the early herders also made pots and used metal items.

Mixed farming with crops such as sorghum and millet and animals including sheep, goats and cattle, spread southwards from East Africa in the same period. African farmers expanded to the Zimbabwe highlands and the coast of Mozambique in the first few centuries AD. There is evidence of settled farmers, making pots similar to those from earlier settlements in East Africa, along the coast of KwaZulu-Natal by at least AD 250. Some of the earliest sites of settled farmers were along the coastal strip, but they gradually settled inland along major river valleys, where rich soils were suitable for agriculture. Their technology included the smelting and working of metal.

African farmers spread into southern Africa about 2 000 years ago. This mid-19th-century illustration of a Zulu kraal shows fat-tailed sheep and Nguni cattle. It reflects a heritage of domesticated breeds, some introduced to Africa and others possibly domesticated in northern Africa about 7 000 years ago.

The production and working of copper and iron seem to have appeared simultaneously in sub-Saharan Africa by the 6th century BC. It was practised in southern Africa by Early Iron Age farmers before AD 500. Many ancient copper mines have been described from Zimbabwe, eastern Botswana and areas north of the Vaal River. Gold mining took place at several thousand ancient mines in Zimbabwe and a few sites along the Limpopo River, while tin was mined at Rooiberg in the Northern Province. Iron ores occur more widely and could be found in the form of pebbles of magnetite, or even iron-rich sand. Various types of smelting furnace have been found in southern Africa. Notably, the earliest mining in Africa can be said to date to Middle Stone Age times, when minerals such as ochre and specularite were extracted as pigments for body paints and possibly for ritual purposes.

Many aspects of society, and the environment, began to change with the emergence of food production, including population growth, wealth and status, political organisation, religious beliefs and rituals, settlement and land use.

Control of scarce resources by a ruling class could lead to state formation, as happened in the Limpopo Valley from the 9th century AD.

Glass beads brought to Africa by Indian Ocean traders were exchanged for animal skins and ivory. Wealth accumulated in the form of cattle and beads gave economic and political power to the rulers of Mapungubwe. Gold gradually became an important commodity in this trade, and the centre of economic power shifted to the Zimbabwe Plateau.

Throughout this time, aboriginal San hunter-gatherers continued to lead a nomadic lifestyle in step with the seasonal availability of plant foods and the migrations of game.

But in their contacts with nomadic herders and settled farmers, patterns of interaction, negotiation and conflict were complex. What resulted were economic, technological and cultural frontiers across which people doubtless fought, but, equally, shared skills, traded and influenced one another's languages and beliefs, eating habits and lifestyles.

It is a reminder that, as archaeologist Nikolaas J van der Merwe noted in 1976:

To look at the history of South Africa [as if it began a few centuries ago] is to look at human events through the wrong end of a telescope.

In some parts of the country, the San shared the landscape with herders but resisted becoming herders themselves, whereas in other regions they adopted herding or were forced into joining farming communities through conquest.

The changing relationships and identities – how people saw themselves – are reflected in the archaeological record by items made and exchanged between groups.

❖

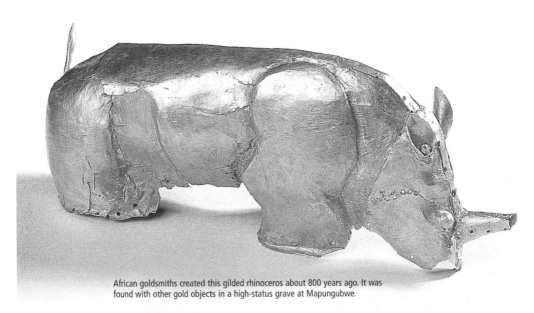

African goldsmiths created this gilded rhinoceros about 800 years ago. It was found with other gold objects in a high-status grave at Mapungubwe.

Ear-rings of copper and iron found in a 350-year-old Khoe-San burial washed open by a flood in the Northern Cape, for instance, suggest possible contact between the community to which this individual belonged and Tswana groups to the north or west.

In the same burial site were some 3 000 ostrich eggshell beads. An increase is bead-making, evident at other contemporary sites of the region, may have been part of more intensive commodity production for exchange. Specularite, a glittering pigment sought after by different communities for body decoration and rituals, was ground to a powder and traded in pots and ostrich eggshell containers. At Mapungubwe, caches of finely crafted bone points were probably obtained in trade with San hunter-gatherers, possibly in exchange for metal items.

In a 'patchwork' pattern, or 'mosaic', of different social, cultural and economic arrangements, San ritual specialists – shamans or 'medicine men' – could become significant agents, managing the stresses of change in their own societies while being rewarded by farmers for their skills, particularly in rain-making. Some of the rock art of this period shows elaborately painted individuals, believed to depict shamans, whose status as mediators had become pre-eminent in situations of social and cultural contact.

The art of the San – often, wrongly, thought to be just pictures of the animals and people in their surroundings – survives as a token of a rich spiritual and even political life that helped shape changes in pre-colonial southern Africa.

'The White Lady of the Brandberg' is neither white nor a lady, but a long-misunderstood example of the sophisticated rock art of southern Africa.

———— ❖ ————

In 1930, Marion How, wife of the magistrate at Qachasnek, witnessed the making of a rock painting by an old man named Mapote. The event is recounted by David Lewis-Williams and Thomas Dowson in *Images of Power, Understanding Bushman Rock Art* (1989). Though Mapote was of Sotho and Pondomise descent, he had half-San stepbrothers and had learned to paint with the San in caves.

Mapote took some trouble in selecting a suitable stone on which to paint. It had to be smooth and, at the same time, porous enough to absorb the paint. In the end, he chose a smooth sandstone. For red pigment he desired what he called qhang qhang, a glistening haemetite dug out of the basalt mountains. It had to be prepared at full moon out of doors by a woman who heated it over a fire until it was red hot. After this treatment, the pigment was ground between two stones to a fine powder. Mapote then announced that he needed 'the blood of a freshly killed eland' but, no eland being available, he had to mix his paint with ox blood. For white pigment he used a white clay and the juice of the plant Asclepia gibba (milk weed). His black paint was made from charcoal and water. Using a different brush (feathers fixed on the ends of tiny reeds) for each colour, he commenced painting an eland. He started at the animal's chest and moved his brush along smoothly without the slightest hesitation. As Marion How watched, the ancient and long-dead art of rock painting came alive, and lived for a fleeting hour or two. Then, his painting completed and having been rewarded with a new pair of boots, Mapote set off on his long journey home and disappeared into the vast valleys of the Malutis.

———— ❖ ————

The 'great efflorescence of Bushman art ... points to the very origin of artistic activity and thence to some of humankind's greatest triumphs,' write Lewis-Williams and Dowson in *Images of Power*. 'Bushman rock art stands at the centre of research into the origins of religion and aesthetics.'

In contrast, the missionary Henry Tindall – who had little success in converting the San to Christianity – complained in 1856 that the San

> has no religion, no laws, no government, no recognised authority, no patrimony, no fixed abode ... no soul, debased, it is true, and completely bound down and clogged by his animal nature.

In the years since, the petty misconceptions of the Tindalls of the world – which lay behind much of the brutal treatment of the San – have been dispelled, and the truer character of the hunter-gatherer cosmos has come to be better understood.

Art is one of its primary surviving expressions. Art on rock – engravings and paintings in more than 30 000 sites throughout southern Africa – forms a rich inheritance. Sophisticated in its detail and depth of meaning, the style and content vary from region to region and through time, but most of the art falls within a single broad tradition.

Engravings – pecked, scored or scraped into the outer crust of rock with a hard stone – are usually found on hills or rocky outcrops, while paintings – painted with brushes, chewed sticks, perhaps quills, or with the finger – are found in caves and shelters in more mountainous areas.

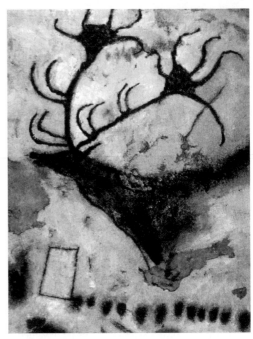

Southern Africa's rock art tradition began millennia before this antlered animal was painted in the caves of Lascaux in France about 17 000 years ago.

As the Blombos and Apollo 11 finds – of between 27 500 and 77 000 years old – indicate, southern Africa has one of the oldest traditions of rock art, long pre-dating famous early European rock art sites such as Lascaux (17 000 years ago) and Chauvet (32 000 years ago).

It is the animal depictions, so often misunderstood, that point to the truer meaning of the work.

Rock paintings in southern Africa represent the flowering of early human creativity and the expression of belief and spirituality.

Animal images are a major symbolic element in Khoe-San art and mythology. In the art large game animals predominate, with the central symbol being the eland.

God, the source of all potency, was a trickster-deity called /Kaggen, and /Kaggen's favourite animal was the eland. (Lewis-Williams and Dowson note that /Kaggen appears in numerous myths in which he can be 'foolish or wise, tiresome or helpful'.) To the San the universe was layered, where spiritual realms existed over and beneath the level of everyday life. Rock art showing snakes and other animals emerging from cracks in a rock or cave wall suggest that the rock itself was an interface, like a veil, between this world and the world of spirits and spirit-animals.

The very making of the art was imbued with a spiritual other-worldliness, and it is linked with the ritual specialists, the medicine people or shamans – perhaps as parts of rites, such as rain-making.

Engravings and paintings were symbols and metaphors for religious beliefs, and some were inspired by visions experienced in trance and depicted on rocks so that others could share and draw spiritual inspiration from them.

This is one of several interpretations of rock art, based in part on detailed knowledge of San beliefs and customs recorded in the last 150 years.

The vast 12 000-page collection of /Xam San beliefs and histories recorded by Wilhelm Bleek and Lucy Lloyd in the late 1800s has been central to understanding the San worldview. Other important records were made by magistrate Joseph Millard Orpen in the Lesotho mountains in the 1870s, and, in the later decades of the 20th century, by a number of researchers working with the Kalahari San and other Khoe-San groups and descendant communities.

These records indicate that, though there are regional differences, and change through time, most of the art 'sprang from the same fundamental system of beliefs', as Lewis-Williams and Dowson describe it.

An important feature of these beliefs was the ritual trance dance. Images of transformation – of men into animals, or vice versa – in paintings and engravings most clearly relate to the religious beliefs and ritual trance dance of hunter-gatherers.

> 'The creature that gazes out over Natal from the Mlambonja boulder is not as enigmatic as it was even a decade ago,' Lewis-Williams and Dowson wrote in 1989. 'It came from the very heart of the Bushman religious experience.'

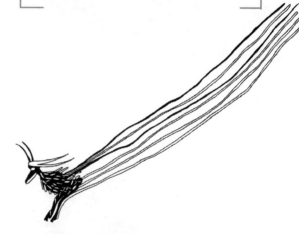

In the 1830s the missionaries Thomas Arbousset and Francois Daumas gave one of the earliest descriptions of the healing or trance dance:

The thousand cries which they raise, and the exertions which they make, are so violent that it is not unusual to see someone sink to the ground exhausted and covered with blood, which pours from the nostrils; it is on this account that the dance is called mokoma, *or dance of blood.*

The trance dance was an important healing ritual. Women sang and clapped 'medicine songs' around a central fire, while men danced around them. The dance increased in intensity. A shaman would feel supernatural potency 'boil' inside him or herself.

'In your back you feel a pointed something, and it works its way up,' as a !Kung shaman described it. *'The base of your spine is tingling, tingling, tingling …'*

Entering a trance state – the spiritual realm – the shaman drew out sickness and 'harm's things' from individuals in the group. Rain-making and out-of-body travel were other ritual skills of shamans.

Ritualistic trance dancing was – and remains – an important element of the San religious experience. This Kalahari healing dance was photographed in the late 20th century.

More than just another kopje, Wildebeest Kuil bears evidence of the long history of humans in the southern African landscape.

Wildebeest Kuil – a hill with a future, a hill with a past.

As the hill rises above the surrounding plains, so the spirit world under the earth may have been seen to 'break through' at a place such as this: some of the engravings show animals of the spirit world as if they are emerging from within the rock, while others 'connect' with the spirit realm above.

From the text of an audio-tour at the Northern Cape Rock Art Trust Centre at Wildebeest Kuil

Wildebeest Kuil, the low hill described as rising from the sweep of grassland surrounding it, commands a view of typical central South African veld to the north, west and south and, to the east, some 15 kilometres away, a modest profile of modernity, an expanse of urban settlement punctuated by half a dozen high-rise buildings.

This is the Northern Cape capital of Kimberley, the diamond city that came into being a little more than 130 years ago.

As a hill, Wildebeest Kuil is unexceptional, barely perceptible from a distance. But it is, in its way, a remarkable hill for the story it tells about the near and very distant pasts of the South African landscape, and the people who have inhabited it.

Its geology is ancient: the burnt-toast coloured rocks in among the grass and scrub vegetation are of andesite, a volcanic basement rock that was formed when the Earth was half its present age, about 2,3 billion years ago, and some 1,7 billion years before

years ago, and these are plausible dates for most of the engravings here.

So notes archaeologist David Morris of the McGregor Museum in Kimberley, and a member of the Northern Cape Rock Art Trust that administers the site.

The engravings, and their setting in the landscape, hint at a spirituality that can be sensed in many thousands of rock painting and engraving sites across the subcontinent.

Partly because of the harsh semi-arid conditions of the Northern Cape, pockets of semi-independent hunter-gatherers and herders lived in parts of the province well into the colonial era. The /Xam San of the upper Karoo were one such group.

In the Kimberley area, descendants of the artists were caught up in the struggle for land as the colonial frontier advanced inland. Frontiersmen from the Cape had come inland as sheep farmers, traders and raiders, through the 18th to the early 19th centuries. For some time before the discovery of diamonds – which changed everything – Khoe-San people were already being marginalised. Some united to form new frontier communities combining San, Korana and other indigenous and immigrant groups or individuals. Subsequently, descendants of the Khoe-San were absorbed into colonial society as labourers on farms and in the mines.

Rectangular stone kraals and ash-heaps at Wildebeest Kuil are signs of later occupation of the hill site by farmers and farm-workers, while from the 1870s there was a 'Half-Way Hotel' at the foot of the hill – it was 'a cross between a canvas tent and a wooden house' – and so called because it was the halfway point between the river diggings of present-day Barkly West and the dry diggings of early Kimberley. Below the hill is a 20th-century farm-workers' house, with a rubbish heap containing archaeological traces of the lives of labourers who were in all probability the descendants of the last independent San and Khoekhoe people of this region. Morris notes:

Along with the changes in way of life, many aspects of culture such as language and religion were eroded away. When the descendants of these people were classified 'Coloured', this imposed Apartheid category demeaned the identities and heritage of the past.

In this way, the hill of Wildebeest Kuil connects the multiple histories of landscape and people.

the first multi-celled organisms appeared on Earth. Some half a million or more years ago, early human ancestors lived here.

Some of the scars on the rocks of Wildebeest Kuil are the result of their stone technology, the flaking of handaxes, many of which are found scattered on the fringes of the pans below the hill. More recent stone artefacts were left on the hill itself by hunter-gatherers, ancestors of the Khoe-San, in Middle and Later Stone Age times, from between one and two thousand years ago until within the last few hundred years. And many of the rocks on the hill are marked and enhanced with a sacred art, rock engravings.

There are also several small circles of stone, and clearings among the rocks on the hill top, which contain many stone artefacts, and, in some, a few potsherds, pieces of ostrich eggshell, and fragments of bone. The stone circles were the bases of simple grass or mat shelters in which it is believed the hunter-gatherer artists lived.

Radiocarbon dates obtained from excavated material suggest that some of the stone circles were occupied between about 1 200 and 1 800

Early South African art contains many clues – if not answers – to its meaning. What is plain is that the paintings and engravings are far more than mere depictions of wild animals and people, or narratives of events. Rather, when 'read' in the light of /Xam and Kalahari San beliefs, the ideas they stand for begin to make sense.

Morris highlights several striking images at Wildebeest Kuil:

Engravings of many large mammals occur, but particularly special are the images of eland. The fat of this animal, its blood, and its sweat, were all believed by the /Xam to be sources of super-natural potency called !gi. In the art, the fatty dewlap below the neck is often emphasized. Shamans would, in their beliefs, draw on this potency for entering the spirit world, to lead the 'rain-animal' to make rain, or to help them in the healing dance.

Water, welling up in waterholes, and falling from the sky, was linked to powerful animal symbolism – rain itself was an animal. In rain-making rituals the mythic rain animal, called !Khwa-ka: xoro, was calmed with ochre or with sweet-smelling herbs called buchu, and 'led', as the /Xam said, from the waterhole to a hill and cut so that the rain might fall.

Rain-bearing clouds embodied the rain animal, leaving watery 'footprints' as it 'walked' across the landscape – so they said – on 'rain's legs'.

One of the unusual images at Wildebeest Kuil is an eland engraved upside down, as if it were dead. It was said by the /Xam that in death the eland releases its power, its !gi, which, through its death, could be harnessed by the shaman.

In more enigmatic images only parts of eland are depicted – a head only, or a headless torso at the edge of a rock – almost as if the animals were being 'lured' out of the rocks, or from cracks between them. Could it be that these represent transitions into and out of the spirit world above and below the earth? That the engravings, perhaps the rocks themselves – or even the hill, clearly a very special place – were in some sense a way into the spirit world under the earth – and over it?

Part of the history of the hill is the history of curiosity about it, and it is significant that when geologist and ethnologist George William Stow copied engravings at Wildebeest Kuil – the first person known to have done so – in the 1870s, and sent copies to Bleek and Lloyd in Cape Town, they saw in the images what Bleek later described as evidence of 'the ideas that most deeply moved the Bushman mind, and filled it with religious feelings'.

Eland engraving at Wildebeest Kuil: a powerful symbol in South African rock art.

For Khoe-San people, who were often marginalised in their encounters with other groups in South Africa, colonial expansion was devastating. Even so, despite fears, once, that they risked becoming extinct, they have survived in communities which, since 1994, have claimed land, political and cultural rights. And, of course, many thousands of South Africans claim a share of Khoe-San ancestry.

Wildebeest Kuil's 21st-century link with its early human associations is telling, but also ironic. It is a link established by people who are newcomers in one sense.

!Xun and Khwe people are members of two San groups, speaking distinct Khoe-San languages and having different histories. Caught up in political turmoil in Angola, they fled to Namibia, only to become embroiled in the conflict there between occupying South African armed forces and the South West African People's Organisation (Swapo), fighting for the independence of Namibia in the 1970s and 1980s.

In 1990 some 4 000 of them (men then employed by the South African Defence Force together with their families) were flown to a tent-camp at Schmidtsdrift, west of Kimberley. Shortly after the democratic elections in 1994, however, Schmidtsdrift was awarded to its former Tswana owners in a land claim, forcing the !Xun and Khwe to move again. In 1996 they purchased the farm of which Wildebeest Kuil forms a part for resettlement.

The communities retain elements of the Khoe-San language, music and other facets of cultural life, and have established a !Xun and Khwe Art Project that produces a variety of traditional and modern arts and crafts.

'As the owners today of the land on which the Wildebeest Kuil engravings occur,' David Morris explains, 'the !Xun and Khwe, who are partners in the Northern Cape Rock Art Trust, see in the art a link – as do others – to a broad Khoe-San cultural inheritance in Southern Africa.'

———— ❖ ————

To experience the breezy quiet of Wildebeest Kuil today is to pause thoughtfully at the rim of a deep and complex southern African past, a history of humanity's first steps, and of its less noble, less creditable marches.

The winds and breezes of their ancestral landscape had a special meaning for the /Xam San of the upper

Karoo, as we learned from //Kabbo, when he spoke of stories as winds that would carry the life-stories of people to other places, other times. 'Then our names, passing behind the mountain's back,' he had told Bleek and Lloyd, 'pass through those people, while we ourselves are invisible to them.'

In many ways, South Africa's first people are all but invisible today.

The engravings of Wildebeest Kuil, as elsewhere, 'survive as but a remnant of a rich inheritance', the audio text at the site tells us, 'a reminder, as they stand silent on the hill, of how much has been lost, and at what human cost.'

———— ❖ ————

In the late 1400s, a southern Africa populated by a variety of complex societies was on the brink of a disruptive confluence with newcomers from Europe whose navigational expertise enabled them to act on their curiosity and develop their trading ambitions by travelling far south from their home ports.

Modern South Africa is, in essence, the product of the consequences of this coming together of people. Archaeological, palaeontological and genetic research suggests that Europeans were coming home to their biological roots.

But it is a matter of record – as //Kabbo's people learned – that the newcomers very largely failed to recognise and honour their innate affinities with people they more often than not regarded as 'other', as inferior, as people whose culture they did not respect, and whose land they took away. There were exceptions among the newcomers, but the exceptions were few.

Violent encounters with white colonists, such as the skirmish dramatically depicted here, prefigured the end of the southern African rock art tradition.

Strangers
on the shore

Strangers on the shore

Ships on the horizon – dim, billowing forms, the first ever seen –
must have been an extraordinary sight.

One of the herders stood suddenly, pointing out to sea, beyond the surf, to the horizon. Others soon caught sight of what he saw and stared hard too.

Nothing like it had ever appeared before. Further along the crest of the hill, from among the grazing herds, another shouted down to them, his words snatched away by the wind sweeping in off the sea. All were now fixed on the horizon, on the dim, billowing form that was clearly approaching the shore.

Perhaps this is how it was, perhaps not.

The dim, billowing form, the dramatic hilltop gestures, are our imaginative attempts at making sense of an event that, truly enough, changed every-thing. And there is a lot to imagine about the first encounters between Europe and southern Africa.

The first ship sighted from the shore might well have been beyond understanding. There was no memory to be ransacked for clues, 500 years ago, about the origins or the meaning of such an object appearing over the horizon.

Out to sea, sailors seeing for the first time the emerging land mass may well have thought of such

a place – so far from their ports, and beyond the limits of what they knew – as another world.

But this, too, is all imagined, and we risk romancing events that are only partially recorded.

Africa below the equator was not entirely mysterious to residents of the northern hemisphere before the first Portuguese voyages.

The Greek historian Herodotus (c 484–c 424 BC) left an unverified narrative of Phoenicians circumnavi-gating Africa 2 600 years ago, so that even if Herodotus himself had doubted the truth of this, the notion, if not the fact, of an African continent was by no means alien to European scholars.

We know from the Chinese map, the Da Ming Hun Yi Tu, created in 1389 and derived from an earlier one dated 1320, that Ming cartographers of the period had already conceived of Africa as a sea-bound continent.

Arab traders and explorers – including the Moroccan Muhammad ibn-Abdullah ibn-Battuta, who voyaged down the East coast of Africa in the late 1320s – traded with or visited east African ports well before the early European voyages. Arab ships are recorded as having sailed as far as 480 kilometres up the Zambezi River in this era. Extensive Arab histories and geographical records reveal a knowledge of Africa as far south as present-day South Africa's border with Mozambique that long pre-date the ground-breaking Portuguese explorations of 1488 and 1497.

Perhaps, even, an awareness of sea-going vessels and visitors arriving from the sea was not a universally foreign concept in southern Africa by the late 1400s, especially if knowledge or stories of the east-coast seafaring had percolated through the region with migration and trade. That may be fanciful. It is certainly entirely speculative.

What is certain is that, when they finally faced each other on the southern African shore 500 years ago, the seafarers from Europe and the coastal communities they met would have recognised one another as fellow human beings, but also as total strangers. They met as strangers on the shore. The scope for misunderstanding was vast.

It was not just that there was no shared language. At first glance, these were people who were poles apart in many other ways: in how they understood the world, in what they knew of life on Earth and how they made sense of it, and certainly in their expectations of one another, and their calculations of one another's intentions.

In these things, it would seem, were the seeds of the contests and conflicts of the hundreds of years to follow – but also, ultimately, the steadily growing idea that they depended on one another. And from that, after centuries, came the political settlement of the past decade, and the efforts at reconciliation, of establishing a sense of single nationhood.

Early contacts at the Cape between Khoekhoe herders and European seafarers were seldom as amicable as this depiction suggests.

Records of the early years are uneven. The only written thoughts and observations to survive – and, often, the mistaken assessments and beliefs – are those of the new arrivals. In their own words, they have left their view of life in what was to become South Africa. The thoughts and memories of the people they encountered are less clear, though not entirely absent either. They were watched, analysed, judged, sketched and described in writing, but they could not 'speak' for themselves on their own terms. They certainly had voices, they had language, they had thoughts and perceptions and a rich mental life. But their literary tradition was an oral, spoken, one. And the nature of the meeting of the cultures and traditions represented by Europe's seafarers and the people of southern Africa did not leave the space for an equal share of the record of the time. The oral tradition was steadily eroded by the literacy, the writing down of things, of Europe.

Looking back, perhaps the single most powerful force in southern African history from the time of the first encounters has been the quest of the silenced to speak for themselves and be heard. It should not be forgotten, though, that the earliest voices, and the ideas, of southern Africa were never entirely silenced or erased. Oral histories, mythologies and art remain expressive. In many cases these are tokens of a long resistance.

This encounter of strangers raises a fundamental question: why did Africans not set out in ships and – to use the words of the American scientist Jared Diamond, who has dealt with this very question – 'conquer, exterminate and infect Europeans'?

Knowledge – if not plain observation – makes it clear that Europeans are not inherently superior to Africans, cleverer or more far-thinking, or more able in using their brains or their hands. So that is not it. The answer Diamond gives is a great deal more complicated, but it rests on a simplicity: farming.

Diamond's book, *Guns, Germs and Steel* (1997), offers an explanation that is fascinating in its detail. The essence of his thesis is that, until about 10 500 years ago, everybody in the world lived by hunting and gathering. When farming emerged, a number of different things happened. People began to settle. There was no need, now, to move constantly after

game or seasonal plants. And with farming came the production of food surpluses, which meant that there were certain individuals who were not themselves obliged to be involved in producing the food.

They might now have begun to do other things, develop other skills, which would have been useful to the food producers and all of the rest of their growing community, since, with settlement, came rapid population growth.

So, gradually, different activities emerged and with them more complex ways of ordering society. Collective interests produced social units, classes, community and eventually national identities, and ultimately competition between nations, the emergence of standing armies, and the desire or need to expand areas of control, to defend or take over productive land, conduct trade, and generally consolidate collective well-being.

Broadly, Africa's history displays elements of these patterns no less than Asia's or Europe's. But Diamond highlights an important, accidental, difference between Africa – along with South America and Australia – and Europe, the Middle East and Asia: not all places in the world had the same share of animals capable of being domesticated, or of plants able to be farmed.

Of the 4 000 species of mammal around the world, only 148 are big enough to be seriously considered for farming, and every continent has at least a couple of them. But 134 of the 148 species are disqualified for farming because they are either too fierce or don't breed in captivity or take too long to mature. Of the remaining 14, 13 were wild animals in Eurasia – the cow, sheep, goat, pig, horse, reindeer, donkey, Arabian camel, Asian camel, yak, water buffalo, gaur and banteng. The only one in the New World was the llama. No big animal was ever domesticated in Australia or Africa south of the Sahara. (Significantly, the world's 'crowd infectious killer diseases' – smallpox, measles, influenza, pertussis, typhoid and tuberculosis – evolved in dense societies of farmers and were, of course, carried round the world by them. Molecular biological research shows that these diseases evolved from diseases of domesticated animals which jumped the species barrier in the last 10 000 years.)

The same pattern as that for animals emerges in the history of the domestication of plants. Of the world's 200 000 species of wild higher-order plants, the most valuable cereals today account for only 56 species and of them 32 were confined to the Mediterranean zone of Western Eurasia.

In complex ways over time, these natural advantages – and the disease factor – had a decisive influence on human societies, and the varying rates of population growth and technological development in different parts of the world.

In the 1400s, African farmers – who had, by then, gained 'imported' domesticated animals and plants – were already mining and working metal and living by complex social arrangements. But, Jared Diamond argues, because of the accident of geography and climate, Africa had not yielded the population growth of Europe, or the technology, the ships and guns and map-making. Or, indeed, the diseases Africans contracted from their one-time fellow hunter-gatherers from Europe. Simply, he proposes, the conditions for colonising Europe had not arisen in Africa, just as they had not arisen in Australia and South America.

So the scene was set for Arabian, Asian and, later, European exploration.

At the time of Bartolomeu Dias's voyage in 1488 – the first from Europe as far as the shores of southern Africa – there was no deliberate strategy to create a settlement, a colony or a state at the southern tip of the continent.

But Dias's voyage was a decisive event.

Typically of human beings, Europeans began to explore parts of the world that were unknown to them because – broadly speaking – they believed they could get something out of it. (The pursuit of self-interest marks the European period of colonialism as much as the period of independence or liberation that has followed it, or, for that matter, any phase of human history before colonialism.) In the second half of the 14th century, there was a great shortage of precious metals in Europe, a shortage that helps explain the huge force the Portuguese used in 1415 to capture the Moroccan trading centre of Ceuta. Thereafter, by order of the king, Henrique, Portuguese sailors and explorers were urged to continue down the coast, round the bulge of Africa, to expand geographical knowledge and extend commerce, to assess the strength of Muslim nations (the prime enemy of Christian Europe at the time, akin in a way

to the Cold War stand-off between East and West in the 20th century), to try to find the source of the gold that reached Ceuta by trans-Saharan trade, and to further the influence of Christianity.

Steadily, then, Portuguese exploration extended further south along the African coast through the 1400s. In 1434, sailors passed Cape Bojador (in what today is Western Sahara), which for a long time had been the limit of Europe's oceanographic knowledge. Portuguese ships reached the mouth of the Senegal River in 1444. By 1460, they had reached Sierra Leone and, within the decade, Principe and São Tomé (off what is now Cameroon). In the early 1480s, the Portuguese spent some effort in turning São Jorge de Miña on the Gold Coast into a trade base and fortress. Already, Portugal was benefiting from trade in African gold and extended political influence. Yet the coast of Africa drew the exploring expeditions ever southwards. By 1486, they had reached present-day Namibia. The prize, by the time Dias set off from Lisbon one year later, was a rounding of Africa, the first step in opening a sea route to India. Overland journeying – by Venetian Marco Polo in the late 1200s and the Arab traders mentioned earlier, among others – had alerted Europeans to the precious commodities of the East, many of which were not available in Europe. There was great demand for them, but the overland route crossed politically hostile and geographically unforgiving terrain. A 'direct' sea route was desired.

Dias's journal and charts have been lost, but some details of the voyage were recorded or mentioned in other documents. From these we know that after leaving his store ship in a bay on the Angolan coast, he continued south, but was blown out to sea by stormy weather. When the weather eased, he steered east, expecting to regain the western coast of southern Africa. After sailing some days without reaching it, he steered north and a few days later, sighted land at or near a bay the explorers called Bahia dos Vaqueiros, so named because of the large number of herds and herdsmen they could make out on land. This was Fish Bay. But they needed fresh water, and since there was none there, they sailed north to present-day Mossel Bay.

Early, distorted conceptions of a much-misunderstood continent made way for a truer profile of Africa in the maps of Europe only after many decades of exploration and conquest.

How did the Portuguese know that by going south along Africa's western coastline they would reach – or had a good chance of reaching – the tip of Africa, beyond which lay the ocean that would take them to India?

Remarkably, there was a map that told them so.

Not surprisingly, given Venice's long history of trading far and wide by land and sea, the northern Italian seaport was a centre of map-making, or cartography. And it was from Venice that the Portuguese king, Pedro, ordered a map of the 'world' in the 1440s. The map that emerged – it was completed only in 1460 – is the so-called Fra Mauro map,

embodying maritime discoveries up to 1448.

Drawing on Arab records of early trade with Africa (and the East), it indicated knowledge of the east coast as far as present-day Mozambique.

Yet, while the shortened, misshapen Africa was not an accurate depiction, it showed the continent surrounded by ocean on the west, south and east … much like the Chinese map of 1389.

The historian OGS Crawford, writing in 1958, notes that 'that was what was believed in his [the map-maker's] time and for at least 170 years before'.

Yet belief, it turned out, was not quite enough for Dias's crew.

What do we know of the very first encounter? Where did it occur, and what actually happened?

The first party of Europeans to go ashore did so at Mossel Bay to get fresh water for their ships. Drawing on a reference in later explorer Vasco da Gama's diary, historian Eric Axelson wrote in 1940 that the herders they met were alarmed at first, and fled.

But the shyness of the natives soon wore off, and as the Europeans were taking in water hard by the beach, a bombardment of stones started from a hillside above. Dias had been strictly instructed in his royal regulations to cause no harm or 'scandal' to the natives of Africa. But so incensed was he at the attack that he fired a crossbow at the assailants and killed one of them – the first victim of white aggression in South Africa.

From *South-East Africa 1488–1530* (1940) by Eric Axelson

Continuing north-eastwards along the coast, Dias's ships reached Algoa Bay (originally Lagoa, but later corrupted) where the weary ships' crews said: 'Enough!' Eventually, a compromise was reached: they would sail for two or three days more and if they had found nothing to make them change their minds, they would turn for home. They got as far as the Keiskamma River or possibly the Kowie River, and turned back. At Kwaaihoek, a little further down the coast, they went ashore and erected a stone cross, or *padrão*, to mark the extent of their travels. It was on the way home that Dias named the southern tip of Africa Cabo de Boa Esperanza, Cape of Good Hope.

❖

At Kwaaihoek, a few kilometres south of present-day Kenton-on-Sea, a replica of Dias's cross stands on the likely spot where he erected the *padrão* on 12 March, 1488. In his poem *Pilgrimage to Dias Cross*, Guy Butler reflects on the significance of this site:

Five hundred years have come, have gone;
the giant light of day,
starry hosts by night,
the changeful moon,
her slavish train of tides,
wind, sea spray, rain,
rubbing to erase
one slight signature
written in stone by Dias,
there, with a mutinous crew.

Portuguese sailors raise a padrão, or cross, to mark a landing on the southern African coast.

He did not guess
what destinies of consciousness,
fleets, empires, tribes, tongues, gods
hung in his rotten rigging, spun
in the salt white sand that filled the space
between the cross's square-cut base
and the ill-fitting socket built
of the bonewhite, soft
indigenous sand.

It marked the limit
to failure and success;
far enough to change the charts
of all ships since.

From *Pilgrimage to Dias Cross* (1987), a narrative poem by
Guy Butler, with woodcuts and engravings by Cecil Skotnes

Almost 10 years after Dias's return to Lisbon, Vasco da
Gama commanded the first ships to sail from Europe
to India in a voyage described by Axelson as one that
'revolutionised trade and relations between Europe
and the East'. Until then, valuable goods from the
East had had to be carried overland for much of the
way to the markets of Renaissance Europe. Opening
the sea route changed that. It also, in a sense, defined
southern Africa as a halfway point, strategically
important, yet not, initially, a destination in itself.

Far inland, well away from the dramatic events at the
southern coast, economic, social and political forces
of a different order had been at work for a long time
changing the way people lived.

Centuries of trade between east-coast Africans and
the Arab world of the Middle East and North Africa,
and with Asia across the Indian Ocean, had helped to
create the conditions for the emergence of powerful
trading states in the region of the middle reaches of
the Limpopo River from more than a thousand years
ago.

Trade, wealth accumulation and political power all
played a part in this.

Among the focal points of such developments was
Toutswemogala, between the years 900 and 1200.

Political centralisation occurred at sites on the
Kalahari fringe and major towns developed where
many cattle were kept. These were surrounded by
smaller settlements.

Further east, in the same period, was the Mapungubwe state. A ruling elite in the present-day northern
provinces amassed wealth in cattle and trade goods,
such as glass beads obtained from Indian Ocean
traders in exchange for ivory and gold. Their control
of this trade led to state formation.

Drought and overgrazing contributed to Mapungubwe's decline in the 1200s, and the centre of
economic power shifted to Great Zimbabwe in the
period between the late 1200s and 1450.

The term '*dzimbahwe*' refers to the home, court
or grave of a chief. At Great Zimbabwe impressive
stone walling encircled the dwellings of the rulers of
this state. Beyond the walls lived an estimated 18 000
commoners in densely packed clay and thatch housing.

From 1450 to about 1800, the focus shifted yet
again to Khami, which was the main centre of trade
when Portuguese mariners reached the east coast at
the end of the 15th century. The architecture of the
Khami period was distinctive, but the underlying
symbols were the same as those of Mapungubwe
and Great Zimbabwe.

By about 1600 Nguni African farmers of the
Tshawe royal clan had established a chiefdom in the
northern part of what later came to be known as the
Transkei, expanding over much of the territory in the
next 200 years. Populations were not static: communities were on the move in one way or another all
the time. This is borne out by discoveries of Iron Age
sites in the Transkei dating to as early as the year 600.

Well before the European settlers met African
farmers – rather than the herders and hunter-
gatherers of the coastal region – there was a vague
notion that the interior of southern Africa was home
to a powerful and wealthy community or state.

And for as long as 300 years after the first
European visits, the idea of a state or a place map-
makers routinely called 'Monomatapa' persisted. It
was not so far-fetched an idea, but its geographical
location was an arbitrary estimation. In 1700, for
instance, the Oxford map-maker, E Wells, produced a
'new map of Affrick showing its present general
divisions, chief cities, towns, rivers, mountains, etc'
that showed a settlement called Monomatapa (in the
vicinity of present-day Bloemfontein) with a stylised
'city' symbol bigger than those for Tunis in North Africa
and Sofala on the east coast. And, nearly a hundred
years later, Monomatapa was still showing up in the
otherwise much-revised maps of the day, such as the
1792 chart by Amsterdam cartographer, JB Elwe.

Powerful myths were forged from Europe's engagement with southern Africa. One of the longest-lasting and most powerful is that of Adamastor in the epic poem *The Lusiads* by the 16th-century Portuguese poet Luis Camões. Adamastor was a fierce and vengeful mythical figure representing Africa's stormy southern tip – and Africa itself, in a sense.

By the time Camões penned his epic, the Portuguese had suffered a bloody setback in the shadow of Adamastor: in 1510, the Viceroy of India, Francisco de Almeida, died after being struck in the throat by a Khoekhoe spear in a skirmish on the shores of Table Bay. It put the Portuguese off the southern African coast for good.

As for Adamastor, his myth lived on, expressing much about Europe's view of Africa, and helping to shape perceptions of generations of settlers.

In one of the most striking interpretations, Roy Campbell's 1930 poem, 'Rounding the Cape', delivered a warning of sorts to a South Africa that seemed intent on denying its African reality:

The low sun whitens on the flying squalls,
Against the cliffs the long grey surge is rolled
Where Adamastor from his marble halls
Threatens the sons of Lusus as of old.

Faint on the glare uptowers the dauntless form,
Into whose shade abysmal as we draw,
Down on our decks, from far above the storm,
Grin the stark ridges of his broken jaw.

Across his back, unheeded, we have broken
Whole forests: heedless of the blood we've spilled,
In thunder still his prophecies are spoken,
In silence, by the centuries, fulfilled.

Farewell, terrific shade! though I go free
Still of the powers of darkness art thou Lord:
I watch the phantom sinking in the sea
Of all that I have hated or adored.

The prow glides smoothly on through seas quiescent:
But where the last point sinks into the deep,
The land lies dark beneath the rising crescent,
And Night, the Negro, murmurs in his sleep.

From *Selected Poems* (1981) by Roy Campbell

Francisco de Almeida, the Portuguese Viceroy of India, died at the hands of the Khoekhoe in Table Bay in 1510, a decisive event depicted in this early rendering.

Quite rapidly, from 1800 onwards, the penetration of the interior by frontiersmen of various kinds and explorers, missionaries, soldiers and administrators banished the romantic visions of the early map-makers.

It would take a much later revision of history to acknowledge the early existence of powerful and wealthy African states in the interior.

❖

The opening of sea routes to 'distant' parts of the world by the first wave of European explorers and sailors – especially to the commodity-rich East, but also to the Americas – galvanised the powerful of Europe, as Spain, France, England and Holland invested much effort from 1500 in establishing world trade networks to the farthest limits of the Atlantic and Indian oceans, and later the Pacific, looking for new commodities or sources of raw materials, taking over new land and exerting extended political control, creating or attempting to create empires.

In the Indian Ocean, of course, Arab traders were veterans when the Europeans were only 'discovering' it. A major black slave rebellion in Iraq in the 9th century, and the growing of bananas and Asian rice in Africa, for instance, testify to the long history of contacts between Africa and the worlds of the Persian Gulf and South and East Asia.

Da Gama was amazed when he arrived at the Mozambican coast in March 1498 – on the last leg of the first European voyage to India – to discover a flourishing harbour in which were moored several traders' ships equipped with charts, compasses and other navigational instruments, and loaded, he was told, with gold and silver, pearls, rubies, cloves, pepper and ginger. The locals, all or mostly Muslims, were dressed in rich linens and cottons. His ragged, sea-worn crews must have been astonished.

This evidence of trade heightened the interest of the Portuguese and, not surprisingly, since the objectives of European exploration were, initially at least, related more to business than politics, to doing trade than to founding distant colonies. Extending the reach of Christianity was an always-present consideration, but business was the main one. It was, in effect, the birth of globalisation.

Some of the surviving stonewall structures of the Zimbabwe citadel.

Within 25 years of Da Gama's voyage, the Portuguese succeeded in ending hundreds of years of Arab dominance in the Indian Ocean. But there was trouble brewing at home. Britain and Holland were emerging as the new commercial powers of Europe. Portugal, already weakening under corruption and mismanagement, was taken over by Spain in 1580, and became weaker. And when, just 15 years later, four Dutch ships rounded the Cape under Cornelis Houtman and pressed on to the East, they found that Portugal's distant and exotic empire was as weak as Portugal itself.

The business-minded Dutch saw an opportunity and took advantage of it.

Within a mere five years of the formation of the Dutch East India Company (VOC) in 1602, the Portuguese monopoly of a century collapsed. And within the next hundred years, the VOC had grown into the largest shipping and commercial company in the world.

With a major base at Batavia, on the island of Java, the VOC had extensive interests throughout the East. But Java was far from home, and the sea voyage to and from Holland was long and hazardous. Thus, in the interests of trade, attention turned to the Cape as a halfway station where ships could take on fresh food and water. It was a business decision that, over the next 350 years, would have far-reaching political, economic and social consequences for the whole of Africa.

The man who was given the task of setting up the halfway station was Jan van Riebeeck.

His arrival at the Cape in April 1652 is usually seen as the most important of the first new arrivals from Europe, and so it was in many ways.

Yet, between the Portuguese voyages in the late 1400s and Van Riebeeck's 150 years later, many ships, mainly English and Dutch, dropped anchor at the Cape and at other bays along the coast. Among the callers was the famous Sir Francis Drake, the writer of whose log in 1580 described Africa's southern tip as 'the fairest Cape in the whole circumference of the earth'. These contacts, the relations and trade, and the impressions and judgements that arose from them, did much to shape the foundations of South African history. And they placed a region poised between East and West within the ambit of the Western Atlantic world.

❖

Visiting seafarers, it seems from early accounts, often got what they regarded as knock-down bargains when it came to trading with the people of the Cape, and they were not shy in bragging about it. Sailor Henry May, with an English fleet which called at the Cape in 1591, notes:

Here we bought an oxe for a knife of three-pence, a sheepe for a broken knife or any odd trifle, of the people, which were negros, clad in cloaks or mantles of raw hides, both men and women.

Much the same sentiments emerge from this account by Willem Lodewijckz, who was on one of four Dutch vessels that anchored in Table Bay in 1595:

That day we bought a fine ox for a poor cutlass, as also one for an old copper adze, and when we wished to have two oxen for a new copper adze they gave us yet a third large ox.

The next day, he reports, they got

three oxen and five sheep for a crooked knife, a shovel, a short iron bolt, with a knife and some scraps of iron, worth altogether perhaps four guilders in Holland ….

Here, it would seem, was the contradiction between two value systems that, in time, would become the foundation of centuries of inequality and exploitation. Of course, there is a risk of assuming the sellers of the oxen were losing out because they were naive. They valued the metals they earned differently.

On the other hand, they had enviable skills of their own, and evidently used them to get their own back. The Khoekhoe herders used elaborate whistling calls to command their herds. In 1616, Edward Terry told of how

they would by the same call make the poor creatures break from us, and run to them again … and by this trick now and then they sell the same beast to us two or three times.

From *Before Van Riebeeck* (1967) by R Raven-Hart

In almost every early account, European observers saw the people of the Cape as godless savages, ugly, smelly, with cannibalistic tendencies, and speaking a language that was more like an animal's than a human's.

So, in 1627, Thomas Herbert wrote: 'Their language is rather apishly than articulately sounded, with whom 'tis thought they have unnatural mixtures.' Science had yet to show it, but, genetically, Thomas Herbert had the same 'unnatural mixtures' as the people he was describing.

In 1595, Franck van der Does said 'their speech is just as if one heard a number of angry turkeys … little else but clucking and whistling'. He also thought 'it looked as if they would have eaten us, since they made little ado of eating raw guts [of animals], from which they had a little scraped out the dung with a finger'.

In 1604, Jacob Pieterszoon van Enkhuisen wrote: 'They clucked like turkeys and smeared their bodies [with animal fat] so that they stank disgustingly.' An anonymous observer in the three-ship fleet that called at the Cape in 1601 under Sir James Lancaster noted:

The people of this place are all of a tawny colour, of a reasonable stature, swift of foot, and much given to pick and steal. Their speech is wholly uttered through the throat, and they cluck with their tongues in such a sort that in seven weeks which we remained here in this place, the sharpest wit among us could not learn a single word of their language; and yet the people would soon understand any sign we made to them.

But even if the Cape's residents showed such intelligence of communication, John Jourdain in 1608 thought they were so horrible that he imagined them resorting to cannibalism without a second's thought:

in so much that my opinion is, that if without danger they could come to eat man's flesh, they would not make any scruple of it, for I think the world does not yield a more heathenish people and more beastly.

Much later, some 50 years after Van Riebeeck's party had arrived, a more generous view of the Khoekhoe emerges from Peter Kolben's writings. Kolben, who spent six years at the Cape, leaving in 1712, praised

'San hunters in the Cape mountains', painted by Samuel Daniell for his African Scenery and Animals, published in 1804.

the indigenous people of southern Africa for their justice, their chastity, and their 'simplicity of manners', and noted that the Khoekhoe themselves had told him that the greed, envy, hatred, injustice and lewdness among Christians were among the things that put them off Christianity.

There seems little doubt that the Khoekhoe worked out for themselves quickly enough that they had to be on their guard as increasing numbers of ships began arriving at the southern tip of Africa.

The scene began to change dramatically after 1652. For the people of the Cape, it must have been a bit like a household waking up one day to discover that a family of strangers who had become frequent and demanding visitors – staying for a few days, but always leaving again – had finally moved in for good.

Indeed, the Dutch were setting up home, and soon assumed rights of ownership. They were staying for good.

However, they quickly realised it was not going to be easy. Without proper shelter, the weather was hard on them. They struggled to grow vegetables or other crops. Wasted or ruined stores and provisions were not easily – or speedily – replaced. There were barely enough of them to do all the work required to set up a refreshment station, especially when illness struck, which it often did. And the Khoekhoe from whom they expected a constant supply of livestock – meat for themselves and for the passing ships they were meant to supply – did not always play along.

What's more, the Dutch East India Company was – like most big companies – concerned chiefly with its own interests, and was a tough employer, demanding a lot from the fledgling settlement at the Cape and showing little tolerance of any deviation from instructions set in Holland.

This combination of factors had a decisive bearing on events in the first decades of the settlement, and on the colony's later history, too.

It was not long before the settlers wanted to break free of the rigid control of the company, and so there was gradual expansion away from the coast. That meant using and eventually occupying land the Khoekhoe regarded, by prior claim, as their own.

It is not hard to imagine what the indigenous people must have felt about the newcomers – who must have seemed rather like squatters – from across the sea. There is virtually no record of what the Khoekhoe thought of the Europeans' language, style of dress, manners, choice of food, and trustworthiness, or their relationships among themselves, but it is evident from the early accounts that they were not innocent or naive about the new risks they faced or, for that matter, what could be gained through trade.

At the time of the arrival of the Van Riebeeck party in 1652, there was among the Khoekhoe already considerable insight into the foreigners.

By as early as 1614, they had the benefit of learning much about the pale-skinned settlers from a Khoekhoe man who had actually spent a year living in England, in the home of one of the most influential businessmen of the day.

Coree (though sometimes spelt differently, his is the first indigenous name to appear in European records) had not been a willing tourist to the northern hemisphere.

From the end of the 1500s, passing ships conducted a flourishing trade at the Cape, gaining cattle for scraps of iron. But within two decades, the Khoekhoe began demanding copper instead, and copper was not as readily available on the ships. How were the English to develop a more advantageous trading relationship? Part of the plan, it seems, was to win over the Khoekhoe by trying to convince some key individuals.

This seemed to be the scheme which led to Coree and another man being abducted in 1613 and taken aboard an English ship, the *Hector*, returning to England from the East Indies.

The second man died on the voyage, but Coree made it to England, where he was put up at the London home of the governor of the English East India Company, Sir Thomas Smythe, who evidently arranged for him to be well clothed, housed and fed. Coree was also given gifts, including a suit of armour and brass ornaments. But, not surprisingly, Coree was not a happy man. He had not chosen this enforced exile. An account from the time describes how 'when he had learned a little of our language, he would daily lie upon the ground and cry very often thus in broken English, "Coree home go, Souldania go, home go."' (Table Bay was originally known as Souldania or Saldania.) Finally, in 1614, about a year after being abducted, Coree was returned to Table Bay.

English crews later alleged that the Khoekhoe became more reluctant or more demanding traders under Coree's influence. And as for Coree himself, it is thought that he was killed in a clash with the Dutch in 1626 after refusing to give them food. A second leading Khoekhoe man, Autshumato – also known as Harry – was taken by the English to Bantam, in Java, between 1631 and 1632. A third, Doman, was taken to Batavia, this time by the Dutch, in the 1650s. He returned in 1658.

———— ❖ ————

Certainly, by the time Van Riebeeck was trying to make a go of the Cape, the Khoekhoe were better informed about European scales of values, and were not so easily enticed into trading cattle for next to nothing.

What is also true, however, is that political or clan rivalries between groups of Khoekhoe in the Table Bay region played into the hands of the Dutch, who formed and changed alliances as it suited them. And men like Autshumato and Doman – and a remarkable woman named Krotoa (called Eva by the Dutch) – were used as interpreters and go-betweens in the discussions about trade and living arrangements.

It was not long before the strangers on the shore had become much more familiar with one another, but the relationship was uneasy. The clans of the Western Cape – people such as the Goringhaicona (whom the Dutch called Strandlopers), led by Autshumato, the Goringhaiqua (whom the Dutch called Kaapmans) under Gogosoa, the Gorachouqua under Choro, the Chainouqua (called Saldanhars) and the Cochoqua, one of whose powerful chiefs was Oedasoa – formed a complex Khoekhoe society that the Dutch could not easily control or manipulate.

On the other hand, there were difficulties among the Dutch themselves.

As the historian CW de Kiewiet wrote in 1941, 'for the first four of five years [Van Riebeeck's] little community lived wretchedly on the brink of failure'.

And, under strict Company regulation, there was little incentive for its employees to do much more than the minimum. That began to change in 1657 when Van Riebeeck urged the Company in Holland to relax its hold a little and allow some employees to go out on their own as so-called 'free burghers', and to enjoy at least some freedom, while still being tied to the VOC's commercial objectives.

Ships at anchor in Table Bay form a deceptively innocent backdrop to this illustration of an early Khoekhoe settlement.

CABO DE GOEDE HOOP.

Khoekhoe independence was steadily eroded from the moment of the first ill-matched encounters with the Dutch.

The VOC did not want an ever-expanding colony to worry about, but the yearning employees at the Cape wanted to escape the Company's clutches, and reasoned that the further inland they went, the freer they could be.

The Khoekhoe must have watched these developments with dismay: their land was being taken from under their noses. Some began to take action, stealing the free burghers' cattle and making life difficult for them. Conflict escalated, with the Dutch forming armed militia to back up their occupation of land. And so, in 1659, just two years after the free burghers were given permission to go farming, the first Dutch-Khoekhoe war broke out. The Dutch, though much harried, gained a special advantage that year with the arrival of a fresh cargo of horses. It was not long before Van Riebeeck was able to host 'peace talks'.

———— ❖ ————

The meeting at the settlement on 5 and 6 April, 1660, eight years to the month after Van Riebeeck's party arrived, was a turning point: it clarified Dutch intentions, and it set the course of the colony's history. Land was at the heart of the matter.

Joining the Dutch in the talks were Gogosoa, Autshumato, 'and all the principal men and elders'.

It comes as a surprise that Van Riebeeck's diarist is so candid in reporting the opinions of the aggrieved indigenous people of southern Africa, and it is a remarkable account. This is how he recorded the discussion:

They [the Khoekhoe leaders] strongly insisted that we had been appropriating more and more of their land, which had been theirs all these centuries ... They asked if they would be allowed to do such a thing supposing they went to Holland, and they added: 'It would be of little consequence if you people stayed at the fort, but you come right into the interior and select the best land for yourselves, without even asking whether we mind or whether it will cause us any inconvenience.' They therefore strongly urged that they should again be given free access to this land … At first we argued against this, saying that there was not enough grass for their cattle as well as ours, to which they replied: 'Have we then no reason to prevent you from getting cattle, since, if you have a large number, you will take up all our grazing grounds with them? As for your claim that the land is not big enough for us both, who should rather in justice give way, the rightful owner or the foreign intruder?' They thus remained adamant in their claim of old-established natural ownership. They said they should at least be allowed to go and gather bitter almonds, which grow wild in abundance there, and to dig for roots as winter food. This likewise could not be granted them for they would then have too many opportunities for doing harm to the colonists, and furthermore we shall need the almonds ourselves this year to plant the proposed protective hedge or defensive barrier.* These reasons were, of course, not mentioned to them, but when they persisted in their request, eventually they had to be told that they had now lost the land as a result of the war and had no alternative but to admit that it was no longer theirs. … Their land had thus justly fallen to us in a defensive war, won by the sword, as it were, and we intended to keep it.

The 'defensive' wild almond hedge planted by Van Riebeeck is still there today. Having been declared what used to be called a 'National Monument', it forms part of the National Botanical Gardens at Kirstenbosch.

The Khoekhoe chiefs were not happy, and told the Dutch negotiators of their ill-treatment by the free burghers, and warned that if this continued, they would continue to steal cattle as 'revenge'. But the Dutch responded that if this happened 'peace could never be maintained between us, and then by right of conquest we should take still more of their land from them'. Eventually, under these harsh terms, the leaders conceded. Finally, the diarist notes:

So peace was concluded and the chief Gogosoa, Harry and all the principal men, numbering about 40 persons in all, were presented with gifts of copper, beads, and tobacco and then treated so well to food and drink that they were all merrily tipsy.

European settlement of the Cape followed within years of the arrival of the Dutch.

DE KAAP STAD
OF
TAFEL VALEY

Tipsy they may have been, and merry for the moment, but this was not, of course, the end of it. If anything, the end of it occurred a mere 10 years ago with the ending of white minority rule in the first democratic elections in 1994.

Back in 1660, the fate of the Khoekhoe was all but sealed. Within a hundred years, they would be conquered, forced off their land – often by white trekboers steadily penetrating the interior – and obliged by the demands of survival to work as labourers on the farms of settlers.

It is thought there were some 200 000 Khoekhoe south of the Orange River in the mid-1600s. By the late 1700s there were perhaps 20 000 within the Cape settlement. Vast numbers died in the smallpox epidemics of 1713, 1735 and 1767.

In the 1760s, the Khoekhoe, along with slaves, were obliged to carry passes, and though the Cape law of 1828, Ordinance 50, scrapped passes for Khoekhoe and freed slaves, it did little in effect to rescue them from impoverishment or economic subservience.

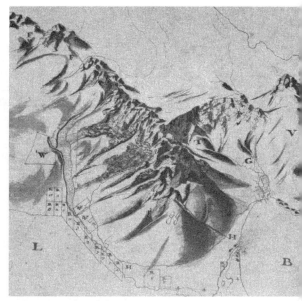

ABOVE: Chart of lands at the Cape of Good Hope in 1658 … the confirmation of possession.

BELOW: Guns and horses gave the settlers the upper hand in the contest with the Khoekhoe, whose survival came to depend on working for the newcomers.

Communities throughout Africa and the East lived in terror of slave traders.

There was significant Khoekhoe resistance against the settlers, which, in some areas, slowed or hampered the whites' advance into the interior, but it was eventually overcome, chiefly by force.

By 1660, when Van Riebeeck was asserting his claims over the Khoekhoe groups of the Cape, the settler community (as much as the indigenous population) was coming under the influence of a damning and decisive factor of South African history: slavery.

A few slaves were already at the Cape as early as 1655. But it was the arrival of a Dutch ship, the *Amersfoort*, on 28 March, 1658, that marked the start of a tragic influx. The 174 slaves who arrived on that date were, in a sense, returning to home soil after an unwelcome adventure on the high seas: they were Angolans who had been enslaved by the Portuguese and were bound for Brazil when their ship was captured by the Dutch off the South American coast. Many of the slaves were young – so young, Van Riebeeck's diarist notes, that they were unsuitable for work for four or five years.

Within a short while, a few made a bid for freedom. It was an act of desperation that would be repeated countless times over the next more than 170 years, until the emancipation of slaves in 1834.

The five men and two women runaways left the Cape and headed north, presumably to try to get home to Angola. They were never caught, and probably did not survive either, but their flight inspired others, and escapes continued. There were strong deterrents. Punishments were brutal, and the Dutch either rewarded the Khoekhoe for helping to recapture runaways or, by threats, coerced them into doing so.

In time, thousands of slaves poured into the fledgling colony. They came, mostly, from five areas: the Indonesian archipelago, Bengal, South India and Sri Lanka, Madagascar and the East African coast. They had been bought in the slave markets of Batavia, Chinsura, Cochin, Boina in Madagascar and Delagoa Bay or Mozambique Island, having been brought there by a network of traders including Bengali Buginese trader-pirates, Chinese junk captains, Sakalava kings, Prazeros on the Zambezi, Portuguese officials in Delagoa Bay or kidnappers in south India.

Often, they were brought to the Cape semi-illegally as the 'cargo' of sailors and officials in Dutch East India ships or in larger French or Portuguese slaving ships which sold off a number of generally sickly slaves on their way to the New World, the new colonies in America.

Events in faraway France in 1685 had a significant impact on the early colony. It was in that year that the Roman Catholic king of France, Louis XIV, revoked the Edict of Nantes, a deal made in 1598 with the Protestants, assuring them a measure of religious freedom. There had been, and continued to be, conflict between the two brands of Christianity. When, in 1685, the deal was broken and the king tried forcibly to convert the Protestants to Catholicism, several hundred thousand Protestants – or Huguenots, as they came to be called – fled France. Many went to Holland and Germany, where they were protected. And, since Holland had control over the Cape, some came to southern Africa, arriving in 1688. They were settled in the area that was named after them: Franschhoek, or 'French-corner'. Though there were not many of them, their impact was marked: with their wine-making skills, they added a new labour-intensive element to the Cape's agricultural economy, which had no great staple product such as the timber of New England (eastern American seaboard) or the sugar of the West Indies (Caribbean).

(The bulk of the other colonists, writer and archivist Karel Schoeman has pointed out, were 'former Company soldiers and sailors who, after completing their period of service, chose to stay on as farmers at the Cape rather than return to an uncertain future in Europe where they made up the lowest class of society'. Most of them were from Holland, northern Germany or Scandinavia.)

Generally, the Huguenots were a cut above these colonists, but in a relatively short time, the settlers merged into a single identity.

Today, the Huguenots' recognisably French names – such as Malan, Du Preez, De Villiers, Du Plessis, Joubert, Roux, Labuschagne, Marais, Viljoen and Lombard – are a fixed feature of Afrikaans society.

Huguenot immigrants fleeing persecution in France enhanced the Cape's wine-making industry, establishing estates such as these in the Franschhoek valley.

Sale of Prize Slaves.
This Day the 3d of October,
Will be Sold by Public Vendue,
At the Garden of F. Kannemeyer,
SEVENTY prime male and female Slaves,
captured in the French vessels, La Raisonable and Le Glaucus, and condemned as prize
in the Court of Vice Admiralty.
Cape Town, 28th Sept. 1801.

The slave trade was a tormenting and complex commerce that turned humans into commodities, so much more, and so much worse, than a life-long prison sentence. 'Everything touched by slavery is brutalised,' notes the historian Robert Ross, masters as much as slaves.

When, in 1717 – there were, by then, already more than 2 500 slaves in the Cape – doubts arose in the Dutch East India Company about continuing to use slaves, only one of the 17 council members argued for the ending of slavery. DM Pasques de Chavonnes believed slaves should be replaced by immigrant labour from Europe. With slaves, he said, colonists had to endure all manner of 'dangers, expense and troubles'.

But he was outvoted. Councillor J Cruse, in a typical argument, put his support for slavery in the following terms:

I cannot believe that farm labourers or other Europeans will be found more useful, industrious, convenient or cheaper than slaves, as one can accomplish everything with slaves (who require only food and a little clothing) even better than with Europeans.

By 1795, when VOC rule ended, there were officially 16 839 privately owned slaves at the Cape. By the time slavery ended in 1834, their numbers had grown to 36 274.

Good profits from the trade in slaves brought misery to millions.

Trading in slaves – though not the owning of slaves – was abolished by the British in 1808. Until then, it was a lucrative and savage business for many, as records of slaving vessels show.

The summarised extract at the foot of this page comes from the log of the Dutch ship *De Drie Heuvelen*, which embarked on a slaving voyage from Cape Town to Madagascar in 1753. The ship left Table Bay on 23 May, arriving at St Augustin Bay on the island's south-western coast about a month later. The crew learned that, while there was much competition from English, French, Portuguese and Moorish traders, the local king was willing to trade slaves for guns and ammunition.

No task was too menial for a slave.

———— ❖ ————

Slaves were bought and sold at auction, like cattle. This first-hand account by a visitor to the Cape in 1824 is a haunting testimony.

Having learned that there was to be a sale of cattle, farm-stock, etc, by auction, at a veld cornet's in the vicinity, we halted our waggon for the purpose of procuring fresh oxen. Among the stock … was a female slave and her three children. The farmers examined them, as if they had been so many head of cattle. They were sold separately, and to different purchasers. The tears, the anxiety, the anguish of the mother, while she met the gaze of the multitude … or cast a heart-rending look upon her children, and the simplicity and touching sorrow of the poor young ones, while they clung to their distracted parent … contrasted with the marked insensibility and jocular countenances of the spectators, furnished a striking commentary on the miseries of slavery …. While the woman was in this distressed situation, she was asked: 'Can you feed sheep?' Her reply was so indistinct that it escaped me; but it was probably in the negative, for her purchaser rejoined in a loud and harsh voice: 'Then I will teach you with the sjambok.' The mother and her three children were literally torn from each other.

From *The Chains That Bind Us. A history of slavery at the Cape* (1996) by Nigel Worden, with Ruth Versfeld, Dorothy Dyer and Claudia Bickford-Smith

5 August: visit to the king of the region; danger of crossing two broad rivers infested with crocodiles.
6 August: king suggested prices for slaves that we think are far too high: eventually beat him down from 35 Spanish realen per adult slave to 20 realen plus knives and ammunition. Several slaves bought.
20 August: king demanded some of the slaves back: we considered it was too dangerous to stay and so we left.
28 August: some of the slaves below deck broke out of their chains and came on deck. They were eventually overcome, but one was killed and seven wounded. We decided to make an example of the leaders of this rebellion by severe punishment in order to frighten the others, since our interrogations revealed that they had plotted to kill all the Europeans on board and then to escape. The leader was tied to one of the gratings and his arms and legs broken. He was then thrown into the sea as food for the fishes, all in the presence of the other slaves. The other leaders were severely lashed.

The ship set sail for the Cape on 14 November, arriving in Table Bay on December 17 with 49 adult males, 41 adult females, 14 young men, four young women and one child.

The slaves' journeys took them, often, from one owner to the next, one corner of the world to another. Their names were changed, and they were usually lost to their families forever. A young Indian girl of nine or 10, sold under the name of China Nagapatnam in India for 15 silver rupees to Jan Tropetter in January 1768, ended up at the Cape in March 1775, where, renamed Rosa, she was sold to a man named Serrurier for 25 rixdollars.

From *The Chains That Bind Us. A history of slavery at the Cape* (1996) by Nigel Worden, with Ruth Versfeld, Dorothy Dyer and Claudia Bickford-Smith

Slaves who resisted the abuse and inhumanity of the men and women who owned them were dealt with harshly. The mildest punishments were severe. Crime, or behaviour considered criminal, carried savage penalties. While Cape slave-owners were forbidden from punishing slaves beyond a certain degree, and slaves could complain when they considered this norm to have been exceeded, allowable (and official) punishment was staggeringly harsh. Slaves could be sent to the *'fiscaal'* (the public prosecutor or police chief) to be flogged or to work on the treadmill (a big wheel, driven by human power). Slaves convicted of theft were likely to be hanged. Those who had murdered other slaves or Khoekhoe would be broken on a wheel, put out of their misery with the 'coup de grâce'. Killing a white carried the same punishment without the 'coup de grâce', and in particularly serious cases this would be preceded by tearing eight pieces of the slave's flesh away with red-hot pincers. When the victim was the slave's master, the condemned man would be impaled on a stake driven up his anus and left to die. It sometimes took two days, or more, for the man to become unconscious.

Homosexuality was regarded by the Dutch as the equivalent of bestiality, and the punishment for both was barbaric: the man was rowed out into Table Bay with enough weights attached to him to ensure he would sink, and would be thrown into the water, often tied to his partner in the 'crime'.

Escapees who were caught were heartlessly treated. Cape-born slave Lea, who 'belonged' to the VOC, had spent some years as a runaway first at Hout Bay and then among a large community of runaways at Cape Hangklip with her husband Jochem, another runaway slave. But when he died, she moved away from Hangklip, and was caught. Her sentence was to spend the rest of her life chained to a block.

Though there were limited revolts by slaves – including, sometimes, setting crops or property on fire – deserting remained the main expression of rebellion. Some runaway slaves reached areas beyond the boundaries of the Colony, joining Khoe-San and Orlam (racially mixed) communities living around the Orange River, as well as Xhosa chiefdoms beyond the eastern frontier. Others escaped on Dutch or English ships, some even managing to reach Europe or the East Indies.

Yet those, the bulk, who remained were not, as might be expected, reduced to machines who in themselves lacked humanity or culture or resolve or skill.

In rough clothing, mostly, and no shoes, and accommodated in spartan quarters, slaves lived out a life of perpetual service.

They worked as domestics for private owners, cleaning, cooking, fetching and carrying water and firewood, looking after children – even breastfeeding babies as wet nurses – or they worked as porters at the docks, or as sellers of vegetables, fish, cloth or other goods for their owners (sometimes being allowed to keep some of the money they made).

The VOC's slaves worked as builders or general labourers (building the Cape Town Castle, for instance), or as gardeners in the Company's garden, developed initially to provide passing ships with fresh produce. A few slaves were skilled carpenters, masons and coopers (making casks and barrels).

Slaves on farms were used for all the hard, physical work of farming – ploughing, planting, pruning, harvesting and herding. They were often supervised by an official – typically a VOC soldier – called a *knecht*, or a trusted older slave, a *mandoor*.

In some cases, slaves developed unexpected bonds. Nigel Worden notes in *The Chains That Bind Us*:

We know that slaves who worked in their owners' houses sometimes became loyal to their owners. Historians have found examples in court records where slaves helped to protect their owners and their families when they were attacked by other slaves or Khoe. Sometimes, slaves were left money or possessions in their owners' wills. Sometimes they were even freed. But we also know that slaves were their owners' property.

Female slaves often had to act as sexual partners for their owners. Their children belonged to their owners. [By the 18th century, many of the slaves in the Cape were not imported. In the records, they would be named accordingly, as in, say, Petronella van der Kaap, or 'of the Cape'.]

We can only guess what the slave women felt about this kind of treatment.

Although they were adults, slaves were treated as permanent children by their owners. The slave owners' legitimate children grew up to be slave owners and farmers. But slaves were always treated as children.

Because they were bought and sold as individuals, it was virtually impossible for slaves to form families. Yet there were bonds and relationships between them that influenced the nature of the whole of society.

Naturally, they all spoke different African and Asian languages, depending on where they had come from. Slaves from India and the East Indies spoke a mixture of Indian and Indonesian languages, and Portuguese. Madagascan slaves spoke Malagasy and African slaves used their own languages. All these languages, along with Khoe, began to influence the way people communicated on the farms. Mixed with Dutch and German, the result was the emergence of a new indigenous African language: Afrikaans. (Afrikaans words such as 'piesang' and 'blatjang', for instance, are rooted in Indonesia.)

Similarly, they influenced the cuisine, the food, of the Cape, the music, the mythology, and the belief systems.

This is especially true of the rise of Islam in southern Africa. Muslim political exiles and slaves from the East Indies spread the word of Mohammed among people the Dutch had made no attempt to convert to Christianity. (There was a VOC rule that baptised slaves could not be sold. That was a good reason for slave-owners not to introduce their slaves to Christianity.)

Historians have suggested that Islam might have become popular because it was a positive link for slaves with the world of so-called 'free blacks' and exiles from the East, and also a way of defying or rejecting the colonists.

By the 1820s, the colonial view was that while 'Muhammedanism' – as it is described in one account – was a political threat, the fact that converts did not touch liquor was a virtue.

— ❖ —

TOP RIGHT: Flogging was the least of the punishments slaves could expect for transgressing boundaries set by their owners. The original caption to this early 19th-century engraving explains that a Dutch slave-owner –the man on the left – would have his slave flogged 'till he has smoked as many pipes of tobacco as he may judge the magnitude of the crime to deserve'.

RIGHT: Anxiety about the emancipation of slaves was widespread at the Cape. Slave-owners' concerns were raised at meetings such as the one reported on here.

THE
ZUID-AFRIKAAN.

CAPE TOWN, MARCH 28, 1834.

THE Public Meeting of Slave Proprietor under the sanction of His Excellency the Go vernor. to take into consideration the prov sions and enactments of the Emancipation Bill pursuant to a previous notice, was held or Saturday, the 22d instant, and terminated not only to the entire satisfaction of those that were present (the number of which we com pute to have been nearly 500); but also of all those whom we have since spoken, we only regret that no more Proprietors of Slaves from the Country Districts attended; although there were a number of the most respectable inha- bitants from Tulbagh, Bokkeveld, Roggeveld, Worcester, Zwartland, the Paarl, &c, and several Field-Cornets, as representing their respective Wards, who heartily joined concurred in the proposed and adopted tions: and surely if the important object be taken into consideration, with harmony displayed on the occa- ngratulate our countr

Slave-owners must often have had a false idea of grandness from having slaves. There is a sense of this in the following description by the Swedish botanist Peter Thunberg, who visited the Cape in 1772:

> Previous to the company's sitting down to meals ... a female slave brings a wash-basin and towel, to wash their hands .... In the houses of the wealthy, every one of the company has a slave behind his chair to wait on him. The slave has frequently a large palm leaf in his hand, by way of a fan, to drive away the flies ....

From *The Chains That Bind Us. A history of slavery at the Cape* (1996) by Nigel Worden, with Ruth Versfeld, Dorothy Dyer and Claudia Bickford-Smith

In an earlier account, from the 1730s, Otto Mentzel, a German resident of the Cape, offers a rather romantic, yet also quite revealing, view of slavery on the grain farms of the Boland:

> [T]he servants themselves know what their daily task is, and it may be said that even the slaves are quite happy in their bondage. This may be clearly perceived in fine weather and on moonlit evenings. For although the slave has worked ... and suffered from the heat ... he is happy and sings, and plays on his raveking (ramkie) and even dances. But on winter evenings they sit round the fire with a pipe of tobacco and tell each other stories of their fatherland in Portuguese.
>
> Sensible slaves want nothing but food, clothing and tobacco; sensible masters do not deprive them of any of these, but take into consideration the heavy yoke of slavery and do not treat them unreasonably nor have them flogged unduly.

From *The Chains That Bind Us. A history of slavery at the Cape* (1996) by Nigel Worden, with Ruth Versfeld, Dorothy Dyer and Claudia Bickford-Smith

It is a very different picture that emerges from the court records of the landdrost of Stellenbosch of 9 January, 1749. The evidence is that of a 60-year-old female slave, Manika of Bengal.

> That about 22 years ago, she was living at Simonsvalleij ... And there she had relations with one of her fellow slaves, Reijnier of Madagascar, and amongst other children they had a daughter named Sabina. Sabina had diligently performed much work for her master's wife, but ... she had been much beaten and abused by the woman; so much so that her man Reijnier had ... asked his master to sell the child to someone else, for she could stand it no longer.
>
> That on a Saturday [the master's wife] took Sabina into a back room after she had laid the table and stripped her naked and tied her to a post and the whole afternoon beat her with a sjambok and rubbed salt on to her.

(Later, when Sabina's father Reijnier found out what had happened, he was enraged, assaulted the slave owner, and fled. This testimony is from his trial after he was caught, having lived as a runaway for almost a quarter of a century. By this time, Sabina, and all Manika's fellow slaves, had died.)

From *The Chains That Bind Us. A history of slavery at the Cape* (1996) by Nigel Worden, with Ruth Versfeld, Dorothy Dyer and Claudia Bickford-Smith

By a process called 'manumission' some slaves were freed by their owners. They were called 'free blacks'. Often they were freed in their owners' wills, or sometimes when their owners wanted to marry them. Some owners freed their slaves in return for money from other free blacks. It was a controlled process, and the VOC had to give permission for it. It was partly for this reason that very few slaves were freed. They made up 7,4 percent of the total free population in 1670, but only 4,4 percent in 1770, when they numbered not many more than 1 000. It is not surprising that they were not as free as the colonists themselves ... a curfew, for instance, applied to 'slaves and people of colour'. They also had to dress in a certain way and pay taxes. Some had plots and farmed on a small scale. And some even had slaves of their own. Most lived in the poorer community of Cape Town among exiles, convicts and traders from the East, working as artisans, small-scale retailers, domestic workers and fishermen.

Early Cape life was not racially divided – as it became later – but there was a sharp division between 'the small number of respectable people – the Company officials at the top, the ships' officers, the merchants, grading down through the various burgher slave-owners, whether lodging-house keepers, small tradesmen or artisans – and the rest, whether they be passing sailors, resident soldiers, free blacks, Chinese or slaves.

> There were free blacks in many of the key positions of Cape Town, as brothel madams, even as publicans. The Chinese, all of whom had been transported from Batavia as a punishment for criminal activities, had much of the retail trade in foodstuffs in their hands, at least at the lower end of the scale, a profession that was good cover for receiving stolen goods.

One case involved a Chinaman Tjo Tsanko, who induced a slave Caatjie to steal from her mistress so that, as she understood it, he could buy her freedom. But Tjo seems to have owed money within the Chinese community, and did not use the money to buy Caatjie's freedom. His intrigue cost Tjo his liberty and he was banned to Robben Island to work for life in chains.

> In a town where that was possible, the Cape slaves had, if in no sense real freedom, at least a certain amount of room to manoeuvre. … The slaves could readily drink their coffee and arak in the huts in the gardens above the town, hold their cockfights or gamble with dice and braai fish on the beach of Table Bay. … But for all this, their masters held great power over them that they were unable to shake off. … The actions of the Cape Town slaves thus grew out of this discrepancy between the relative absence of supervision within the urban environment and the savagery of their subordination to the masters. Given this contradiction, they shared the fate of many of the lowest of the company employees, soldiers, sailors, woodcutters and so on, and it is thus not surprising that occasionally slaves and Europeans deserted together and lived together in their precarious, often short-lived freedom.

From *Cape of Torments, Slavery and Resistance in South Africa* (1983) by Robert Ross

A significant group of people to find themselves at the Cape – though, unlike the Huguenots, not by choice – was a remarkable assembly of kings, princes and religious leaders of Muslim states in the Indonesian islands which were either defeated or subverted by the VOC. They ended up at the Cape as political exiles whom the Dutch wanted to be kept as far away as possible from Batavia.

Those the Dutch regarded as having moderate opinions enjoyed relative comfort, but radicals were sent to Robben Island.

One of the most prominent political prisoners of the time was the Rajah of Tambora, sent to the Cape in chains in 1697 after resisting VOC rule. When he arrived, though, Governor Simon van der Stel (whose grandmother was a Javanese woman) treated him relatively leniently. The rajah's wife was allowed to join him, and they lived for a time at the company gardens at Rustenburg, in present-day Rondebosch. When Simon van der Stel was replaced as governor by his son, Willem Adriaan, the rajah and his family moved to the governor's country estate, Vergelegen, where – according to the French traveller Francois Valentyn – the rajah's wife had some sort of authority in running the household.

Repeatedly during his 22-year exile, the rajah begged to go home to Tambora, but the Dutch would hear none of it, and he died at the Cape in 1719.

> Loring Passir was exiled to the Cape in 1723 for no greater reason, apparently, than having angered his influential mother-in-law. His father-in-law, the Sultan of Pakabuana, paid his living expenses at the Cape, and the company gave him a place to live in at Stellenbosch.
>
> Prince Achmet of Ternate, who was exiled to the Cape about the same time, lived lavishly to begin with and was even allowed to keep slaves, but finally his style of life so angered the authorities that they had him beaten and sent to Robben Island, where he remained for 65 years.
>
> From *Forgotten Frontiersmen* (1978) by Alf Wannenburgh

A berobed Sheik Jusuf and his followers arrive at the Cape, exiled for defying the Dutch in Java.

Sheik Jusuf, regarded as the founder of Islam in South Africa, was already an elderly man of 68 when he was landed at the Cape in 1694. He was a relative of the King of Goa and had been born … at Macassar in the Celebes. … [H]e had married one of the daughters of Sultan Ageng of Bantam and come to be venerated as the leading religious authority there. He had lived at Ageng's court for many years when, in 1680, the chain of events which was to end in his exile to the Cape was set in motion.

Ageng, one of the last of Java's independent Sultans, was overthrown by his son with the backing of the Dutch. … Sheik Jusuf took to the jungles and mountains with 4 000 followers to wage a guerrilla war. It was tough, and his forces dwindled rapidly. The Dutch persuaded him to give himself up with the promise of a pardon, but the promise was not kept. He and his family were taken first to Batavia, then Ceylon, and finally, in 1694, to the Cape. With him were 48 followers, including two wives.

They were settled well away from Table Bay, on the farm of a Dutch Reformed minister at Faure. The name of the nearby Macassar Beach dates from that time.

Tradition has it that Sheik Jusuf performed many miracles here during the remaining five years of his life, and the settlement at Faure became a haven for runaway Indonesian slaves, and the first Muslim religious community in South Africa.

Two other intriguing and influential men to be exiled at the Cape in the 1700s – there is no record of their 'crimes', but they are thought to have been political – were Tuan Said, who arrived in 1747, and Tuan Guru, who arrived in 1770. Tuan Said was the first imam at the Cape and Tuan Guru the founder of the first mosque. Both were buried on Signal Hill.

From *Forgotten Frontiersmen* (1978) by Alf Wannenburgh

The beginning of the end of slavery came in 1808 when the British, who had taken control of the Cape two years before, abolished slave trading throughout their expanding empire.

But it was a full 30 years before slaves at the Cape were actually freed. By the 1820s, new so-called 'amelioration laws' had been passed to ease the plight of people in bondage: hours of work were limited; clothing and food requirements laid down; slaves were allowed to marry and their owners forbidden from selling young children separately from their mothers; slaves were given the right to buy their own freedom; punishments were controlled, and some slaves in Cape Town were given basic education.

History suggests that whenever a bad or unpopular system is reformed, and therefore has the appearance of weakening, its victims are often inspired to revolt. This is no less true of the slaves of the Cape.

A couple of Irish sailors, having a drink in a tavern in Cape Town one day in 1808, are credited with providing the spark that led to the first of two slave uprisings. Two slaves, Louis van Mauritius and Abraham van der Kaap, got chatting with the sailors, who told them that the ending of the trade in slaves that year meant slavery itself was going to end soon. The slaves also learned that in countries such as Britain there was no such thing as slavery. This information fired the imagination of the two slaves and they decided it was time to fight for their freedom.

They persuaded 300 farm slaves from the Koeberg region to join them, and they set out for Cape Town to demand their freedom, attacking other farms on the way. The alarmed colonists confronted the rebels at Salt River and defeated them.

The second uprising, the so-called Galant rebellion, took place in 1825 on a remote farm in the Bokkeveld. A group of slaves and some Khoekhoe labourers under Galant van der Caab killed the farmer and some of his family and threatened to take over other farms, believing that their freedom had been promised but withheld. The rising was shortlived: the slaves were caught and publicly executed. The severed heads of Galant and another were 'stuck upon iron spikes' for people to see.

By the same token, reform can have unsettling consequences for those who have benefited from the old way of doing things.

Slave-owners at the Cape became increasingly indignant at the British government's reforms, rules such as the 1830 regulation that female slaves could no longer be physically punished, or the regulation that a record had to be kept of every punishment inflicted on male slaves. Owners were so resistant to this rule that they rioted in Stellenbosch in 1831 and in Cape Town a year later 2 000 owners protested against Britain passing new laws without asking them what they thought about it. But there was no stopping the gradual reforms. Ultimately, slave-owning farmers who refused to accept the ending of slavery decided to leave the colony altogether. It was one of the main reasons for the Great Trek into the interior from the late 1830s.

Emancipation offered some, but not much, comfort to many former slaves. The sense of a wearying lifetime of bondage is evident in this portrait of Petrus Frans and his wife.

Why was it, then, that a system the Dutch believed provided 'useful, industrious, convenient [and] cheaper' labour than any other came to an end?

Rather like the ending of apartheid, a combination of factors, rather than any single one, led to the ending of slavery.

On one hand, pressure mounted steadily on the British government from people who thought slavery was inhumane, cruel and immoral. Some of these were strongly influenced by Christian ideas of equality, love and humanity. Vigorous campaigns were launched by abolitionists such as Dr John Philip and William Wilberforce.

On the other hand, the economy – the ways of making money, doing business, producing goods and services, and of farming – had changed in the years of slavery. While, in Britain and Europe, the Industrial Revolution was changing the patterns of work, money-making and spending, the slave-owning colonies were stuck in the rut of an old system based on the manual labour of people who did not have the money to participate in the new kind of economy. Slave-owners, who invested their money in slaves, had little to invest in new technology. And unpaid slaves could not contribute to economic growth, because they were not wage earners.

So slavery was increasingly seen to be economically inefficient, old-fashioned and cruel. The end was inevitable, yet, typically for such historical processes, it was not clear-cut. Formally, slaves were emancipated – or freed – in 1834, but there was anxiety in Britain and in the colony about the impact of freeing nearly 37 000 people into society – into the economy – in one day. As a result, the freeing of slaves on 1 December, 1834, was compromised: they had to work for their owners for another four years as apprentices.

When, finally, on 1 December, 1838, the thousands of slaves at the Cape were freed, their options for exercising their freedom were limited. They did not have the money to buy land in an economy dominated by farming, and because there were so many others looking for jobs in Cape Town, work was hard to find. One popular option was to go to mission stations, where the slaves were given plots of land. But many simply returned to their former owners – or went to other farms – to work as wage labourers on the land.

The colonists were also quick to pass laws to try to control the new society that was emerging. The Masters and Servants Ordinance of 1841 – which survived until 1974 – established, as its name makes clear, who the 'baas' was. Offences included desertion, 'insubordination' and even the 'use of insulting language' by workers. The law became steadily stricter throughout the 1800s.

❖

The historian CW de Kiewiet believed that white South Africa's experience of slavery was a precursor to the constructed, or consciously fashioned, system of discrimination that apartheid was:

As the entire community of Hottentots, slaves and Europeans grew more numerous without becoming appreciably richer, it began to create within itself a privileged white caste, depending upon an excessive number of slaves and servants, whose labour was wastefully and inefficiently used. Little effort was made to raise the standard of living or increase the opportunities of the class of slaves and servants. In this manner, the limited wealth of the Colony became the privilege of its white population, whose higher standard of living was at the expense of the economic and social welfare of a numerous servile population. Thus early did South Africa learn that a self-conscious group may escape the worst effects of life in a poor and unprosperous land by turning distinctions of race and colour into devices for social and economic discrimination.

From *A History of South Africa Social and Economic* (1941) by CW de Kiewiet

Order and permanence pervade this panorama of Cape Town at the end of VOC rule.

Some men flourished at the Cape, though it was not an environment in which individual success was encouraged. The rewards, but also the penalties, were obvious under the Van der Stel governorships. Simon van der Stel, governor from 1679 to 1699, and his son, Willem Adriaan (1699–1707), did much to modernise farming and consolidate the colony's agricultural economy. Willem Adriaan especially is seen as the first entrepreneur of southern Africa, forming with his father and his brother a monopoly that encompassed a third of the colony. He became the biggest landowner, the biggest cattle and wheat farmer, the biggest wine grower and slave holder.

But he was seen to have become too big for his boots, threatening the interests of the VOC, and angering the bulk of – poorer – colonists. He was finally dismissed.

Writing in the mid-1800s, Cape judge EB Watermeyer said of VOC rule at the colony: 'The government of remote provinces on the principles of the counting-house had failed.'

As a whole, the Cape was not a profitable colony, partly because of the difficult geographic conditions and climate, the fact that there was no natural resource of any significant scale, and partly because the VOC, in its keenness to maintain its monopoly, limited the scope of individuals to make money for themselves and administered an increasingly complex settlement with often absurd rigidity.

A strange token of this is the regulations passed under Ryk Tulbagh, who started out life as a common soldier and rose to the rank of governor, to limit 'ostentation and luxury' (*pracht* and *praal*). It concerned, among other things, the use of umbrellas. In a population of some 45 000 people, of whom 12 000 were of European extraction, no more than 50 men and their wives were entitled by law to the privilege of using an umbrella at all, in any weather.

Women had to watch their dress:

> No women below wives of junior merchants, or those who among citizens are of the same rank, may wear silk dresses with silk braiding or embroidery, nor any diamonds nor mantelets; and although the wives of junior merchants may wear these ornaments, they shall not be entitled to allow their daughters to wear them. All women, married or single, without distinction, are prohibited, whether in mourning or out of mourning, under a penalty of 25 rixdollars, to wear dresses with a train.

A regulation cited in *Selections from the Writings of the late EB Watermeyer* (1877)

This was the least of the restraints that for many made life at the Cape intolerable.

Colonists rebelled – or sought better opportunities – by moving steadily further away from Table Bay into the interior. 'On the slowly widening frontier of the Colony,' De Kiewiet writes,

> developed an economy in which self-sufficiency was more important than profit. For men who gave up trying to raise cash crops and used what they produced mainly for their own consumption, the Company's monopoly had few terrors.

Armed conquest brought the Cape under British rule. This depicts the battle of Blaauwberg in 1806.

As a sum, the social, political and economic factors of the early years, he suggests, forged not a European colony, but 'a totally new and unique society of different races and colours and cultural attainments, fashioned by conflicts of racial heredity and the oppositions of unequal social groups'.

As the yearning colonists spread out, so the administration, the government of the Cape, was obliged to reach out after them, partly in a vain attempt to limit the extent of the colony and thus its own administrative pains, and partly to hold on to the advantages of controlling the settlers' farming activities. It was a lost cause.

Though increased sea traffic, and free-spending French soldiers visiting the Cape, during the Seven Years War (1756–63) and the American War of Independence (1775–83) created a sudden boom at the colony, the VOC was on its last legs. Struggling under the burden of huge debts and facing stiffening English and French competition in business, the once mighty Dutch East India Company was collapsing, finally going bankrupt in 1794.

In 1795, just over 300 years from Dias's first landing, a British force invaded the Cape, turning southern Africa into a territory of dispute between European powers, an object of the imperialist scheme and the politics of European economies.

The herders and hunter-gatherers who were the first to meet the pale-skinned newcomers from across the sea were all but conquered and dispossessed. In the next 100 years, conflict with the African farmers of the interior and dramatic economic change after the discovery of gold and diamonds would shape the profile of modern South Africa, and set the scene for the political showdown of the 20th century.

Being in touch

chapter three

Being in touch

Ray and Diana de Proft with a photograph of their son, Graham, and his white girlfriend, Sonia. Theirs was an outlawed, and tragic, love.

One winter's day in 1974, a young Cape Town man made his way to a suburban railway station with a desperate idea in his mind.

He was in love, but his love was a secret. Soon it would be a secret he would no longer be able to conceal. As the next train thundered down the tracks, 20-year-old Graham de Proft leapt from the platform.

It was the price of being in touch in a South Africa that had become coldly obsessed with keeping people apart.

De Proft had just learned that his girlfriend was pregnant, but because he was classified 'coloured', he could not marry her as the Mixed Marriages Act forbade marriages across the colour line. He took his life instead. As a last token of his love, he left the girl all the money he had – about R40 – to help her buy clothes for the baby. But the girl's father took the money and used it to pay for an abortion: a legal

abortion could be obtained only because the father was classified 'coloured'. The girl, who learned of her lover's death only when he failed to arrive to take her to the cinema, tried to commit suicide by cutting her wrists, but failed.

The story of Graham de Proft and his girlfriend, Sonia, was repeated in different forms in countless cases in the second half of the 20th century. But the tragedy and anguish of the Graham de Profts of the time were heartlessly weighed in some quarters.

'I have a great deal of sympathy with people who have suffered under this Act, and who have committed an offence under this Act,' JT Kruger, National Party MP for Prinshof, told the House of Assembly on 26 February, 1971. But, in defence of the Immorality Act and Mixed Marriages Act, he added:

> My attitude towards people is not a callous one, but the fact that people commit suicide means in actual fact that they realise that they have contravened a code of social behaviour. That means that the code of social behaviour is so strong that it can move a man to commit suicide. That is once again the justification for this Act.

But it wasn't always like that. Graham de Proft's very existence is evidence of social interaction that, though taboo in his time, was once unexceptional.

————— ❖ —————

Intimacy – conversationally and intellectually, emotionally and physically – is what makes families and communities and, ultimately, societies, what they are. It is part and parcel of being human, yet, under conditions of mistrust, suspicion and ignorance, it is not always easy or commonplace.

In the first decades after European settlement in southern Africa, the barriers of language and culture – and, often, false perceptions – were not easily overcome.

Yet there were people from the sharply contrasting communities coming into contact in the second half of the 17th century who did bridge the divides.

The degree of intimacy varied, and so did the reasons for being in touch. From early on there was a measure of interdependence, of people doing things in certain ways because they had begun to depend on one another. Often, without doubt, intimacy was involuntary, not chosen.

The one-sidedness of the written record makes it difficult to be sure just what 'being in touch' really meant. In some cases, people were friends of sorts. Some were allies, or partners in business arrangements. Some came together against their will, by force, especially in the years of slavery. But some went as far as marrying each other and having children.

Romanticised ideas about intimacy in the early years of the Cape risk obscuring its abusive aspects, yet intimacy across cultural and racial barriers was often unexceptional.

Historian Robert Ross notes that in the early years 'a number of slave women were able to exploit the relative scarcity of their sex to achieve upward mobility for themselves and their offspring': between 1657 and 1807,

408 women of apparently 'black' descent married into the white population … [and] their descendants could reach the highest positions in the Colony, as, for instance, occurred with the Bergh family.

Olof Bergh married Anna de Koning, daughter of Anna van Bengal. One of his descendants became landdrost of Stellenbosch and another a burgher lieutenant. There were many such family histories.

In different ways, these bonds all played a part in the unfolding story of what was to become South Africa and what it meant to be South African.

❖

Krotoa, who became a tragic Eva.

The wedding took place in the hall inside the fort. The bride was 21. She was a remarkable woman who, in six or seven years, had bridged the divide between Europe and Africa and was a symbol of sorts of what the new country could become, and would become. Her name was Krotoa. Hers is, ultimately, a tragic story.

But on 2 June, 1664, her marriage to 27-year-old Danish soldier and explorer Pieter van Meerhof, and the 'little marriage feast' in the house of the com-

mander Zacharias Wagenaer, was a joyous occasion.

The keeper of Wagenaer's diary hints at the significance of the union: 'the first marriage,' he writes, 'contracted here according to Christian usage with a native.' It was just 12 years after Van Riebeeck's landing at the Cape.

The young Khoekhoe girl had been taken in by the Van Riebeecks in the first days of the settlement, working as a servant to the commander's wife, Maria de la Quellerie. She was about 10 or 11 when the Dutch settlers arrived, and is first mentioned in Van Riebeeck's diary in January 1654, described as 'a girl who had lived with us' in the first hastily erected fort. Three years later, the diarist notes that Krotoa 'has been in the service of the commander's wife from the beginning'.

Soon, her familiarity with the settlers would complicate her existence. She was the first indigenous southern African to be baptised a Christian – the Van Riebeecks named her 'Eva' – but her role, and her importance, had as much to do with her identity as a person who was not of Europe as with her identity as a newly christened, Dutch-speaking indigene.

In his account of her life, *Krotoa, Called 'Eva', A Woman Between* (1990), VC Malherbe notes that she 'pioneered a hazardous terrain: the frontier between the Cape's Khoekhoe herders and Europe's premier trading nation, the Dutch'. As Krotoa's command of the Dutch language and her familiarity with Dutch ways grew, so did her usefulness as an interpreter, a go-between. This was not an easy time for such delicate work. The people who had taken her in, dressed her in new clothes and taught her their language were, in the late 1650s, gradually taking over her own people's land and forcing their will on them. Krotoa often struggled to maintain trust on either side.

The measure of her difficulties emerges from an accusation later levelled at her (and reported by Van Riebeeck's diarist) by Khoekhoe chief and sometime interpreter Doman. 'I am a Hottentot and not a Dutchman,' Doman is reported to have declared, 'but you, Eva, try to curry favour with the Commander [Van Riebeeck].' He regarded her as a traitor.

Yet Van Riebeeck, who understood that Krotoa was the niece of the Goringhaicona chief Autshumato (called Harry, first by the English, then by the Dutch), felt she was overly devoted to her uncle. He often treated her revelations 'with reserve' as a result. Ironically, it was on Krotoa's advice – supported by

Doman – that Van Riebeeck once had Autshumato captured and sent to Robben Island. This, too, illustrates the precarious politics the teenage Krotoa became embroiled in.

Later, abandoning the European clothes the Van Riebeecks had dressed her in and changing into the animal skins of her own people, she would leave the fort and spend time with her Khoekhoe relatives. She would always return to take up her Dutch ways at the fort, and information she brought back with her was useful to them, but these comings and goings reflected, perhaps, the conflicts of loyalty and identity she was grappling with.

The departure of the Van Riebeecks, her 'Dutch family' in a sense, in 1662 must have left Krotoa feeling vulnerable. She had been recommended to Van Riebeeck's successor Wagenaer, but the new governor was suspicious of her. This was partly because of her going off to live with her own people from time to time.

It became especially hard for Krotoa when, after the death of both Autshumato and Doman in 1663, she was left as the only experienced go-between at the Cape.

Still, the prospect of a better life was offered by her relationship with Pieter van Meerhof.

Van Meerhof, who arrived at the Cape in 1659, was to gain a reputation for perseverance and bravery for his part in six expeditions into the interior over the next six years. Krotoa's information was often of importance to these expeditions, and probably explains why or how they met.

Their relationship grew more intimate, and on 26 April, 1664, three months after Van Meerhof's sixth expedition, Krotoa's engagement to the explorer was announced. They were married less than two months later.

A year later, the young family went to live on Robben Island when Van Meerhof was appointed superintendent there. It was the beginning of a tragic end for Krotoa. The bleak and windswept island was not a pleasant place to live and while her husband was kept busy running a small garrison and overseeing convicts whose work was to collect shells for making lime and stones for the building of the fort on the mainland, there was little for Krotoa to do, and she didn't have much company.

When Krotoa, who already had two children, gave birth to another child in 1666, the family returned briefly to the mainland to have the baby baptised.

Just one year later, Krotoa's sad decline began.

Evidence suggests she had started drinking, possibly out of despair and loneliness. Her sense of hopelessness must have been deepened when her husband, who had been commissioned to lead a slaving and trading expedition up the east coast of Africa, was killed in a skirmish in Madagascar.

Krotoa and her children returned to the mainland in September 1668. She was a shattered woman. One day in February 1669, her drunken behaviour at the dinner table of Commander Wagenaer was the last straw. This, coupled with her increasingly bitter outbursts against the settlers, provoked a warning from the Dutch that if she did not correct her ways, she'd be banished. Krotoa ran off, leaving her children behind, but was soon hauled to the fort as a prisoner, and, at the end of March banished to Robben Island. Several similar banishments followed until, five years later, she died on the island.

'This day departed this life, a certain female Hottentoo, named Eva,' wrote the Dutch diarist on 29 July 1674, *'long ago taken from the African brood in her tender childhood by the Hon Van Riebeeck and educated in his house as well as brought to the knowledge of the Christian faith, and being thus transformed from a female Hottentoo almost into a Netherland woman ....'*

Almost into a Netherland woman, but not quite, the Dutch believed, since her life was 'a manifest example that nature, however closely and firmly muzzled by imprinted principles, nevertheless at its own time triumphing over all precepts, again rushes back to its inborn qualities'.

For centuries, this fundamental prejudice would persuade generations of whites that African people were inconvertibly savage. It was an ironic contradiction of the popular mythology of the 'noble savage', the idea that people living in a more natural state were untainted by the vanity and greed of 'civilisation'.

Despite all, Krotoa was, a day after her death, buried 'according to Christian usage in the church of the new Castle'.

Krotoa's legacy is, of course, a living one.

The two younger children of her marriage to Pieter van Meerhof, Pieternella and Salamon, were taken in 1677 to Mauritius by a man named Bartholomeus Born. The children grew up there. Pieternella later married the free burgher Daniel Saayman. They had four sons and four daughters, naming their second daughter Eva after her extraordinary grandmother. The story came full circle in 1709 when Pieternella and her family returned to live at the Cape.

While little is known about the lives of Pieternella's brothers and the half-brothers and sisters Krotoa produced out of wedlock, what we do know is that Krotoa's bloodline continues today in families who are neither Dutch nor Khoekhoe, and who are, conceivably, both 'coloured' and 'white'.

Guillaume Chenu de Chalezac was just 14 when he left France in haste. His life was at stake. In 1685 there were hundreds of thousands just like him, Protestants who, after 87 years of living in relative security in Roman Catholic France, were now suddenly and unexpectedly vulnerable again.

They had been given a measure of religious freedom under the Edict of Nantes, an agreement signed in 1598. But that assurance was shattered in 1685 when the Catholic king, Louis XIV, revoked the agreement.

If they wanted to remain true to their faith, and live, there was nothing for French Protestants to do but leave. As many as 500 000 of them eventually left the country.

Young Chenu had an older brother in Germany, so the family hatched a plan to get him on a ship bound for the island of Madeira, from where he could take another ship back north, to Holland, and then travel overland to Germany.

The first part of the plan worked out well. He got to Madeira. But when the French put pressure on the island authorities to hand over fugitive Protestants, Chenu had to leave sooner than expected. Fatefully, he secured a berth on an English ship, the *Bauden*, bound for the East Indies. It was to be an extraordinary adventure.

Disaster struck when the *Bauden* encountered pirates soon after leaving Madeira, and though the ship evaded capture, the captain and first pilot were killed in the fierce engagement. This was to have grave consequences later when the ship reached the coast of southern Africa.

In the absence of the dead officers, nobody on board knew exactly where they were when, after many days' sailing, they approached the African mainland. They were, in fact, off what would later be known as the Transkei coast, but, of course, they didn't know it.

Chenu and seven others were sent off in a boat to find a suitable anchorage. For three days they struggled to get ashore and decided finally to return to their ship. But, to their horror, a storm had driven the *Bauden* away. They had become castaways.

Theirs was among the very first encounters between Europeans and the African farmers of what is today the Eastern Cape. It was just 34 years after the beginning of the Dutch settlement in southern Africa, and Chenu's story was the first the Dutch knew of Xhosa people in the region. (In the report he produced later, he vividly describes clothing, war-making, kingship, attitude to cattle, settlements, dwellings, marriage customs, circumcision, diet, beer-drinking, hunting, religious rites, fear of death, burial customs, witchcraft as cause of death, punishment of witches, laws and manners.)

Chenu's account of what happened reveals the uncertainty, lack of understanding, fear – and therefore suspicion – that seems typical of most early contacts.

A picture emerges of an ill-matched encounter between the settled people of the region, and newcomers equipped with better weapons, and hidden or at least unclear objectives and intentions. Yet, what is remarkable about Chenu's fuller account is that, unlike so many early observers, he is full of praise for his African hosts, under whose protection he lived for a whole year – as the foster son of a local chief – and reveals the warm, human bond that existed between them.

But to start with, when Chenu and his comrades, realising their ship was gone, finally went ashore, their encounters with the Africans were beset with fear and confusion on both sides. This is how he described it:

We had not gone far when we saw six blacks herding a large herd of cows. As soon as they caught sight of us they fled, but one of them, braver than the rest, came towards us, as we had tried to call him by shouting and gestures of supplication. We tried with all manner of signs to make him understand our need, to which he made no reply but put out his hand towards us. We took this for a sign of friendship and pressed it heartily, but this was not what he wanted. We soon comprehended this and put in his outstretched hand a small piece of copper. We were astonished, however, that he thereupon departed from us with amazing speed, and at first we believed he had cheated us. We soon saw him returning with a large leather bag filled with curdled milk. We went back to rejoin our comrades and made a meal which we all confessed was the best we had ever eaten in our lives.

The next morning, Chenu and his companions woke to find 'the beach was full of blacks'. They reached for their guns, 'more to wake fear in them than to do them harm'. (Their gunpowder was wet, anyway.) The visitors fled. But the marooned seamen realised they would need help from the Xhosa if they were to survive, so they put their weapons aside. In due course, the people 'returned in great numbers and brought us all kinds of birds, sheep and oxen to trade with us'. (It was, Chenu notes, 'easy for us to obtain stores at little cost, for they sold us a whole ox for a piece of copper only as long as a finger'.)

So far, then, the encounter had gone smoothly enough. There had been some tension, but it seemed now to have eased.

Then it turned ugly.

Having concluded their trading, the seamen were waiting for the high tide to float their boat off when 'an old woman brought us an earthenware pot which we filled with meat in order to cook ourselves something'. This they did, and had just sat down to eat it when

the old woman [seeing] we had served the meat and the pot was still lying near the fire, ran up in order to take it away, but our helmsman, thinking we would frequently have need of this utensil,

got up abruptly in order to prevent the woman from taking the pot.

She then obviously became afraid, seized the pot suddenly and ran away. The helmsman pursued her and in fact called to her that he wanted to pay for the pot. The blacks, however, did not understand him, imagined he wanted to lay violent hands upon her and therefore came to us in a crowd. Without giving us time to pick up our guns they attacked us with stones, spears and sticks.

All Chenu's comrades were killed. The young French boy himself was badly beaten, but managed to flee down the beach. He was later overtaken by two men, who urged him to return. When he refused, they beat him again, and 'left me lying there, more dead than alive'. Not long after, two other men appeared. He thought he was to be attacked again. But 'these two … with great humanity, raised me up and, since I had no strength left to walk, dragged me to their huts. They made a little fire for me and applied cow dung, as a dressing, to my head wounds. They also gave me a little to eat.'

In due course, he was taken into the local chief's household.

A year later, he and the survivors of other wrecks along the coast made their way to the Cape in a vessel, the *Centaurus*, which had been built by stranded sailors on the Natal coast.

In an extraordinarily poignant passage about the moment of his rescue, when, after his year with the

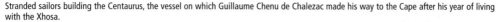

Stranded sailors building the Centaurus, the vessel on which Guillaume Chenu de Chalezac made his way to the Cape after his year of living with the Xhosa.

Xhosa, Chenu joined other stranded sailors on the coast to board the *Centaurus* and leave for the Cape, the young French boy describes how the chief who had been his host carried him to the ship, in tears:

> As the ship could not come close up to the land, it was necessary to wade out into the sea. He [the chief] sat me on his neck and carried me out to the ship, albeit against my will. During this journey his face was no less wet with tears at my parting from him than his body was with sea water. Until we parted he rent the air with his cries, and I in turn could not refuse the love of a man to whom I owed so much.

From *Guillaume Chenu de Chalezac, The 'French Boy'* (1993) by Randolph Vigne (editor)

Chenu's recollections from the late 1600s have an almost haunting quality since they express a sense of the common humanity that would be deeply eroded by the conflict and bitterness of the centuries to come.

❖

Piet Retief is remembered either as one of the heroes of the Great Trek or as an agent of the invasion and dispossession of the interior of southern Africa. The light always catches different facets of history, depending on how it falls or how it is shone.

But there is another element to Piet Retief that is not obvious, and the examination of which was once actively discouraged.

It concerns a princely figure who became an unlikely inhabitant at the Cape. The Rajah of Tambora – among the exiles described in chapter two – was a member of the Muslim aristocracy in the Indonesian island states when the Dutch began building their empire there. Tambora, the third largest island east of Java, fell under the Sultanates of Macassar, and when the Dutch took over the Sultanate of Goa, Tambora fell to the European power, too.

The rajah resisted the invasion, but was overcome and sent to the Cape as a prisoner in chains in 1697. Though he had been sentenced to hard labour, the Dutch at the Cape, under Simon van der Stel, took a more lenient view: he was given more reasonable accommodation and his wife was allowed to join him. Of course, he desperately wanted to go home, but was kept at the Cape until his death 22 years later. He left many descendants in both the white and the coloured communities.

This is a story told by Alf Wannenburgh in his

book *Forgotten Frontiersmen* (1978). 'His most notable connection with the white community,' Wannenburgh writes, 'was through a great grand-daughter who married into the family of Piet Retief, the Voortrekker leader.'

It's a connection, intriguingly, that involves another important exile of the early years, Sheik Jusuf, regarded as the father of Islam in southern Africa.

The rajah took the Sheik's daughter Zytia as his second wife, in the late 1690s, just a few years after arriving at the Cape. After the rajah's death in 1719, her requests to be sent back to Batavia were declined, just as her husband's had been, and the family remained at the Cape. Having lived in virtual isolation from the rest of the Muslim community, most of the family ultimately converted to Christianity. The oldest son, Ibraim Adahan, was baptised Abraham de Haan.

Wannenburgh writes:

Abraham married Helena Valentyn, the daughter of 'free blacks' Hercules Valentyn and Cecelia of Bengal. Two of Abraham and Helena's daughters married young Hollanders, and one son married and had two children by Christina Alesia Everskyk, from Amsterdam.

The third daughter married first a Hollander and then a German, having four children by her first husband and five by her second. One of the daughters by her second husband married Francois Johannes Retief.

Though she had married into the family of the Voortrekker leader, she was not related to him by blood, because her marriage to Francois Retief produced only a daughter.

———— ❖ ————

Perhaps the most unlikely bonds were those formed between slaves or former slaves and their masters or former masters, and there were many of them.

Johannes Vanderkemp

During the first 20 years of European settlement, three-quarters of the children born to slave mothers had white fathers. It was often quite matter of fact, though some of the individuals involved were regarded as odd or eccentric, perhaps because they were also politically liberal.

This was probably the case with the missionary and former soldier, Johannes Theodorus Vanderkemp, the son of a Rotterdam theology professor, who arrived at the Cape at the age of 53 in 1799. Within a few years he had established a mission station on the eastern frontier (in what today is the Eastern Cape at Bethelsdorp). His idea, as he once described it, was to create a settlement where refugees from what had been a war zone in the conflict between colonists and the Xhosa, could be 'perfectly free, upon an equal footing in every respect with the colonists'.

Many farm labourers took refuge there, but, with insufficient water and grazing, there often wasn't much for them to do. Local farmers came to resent the mission and, in 1805, the Dutch governor Janssens had the missionaries withdrawn to Cape Town to avoid conflict. Vanderkemp worked in the slave community in Cape Town, buying the freedom of several slaves, and marrying one, a 17-year-old girl named Sarah, whose mother had come from Madagascar.

They returned later to the Bethelsdorp mission, which continued to struggle and draw criticism from the colonists. This was partly because of Vanderkemp's campaigning efforts on behalf of farm labourers. Vanderkemp died while visiting Cape Town in 1811 to give evidence on the mistreatment of farm workers. His young wife, who had had three sons and a daughter with him, later married the son of a Dutch artillery officer.

Vanderkemp's assistant at the mission, James Read, married one of his Khoekhoe converts in 1803, and had three sons and five daughters by her. (Read later admitted to 'being seduced' by a young black girl in the church at Bethelsdorp and was transferred

James Read

eldest son became a missionary like his father.

This pattern – of race or the mixing of races being irrelevant to the capabilities and achievements of people – has been borne out repeatedly in South Africa's past, even though the philosophy of apartheid, and colonial thinking before apartheid, tried to deny it.

———— ❖ ————

Millions of South Africans today, of all skin colours, owe their identity, their language and their culture – their heritage, and their inheritance in the truest sense – to the human impulse that moved their distant forebears to be in touch. It was not always how some of them would have chosen it.

What is certainly true is that it was an intimacy that, though often unremarkable and socially acceptable in the early years of the meeting of cultures in southern Africa, would in time be severely tested, stigmatised, even outlawed, yet ultimately celebrated.

by the London Missionary Society to Kuruman in the Northern Cape.)

One of Read's sons later served with distinction as a commandant in the 8th Frontier War, while the

'This was part of my genealogy of which we did not speak – and of which I did not know – when I was a child.'

These are the words of Frederik Willem de Klerk, President of South Africa from 1989 to 1994, a staunch and successful Nationalist politician under apartheid for much of his political career, and the man credited with having the courage, in submitting to political, social and economic pressures, to signal the end of apartheid in 1990 by unbanning the liberation movements and freeing the man who later replaced him as the first democratically elected president, Nelson Mandela.

The 'genealogy of which we did not speak' – and which FW de Klerk revealed in his autobiography, *The Last Trek – A New Beginning* (1998) – concerned a woman named Susanna. The story of the De Klerks, he writes, is 'the story of the emerging Afrikaner nation'. And this is no less true of Susanna.

Former President FW de Klerk

She was the daughter of Diana of Bengal, an Indian slave who was sold to one Augustin Boccart in 1667. Her father was Detlef Bibault and she was raised with her white half-brothers and -sisters by Bibault's Dutch wife Willemyntjie de Wit, 'apparently without any problem or discrimination'.

De Klerk writes: 'Susanna married Willem Odenthal in 1711 and was the mother of Engela Odenthal, who married my direct ancestor, Barend de Klerk, on 7 April 1737.'

As far as the eye could see

[chapter four]
As far as the eye could see

'You were a lord if you had a horse,' the English writer DH Lawrence once wrote. 'Far back, far back in our dark soul the horse prances … The horse! The horse! The symbol of surging potency and power of movement, of action in man.'

By an accident of geography, there were no horses in southern Africa before European settlement. And horses gave the newcomers an advantage that must often have been decisive. It was not just horses, but technology – guns, mainly – that enabled them to be more assertive in lording it over the landscape.

Yet, as Lawrence saw it, horses may well have made them feel like lords, confident, superior, civilising, bringing light to dark corners never lighted before. From the saddle, the horseman looks down on everyone else, but he can also cover ground more quickly, carry more with him, and go further.

In this, Lawrence's 'symbol of surging potency and power of movement' was an essential element in what for many people was a spreading gloom rather than a spreading of light. It was a period of fear, of being chased, of being stolen from – though not always and not only by white European settlers – of being on the move, and being made to live very different lives.

This, at any rate, is one way of looking at the period of expansion into the interior of southern Africa from the coastal settlements at the Cape and Algoa Bay. Horses, wheels and weapons were significant. However, they did not fully account for the unfolding story.

Nor does the image of fear and gloom explain the thoughts of the men and women who came to make maps, explore, record what they saw by drawing, painting and writing, hunt or trade, learn the languages of southern Africa, build roads and passes through the mountains, convert people to Christianity, administer the 'virgin' colonial territories, wage war against opponents, and even look at the stars from the southern hemisphere … the people who, in one way or another, were the agents of European colonialism.

Symbol of surging potency and power of movement … the horse was a decisive instrument of colonial expansion and control. This 19th-century depiction shows Lieutenant-Colonel – later Governor – Harry Smith in pursuit of Xhosa ruler Hintsa.

Similar processes were happening elsewhere in the world in the 1700s and 1800s: Europeans were trekking west in waggons in North America, and into the interiors of South America and Australia.

Most of those who went north in southern Africa would have regarded their life and work as a response to the opportunity, or what they might even have seen as the duty, that confronted them. Yet, collectively, they helped change the region utterly, for good.

And, broadly, everything as far as the eye could see was within the range of curiosity, conquest and control.

It was a world that must have seemed uncomplicatedly accessible, as this anonymous childhood recollection of the travels of a trekboer family suggests:

It is a wonderfully restful and unforgettable experience to lie in the wagon, looking at the silhouette of a strong father sitting on the box seat with a handful of reins and a long bamboo-staff whip in his hands, gently calling the oxen in the span by name, or softly whistling to while the time away. Gradually you fall asleep to the singing of the wheels in the soft sand of the road. Your family is around you, your whole world is in the wagon and your father has the reins of it all in his hand.

Trekboers were among the first European frontiersmen to venture over the mountains and penetrate the southern African interior. They were followed or accompanied by – or they impinged on – other individuals whose lives reflect the changing scene.

History is not the story of the few prominent people of their time, but of the collective behaviour, the actions and reactions, of all people. Yet it is possible to trace in the lives of individuals – in this, and the next, chapter – the themes of the larger narrative.

One way of categorising these individuals might be to call them victors and victims. But the kings and chiefs, soldiers and administrators, servants, explorers, journalists, subjects, road-builders, slaves, missionaries, map-makers and others would probably have seen themselves in a different light, as being more complex than the simpler categories that might seem sufficient today.

———— ❖ ————

[JOHN BARROW, MAP-MAKER]

Knowledge is power, and of all forms of knowledge of the landscape the map is among the most powerful.

In the map, there is a record of the terrain the map-maker observed, and a trace of the map-maker in the terrain. In this, the map both confirms and enables conquest.

These key ideas are highlighted by the historian Nigel Penn in his assessment of the first comprehensive mapping of portions of the Cape colony by the Englishman John Barrow, who set off for the eastern frontier in 1797.

To start with, the first British occupation of the Cape – from 1795 to 1803 – immediately following the collapse of the VOC was a strategic move that had more to do with events in Europe than in Africa. It was a move to deny the former Dutch colony to revolutionary France. But it is evident that in these eight years – before Britain returned at the second occupation in 1806 for an extended and decisively influential stay – the Cape was regarded as being what Penn has described as 'a British responsibility'. And one of the most telling indications of this was the production of a comprehensive report on the state of the colony, and the making of an accurate map.

So it was that 'with his compass, pocket sextant, telescope, artificial horizon, chronometer and measuring chain Barrow sought to seize the country with the vision of exact science'.

John Barrow

Few documents more readily confirmed the project of conquest – and consolidated it – than John Barrow's map of the Cape Colony.

Born to a modest family in Lancashire in 1764, Barrow left school at the age of 13, but was driven to become something more. Developing his talent for mathematics, he took up teaching at a school in Greenwich in London. It was on the strength of his industriousness and skill there that he secured a posting on a diplomatic mission to China. He made a good impression, and when the man who led the Chinese expedition, Earl George Macartney, was appointed to the Cape in 1796, he brought Barrow with him.

Barrow threw himself into the task set for him. He wrote from Graaff-Reinet on 12 October, 1797, that

I have scarcely rested half a day on any spot since our departure ... I find not a vacant moment ... The geography, nature, and produce of the country fill up every moment of my time.

And when he was done, his map gave Britain a clearer idea of what it now possessed and, perhaps, what it intended to keep.

In describing the 'borders' of the colony for the first time, the map reflected the British intention, or

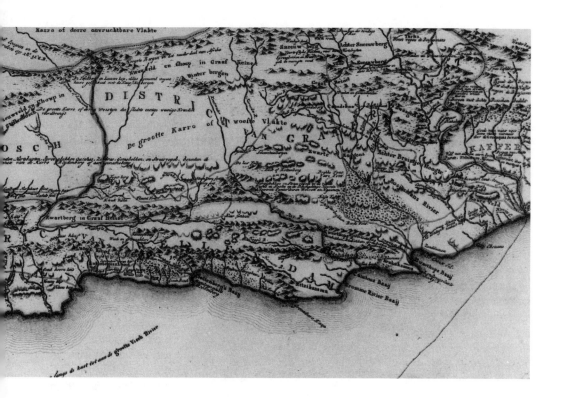

hope, that mutually acceptable boundaries could be decided on and respected as a step towards preventing conflict between settlers and the Xhosa, and settlers and the San. To this end, Barrow travelled as far as present-day King William's Town to meet the Xhosa leader Ngqika. As Penn notes:

It was hardly Barrow's fault that lasting peace eluded the antagonists. But his intervention ensured that, before too long, British troops would be marched eastwards to play their part in the interminable frontier wars.

Intentionally or not, then, Barrow was an important figure in securing the conquest of southern Africa.

Yet his thoughts about the people of the region are sympathetic. He wrote with 'considerable feeling' about the plight of the San and the Khoekhoe. He was appalled at witnessing a commando raid on the San in the Sneeuberg, and was convinced that the theft of colonists' cattle was a natural response to the way the colonists treated the indigenous communities. He also thought slavery was pernicious and degrading, and noted disapprovingly that only Christians, or whites, were treated as human beings. In these things, Barrow reflected something of the philanthropic spirit

at large in Britain.

On the other hand, his thoughts about the Dutch colonists, or 'Boors' as he called them, were harsh:

unwilling to work, and unable to think; with a mind disengaged from every sort of care and reflexion, indulging to excess in the gratification of every sensual appetite, the African peasant grows to an unwieldy size, and is carried off the stage by the first inflammatory disease that attacks him.

As it happened, in August 1799 he married Anna Maria Truter, the daughter of a senior Dutch official at the Cape, Petrus Truter.

Beyond his map-making, Barrow produced a detailed assessment of the finances of the Cape, which proved vital to Britain's reforms in the colony. His records and memoirs helped to generate support for the second British occupation in 1806 and, within a decade and a half, his researches helped prepare the scores of 1820 settlers who sailed out to Africa to make new lives on the contested eastern frontier.

Penn concludes that 'if any one man may be said to have 'captured' the Cape' and placed it in the context of Britain's international relations of the time, it was John Barrow.

[WILLIAM BURCHELL, EXPLORER]

In every age, there are men and women who want more than anything to cross the next ridge of hills, and the next, to see what lies beyond, to discover, to explore.

And in the first 200 years of European settlement in southern Africa, the explorers who went beyond the coastal towns and farming communities to 'discover' what they considered to be an undiscovered interior formed an intriguing assembly.

Of course, the terrain they explored was not undiscovered: Africa had been populated for millennia. But for Europeans ignorant of Africa, the explorers provided, often, the first accounts of what it was they thought of as unknown and strange.

Explorers, like map-makers, were in one sense the first agents of conquest: what they learned was useful to others who wanted to gain control politically, commercially or militarily.

But it is also true that the explorers' curiosity left information and insights that would not otherwise be available, partly because the oral record that was the literacy of Africa was being steadily eroded by the advance of European literacy, of reading and writing.

One of the classic texts of early travel in southern Africa was written by William John Burchell, the son of a nurseryman, who came to the Cape colony in 1810 after spending five years on the island of St Helena.

How much, for instance, would we know of the actual mechanics of the working of metal by blacksmiths in pre-industrial Africa without Burchell's account of it from 1812 in his *Travels in the interior of Southern Africa*? His visit to the 'workshop' of the only *moturi* or blacksmith at Dithakong on 29 July,

William Burchell, drawn into an 'undiscovered' interior.

1812, provides a rare view of the extent of trade in the interior, the commercial arrangements of the Tlhaping people he spent much time with at Dithakong, their capital, and the skills and industry of people who would later be drawn into the life of manual labourers by the creeping industrial capitalism that followed the conquest of their land and the beginning of mining towards the end of the 1800s. This is how Burchell described what he saw that day:

This man obtained his knowledge from the north-eastern nations; and though he was at this time but a beginner and an imperfect workman, he was, notwithstanding, overwhelmed with work from every side. ... His work consisted generally of making hatchets, adzes, knives, hassagays [assegais] and hoes or mattocks for breaking up their corn-land. For this he was paid either in unwrought iron obtained by barter from the north-eastern tribes, or in corn, oxen, cows, goats, tobacco, beads, koboes, leather or undressed skins ... I satisfied my curiosity by paying a visit to ... this industrious moturi ... [who] was sitting in the open ... having on one side of him a slight hedge of dry branches to screen his fire from the wind. This fire was made in the open air ... without anything for retaining its heat. The fuel was charcoal; the art of making which he had also learnt from the Nuakketsies.

The most ingenious contrivance was his muubo, *or bellows: this was formed of two leathern bags made from goat skins taken off entire or without being cut open lengthwise. The neck was tight bound to a straight piece of the horn of an antelope, which formed the nozzle of the bellows. These two nozzles lay flat upon the ground, and were held in their place firmly by a large stone laid upon them: they conveyed the wind to a short earthen tube, the end of which was placed immediately to the fire. The hinder part of the bag was left open, as a mouth to receive the air, and was kept distended by two straight sticks. … These sticks are so held … that they may be opened on raising the mouth, and closed on depressing it. … By taking a bag in each hand, and continuing this action of raising and depressing them alternately, a strong and constant stream of wind was produced, which presently raised a very small fire to a degree of heat equal to rendering a hatchet red hot in two minutes. … A stone for his anvil, a horn of water for cooling the iron, and two or three very small iron hammers, were the only apparatus, and all the tools, which he made us of.*

From *Travels in the interior of Southern Africa* (facsimile, 1967) by William John Burchell

Burchell was enchanted by the sight of the blacksmith at work, but he makes a telling judgement of the scene. The *moturi* was,

in the midst of a nation which sought to enrich itself only by the plunder of its neighbours, so rare a specimen of honest industry, one of those moral virtues which elevate the character of a people upon a basis incomparably more firm and respectable than any which can be raised by the sword, and in the same proportion in which the arts of peace stand morally higher and more honourable than the arts of war.

It is an ironic view, since even as Burchell was forming this judgement of their war crafts and plundering, Africans throughout the region would have had ample evidence for a much harsher view of the white man's war-making, evidence that would be brutally confirmed in the next century and more.

Burchell would, indirectly, be an agent of this. In June 1819, he appeared before the British House of Commons' Select Committee on the Poor Laws to advise on the suitability of South Africa for the settlement of British emigrants. He recommended the Albany district in the Eastern Cape, which would soon become the centre of the 1820 Settler programme, at the heart of a bloody frontier conflict.

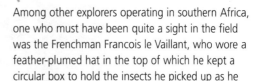

Among other explorers operating in southern Africa, one who must have been quite a sight in the field was the Frenchman Francois le Vaillant, who wore a feather-plumed hat in the top of which he kept a circular box to hold the insects he picked up as he went along.

Le Vaillant's three years in the region, from 1781, took him through the Karoo, Namaqualand, the Kalahari and the Eastern Cape, and his special interest was birds. A notorious footnote in his history of travelling is that he went as far as inventing some species, back in Paris, giving names to birds which did not actually exist but which a taxidermist had created by combining the body parts and plumage of different specimens.

The flourishing interest in getting to the heart of the 'unknown' world was allied to the sweeping scientific and social possibilities of the time for actually understanding how the world worked. And, to a greater or lesser extent, that meant classifying things as objects and fitting them into the grand puzzle of life on earth. It covered everything from flowers, plants and insects to people.

Two early explorers who were particularly interested in plants were Swedes: Carl Peter Thunberg visited the Cape in the course of wider travels in Europe, Africa and the East between 1770 and 1776, and Andreas Sparrman trekked to the eastern frontier in the same period. (Both were students of the famous Swedish botanist Carolus Linnaeus, father of the classification of plants and animals.)

Other famous names among explorers are Dr Martin Karl Heinrich Lichtenstein, a German who arrived in 1802 and spent four years in the region; and Robert Gordon, born in Holland of Scottish emigrants, who arrived at the Cape in 1777 and is credited with naming the Orange River (until then – and now, quite widely – known as the Gariep).

[JOHN PHILIP, MISSIONARY]

God – the Christian God – became one of the most penetrating ideas in the southern Africa of the 1800s.

And the missionaries who took the Word of God to the heathens, as they would have seen them, the unbelievers, of southern Africa were also taking the good and the bad of Western European society with them.

The Christian influence in southern Africa did much to undermine African beliefs and structures of authority, but it often equipped poor and marginalised people with the means or insight to confront colonialism, or survive better within it. (Later, mission and church schools played a key part in the emergence of articulate, politically conscious leaders in the early years of the struggle against racism.)

The Bible, as a written 'truth', was powerful in shifting the authority of story-telling, as a literary culture, to reading and writing. And the missionaries were the first to use printing presses at remote stations, producing written texts – and Bibles – in African languages. A visitor to Robert Moffat's mission at Kuruman in 1849, marvelling at the 'fountains of civilisation' rising up in the interior, describes 'scores of men, women and children, having renounced heathenism, intelligently reading the Word of Life'.

The first 'infant schools' for children under normal school-going age were established at mission stations as early as 1829. And missionaries often served as go-betweens in political deals and in the signing of treaties that, effectively, extended British influence.

All these things gave the men of God, who had arrived from distant and unimaginable places, an important status.

A striking image of this is the account by John Campbell of his first meeting with the chief of the Tlhaping people in the northern interior in 1813. The missionary brought various gifts for the African ruler – a copper comb, a silver headband and a chain, and

Christianity and civilisation were one and the same thing, in missionary John Philip's view.

after placing these things on the chief's head and around his neck, his last gift was a mirror (what was called a 'looking-glass' then) so that the chief could see for himself how he had been transformed. Such encounters were tokens of the incorporation of Africans into the culture of Western Europe.

And so the spread of Christianity came to be a key element of colonial ways in the region.

Yet, the influence of Christian missionaries was more complicated. Another missionary, Isaac Hughes grappled with the difficulties when he wrote in 1851:

We missionaries are blamed by the Natives as forerunners to them of oppression and destruction from the hands of our fellow white men. The Colonists, on the other hand, blame us for sacrificing their interests for the Natives.

The life and work of John Philip illustrates the complexity.

Philip, a Congregational minister from Aberdeen in Scotland, arrived at the Cape in 1819, and soon became a very influential superintendent of all London Missionary Society (LMS) mission stations in the region.

Philip had had to leave school when he was 11 to work in his father's weaving mill, but, after converting from Anglicanism to the Congregational Church, he became interested in missionary work, and decided to go back to his books, at the Hoxton College in London.

He was an able and much-admired churchman by the time he arrived in the Cape. The LMS missions had become controversial, with claims of malpractices, disorder, and the moral and spiritual decline of missionaries themselves.

A serious, principled man, Philip was determined to sort out whatever mess the missions were in. But in his first year in southern Africa his view changed:

there were problems at some missions, he conceded, but the main problem was the oppressive measures of colonial officials. Philip soon began to play more of a political role.

He made it his business to work closely with the governors of the colony, but his political support for greater freedom for the Khoe-San, Xhosa and Griqua people, and the slaves, made him increasingly unpopular in the Cape. (Soon after arriving at the colony, he helped found the Cape Philanthropic Society, which tried to buy the freedom of as many slaves as it could.)

Philip, like others in Britain – and a few in the colony – believed that slavery was inhumane, a denial of humanity and contrary to Christian values, and that the treatment of people who were not white was wrong and oppressive.

Missionary and traveller
John Campbell

Most colonists did not like him because his opinions threatened them: Philip was a threat to the pattern of life that suited the farmers.

In 1828 – when the Cape government issued Ordinance 50, which, though it scrapped passes for Khoekhoe and freed slaves, did not protect them from impoverishment or economic abuse – Philip stepped up his campaign.

His controversial report of that year, *Researches in South Africa*, was intended to persuade the British government of the injustice of colonial policies.

It was largely dismissed at the Cape – one critic said of Philip and his opinions that it was 'the unauthorised quackery of conscienceless agitators'. (One keen supporter was Philip's son-in-law, the journalist John Fairbairn.)

Philip succeeded in 1830 in stopping the colonists from passing a vagrancy law against the Khoekhoe, but, despite the influential support he received in Britain for progressive changes, colonial policy did not change much.

Philip warned that robbing the Xhosa of their territory by white settlers was the primary cause of the conflict on the eastern frontier, the region that is today the Eastern Cape, and tried many times to convince the British government to limit white expansion and recognise the independence of Xhosa chieftainships.

His ultimate goal was that through treaties of friendship missionaries would be able to expand their influence, and the benefits of British civilisation, further into Africa. He vigorously opposed the trekker colonists who left the Cape in the Great Trek, but he also eventually opposed the Xhosa resistance to colonialism.

Philip's ideas, as historian Robert Ross argues, were 'typical … of the cultural imperialism' of the mission-aries of the time, that Christianity and 'civilisation' were one and the same thing. As Philip wrote:

I am satisfied, from the abundance of incontrovertible facts, that permanent societies of Christians can never be maintained among an uncivilised people without imparting to them the arts and habits of civilised life.

To be civilised meant, among other things, to work and be productive, to be clean, sober and morally upright, to go to school and to wear clothes, to have European possessions. Philip once wrote of the Griqua: 'By increasing their artificial wants you increase the dependence of the Griqua on the Colony.'

As a sum, all this meant changing the way Africans lived, making them live the life of a typical European worker. Many resisted. In some parts of the country, and for a long time, missionaries had little luck in drawing people into the flock.

From as early as the mid-1840s, the LMS was on the wane – though Christianity continued to spread and flourish through other English, French, German and American missions – as was public and political support in Britain for philanthropy in Africa.

But Philip is remembered for speaking up for the unfree, the dispossessed and the oppressed when so few others spared them a thought.

[ANDREW GEDDES BAIN, ROAD-BUILDER]

Capable Scotsman Andrew Geddes Bain, a pass-builder and much more besides.

Control of the landscape is not much more than an idea unless people actually experience it.
And, for scores of people who fell within the ever-widening boundaries of colonial control and the succession of annexations that claimed huge chunks of southern Africa in the 1800s, the idea that they fell under the law of a distant British government must often have seemed remote.

They knew it as a hard fact when soldiers were sent against them or magistrates were sent to outposts to enforce strange-seeming regulations.

But what turned the idea into a steadily more fixed reality was the building of networks of communications, of roads and railways and telegraph lines, that linked the far reaches of the landscape to the centres of control and decision-making.

As the engineers worked their way inland so the countryside was brought under the influence of useful science. Telegrams, government pronouncements, military orders, newspapers, personal letters, Bibles, school books – but also guns, gadgets, clocks, food, liquor, clothing, money – all these reached further inland, more quickly, as engineering tamed the veld.

To start with, though, between the sea and the uplands of the interior, chains of mountains raised a barrier against travellers. The mountains didn't ever stop the early trekkers or runaways, the explorers or mounted troops, but getting inland was hard going, and slow.

One of the men who began to change that was a Scotsman named Andrew Geddes Bain. He is described first as a road-builder, but also as a geologist, explorer, trader, soldier, writer, palaeontologist and artist.

The son of a joiner, he arrived at the Cape as a soldier in 1816. Six years later, he and his family were settled at Graaff-Reinet where he worked as a saddler. But he was bored, and over the next more than 10 years took to exploring. It was in the course of journeying far and wide that he found his talent for drawing and writing. He became a regular correspondent for John Fairbairn's *South African Commercial Advertiser*, though his cutting wit got him into trouble sometimes. In one of several libel suits, he lost to Gerrit Maritz, who became one of the leaders of the Voortrekkers. (Bain wrote other things, too: he later penned a satire of John Philip and other missionaries, in Afrikaans, called *Caatje Kekelbek; or life among the Hottentots.* 'Kaatjie Kekkelbek' has since become a byword in Afrikaans.)

On his last hunting trip to the northern interior in 1834 – to get live animals and rare skins for American buyers – he had a brush with a Matabele impi after his Griqua guides stole cattle belonging to Mzilikazi.

A year later, he was back in the army, serving at Graaff-Reinet in the 6th Frontier War. He then took to farming in the recently annexed Queen Adelaide Province, but lost the land in 1836 when the province was returned to the Xhosa.

So, finally, he turned to road-building.

He had, in fact, already built the Oudeberg Pass and the Van Ryneveld Pass, both leading north from Graaff-Reinet.

Joining the Royal Engineers, Bain worked extensively on military roads throughout the eastern frontier, built the Fish River bridge, then the largest in the country, and constructed several roads leading north from Grahamstown.

(It was in the course of building roads that he took to geology – he is known as the 'father of South African geology' – and palaeontology. He was self-taught in both fields. One of his finds, near Fort Beaufort, was a reptile skull with only two large teeth: it was an important discovery, becoming famous as the dicynodon.)

To the south, in the Western Cape, passes were needed through the mountains to ease traffic from the colony's capital into an interior that was gaining in importance. So Bain joined the staff of colonial secretary John Montagu, and set to work on his most important projects.

The first was the completion of the Mitchell's Pass, following the Breede River through the Skurweberg range, in 1848. While working on this project, he constructed two other passes – the Gydo Pass between the Warm and Koue Bokkeveld, and the Houw Hoek Pass between Elgin and Bot River.

But his most acclaimed project was the more than 30 kilometre pass through the mountains between Wellington and Worcester, opened in 1854, and named after him. It originally featured South Africa's first road tunnel, but that was changed because draught animals pulling waggons and coaches did not like going through the unlit tunnel.

❖

Fixing the land in the scheme of science was matched by scientific curiosity about the stars of the southern hemisphere. It was this that brought the renowned astronomer, Sir John Frederick William Herschel, to the Cape. Herschel, and his self-taught astronomer father, had contributed extensively to mapping the stars of the northern hemisphere. In 1833, he decided it was time to look at the southern night skies.

He arrived at the Cape the next year, bought a country estate in what is today the Cape Town suburb of Claremont, and erected a huge reflecting telescope. Working closely with the government-appointed astronomer, Thomas Maclear, Herschel spent the next four years measuring and describing the stars twinkling above Britain's far possession at the southern tip of Africa.

In this time, he identified 2 000 double stars, 1 700 nebulae and clusters, made the first measures of direct solar radiation, and developed new theories, since accepted as valid, based on observations of sunspots and of Halley's comet.

He was also very influential in reforming the way schools were set up and run in the colony, including having all schools fall under a professional superintendent. This innovation put South Africa ahead of Europe and America at the time.

In the broader picture of colonialism in the 1800s, Herschel's part is small. But his work helped to place the colony firmly within the realm of modern European science, and the rational ordering of the universe.

Traversing the Cape's mountain ranges was perilous, as this 1840 etching graphically suggests.

[JOHN FAIRBAIRN, JOURNALIST]

Even in the era of television and the Internet, newspapers are still the first chatroom of choice for society's conversation with itself.

Before television and the Internet, or the radio, the telephone and even the telegram, newspapers in the Cape were alone in representing the colony to itself, in easing trade and commerce by carrying news of shipping, new business ventures and products, and in keeping colonists up to date with news from Europe and the policy-making in Britain that affected them directly.

It was also a forum for them to say what they thought, which was not always encouraged by the authorities, as Fairbairn would discover.

Father of the tradition of a free Press in South Africa, John Fairbairn.

He came to the Cape from England in 1823 at the invitation of his university friend, writer and poet Thomas Pringle. Their first venture was a school, the Classical and Commercial Academy, and it did quite well, but had to close down within the year after the two men made themselves unpopular with the governor, Lord Charles Somerset. The source of his disfavour was the political tone of a literary magazine they had launched, the first in the colony, called the *South African Journal*.

It was not their last brush with Somerset and the authorities over free speech.

In 1824 the colony got its first independent newspaper, *The South African Commercial Advertiser* and, right at the start, its publisher, George Greig, asked Fairbairn and Pringle to edit it.

Across the top of the front page, every issue carried the words of the famous 18th-century English intellectual, Samuel Johnson: 'The mass of every people must be barbarous where there is no printing.' It was like a motto.

Initially, the paper ran for only 18 issues, until May.

Its editors ran into a snag because of their decision to cover court cases and one of them at that time was a libel case involving Somerset. Before the 18th issue was printed, the authorities demanded to see, and approve, what had been written. Although the material was approved, and the paper printed, Greig, Fairbairn and Pringle added a postscript saying it was impossible to produce a newspaper subject to such political interference. In the face of further threats, they decided to stop publishing altogether.

Greig went to England to protest against the action and, a year later, the paper was back on the streets, this time under Fairbairn's sole editorship. But there was trouble again in 1827: even though Somerset had by this time left the colony, he used his influence from England to shut the paper down again. The colonial administration was still insisting that *The South African Commercial Advertiser* steer clear of personal or political controversy.

Fairbairn would not give up. His determination paid off when, in April 1829, the Press was freed from the control of the governor and council of the Cape, though with the condition that publishers provide a substantial financial security in case of libel actions against them.

Fairbairn remained editor of the paper until 1859, the year in which he had the satisfaction of piloting through the Cape parliament a law to abolish the requirement that newspapers could be printed only if their publishers provided securities.

Politically, Fairbairn was strongly influenced by his father-in-law, the outspoken missionary John Philip.

In part, as the historian Robert Ross has written, they 'saw their task as protecting the Cape's Khoe-San and ex-slaves, as well as the Xhosa and others across the border'.

His stance was, nevertheless, shaped by the idea that, through treaties and deals, the people of southern Africa were better off within the British Empire and the values of 'civilisation', as he saw it. Perhaps for this reason, he, like Philip, became less supportive of the Xhosa resistance from the mid-1840s.

He opposed slavery, from both a humanitarian and an economic point of view. He thought it was morally wrong, but also bad for the economy of the Cape.

Fairbairn was an ardent advocate of representative government – the simple idea that the people of the colony, not legislators in faraway London, should run the Cape – and was elected to the first Legislative Assembly when it finally came into being in 1854.

In the run-up to the first Cape parliament he fought against a property qualification – the requirement that politicians must own property – but was overruled.

Fairbairn also had a significant role in local business: he founded in 1845 the insurance company that, today, is the mammoth corporate, Old Mutual.

But his chief legacy was in establishing the idea that a free Press is desirable. It is expressed in an editorial in *The South African Commercial Advertiser* in April 1824 devoted to a discussion of open government.

> *But how are discordant opinions to be assimilated? How are weak prejudices to be overcome? And how are a body of people who have exactly the same interests, to be brought to feel the same way? It can only be done by an open discussion of differences that exist. We repeat, it is only to be effected by means of a Free Press.*

It was a goal successive generations of journalists would have to continue fighting for, right up to the Internet age.

——— ❖ ———

Poet and journalist Thomas Pringle.

Fairbairn's writing was a very public affair. Others wrote privately, and some with great insight. One of these was a remarkable woman named Lady Anne Barnard, who visited the Cape between 1797 and 1800 as the wife of Colonial Secretary Andrew Barnard. Her journals contain telling evidence of the mechanics of the new society emerging in the colony at the start of British rule, though as a woman she would not have been taken seriously at the time as a writer and thinker on political matters. Some of her most interesting reflections, for our time, are those on class and racial divisions, and on slavery, which – as the editors of her *Cape Diaries*, Margaret Lenta and Basil le Cordeur, note – 'portray the moral blight inflicted upon the whole society, both masters and slaves, by the institution of slavery'.

Fairbairn's public and Barnard's private writing represent the big themes of South Africa's future debates from which emerged the political resolution encompassed in the Constitution of the Republic of South Africa of 1996 – of

> *freely elected representatives [laying] the foundations for a democratic and open society in which government is based on the will of the people and every citizen is equally protected by law.*

The rationale of the democratic and open society envisaged and enabled by post-apartheid South Africa's Constitution was plainly understood by Fairbairn back in 1824. Above all, he wrote,

> *in order to secure [the advantages of government by informed consent] and to guard against abuse of every description, every honest man desires that public measures may be open to discussion, and that it may be lawful for him to speak and write what he pleases, so long as he does no injury to his neighbour; or, in other words, that the liberty (not the licentiousness) of the Press may be protected by law.*

From *The South African Commercial Advertiser* (7 April, 1824)

[KATIE JACOBS, SLAVE]

One day in 1910, a journalist visited a run-down house at 63 Hanover Street, District Six, Cape Town. The woman he had come to see was sitting on a low stool in the yard nursing one of her great-grandchildren. She was very old, but her mind was lively. She remembered well, and she had much to remember. In this, Katie Jacobs was a remarkable link with a past many people might have preferred to forget.

While the John Barrows and William Burchells, the John Philips and John Fairbairns, explored and made maps or converted pagans and argued about justice, many thousands of Katie Jacobses lived out hard, largely unwritten lives in a society that mostly overlooked their plight, or regarded it as an unremarkable or unchangeable fact of life.

Katie Jacobs was born a slave in 1814. Her father was a Malagasy (from Madagascar) and her mother a Cape woman. Both her parents, too, were slaves, and all three were the 'property' of a Mr Mostert, a farmer, according to *The Chains That Bind Us. A history of slavery at the Cape* (1996).

When she was a young girl, and already working, her master, who was now old, decided to give up farming, and handed out his 'chattels' to his sons, who were all farming in the district. In the process, Katie lost her mother for good.

She recalled:

I and some cattle and horses were given to baas Kootje; my mother and some more cattle were presented to another son in Frenchhoek. From that day I never saw my mother, nor do I know what became of her. Though I did not know how long it would take to perform the journey to Frenchhoek, I often desired to see my mother.

Former slave Katie Jacobs with two of her great-grandchildren.

This was always refused. 'I think he was afraid that I would not return.' The young Katie's life was hard. The new farm had never been cultivated, so it was overgrown. For the first year she had to help the men, working with a pick and shovel from sunrise to clear the land, and then help in the kitchen in the evening.

She also had to help herd cattle, and was thrashed once for allowing the young horses to run away.

There were opportunities for recreation, she remembered: 'Well, I was often allowed to go to dance parties, but we had to be home before 2 am.'

She had a husband, too, though they were not legally married.

My first child died in infancy. I was a healthy woman, and as my missus was in rather delicate health, I became foster mother to her first-born son and heir. During this time I was well looked after, and became one of the family; that is, I was made to sleep on the floor of the dining room near the bedroom to be on hand when the young baas wanted another drink [of milk].

Summoned one day to the dining room in their best clothes, the slaves were told they would be freed in four years' time. The year was 1834, the date of the emancipation of slaves. Katie Jacobs remembered that her old father did not live to 'enjoy the God-given freedom which is the right of every human being'.

She herself was not keen to leave her 'baas and missus', who she said were 'on the whole kind'. Her husband Jacob's owner, however, was a nasty man who 'sjambokked his slaves as often as he fed them'. From 1 December, 1838, then, both worked for her 'master'.

Jacob at first appeared determined to leave the district where he had suffered so much. My missus wept at the idea: 'No, you must stay!' she cried. 'Think of my son, whom you have suckled and nursed, and who has now grown so fond of you. What will become of him? No, you must stay, you cannot go!'

So she and her husband stayed. Shortly after their liberation they were baptised and married: 'The Rev Beck, who performed the ceremonies, was kept busy from morning to night, as there were hundreds of ex-slaves gathered together for the same purpose.'

After working for several other 'masters', Katie Jacobs and her husband made their way to Cape Town and settled in District Six.

Their new life was a mixed blessing. 'There was more love in the old slave days,' Katie remembered. 'It was more peaceful. Now the electric trams pass my door from early morning till late at night, and the whole day long people shout at one another.'

Perhaps city life did not agree with the old lady, but had she lived another 60 years, her life would have been shattered once more with the bulldozing of District Six itself, and the unforgiving conditions of the apartheid era.

Against her vivid memory of the slaves' day of freedom in 1838, it is striking that it was not until 1996 that there was a law to state as simply and unequivocally as the Bill of Rights does: 'No one may be subjected to slavery, servitude or forced labour.'

[WILHELM BLEEK and LUCY LLOYD, PHILOLOGISTS]

Loss and recovery are the themes of the lives and work of Wilhelm Bleek and Lucy Lloyd.

Bleek was a German immigrant, and a philologist (one who studies languages). Lucy Lloyd was his sister-in-law. And in the Cape Town of the second half of the 1800s they made a most unusual pair: of all the tens of thousands of Europeans then living in southern Africa, they were the only ones to take the trouble to learn a San language. In fact, they went much further than that.

Well before coming near Africa, Bleek had developed an interest in, and an extensive knowledge of, the continent's languages, as a student in Bonn and

German philologist Wilhelm Bleek with his family.

Berlin. (His thesis on the grammatical gender in African languages, was written, as was the custom then, in Latin.)

His first visit to Africa was to Nigeria in 1852, but ill-health forced him to return to Europe. In Britain, he fortuitously met Bishop JW Colenso of Natal, at whose request he sailed south to Natal in 1853 to compile a Zulu grammar. While there, Bleek acquired a sound understanding of Zulu, and wrote much about the language. He also dabbled in journalism, helping to produce the *Natal Witness*.

In 1855 he left for Cape Town, where he was appointed interpreter to the governor, Sir George Grey, with whom he developed a close working relationship. Grey was a phenomenal book collector, and Bleek set about cataloguing the governor's extensive collection of books on the languages of Africa, Madagascar, Australia, Papua, Borneo and the South Seas, and continued collecting new material in southern Africa, particularly items printed at outlying mission presses.

It was in this period, the 1850s and 1860s, that Bleek developed ideas about the evolution of languages and races, and the classification of races – he coined the term 'Bantu' as a language category – using words such as 'primitive' and contrasting 'lowest' and 'highest' conditions of humanity.

In recent years, in some quarters, this work has been criticised as forming the intellectual backdrop to intensifying racial discrimination.

Some may argue it was a failure on his part that he did not foresee the destructive force of racial classifications – particularly in the 20th century – in the ordering of society, socially and politically, into upper and lower categories based on physical appearance.

But even if he did not resist the Victorian intellectual climate in which classification was a common impulse, his work in the late 1860s and 1870s with /Xam San men and women made possible a more sophisticated understanding of southern Africa's indigenous people as a complex, culturally rich community.

This arose mainly from contacts between Bleek and Lucy Lloyd and six /Xam-speaking people, some of whom had been arrested for stock theft in the Karoo and sent to the Breakwater Prison at the Cape Town harbour. (The hunting out of the San's food resources prompted many starving hunter-gatherers to hunt the new settlers' sheep.) By special arrangement, they spent extended periods at the Bleeks' home in the Cape Town suburb of Mowbray, where Bleek and Lloyd learned their language and recorded their folklore and personal experiences.

Over a number of years, they amassed an 11 000-page collection of lXam San histories and stories.

Near the end of his life, Bleek wrote of rock art that it 'shews us the Bushmen at once in a thoroughly different light from the commonly adopted view of regarding them as the lowest of

Lucy Lloyd, Wilhelm Bleek's devoted helper.

mankind'.

Bleek himself died in 1875, but work on the material was continued by Lucy Lloyd (it earned her an honorary doctorate from the University of the Cape of Good Hope in 1912), for whom it was virtually a life-long task, and Bleek's daughter Dorothea.

This work remains central to understanding the San worldview, and links modern South Africa with its ancient past.

The recovery of the /Xam folklore is also a reminder of the loss of much cultural heritage in the region through the dispossession, and the indifference, of the colonial period.

[DIÄ!KWAIN, THE 'SOFT-HEARTED' PRISONER]

Prisoner 4434 was a murderer.

That he killed a man was not in doubt, but what was intriguing about Diä!kwain was that people found it hard to believe. There was more to him than met the eye.

Diä!kwain, also known as David Hoesar, was a /Xam man who grew up in the Kenhardt district of the Karoo.

He was arrested for shooting and killing a farmer, Jacob Kruger, but convinced the judge that he had acted in self-defence. He was admitted to the Breakwater Prison at the Cape Town harbour on 1 November, 1869. He was about 25, and relatively tall, taller than most of the other /Xam San prisoners. He also had a large scar on his right cheekbone.

More to Diä!kwain than met the eye.

Archaeologist Janette Deacon, drawing on the records of Wilhelm Bleek and Lucy Lloyd, says of Diä!kwain that he was the most enigmatic of the /Xam men who shared their life stories with the two researchers.

He was 'remembered as "a soft-hearted mortal, who would not, unprovoked, have hurt a fly"'.

Something of the gentle concern of the prisoner Diä!kwain emerges from a letter transcribed to his sister Rachel, via a Dr H Meyer of Calvinia, in August 1875.

I have been wanting to say, why can it be that Rachel and her family do not send me a letter? That I might hear whether they went to the place to which they intended to return; if they had returned, they would have sent me a letter. Therefore, I am thinking that I want to hear whether they have returned; for, if they had returned, they would have told me, that I might know that they had got home: they must please speak to me.

Wilhelm Bleek had just died, and Diä!kwain felt he could not make his own way home just yet:

Therefore I know not what I shall still do about it;

for my mistress still weeps; this is why I still sit melancholy on account of it.

From *Stories that Float from Afar, Ancestral Folklore of the San of Southern Africa* (2000) by JD Lewis-Williams (editor)

Still, he was not a model prisoner: the records show that in June 1870 he was given three hours' extra labour for disobeying orders and, in May the next year, was kept for two days in the cells on a spare diet for having dagga in his possession.

Discharged from prison in November 1873, Diä!kwain stayed at the Bleeks' home for about three months, and then went home to fetch his sister and mother-in-law and returned for a second period of nearly two years, until March 1876.

When Diä!kwain left Cape Town for the second time, it was to be his last journey.

He had gone to work for Dr H Meyer in Calvinia, but when Lucy Lloyd wrote to the doctor to ask if Diä!kwain could return, the doctor explained that he had left to visit his sister and not returned, and there was no trace of him.

It later emerged that friends of the farmer Diä!kwain had killed had heard he was back in the vicinity, tracked him down and killed him near Kenhardt, in revenge.

It was an echo of the commando raids – hunting trips, it often seemed – mounted in the late 1700s by white farmers to ruthlessly track down and kill San people.

In the work of Bleek and Lloyd, though, Diä!kwain remains a presence. While he and the other /Xam informants represented what Janette Deacon has called 'a very small sample of the descendants of the tens of thousands of Southern San who lived throughout southern Africa at the time of European contact', he plays a part in reminding South Africans today of the significance and origins of the new national motto: !ke e: /xarra //ke (people who are different join together/unity in diversity).

[SARAH BAARTMANN, ICON]

It was a sad and degrading spectacle, but the people of London were drawn to it in droves, fascinated by the latest live offering from Africa.

'The Hottentot was produced like a wild beast,' as *The Times* newspaper described part of the show,

> and ordered to move backwards and forwards, and come and go into her cage, more like a bear on a chain than a human being. And one time, when she refused for a moment to come out of her cage, the keeper let down the curtain, went behind, and was seen to hold up his hand to her in a menacing posture: she then came forward at his call, and was perfectly obedient.

And so the 'Hottentot Venus' became famous.

Sarah Baartmann was born in or about 1789 near the Gamtoos River, which was then about the limit of Dutch penetration into what is today the Eastern Cape.

About the time of the first or second British occupation of the Cape – between 1795 and 1806 – she moved to the Cape Town area and by 1810, aged about 20, she was working on the farm of Peter Cezar, as a servant.

One day Cezar's brother, Hendrik, visited the farm with an English ship's

surgeon named Alexander Dunlop, and they were so impressed by Baartmann's body that they persuaded her to go with them to England and exhibit herself. The degrading quality of the 'Hottentot Venus' show incensed the African Association in London and they took Cezar and Dunlop to court.

They alleged that Baartmann had been brought to England against her will, that she performed only because she was threatened, and that the whole affair was a 'peculiar disgrace to a civilised country'.

In court, though, she herself testified that she had agreed to visit England for six years, that Cezar and Dunlop had convinced her that she could make some money appearing as the 'Hottentot Venus', that she was not being held against her will, and was happy in England. There remains doubt that she felt free to speak the truth in court, but on the strength of her evidence the case was dismissed. The court did warn that if there was any indecency, 'the law would afford another remedy'.

In London, at least, there were no more exhibitions. The records show that Sarah was baptised in Manchester on 1 December, 1811, and she appears to have married a West Indian man by whom she had two children.

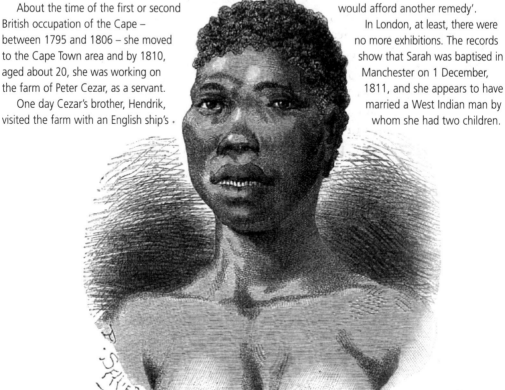

Sarah Baartmann, an iconic figure of colonial exploitation.

Then, in 1814, Cezar took Baartmann to Paris and, as renowned palaeoanthropologist Philip Tobias described it in an article in the *South African Journal of Science* in 2002, 'sold her to an animal trainer who exhibited her in the rue Neuve de Petits-Champs, and hired her out for dinner parties'.

It was claimed her working conditions were improved.

According to one Parisian journal, she was treated in a manner befitting a lady: 'The

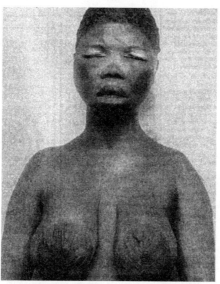

Robbed of her dignity, Sarah Baartmann became a mere exhibit.

doors of the salon open, and the Hottentot Venus is seen to enter. Some sweets are given to her in order to induce her to leap and sing, and she is informed that she is the prettiest woman in society.
The French public was 'as captivated by Baartmann as the English had been'. She was even portrayed in a musical melodrama at a Paris theatre.

But there was another category of individual captivated by Sarah Baartmann: the European scientist. One in particular was Georges Cuvier. He arranged to meet her at the Jardin du Roi in March 1815, where she undressed and was painted in the nude. Cuvier made a number of 'scientific observations', which were latterly published.

He wrote of her 'monkey-like' and 'orang-utan' features, but also that she was an intelligent woman, with an excellent memory, that she could speak Dutch and some English and was learning French.

Cuvier was especially interested in her sex organs, partly because it was thought this would shed light on whether she was fully human or more like an animal. He would have to wait to satisfy his curiosity, though not for long.

Within less than a year, Cuvier had his chance to examine her fully: Baartmann fell ill and died on 1 January, 1816, and he got permission to dissect her body.

A cast was made of her, the skeleton preserved, and her external genitalia removed and preserved in a bottle. Her remains were kept at the Musèe de l'Homme in Paris.

Cuvier's preoccupation with her sexual characteristics is borne out by the fact that nine pages of his 16-page report deal with her genitalia, breasts, buttocks and pelvis. Ultimately, he decided, she was a human being.

But, for nearly two centuries, she was a human being denied her dignity.

In South Africa and internationally, as Tobias argues, Sarah Baartmann 'has become a symbol of colonial and imperial excesses'. She became an icon, the subject of films, books, articles, exhibitions, protests – and, ultimately, negotiations. In 1996, the South African government expressed its desire to have Sarah Baartmann's remains repatriated.

It would have astonished the young victim of European prurience to know that she eventually became the subject of a debate and a decision of the French parliament, no less.

Finally, after a long journey, and moving rituals, Sarah Baartmann came home: she was buried beside the Gamtoos River, on 9 August, 2002, in a ceremony presided over by President Thabo Mbeki.

It was National Women's Day, and a moment, Mbeki noted, for South Africans to recognise that

a troubled and painful history has presented us with the challenge and the possibility of translating into reality the noble vision that South Africa belongs to all who live in it, black and white. When that is done, then it will be possible to say that Sarah Baartmann has truly come home.

Do people, individuals, make history, or does history make individuals?

There may not ever be a clear answer to the question, but – looking back at the events that shaped a history of inequality from an era which has the assertion of equality at its core – it may be an important question to ask about the past as much as the present.

What is beyond doubt is that only individuals think and act, not groups. Certainly, each individual's thinking and acting is influenced by other individuals, to varying degrees and in varying ways. But how does social and political change arise? What drives it, and what steers it?

Looking back, we may be tempted to think that if people, individuals, had been wiser, kinder or more intelligent in the early years, the events of 1994 could have happened in 1894, and the conflict and tragedy and human cost of the 20th century, the losses, the discrimination, the deaths, could have been avoided.

It is difficult to recover the atmosphere of a past age, but in surveying the lives of Sarah Baartmann, John Philip, Diä!kwain, John Barrow, Lucy Lloyd, William Burchell and others, is it possible to identify certain avoidable 'mistakes' of history, and can these be judged by what is commonplace and accepted in 2004?

Perhaps the questions are better asked about our own time.

Are our opinions today – about whether driving motor cars is bad for the global environment, say – shaped by the time we are living in or shaped by us? And if we disagree with the prevailing thinking, how feasible is it to live differently, or what does it take to try to reshape conventional attitudes to roads, oil companies, motor-car technology, or reshape consumer tastes? Are today's governments merely dancing to the oil companies' tune, or do the voters who can change governments merely want to hang on to the comforts and convenience of car travel for as long as possible?

What certainly seems true is that if the prevailing view is that using petrol-driven vehicles is a good thing, the most successful car manufacturer, the most persuasive car dealer, and the most efficient mechanic will be the purest expression of the will of even the most half-hearted supporters of petrol-engine technology.

On the other hand, the most outspoken and perhaps even reckless critics of the technology will probably be unpopular people in their time, but could well be celebrated later as having foresight or courage or wisdom that was rare when they were alive.

The record does suggest that even in the early 1800s there were people within the community that had most to gain from oppression who did actually oppose it.

Clearly, the opposition never went far enough. But why not?

If the ideas that eventually formed the hated system of apartheid were already taking shape in those early years, it is fair to say the ideas that rose up to oppose inequality and eventually overthrow it were there, too.

But how much sooner could South Africa have had a Bill of Rights and the commitment to equality of the Constitution of 1996 if individuals had decided it was desirable? And what would have succeeded in making them think that way in the circumstances of their time?

Finders keepers

Finders keepers

Right at the heart of British imperialism, in the capital of the 19th century's superpower, there were serious moral doubts.

A group of MPs who formed the Select Committee on Aborigines at Westminster in London took a long, hard look at what it was the British Empire was all about, and they didn't like what they saw.

'It might be presumed,' the committee wrote in 1837, 'that the native inhabitants of any land have an incontrovertible right to their own soil: a plain and sacred right, however, which seems not to have been understood. Europeans have entered their borders uninvited, and, when there, have not only acted as if they were the undoubted lords of the soil, but have punished the natives as aggressors ....'

'Too often,' the MPs noted,

> their territory has been usurped; their property seized; their number diminished; their character debased; the spread of civilisation impeded. European vices and diseases have been introduced amongst them, and they have been familiarised with the most potent instruments for the subtle or the violent destruction of human life, namely brandy and gunpowder.

It was powerful stuff, but it was not a popular view. Gunpowder and brandy still had a long way to go in southern Africa.

———— ❖ ————

There used to be a tough playground rule that if you lost something and someone else found it, they could keep it. It was called 'finders keepers, losers weepers'.

But even children knew that it wasn't a right in the legal sense, and it was not a rule that could be applied elsewhere in life with any success.

Ownership never was as simple. And the larger story of loss and gain in the history of whole communities is never as simple either.

But for many people in southern Africa – especially as the competition for land and resources intensified in the decades after the second British occupation of the Cape in 1806 – it must often have seemed as simple as 'finders keepers, losers weepers'.

Whole communities lost their land – and their livelihood – not out of negligence, but because someone else more powerful 'found' it.

The agents of this process were Africans as much as Europeans, ex-slaves, runaways and bandits. It was the result of government orders, from the Cape, or London, and incursions by newcomers, including those who emerged from the political and military upheaval – the *Mfecane* – that in the early 1800s held southern Africa in a state of conflict.

There was creeping colonial expansion and dispossession from the south, and clashes and conquests of chiefdoms and kingdoms in the north. In time, especially as the trekkers penetrated northwards, the bloody competition between armed settlers, colonial armies and powerful African leaders for land and power intensified.

Often, as the historian CW de Kiewiet has suggested, the conflict arose over the basic needs of water and grass – 'the first principle in the life of Boer and Bantu, for it was in their herds that both counted their wealth'.

And he goes on to argue that in the competition for water and grass, '[e]very blow that struck at native life had its repercussion on the white community as well. This is the deepest truth in all South African history.'

Before the British came at the end of the 1700s, the Dutch had tried to limit the size of the colony and the conflict between whites and blacks. There was one ruling after the next – in 1727, 1739, 1770 and finally 1779 – to say: so far and no further. Each line was overrun. And the deeper the penetration, the more complex the disputes – over grazing rights, cattle thefts, conditions of labour, civil law – with each clash leaving 'a larger number of natives embedded in white society'.

For the British, who took over a steadily expanding possession at the start of the 1800s, the administrative costs of the colony rose steadily. The expense of keeping soldiers in the field went up as the increasing settler presence led to more frequent disputes, and there were times when it must have seemed an unrewarding investment.

On the eastern frontier, however, flourishing merino sheep farming provided a steadily industrialising Britain – whose fabric mills were at the core of the Industrial Revolution – with a good economic reason to promote settler farmers' interests. Four Spanish merino sheep – alien to Africa – had been imported in 1789. The wool-bearing animals took to their new home, though the farming was labour-intensive. Within 60 years, by 1851, merino wool accounted for nearly 60 percent of all Cape exports. (Merinos from the Cape were later exported to Australia, forming the basis of that country's gigantic wool industry.) In what became the Eastern Cape, though, some of the best grazing was in Xhosa hands and labour was not abundant. Farmers saw that if they took the land, the landless Xhosa might be compelled to work for them. If it seemed to them a recipe for success, it was also a key factor in a century of wars.

A much more compelling economic proposition emerged towards the end of the 1800s, in the interior: in the last 20 years of the century, the discovery of diamonds and gold north of the Orange River spurred Britain on to gain total control over the whole region – its natural resources, but also its labour.

Reflecting on the Tswana experience, the 20th-century intellectual and political leader Zachariah Keodirelang ('ZK') Matthews noted:

> *The coming of the British was a rescue from the conquest of the* maburu *[Boers] and was regarded by our people as very much the lesser evil. But still … it meant that we had lost forever power over our own lives. This power passed to the* mokgethi, *the tax-gatherers, who more often than not were* manyesemane *who acted like* maburu, *Englishmen who acted like Boers.*

From *Freedom for My People, The Autobiography of ZK Matthews: Southern Africa 1901-1968* (1981) by Monica Wilson (editor)

That came later. In the interior of the early 1800s, African politics dominated the scene.

[SHAKA]

Rather like Napoleon, though not on the same scale, Shaka has remained a fascinating figure to successive generations who have been drawn to the man, and the myth, through films, books, art, legends, poetry, plays, popular songs and even a guide to doing business that suggests Shaka's style of leadership is a recipe for success in the corporate world of the 21st century.

The poet Oswald Mtshali wrote of him that

The gods
boiled his blood
in a clay pot of passion
to course in his veins.

He is perceived as a no-nonsense man, ruthless yet also heroic, who gained a reputation for knowing what he wanted, and getting it.

His early life was marked by bullying and ill-treatment, especially after his mother Nandi was expelled from the royal household of Senzangakhona. But life took a different turn once he had proved himself as a fearless and able warrior in one of Dingiswayo's regiments.

Shaka, ruthless and heroic.

It was the springboard to his creating one of the most militarised and powerful states of the region in the early 1800s.

His military innovations – the short stabbing spear and large shield, coupled with tactical refinements that enabled decisive close-order fighting, and the drafting of all young men within his growing empire – enabled his formidable regiments to crush neighbouring rivals.

In time, his conquests brought within the Zulu kingdom all the northern Nguni between the Drakensberg and the sea, from the Phongola River in the north to the Thukela in the south. South of the Thukela he kept a buffer zone of cleared land. His armies raided as far south as Mpondo country, in what became the Transkei, and far to the north, enabling Shaka to control much of the trade between the interior and the Portuguese at Delagoa Bay (in present-day Mozambique).

These conquests were part of, and contributed to, the large-scale upheaval known as the *Mfecane* (or *Difaqane* in Sotho). The *Mfecane* was long thought to have been driven by the rise of the Zulu kingdom in the early 1800s, but is now regarded as the consequence of a broader range of developments, including a population increase following the introduction of maize, competition for resources, a severe drought in the first decade of the century, and the impact of growing trade – in slaves too – with Delagoa Bay.

The prelude to Shaka's rise was conflict between rival northern Nguni states – the Ndwandwe under Zwide and the looser Mthethwa confederacy under Dingiswayo (under whom Shaka rose to prominence as the leader of a regiment) – which came to a head with the Mthethwa's defeat in about 1818. With the death of Dingiswayo, though, Shaka was determined to better the Ndwandwe. Drawing Zwide's forces deep into his own territory, he routed them at the Mhlathuze River, shattering Ndwandwe power for good.

As Shaka's conquests continued, they compounded the other elements of the *Mfecane*, and war and dislocation spread in waves throughout much of southern Africa and even as far north as central Africa. Tens of thousands of displaced people were on the move, some seeking refuge elsewhere, others marauding and killing and taking over land

from whoever was in their path. Livestock losses by chiefs cost them prestige and authority. In time, new social categories such as peasant farmers, sharecroppers and migrant workers began to emerge. The political map of the region was dramatically altered. It was into this turbulent landscape that the Voortrekkers ventured. The consequences of the *Mfecane* deceived them into thinking the extensively depopulated interior was unclaimed and could be occupied without much resistance.

Elsewhere, the upheaval led to unlikely alliances. An invading Sotho army was stopped in its tracks by a combined force of Africans and Griqua (descendants of European, Khoe-San and ex-slave migrants from the Cape in the late 1700s) at Dithakong, near present-day Kuruman, in 1823. And, on the eastern frontier, displaced northern Nguni people moving south formed themselves into the Mfengu (or Fingo) grouping. In the absence of traditional leadership, they were quicker to convert to Christianity and acquire Western education, and, in three of the Frontier Wars between 1846 and 1878, fought on the side of the colonial army.

Two major new states emerged from the *Mfecane*: the Ndebele under Mzilikatsi (a rival of Shaka's and a feared military man who eventually created the new state of Matabeleland in southern Zimbabwe) and Basutoland under Moshweshwe.

Perhaps, as historian Christopher Saunders notes, the most important consequence was that 'the *Mfecane* gave to millions of Africans new identities – Zulu, Swazi and Ndebele – which would be long-lasting'.

As for Shaka's legacy, it was the self-conscious militarism and the political unity of the powerful Zulu kingdom that presented settlers with a lasting challenge: first the Voortrekkers, whose leader Piet Retief was killed in 1838 by Shaka's successor and half-brother Dingane (who, with another brother, had assassinated Shaka in 1828), and later the British, whose first attempt to subdue Dingane's successor Cetshwayo ended in bloody defeat at Isandhlwana in 1879. Having annexed Natal in 1843, Britain finished the job by annexing Zululand in 1887. Even so, the cohesion and the identity of the Zulu 'nation' is in large part the legacy of the will and the exploits of Shaka.

[MOSHWESHWE]

Much less of a warrior king than Shaka, Moshweshwe was shrewd, statesmanlike and wise, a clever strategist and an astute diplomat who created and preserved his kingdom in the face of threats from African rivals, settler incursions and far-reaching socio-political change.

Born in the late 1780s, Moshweshwe was the son of a minor Sotho ruler in the upper Caledon River valley. At his initiation he was named Tlaputle (the energetic one), but the name by which he is remembered is from a praise song in his honour after a particularly daring and successful cattle raid in which he 'shaved off' a large number of beasts from a neighbouring community: Moshweshwe is an imitation of the sound of a knife shaving off a beard or hair. He and his close friend, Makoanyane – later his trusted general – gained a reputation for their feats in raids.

If the conditions of his early manhood were difficult and challenging, with the fall-out of the *Mfecane* threatening the livelihood and the very existence of communities across the interior, Moshweshwe had both the bravery and the strategic wisdom to manage the risks.

His rise to prominence owed much to his success in holding his followers together, seeing to their collective interest. By offering protection to refugees fleeing pillage and famine elsewhere, he increased his following. He was careful not to take on rivals who might destroy him, and would disarm them by sending them gifts of cattle.

In about 1820, he and his people were settled at Butha Buthe, but, threatened by aggressors four years later, he withdrew in mid-winter in a gruelling 120 kilometre march to Thaba Bosiu, a nearly impregnable flat-topped mountain east of the Caledon River. There were only a handful of routes to the summit, which could be blocked by boulders in times of war; there was a water spring at the top, as well as grazing and soil enough for growing crops. Moshweshwe and his people could survive any siege there indefinitely.

But it was not only an astute defensiveness that

Moshweshwe, brave and astute.

counted in Moshweshwe's favour. Having expanded his wealth in cattle through raids, he built up his kingdom by loaning his cattle to neighbouring clans through a system of patronage known as *sisa* or *mafisa*.

According to this system, the cattle or the milk could be recalled at any time, but the holder of the cattle had the use of the herds without owning them. In this way, Moshweshwe acquired a following of people who depended on him, and, as he saw it, the territory in which they lived.

Moshweshwe himself claimed in later life that he had incorporated no fewer than 23 distinct communities under his patronage. It may be mere legend that he even welcomed cannibals accused of capturing and eating his own grandfather. He was, as Christopher Saunders notes, 'magnanimous to his enemies, and a humane and tolerant ruler of a relatively loose-knit federal state'.

He developed a close and useful relationship with Paris Evangelical Missionary Society missionaries – who became crucial intermediaries in his dealings with white settlers – and eagerly developed trade, mainly in grain, to procure guns, horses and blankets.

But, from the 1840s, the pressures of change intensified.

He faced two new threats in particular: Britain, which, by proclamation, was absorbing large pieces of southern Africa into its expanding colony; and the Boers

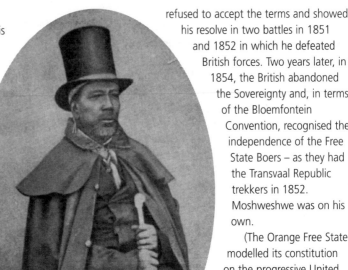
Statesmanly king, Moshweshwe.

who had trekked north from the 1830s and were laying claim to vast stretches of the countryside. Initially, they merely crossed Moshweshwe's territory on their way north to Natal. But when the British annexed Natal in 1843, many Boers returned to what would become the Orange Free State, between the Vaal and the Orange rivers.

Moshweshwe's mountain bases were not attractive to the newcomers, but they wanted the farmland west of the Caledon River.

Britain had initially recognised that this land belonged to Moshweshwe, but by the late 1840s there were other considerations: trekboers and Griqua had clashed north of the Orange, and Britain wanted to – or felt it needed to – assert itself in bringing order to the colony's northern frontier. In this way the high commissioner at the time, Sir Harry Smith, justified the proclamation in 1848 of the Orange River Sovereignty. It cost Moshweshwe his land to the west of the Caledon. Angered, he

refused to accept the terms and showed his resolve in two battles in 1851 and 1852 in which he defeated British forces. Two years later, in 1854, the British abandoned the Sovereignty and, in terms of the Bloemfontein Convention, recognised the independence of the Free State Boers – as they had the Transvaal Republic trekkers in 1852. Moshweshwe was on his own.

(The Orange Free State modelled its constitution on the progressive United States constitution, but citizenship was for whites only.)

Through the 1850s and 1860s, Moshweshwe was embroiled in armed conflicts and inconclusive negotiations over land. In 1868, he was convinced that to save his kingdom the only option left was to appeal to Britain for protection. The territory was annexed. It sheltered him from the Boers but it also confirmed his loss of the fertile lands west of the Caledon.

Two years later, the year of Moshweshwe's death, Basutoland was taken over by the Cape. Resistance and conflict continued to flare up through the 1870s and 1880s, until the Cape asked Britain to take over the territory again. Finally, nearly a century later, Lesotho was granted independence from Britain in 1966.

It is noteworthy that, in the 1870s, Basutoland supplied large quantities of grain to the diamond diggings of the Northern Cape, but within less than half a century its main export was migrant workers – for South Africa's mines – and it was importing food.

The kingdom itself, the nation of people, is Moshweshwe's monument. Its formation in the 1800s was, as historian Robert Ross has described it, a 'most remarkable success'.

An aspirant nation-builder in his own right, Piet Retief – like other Voortrekker leaders – was perhaps driven by much the same impulse that stirred Shaka and Moshweshwe: a desire to find a place to settle with his people and call the shots without inter-ference from anyone else.

The dynamics were, of course, more complicated. The context in which Retief's well-armed trekkers pursued these goals – occupying land and exerting their independence, by force if necessary – casts him more obviously in the role of an exploiter. He would ordinarily have

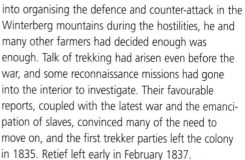

Voortrekker leader Piet Retief.

expected to pay a good price for land and live under laws that would have limited his scope for using force against people armed with spears and sticks.

Born in 1780, he grew up in Wellington in the Cape, a town that was meaningfully called *Wamakersvallei* (waggon-makers' valley) then. As a young man, he had lost a lot of money in property deals in the Stellenbosch area, so that when, in 1812, he led a commando to the eastern frontier to relieve civilians helping troops in the 4th Frontier War against the Xhosa, he was on the lookout for new opportunities. His initial idea was to provision troops, which he did by government contract in 1813, but it was not a financial success.

He stayed, though, and became a general dealer, baker, miller, butcher, liquor trader, auctioneer, timber merchant and building contractor. There was no doubt a demand for all these things on a frontier in which white settlers with all their consumer demands were growing steadily in number. Yet success eluded him. Though the business folded eventually, he still had his farm – and the respect of fellow-farmers and the authorities.

As a field commandant from 1822, he acted as the spokesman of settler farmers. They were not a happy lot. It was a discontent that spurred the Great Trek.

They were unhappy about Ordinance 50 of 1828,

giving rights to Khoe-San people and freed slaves, which they believed was not in the farmers' interests, nor those of poorer whites whose access to land was narrowing. They did not feel the government was doing enough to protect them from Xhosa attacks. And they were angry that missionaries such as Dr John Philip kept blaming them for the conflict, accusing them of angering, and stealing land from, neighbouring Xhosa.

The outbreak of the 6th Frontier War in December 1834 – the year that marked the beginning of the end of slavery – was a turning point for Retief. While he threw himself into organising the defence and counter-attack in the Winterberg mountains during the hostilities, he and many other farmers had decided enough was enough. Talk of trekking had arisen even before the war, and some reconnaissance missions had gone into the interior to investigate. Their favourable reports, coupled with the latest war and the emanci-pation of slaves, convinced many of the need to move on, and the first trekker parties left the colony in 1835. Retief left early in February 1837.

In Britain, the brazen single-mindedness of the trekkers was viewed with anxiety.

In a speech to the House of Commons on 6 March, 1838, Sir William Molesworth, a campaigner for social and colonial reform, warned that

[O]ur colonists are producing in southern Africa, by seizing the cattle of the natives, evils similar to the worst of those created in central Africa by the slave trade. Besides these evils, which have long existed and for which it may be difficult to find an adequate remedy at the present moment, the most extraordinary events are taking place in the colony, which prove the inability and feebleness of the Colonial Government. A formidable body of Cape boors … have left the colony, and set our authority at defiance.

Conflict, chiefly over land and grazing, was an inevitable consequence of the Voortrekkers' penetration of the interior.

Retief's own manifesto, published in the *Graham's Town Journal* on 2 February, 1837, left no doubt about that:

> *We quit this colony under the full assurance that the English government has nothing more to require of us, and will allow us to govern ourselves without its interference in future.*

He complained of the 'severe losses' resulting from the freeing of slaves, and the absence of any prospect of peace and security in the colony.

While he assured that the trekkers would 'take care that no one shall be held in a state of slavery', the trekkers said they would 'maintain such regulations as may suppress crime and preserve proper relations between master and servant'.

There was surely an element of wishful thinking, even of naivety, on Retief's part in his saying in his manifesto that 'we quit this colony with a desire to lead a more quiet life'.

Linking up with other trekker leaders at Thaba Nchu, Retief was elected 'governor', the chief leader, but failed to convince all the others that Natal ought to be their destination. (Earlier treks had already penetrated the region later known as the Transvaal.)

Concluding treaties with African rulers wherever they could – and sometimes operating in alliances with them – the trekkers hoped to secure a place for themselves by agreement.

This was what Retief hoped to achieve when he reached the territory of Shaka's successor Dingane towards the end of 1837. The first meeting at the royal settlement of uMgundgundlovu seemed promising enough: the Zulu ruler reportedly agreed to give land to Retief if the trekker leader recaptured cattle stolen by a neighbouring rival, Sekonyela of the Tlokwa.

But the trekkers may have acted prematurely in response to news of the negotiations by moving down from the Drakensberg range and fanning out over a wide area. Retief succeeded in recapturing Dingane's cattle, but his second meeting with the now anxious Zulu king was a disaster. Dingane clearly had grave misgivings about the sudden influx of settlers, and when Retief and his party returned to uMgundgundlovu in early February 1838 to have the king sign the title deed for the territory they believed he had promised them, their end was near. As the trekkers sat and watched the warriors dance, the king stood suddenly and shouted: '*Bambani aba thakathi!*' ('Kill the wizards!')

That same day, Zulu regiments attacked the trekker settlements at great cost. Though the outlook in Natal was grim, the trekkers avenged the killing of Retief and his party at the battle of Blood River some nine months later, on 16 December, 1838. The battle was so named because the Ncome River on the banks of which it was fought was said to have run red with the blood of killed or wounded warriors. It would become an elemental image of Afrikaner nationalist mythology of the 20th century.

The defeat cost Dingane his throne. He was overthrown by his half-brother Mpande, who was more amenable to the trekkers. Soon, the trekkers declared the Republic of Natalia.

Later – in Natal and elsewhere – their old colonial foe, Britain, would eventually return to harry the trekkers.

It has been said of Piet Retief that his significance lies not in what he accomplished but in what he represented. He did not personally realise the aims set out in his manifesto. But the Great Trek that he personified had a major impact.

'Its result,' as historian Robert Ross notes,

> *was a massive increase in the extent of the proportion of modern South Africa dominated by people of European descent. It was thus one of the crucial events in the formation of the country.*

[CAROLUS]

Not much is known about Carolus, and he is not a decisive figure in the events of the cataclysmic 19th century.

He was an 'apprentice' to Coenraad Scheepers when that discontented farmer left the eastern frontier in April 1837 to join the Great Trek. (The term 'apprentice' refers to children of Khoekhoe slaves and servants who were compelled to work for their 'masters' until they were 25.)

Carolus eventually escaped, and made a statement on 28 February, 1838, on his return to Port Elizabeth that describes a feature of the risky migration to the north that is overlooked in most Voortrekker histories.

He did not want to trek, but Scheepers told him he had no choice.

Eventually, when they were about four days' ride from Port Natal (latter-day Durban), Carolus once more 'asked my master to let me go back to the colony'.

For his trouble, he was tied to a waggon wheel, given 20 lashes, and told that Scheepers 'had me now where he could use me as he pleased'.

A week later, when his 'master' was at church, Carolus ran away. He left behind his wife Sareen, his son Jacob and another old 'apprentice' named January.

I have left behind … very many apprentices, but I have not the means of ascertaining their number. The apprentices are occasionally in the habit of endeavouring to effect their escape, but are generally caught by the trek boers when they are secured in irons and severely flogged.

'Apprentice' was the misleading term for former slaves who were compelled to join the Voortrekkers. The bare-chested man on the right was probably one of them.

[SIR GEORGE GREY]

The Voortrekkers had long driven north in their quest for freedom from Britain and the reformist zeal of missionaries, Shaka had come and gone, and Moshweshwe was anxiously negotiating his kingdom's survival when Sir George Grey arrived at the Cape to assume control of a colony that seemed, often, to be at war with itself.

His greatest challenge – and the source of the bitterest criticism of his governorship – was the unresolved conflict on the eastern frontier between white settlers and the Xhosa whose land they wanted.

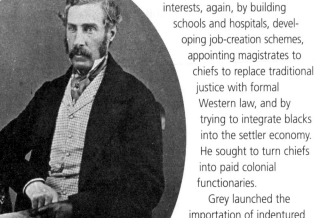

Sir George Grey's legacy is complex and difficult.

Born in 1812, Grey had started out as a soldier in the army of occupation in Ireland. In his twenties he undertook two expeditions as an explorer to Australia, where, in 1841, he was appointed governor. His keenness to 'civilise' the native inhabitants of Britain's far-flung colonies was born there, too, with his building schools for the aborigines. After four years, he was sent to New Zealand as governor, where settlers were struggling economically and faced a Maori rebellion. His response was a prelude to his activity at the Cape: drawing opponents of the settlers into the 'civilised' way by using education and work-for-pay schemes to replace indigenous authority and belief with Western values, laws and economic activity.

Ironically, the white settlers were not happy with him, for he was seen to be overly sympathetic to the Maoris, though he undermined the Maori chiefs' authority. For the time being, however, New Zealand was better off economically.

Would he do the same at the Cape, his next appointment, from 1854?

Sympathetic histories credit Grey with doing much to 'civilise' the Africans whose hostility threatened the Cape settlers' interests, again, by building schools and hospitals, developing job-creation schemes, appointing magistrates to chiefs to replace traditional justice with formal Western law, and by trying to integrate blacks into the settler economy. He sought to turn chiefs into paid colonial functionaries.

Grey launched the importation of indentured labour from India for Natal's fledgling sugar-cane farms; he improved the colony's harbours; had the first railway line built between Cape Town and Wellington; and the first telegraph link between Cape Town and the eastern frontier.

Some of his ideas might even seem progressive, ahead of their time:

'We should try to make [the Xhosa] part of ourselves,' he wrote, 'consumers of our goods, contributors to our revenue; in short a source of strength and wealth for this colony ... We should ... use our time of strength, when our generosity cannot be misunderstood, to instruct and civilise – to change inveterate enemies into friends, alike from interest and increased knowledge – destroyers of our crops and produce into consumers of our goods and producers for our markets ... Should this plan be carried out, our ultimate frontier defence would be a fertile and populous country, filled with a large population, partly European, partly native.'

But these things chiefly reflected settler interests. And they have been seen to have been achieved at the appalling expense of Africans.

When Grey arrived, the lie of the land on the frontier was like this: all the Xhosa territory between the Great Fish and the Keiskamma rivers had been annexed and given to white settlers and their Mfengu allies. The Xhosa, whose chiefs' power had been restricted, were forced into the territory called British Kaffraria, between the Keiskamma and the Great Kei rivers. Across the Kei, to the east, the Xhosa under King Sarhili were still independent but under constant threat.

If it was Grey's vision to turn this disputed territory into a model colony, the stain on his reputation arises mainly from his response to the disastrous cattle killing of 1856–57.

In April 1856, a young girl named Nongqawuse and her friend let it be known that they had been approached by 'two strangers', ancestors, who had delivered a prophecy to

Tragic prophetess Nongqawuse.

them, that if the Xhosa slaughtered all their cattle, and destroyed their crops, all the ancestors would rise up and, by implication, rid them of their settler enemy. It was an infectiously hopeful vision.

Throughout the frontier region, after more than 50 years of conflict with the settlers, the embattled and weary Xhosa had seen their herds decimated by lung sickness in the early 1850s, had endured the suffering of the 8th Frontier War of 1850–53, and had seen their crops die from disease.

Furthermore, in the past half-century, two important prophets – Nxele (Makana) and Mlanjeni – had predicted that a great day would come when the dead would rise up and herald a future of freedom and plenty.

The prophecies also rang true with the Christian idea (circulating then, if not embraced) of resurrection.

Thus Nongqawuse's promising prophecy gripped their imagination. The Xhosa King Sarhili became a firm believer and told his people to slaughter their herds. Where some chiefs and communities refused, they were blamed for delaying the prophecy. Dissension and anger mounted along with starvation. Conditions were appalling. People were eventually grubbing for roots, and eating bark, to survive. As Grey watched

the unfolding catastrophe he believed 'we can draw very great permanent advantages from the circumstance, which may be made a stepping stone for the future settlement of the country'.

When the cattle killing ended in June 1857, about 40 000 people had died of starvation and more than 400 000 cattle had perished.

Grey had stockpiled food to meet the needs of the starving, but only on condition that they signed labour contracts to work on farms and towns throughout the colony. Almost 30 000 survivors went off to other parts through this scheme. Charitable whites were told their efforts to organise relief were not needed. Deaths, and the work scheme, reduced the population of British Kaffraria from 105 000 in January 1857 to slightly less than 26 000 in December 1858.

Much of the land was cut up for white farmers. Xhosa communities were forced to live in villages under close colonial supervision. A hut tax was introduced, effectively forcing people into working in the cash economy. Charges were brought against chiefs for 'hatching' the cattle killing as a 'plot' to ferment conflict and they were sent to Robben Island. And, across the Kei River, the starving King Sarhili's plea for help was answered with violence: in February 1858, Grey's forces crossed the river and took over the independent territories, forcing Sarhili into exile.

The military power of the Xhosa nation, which had resisted the white advance for more than 80 years, was broken forever.

The lasting anger towards Grey is reflected in a Black Consciousness song from the 1970s, more than a century after his governorship:

Sir George Grey took our country
He entered in through Nongqawuse
The cattle died, the sheep died
The power of the black people was finished off.

Examining the complex combination of fact and metaphor, historian JB Peires writes:

It is not true that Sir George Grey hid in the reeds pretending to be a Xhosa ancestor [misleading Nongqawuse into conveying the prophecy]. Nor is it true that his agents handed brown sugar around pretending it was a new sorghum [to replace destroyed crops]. But it is true that the Xhosa themselves must bear a large share of the responsibility. It is true, but it doesn't matter. Because it is also true that the Xhosa were never defeated on the battlefield. And that a young girl under indirect Christian influence told them that the dead would arise if they killed their cattle. Above all, it is true that a foolish mistake was converted into a national catastrophe through the ruthless and implacable policies of Sir George Grey. These latter are the important truths, and all else is detail.

In a sense, the division Grey confronted – or sought to exploit – remains today in the 'memory' people have of him: to most descendants of the Xhosa who suffered during his time as governor, he is akin to a murderer for having taken advantage of a national crisis.

To others, conceivably the descendants of the settlers who benefited from his actions, he is seen in a very different light. This view is of an enlightened man who built schools and hospitals and created jobs (the very infrastructure at the heart of the post-apartheid drive to 'deliver', to eradicate poverty, crime and disadvantage), who wished to overcome 'superstition' and replace it with 'civilised' laws, and who bequeathed to future generations his priceless collection of medieval manuscripts and rare books, including rare specimens of printed material in African languages. Could such a man have wilfully sponsored genocide, his supporters ask incredulously? And could he be held responsible for the killing of the cattle?

Grey's complex, difficult legacy is, perhaps, precisely the idea that the past reaches far into the future, where successive histories compete for attention and predominance … or demand to be rewritten if they are to speak the 'truth'.

[SARHILI]

Many great names signpost the road travelled bitterly by the Xhosa in the 1800s.

Of the princely figures who resisted the colonial advance, and paid dearly for it, Hintsa, Makana, Phato, Sandile, Maqoma, Stokwe … are among the many remembered for their successes and their mistakes, their warriorship, diplomacy, betrayal and defeat in a contest, and one war after another, that lasted a hundred years.

Sarhili, chief of the Gcaleka, paramount chief of all the Xhosa, and the last leader of independent Xhosaland, is one among them.

Born in about 1814, he was the son and heir of Hintsa, whose death in 1835 at the hands of British troops deeply affected him.

Under an assurance from Governor Benjamin D'Urban, Hintsa, accompanied by the young Sarhili, went to a British camp to negotiate a settlement which involved the return of cattle. When only a few cattle were returned, Hintsa offered to leave his son behind as a hostage and accompany Lieutenant-Colonel (later Governor) Harry Smith and a detachment of soldiers to persuade his people to surrender cattle. What followed is still uncertain in part: Hintsa's horse either bolted – or he tried to escape – and Smith raced after him and pulled him from his horse. In agony from a broken jaw, he tried to get away, but was shot twice by a soldier. He staggered on to a stream, where he collapsed, and was cold-bloodedly shot in the head. Harry Smith, an inquiry a year later was told, decided to leave Hintsa's body to the vultures, but before the army detachment withdrew Hintsa was mutilated. His head was hacked off. None of the witnesses at the inquiry into Hintsa's death – ordered by Colonial Secretary Lord Glenelg – was prepared to reveal who had mutilated the Xhosa ruler.

This atrocity did much to shape Sarhili's view of the colonial authorities, and the implications of the white settlement on the eastern frontier. But it was not an isolated, or accidental, event.

It had come at the end of the 6th Frontier War (1834–35), the 7th was eight years away and the 8th just three years after that. It was an era, and a landscape, defined by a bloody and seemingly perpetual conflict.

Sarhili was said to have had a mild manner and a quiet sense of humour, but as a staunch defender of his people and his land against the settlers and their African allies he fought whenever he had to – and negotiated, too – in the hope of preserving his independence.

It was possibly his keenness to reject colonial values that drew him to the fatal prediction of the tragic prophetess Nongqawuse.

His role in the cattle killing, in giving his influential endorsement to the prophecy of Nongqawuse, was telling and controversial.

He had always been strongly swayed by diviners and magicians, and though fascinated by elements of Christianity, he was impressed neither by the behaviour of white colonists nor the missionaries who crossed the Kei River in the hope of drawing converts into the fold.

He saw a return to Xhosa beliefs as a way of resisting the colonial advance, and he was among those who claimed he himself had seen visions that corroborated the prophecy. His support for the killing of cattle and the destruction of crops convinced many.

The disastrous consequences touched his household directly, too, and in October 1857 Sarhili dictated to a trader John Crouch a desperate letter of appeal to the governor, Sir George Grey. He begged for forgiveness and appealed to the governor to send food and seed for his family and his people.

'If he does not assist us, we must all die of starvation. I this day place myself entirely in his hands.'

Grey's response – an armed attack, assisted by the Thembu, on Sarhili's territory across the Great Kei River – forced the king into exile east of the Mbashe River.

The Cape government eventually allowed the

His support for the cattle killing cost Xhosa paramount Sarhili dearly.

much-depleted clan to return to their territory in 1864, but most of their land had been resettled by the colonists' Thembu and Mfengu allies. In 1878, after a war with the Mfengu, Sarhili was 'deposed' from his paramountcy by colonial proclamation and, though pardoned in 1883, his power had really already been taken from him with the incremental annexation of the Transkei by the Cape from 1879.

Sarhili's fate was, ultimately, a consequence of the cattle killing that he endorsed and of the colonial response to it.

The cattle killing, as historian Robert Ross sees it,

marks the end of the beginning of South African history. For the first time, an African society (other than the Khoekhoe) had been broken. Much land had already gone, but now Africans began moving out as labourers, while paying heed to the message of the missionaries as never before.

[ADAM KOK III]

Unacknowledged trek leader, Adam Kok III.

Among the people who trekked north, crossing the Orange River in the early 1800s, were the Griqua, who had formed themselves in the later decades of the previous century from the descendants of European, Khoe-San and ex-slave migrants from the Cape. They were initially called Basters or Bastards.

As they trekked inland, they were accompanied by missionaries of the London Missionary Society. Settlements were established at Klaarwater (later Griquatown) and Campbell, named after the missionary John Campbell.

Their Western clothing and customs, rifles, horses and waggons set them apart from other people in the area.

They even had their own 'Griqua Town' coins minted in England in about 1814. Organised by Campbell, two consignments of coins were received, one in 1815 and the other a year later.

They were mainly herders, traders and hunters. To some extent, indigenous people and groups were absorbed into their community. Campbell once noted that in the village later named after him: 'the people … seem to live as one family … [where] five languages are spoken … namely Dutch, Coranna, Bootchuana, Hottentot and Bushman.'

In the first half of the 1800s, the Griqua divided into separate captaincies. Andries Waterboer was appointed captain at Griquatown in 1820. (It was his son, Nicholas Waterboer, who was persuaded in 1868 to lease farms to English colonists, ostensibly to prevent Free State farmers from encroaching on Griqua-land. It turned out to be the first step towards British annexation of Griqualand West and the diamond fields in the 1870s.) Further to the north, Adam Kok II was the first captain at Klaarwater. Eventually, out of distrust for the missionaries as colonial agents, Adam Kok II moved his captaincy to Philippolis. When he died in 1835, his son, Adam Kok III, became leader. Times were hard, with the Griqua coming under threat from trekker settlers. Britain initially promised to protect them and treaties were signed, but eventually, in 1854, the British cleared the way for an independent Orange Free State. And, in terms of a secret deal between the Boers and Britain, the Philippolis Griqua lost their land.

Six years later, the Free State government made the deal known to the Griqua, which the Griqua believed left them three choices: they could give up their land and work for farmers as servants; they could stay and fight; or they could leave and find somewhere else to live. They opted for the last.

More than 2 000 people, with some 300 carts and waggons and more than 20 000 head of cattle, left Philippolis on what turned out to be a two-year trek across the Drakensberg to a territory called Nomansland, between the Transkei and Natal, and later renamed Griqualand East. (The colonial government thought of Nomansland, as its name suggests, as nobody's property, but it did in fact fall under the territory of the Mpondo chief Faku.)

The hard journey left many of these trekkers exhausted and poor, but their freedom was at stake and it was a price they were prepared to pay. The colonial governor Sir George Grey favoured the Griqua's choice of destination – over alternatives such as Namaqualand – because he felt they would create a buffer between the Natal colonists and the Xhosa. But he insisted that they submit to British authority as subjects, not merely as allies. The Griqua resisted, but Grey was firm.

A 100-strong scouting expedition reconnoitred the route, secured Faku's support, and reported back to Philippolis in December 1859 that Nomansland did indeed offer promising prospects. The Griqua sold their farms, secured Moshweshwe's approval to cross his territory, and began preparations for the main trek. Adam Kok III travelled to Cape Town where, among other things, he bought three ship's cannons to be fashioned into artillery pieces as protection.

The first trekkers left Philippolis towards the end of 1860 and established a base near present-day Zastron. Once joined by the others, they decided to wait out another winter – which proved severe, costing them thousands of cattle and sheep – before tackling the mountain barrier before them in the spring.

It was hard going. They had sometimes to blast a way through the mountains, using gunpowder to shift rocks and boulders and create passes for their waggons. They were also preyed on by Sotho cattle-raiders.

But, eventually, in the summer of 1862–63, they crossed Ongeluk's Nek and descended to the plains below. It was indeed promising. Game, grazing, water and timber were plentiful. But it was a tired and weakened community. Eventually, after a slow start, the Griqua began to organise their lives, planting crops, establishing an administration and laying out the new town, Kokstad.

But the number of white traders and farmers was increasing, too. By the 1870s, the colonial administration was also showing an interest and, in the pattern repeated everywhere else, annexed the territory in 1875. Kok would remain the nominal leader and receive a salary.

When he died at the end of the year after falling from his horse-drawn buggy, his cousin Adam 'Eta' Kok delivered a prophetic graveside homily:

He is the last of his race. After him, there will be no coloured king or chief in colonial South Africa … Do you realise that our nationality lies buried there?

Alf Wannenburgh notes in *Forgotten Frontiersmen* (1978) that, when Adam Kok III set off in 1860, his people little realised that their promised land 'was a false promise, a land they would be able to call theirs for barely 15 years, though it bears their name to this day'. But the trek of the Griquas from Philippolis across the Drakensberg into the territory that would later be named Griqualand East

is one of the great epics of the South African interior in the 19th century. Only the fact that its participants were coloured people has denied it its proper place in standard histories beside the other great migrations of the period ….

[SIR ANDRIES STOCKENSTRÖM]

Few in his time had Andries Stockenström's breadth of vision.

The difficulties of trying to change the political spirit of an era are reflected in the achievements and frustrations of Andries Stockenström. He was always in the thick of things, in war and in politics, yet he maintained a view of the bigger picture and was never afraid of unpopularity.

Born in 1792, he had only a rudimentary education in Cape Town before joing his landdrost father Anders Stockenström's office in Graaff-Reinet as a clerk.

He wanted to become a soldier, and in 1811 joined the Cape Corps and took part in the 4th Frontier War that broke out in that year. It was in 1811 that his father was killed in a Xhosa ambush. The young Stockenström, with other mounted burghers, rushed to the scene and shot dead 13 of the attackers.

In 1815, at the age of 22, he was appointed in the post his father had had, as landdrost. It was his job to regulate relations between the settlers and the Xhosa and see to all other government business, from education to law.

The first sign of a major difference of opinion between Stockenström and the settlers and the colonial authorities was his strong opposition to what was called the 'reprisals system', a new frontier policy which allowed white farmers to reclaim any cattle from a kraal to which the spoor of stolen cattle led, even if the stolen cattle were not actually there. Maintaining a fair, strict frontier policy was a key theme of his role in the region.

He had a role in promoting Ordinance 50 in 1828 – granting to Khoe-San and free persons of colour the right to own land. In effect, they had no access to land outside mission stations, so Stockenström established the Kat River Settlement on the eastern frontier a year later so that the Ordinance's intended beneficiaries could have land and develop their own farms. It was not liked by white settlers.

He was appointed commissioner-general of the Cape's eastern districts from 1828 to 1833, but resigned angrily over the defiance and recklessness of army officers who insisted on crossing into Xhosa territory and stealing their cattle as 'punishment' for attacks on settlers.

Stockenström travelled to London in 1833 to try to gain more independence for his commissioner-general's post, but failed.

After spending some time in Sweden – where he was thinking of settling – he was on his way back to the Cape to wind up his affairs when he stopped over in London. While there, he gave evidence to the Select Committee on Aborigines at the House of Commons.

His criticism of the colonists drew bitter attacks from the Cape farmers. Equally, however, Stockenström often disagreed with the views of philanthropists. He believed that the authority of the chiefs had to be maintained and that frontier relations were to be strictly regulated and not left to simmer in an endless sequence of attacks and reprisals.

This was broadly the view of the colonial office in London, which decided to appoint Stockenström lieutenant-governor of the eastern districts, a job he did for three years from 1836. Colonists reviled him during this time.

In 1839, he was made South Africa's first baronet and, a year later, retired to his farm. His public life was far from over, however.

When Sir Harry Smith was appointed governor in 1847, and immediately abandoned the treaty system with Xhosa chiefs, Stockenström warned him he was courting trouble. Escalating conflict proved him right.

Stockenström now devoted his energies to agitating for representative government at the Cape, which eventually came about with the first Cape parliament in 1854. As a member of this legislature until 1856, Stockenström defended the Kat River Settlement and tried to resist its abolition, attempting to expose frontier warmongers and land speculators with the appointment of a commission of inquiry.

He failed in these attempts, but his fearless airing of his views kept attention on critical issues that would shape future events.

His death in England in 1864 brought a controversial life to a close.

Stockenström stands out as a remarkable figure of the 1800s.

'No man in the 19th century Cape,' historian Christopher Saunders writes, 'had greater breadth of vision, none gained the respect of a wider constituency, black as well as white.'

It is little wonder that, back in London as early as 1837, some at least were distressed by the history of colonialism, by a record showing that …

Europeans have entered [countries peopled by others] uninvited, and, when there, have not only acted as if they were the undoubted lords of the soil, but have punished the natives as aggressors ….

Things were to get a lot worse in South Africa before this basic injustice would, as a principle, be set aside. It came more than 150 years later in a deceptively simple, yet powerful form unimagined in 1837.

'We, the people,' the preamble to the Constitution of the Republic of South Africa of 1996 asserts, *'… believe South Africa belongs to all who live in it, united in our diversity.'*

Many divisions and inequalities remained in 1996, and still do today. But the simple idea of belonging, for everybody, was a new departure. The preamble to the Constitution is a strikingly plain statement against the traumas of the 1800s – wars and invasions that, by the 1890s, had largely destroyed indigenous independence and created the political conditions that would assure the dominance of 'white' South Africa's interests for much of the 20th century.

Sparks from the earth

[chapter six]
Sparks from the earth

Fleetwood Rawstorne's Red Cap party at work on Colesberg Kopje.

Damon, a man whose full name is forgotten, was just a cook when he probably found the very first gems at the site of what would later become the biggest man-made hole in the world.

Banished to a *kopje* for his drunkenness, the story goes, the lucky cook got on with his own dig and left the rest of Fleetwood Rawstorne's Red Cap party in peace at their camp down on the plain.

A few nights later he stumbled down to the tents. 'Fleet,' he hissed, summoning Rawstorne, 'I want to see you.'

Word spread rapidly about the latest finds at Gilfillan's Kop on Johannes Nicolaas de Beer's farm, *Vooruitzigt*. Soon enough it became the centre of a bustling diamond-seekers' settlement aptly named New Rush. In time, the hill – renamed Colesberg Kopje by Rawstorne himself after his home town – attained an awesome significance as the Big Hole, a vast, shadowy crater hacked into the blue kimberlite rock that would yield the De Beers diamond empire.

In the famous black-and-white photograph of Rawstorne's party, posing on the crest of the *kopje* in

the second half of 1871, their signature red hats have to be imagined. It's a portrait almost of leisure. And it is not clear whether Damon is even in the picture, being perhaps merely incidental to the scene, to the fame and fortune that beckoned thousands of new settlers across the hot, dusty veld of the interior.

Yet if diamond mining gave anyone a primary role in southern Africa, it was the black men whose labour became indispensable in the extraction of the mineral wealth of southern Africa, diamonds from the 1870s and gold from the 1880s. It was not obvious in the early years, and it would take a long time for that truth to be realised.

The diamond – and, soon, the gold – mines were the foundation of South Africa's future national wealth. They were also at the heart of the war that led to the unification of the Boer and British territories into a single country, the Union of South Africa. And they marked the beginning of the exploitation of mass, migrant labour which, within a century, spawned a potent political element in the forces ranged against white minority rule.

More immediately, in the late 1800s, the massed labour of Africans – never before organised on such a scale to match the needs of an industry – assured the fortunes and the status of a handful of powerful capitalists. It was an industry that elevated both the colony in Britain's global empire and southern Africa's significance in world affairs. And it deepened and hastened far-reaching socio-political change through-out the region.

Like sparks from the earth, the precious glitter of diamonds and gold set off a revolution in southern African life.

———— ❖ ————

Mining is among the oldest 'industries' in southern Africa. But it was not, in its earliest form, an industry in the 19th-century sense.

Sites across the region show that from at least 200 000 years ago early modern humans searched for natural pigments – such as red ochre and glittering black specularite – and ground them down to powder to decorate their bodies. Evidence at Lion's Cave in Swaziland suggests that the demand for such cosmetics led to the actual mining of specularite with stone tools by 110 000 years ago.

It was the basis of trade, too: nodules of specularite were traded or carried up to 200 kilometres from their source to sites in the interior at even earlier periods.

Specularite, mined at Blinkklipkop or Tsantsebane, near Postmasburg, was highly prized as a cosmetic and for ritual purposes by different groups in the Northern Cape. In 1815, missionary John Campbell noted that 'Blink Mountain' was 'a kind of Mecca to the nations around, who are constantly making pilgrimages to it to obtain fresh supplies of the blue shining powder and the red stone'.

And the recovery, smelting and working of metals – iron, gold and copper – had long been a feature of African economies when the first frontiersmen from the south made their way across the veld of the interior in the late 1700s. Arab traders were familiar with southern African gold, which was part of the trade between the region and the Arabian Peninsula and the Persian Gulf.

Metal ores were smelted in furnaces at high temperatures, separating the metal from the impurities in the rock. Copper, too, was sometimes cast into ingots which were then traded widely.

Metal obtained through smelting was reheated in a forging, or smithing, process and worked by beating or cutting into agricultural implements, spears, knives, and other tools or ornaments. Copper wire – made by drawing, or pulling, the hot metal through a hole – was used to make jewellery such as bangles.

———— ❖ ————

Diamonds, though, may not have been regarded as valued objects in the pre-colonial era. In their rough state they were not the sparkling, faceted gems of the European jewellery trade.

Certainly, the diamond that was among the pebbles Erasmus Jacobs and his young siblings used in their games of 'klip-klip' (or five stones) at their home on a farm on the Vaal River in 1867 was, to all intents and purposes, just another stone. But there was something about it that intrigued neighbouring farmer Schalk van Niekerk when he visited the Jacobses to discuss a property deal. Van Niekerk had an amateur but discerning interest in stones. He offered to buy it, but Mrs Jacobs scoffed at the idea and gave it to him. His conviction that this particular stone was a diamond was shared some months later by a passing trader, John O'Reilly, who took it on himself to verify the hunch. There was ridicule at first from all who looked at it in the bars of Hopetown and Colesberg. But eventually it was posted to a surgeon in Graham's Town, Dr William Atherstone, who, along with the local jewellers, was convinced. The stone made its way first to the Cape, then to London. Bought eventually by the governor of the Cape, Sir Philip Wodehouse, for the princely sum of £500, it became famous as the Eureka diamond. (*Eureka* is Greek for 'I have found it'.)

But was it just a chance find, rather than evidence of a diamondiferous landscape? For a while, the experts were sceptical.

That changed two years later with the appearance of the diamond that came to be called the Star of South Africa, a bigger stone bought by Schalk van Niekerk from a Griqua shepherd for 500 sheep, 10 head of cattle and a horse, and eventually sold in England for £30 000.

This was indeed confirmation of unexpected riches in the South African veld.

Mounds of washed ground soon built up along the river diggings.

It was the earlier Eureka diamond that moved Colonial Secretary Sir Richard Southey to declare: 'This diamond is the rock upon which the future success of South Africa will be built.'

Damon's solitary discoveries at Gilfillan's Kop in July 1871 helped make sure of that. In a sense, Southey was right, though it does depend on how the idea of 'success' is defined.

———— ❖ ————

As the story of the Star of South Africa spread, so fortune-seekers from around the country, and the world, began converging in large numbers on the Vaal River in the vicinity of present-day Barkly West. By 1870 there were some 10 000 diggers sifting through the ground along a 160 kilometre stretch of the river.

There were also dry diggings away from the river. But the Gilfillan's Kop finds in July 1871 decisively shifted the focus from the Vaal to New Rush, later named Kimberley after the secretary of state for the colonies, the Earl of Kimberley. Within a year, Kimberley was second only to Cape Town in size, with a population of 50 000. (Intriguingly, there were no fewer than four future prime ministers at the diggings in the 1870s, men who would be key figures in the

politics the mineral wealth of the country helped to fashion. They were Cecil John Rhodes, William Schreiner, John X Merriman, and a young boy, the only one to be a prime minister of the Union, JBM Hertzog.)

The crush of people, and the immense potential wealth of the area, raised a pressing political question: who did the territory belong to?

The first inhabitants of the land were hunter-gatherers who had no conception of the earth belonging to anybody. By 1871, there were few of them left. None laid claim to the diamond fields. The Tlhaping had been settled in the area for hundreds of years, and one of their chiefs, Jantjie Mothibi, asserted a claim.

The Griqua, relative newcomers who had crossed the frontier from the south at the end of the 1700s, believed they had a right to the land, and they made a claim. Their shrewd agent, David Arnot – the son of a Scottish immigrant and his Khoekhoe wife – played a key role in the claims dispute. (Even before the discovery of diamonds, Arnot had asserted the Griqua's land rights in the area.)

The Orange Free State, the Boer republic that had come into being with the Bloemfontein Convention of 1854, put in a claim. So did the other Boer territory, the South African Republic, later called the Transvaal.

The British persuaded the claimants to submit to an arbitrator, who would decide the matter. So it fell to Robert Keate, lieutenant-governor of Natal, to weigh up the matter. Arnot duly convinced him, and the territory was awarded to the Griqua, who, in turn, asked Britain for protection. The awarded land was declared a Crown Colony at the end of October 1871. But the dispute was still not resolved, since the Orange Free State rejected the Keate decision. A fresh survey was done, and though it was based on breathtaking inconsistencies which 'confirmed' the Orange Free State border as being well clear of the diamond fields, Griqualand West, as the new territory was now called, remained. And it remained under British control. (Orange Free State president Johannes Brand went as far as travelling to England to protest. He failed to gain the land, but was given compensation of £90 000.)

Not surprisingly, perhaps, Arnot was rewarded for his efforts: he was given a vast tract of farmland, a cash payment and a pension.

The settling of the territorial claim to the diamond fields matched the pattern of Britain's annexations through the 1800s elsewhere in southern Africa. Protection by Britain was always a prelude to control by the imperial power, and Griqualand West was formally annexed to the Cape in 1880.

While the dispute over the territory continued between the politicians and their agents, the diamond town was growing.

In his memoir of the first days of Kimberley, Richard William Murray described in 1873 the 'grand sight' of the camp from the top of a mound of discarded ground, which the diggers named Mount Ararat:

The main street, a mile long, stretched away in the centre of the camp. That street is lined with places of business, diamond merchants' offices, the stores of general dealers, jewellers, and watchmakers, hotels and billiard-rooms, doctors' and chemists' shops, and bazaars. The post office is in the centre of the street, the Mutual Hall, capable of seating six hundred people, in the far beyond; here and there, dotted about the camp, are churches and chapels. The New Rush has been in existence but about a year and a half,

and it has the appearance of a town of at least ten years old.

But it's a deceptive picture of urban order. Life was hard. Water was in short supply. So was food, and firewood. The whole district was soon stripped of trees, and waggon-loads of wood had to be brought in daily from further and further afield. Africans living in the region – and as far away as Basutoland – did well initially out of selling grain and other food to the growing market.

But Kimberley was isolated. Coaches took nine days from Cape Town, a waggon six weeks. Port Elizabeth was closer, but it still took a waggon of provisions four weeks from the Eastern Cape to reach the diamond fields.

Even so, thousands were prepared to give it a go.

And on the heels of the diggers came the diamond dealers, and behind them the whole range of business-minded people who saw opportunities for a living, or a killing.

One among them was a young Englishman who came to South Africa in 1870 – to his brother's farm in Natal – as a remedy for a tubercular condition. He had ambitions to become a lawyer or a priest. But that changed when he arrived at the diggings in November 1871, aged 19, to look after his brother's three claims, which were among the first to be pegged out on Coles-berg Kopje. His name was Cecil John Rhodes, and he was destined to be the lord and master of this vast enterprise in the veld. It was partly the very nature of the mine that spurred his ambitious imagination.

What the diggers did not immediately appreciate was that they were hacking into the surface of a diamond-bearing volcanic pipe that reached deep into the crust of the Earth.

By 1872, claims at Kimberley mine were between 15 and 25 metres deep, and the roadways that were meant to provide access to the claims had become walls with cliff-like edges. Within two years the roadways had gone, and the vast pit was serviced by a web of thousands of cables by which the buckets of ground were hauled to the surface, to be crushed and passed to teams at sorting tables. The mining was becoming increasingly challenging.

Murray described as the 'greatest danger' the risk of rockfalls. 'Several pieces have fallen in,' he recorded, 'and men have been buried in the ruins.'

Part of the problem arose from the allocation of claims to individuals.

ABOVE: Cecil John Rhodes, flawed in his single-minded pursuit of imperialist interests.

TOP LEFT: Dangers increased as the claims drove ever deeper into the Kimberlite rock.

BOTTOM LEFT: Hundreds of cables, by which the diamond-bearing rock was drawn to the sorting tables, linked individual claims with the surface at the Kimberley mine.

Although only 500 claims were allocated initially, they were subsequently subdivided. Eventually, there were some 1 600 claims.

And the deeper the miners went, so rockfalls and flooding presented increasing difficulties that individual claim owners could not afford to deal with.

Rhodes and others like him saw that consolidating the claims and working the mine as a unit was the answer not only to technical problems in the mining operation itself but also to regulating the supply of diamonds to the market to avoid price collapses. There was also the problem of extensive illicit diamond buying (IDB).

And in the minds of most claim owners – and others whose livelihood depended on the legitimate

diamond market – IDB was a problem entirely associated with the black workers.

Without doubt, the possibility of secreting a stone between their toes, say, and making more money on the side through a shady dealer must have been an attractive option for workers whose wages were not spectacular and whose prospect of making it rich on the mines was nil.

Entrepreneurs like Rhodes recognised that if diamond mining was to be made more efficient and profitable, two things were necessary: rivals must be bought out, and the labour force must be kept under firmer control. It was a vision that gave birth to industrial capitalism in South Africa.

───── ❖ ─────

'Almost every nation,' a traveller recorded in 1877, 'finds its representatives [at the diggings], English, French, German, Italian, the Colonial Dutch, and "Africanders", and as for the numerous Native races, I would scarcely like to say what African race was not there.'

The attraction of the diamond fields was no less strong for Africans, though it represented a different opportunity.

Migrant workers were not new to southern Africa in the 1870s. From the far north of what later became the Transvaal, Cape farms had long attracted young men who would make their way south on foot. The discovery of diamonds brought the opportunity of work closer.

Between 1871 and 1875, some 50 000 Africans – from the north, but also from Basotuland and Natal – arrived at the Kimberley mines each year, with the same number heading home.

Chiefly, their objective was to earn enough to buy guns, acquire farming implements or amass bride-wealth. In the decade of the 1870s, it is estimated some 75 000 guns were acquired by migrant workers on the diamond fields.

Some Africans actually owned claims. One of them was the Reverend Gwayi Tyamzashe, who left a vivid description of the mine in 1874:

The hurry and din of the wheels, pulleys, wires and buckets, in conveying diamondiferous ground out of the gigantic mine; the noise of wagons, carts, carriages, sieves, sorting tables and all the like, combined with the ... yells of the labourers.

African Natives bound for the Goldfields.

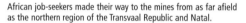

20

African job-seekers made their way to the mines from as far afield as the northern region of the Transvaal Republic and Natal.

DINNER TIME, IN DE BEERS COMP

Mine compounds were not unlike prisons for the miners who were compelled to live in them.

He had misgivings. The raucous amusements of the night suggested to him that the

> life of both coloured and whites was so rough that I thought this place was only good for those who were resolved to sell their souls for silver, gold and precious stones, or for those who were determined to barter their lives for the pleasures of a time.

By 1883, Tyamzashe was the last black man to hold a diamond claim. In that year he lost it.

From early on at the diggings, African workers came under steadily stricter controls. From 1872, they were obliged to carry their labour contracts with them. It was an early form of the pass law. At that time, they lived in open barracks near the mines.

It was typical of the Victorian view that, as English novelist Anthony Trollope (who visited Kimberley in 1877) put it, the pursuit of wealth through the discipline and regularity of wage labour worked better than religion or philanthropy in civilising the 'Natives'. Surveying the vast mine in which three or four thousand Africans were at work, he wrote:

> Who can but doubt that work is the great civiliser of the world – work and the growing desire for those good things which only work can bring? If there be one who does he should come here and see how those dusky troops of labourers, who ten years since were living in the wildest state of unalloyed savagery, whose only occupation was the slaughter of each other in tribal wars, each of whom was the slave of his chief, who were subject to the dominion of most brutalising and cruel superstitions, have already put themselves on the path towards civilisation.

From South Africa (1878) by Anthony Trollope

DIAMOND MINES, S.A. 2,349. G.W.W.

❖

If the African workers ever thought of it quite like this, they would certainly have begun to think differently as the more sophisticated economics of mining began to impinge on them.

With the emergence of companies that began buying up claims and working the mine more efficiently, the workforce came under increasing control.

This was especially so after Brazilian diamonds flooded the market and prices dropped. Mining costs were rising, and so was IDB.

A parliamentary inquiry keenly supported by Rhodes – who became an MP in the Cape parliament in 1880 – suggested the solution was to house workers in compounds. As a result, from the mid-1880s, all African – though not white – workers were obliged to live in closed compounds, which they could leave only to go down the mine or to go home at the end of their contracts. Conditions were inhumane and unhealthy, but the system endured. It would later be applied on a much larger scale on the gold mines soon to reach into the reefs of the Witwatersrand.

Rhodes's rise began with an ice-making plant. Given the temperatures of the Kimberley summer, it was a smart business venture. He also made money through a contract to drain flooded portions of the mines – there were four, eventually, in Kimberley – using new steam-driven pumps. But his chief success was in buying up steadily greater portions of the claims themselves.

There was a bumpy period in the early 1880s when umpteen diamond companies owning large chunks of the mines collapsed because of wildly fluctuating share prices. But among the survivors was Rhodes's De Beers Mining Company. By 1888, he had full ownership of the De Beers Mine. A year later, having secured ownership of all the dry diggings, he formed De Beers Consolidated Mines. 'From being seemingly anarchic,' historian Robert Ross notes, 'Kimberley had become a Company town.'

Mining turned technology to productive ends in every conceivable way and helped pull the whole country into the industrial age. It is striking that Kimberley was the first town in the southern hemisphere to have electric street lighting, installed in September 1882.

Increasingly sophisticated mining machinery eased the processing of diamondiferous blue ground. And the first railway line to the north was drawn to Kimberley by the demands of the new market in 1885.

Another measure of the young town's place in the expanding modernity of southern Africa was that it was the birthplace of professional nursing: Sister Henrietta Stockdale, of the Anglican nursing order of

Individually owned claims soon made way for consolidated ownership by powerful and wealthy mining companies.

St Michael and All Angels, first worked in the town in 1876, returning as matron at Kimberley's Carnarvon Hospital in 1879. The first state registration of nurses in the world, by Act of Parliament in 1891, resulted from her efforts in Kimberley.

Huge increases in imports from overseas boosted the harbour economies of Cape Town, Port Elizabeth and Durban, and a multitude of new businesses grew up on the strength of mining. And a group of so-called 'mining magnates' – Rhodes, but also others such as Alfred Beit and Charles Rudd – were poised to go on to greater things.

The discovery of gold on the Witwatersrand in 1886 opened up new opportunities.

Because the concentrations of gold were low – it took three tons of ore to yield one ounce of gold – extracting it required expensive underground mining that only huge capital investment could accomplish, and a complicated chemical process to free it from the rock.

'Once again,' Ross notes, 'history had to work itself within the confines provided by geology.'

And it was the companies that had made lots of money from diamond mining in Kimberley which now had the resources, access to technology and experience in handling a massive workforce on which exploiting the gold reefs would depend.

Within six years, no more than eight large companies controlled all the gold mining of the Witwatersrand. Cooperation between the mine-owners was secured through the formation of the Chamber of Mines in 1887, among the primary goals of which was to avoid wage competition and keep wages down.

And the Chamber helped to create a sense of mutual interest with Paul Kruger's conservative South African Republic government, which was mistrustful of the big league mining companies, their foreign backers and the hordes of foreigners (Uitlanders) drawn to the gold fields.

By 1895, Rhodes's Consolidated Gold Fields company was a greater source of income than his diamond interests. For Rhodes, though, mining was a means more than an end. He was driven by the idea

TOP RIGHT: With more sophisticated mining technology, the quest for diamonds went deep underground, via shafts and tunnels.

BOTTOM RIGHT: Randlords, the powerful men who directed the gold industry, included (seated, from left) Alfred Beit, Lionel Phillips, Frank Rhodes and Abe Bailey, and (standing) John Hays Hammond and George Herbert Farrar. There is no record of the name of the African man in the centre, a token, perhaps, of his apparent insignificance in the world of industrial capitalism.

Johannesburg thrived on the wealth of its gold.

of a benevolent, civilising British imperialism spreading through Africa for the good of all people and the success of the system of which he had proved himself a master.

It was with this in mind that, in 1889, he founded the British South Africa Company to extend imperial influence to the north. (The 1880s marked the start of the 'scramble for Africa' by several European powers. Within 30 years, only Liberia and Ethiopia would remain independent.)

But the mines had to fund Rhodes's ambitions. And – unlike the diamond market, where prices were determined by fluctuating supply and demand – the gold price was fixed, and the only way to ensure profitability was to reduce costs. And the only way that could be done was by reducing the cost of labour.

Paul Kruger's South African Republic had made a law preventing Africans from having any stake in the gold industry, other than as workers. The republic also passed legislation limiting the number of black tenant farmers on white farms, forcing more peasants into the capitalist mining economy.

But the more powerful measure to assure migrant labour for the mines was a Cape law sponsored by Rhodes himself in the Cape parliament.

The hated Glen Grey Act of 1894 appeared to offer Africans the promise of development and more political say in their own affairs, but actually limited

their political voice in the Cape (where, with a property franchise, a small minority had the vote) and drastically reduced their hold on the land. It changed rules of inheritance so that, in future generations, all but one member of an African family would be made landless. And it imposed a labour tax.

The effect – and, indeed, the intention – of the law was to limit African influence politically and to force rural Africans into a labour market hungry for new recruits, especially on the mines.

It coincided with the defeat and subjugation in the last decades of the century of the Tswana, the Pedi and the Zulu, a fate that obliged increasing numbers of Africans to seek paid work to survive.

On the gold fields, African workers were squeezed. Though compounds were not closed, pass laws became stricter, they were prevented from moving from one mine to another offering higher wages – before mine-owners colluded through the Chamber of Mines to limit wage competition – and no trade unions were allowed.

Against this harsh life experience, there's a cruel irony in the offensive, yet curiously innocent, terminology of the gold market: For a long time, South African gold shares on the London Stock Exchange were called 'Kaffirs', and the section of the Stock Exchange specialising in the trading of these shares was called the 'Kaffir circus'.

Novelist Anthony Trollope ended his tour of 1877 with a positive view of the arrival of industrial capitalism in southern Africa:

Our duty to the [African] of course is to civilise him – so to treat him that as years roll on he will manifestly do the better for our coming to his land. I do not think missionaries will do this, or fractions of land – little Kaffrarias separated off for their uses. But equality of law, equality of treatment, will do it – and I am glad to say, has already gone far towards doing it. The [African] can make his own contract for his own labour the same as a white man … Encouraged by this treatment he is travelling hither and thither in quest of work, and is quickly learning that order and those wants which together make the only sure road to civilisation.

From *South Africa* (1878) by Anthony Trollope

Historian Leo Marquard presents a different picture, after half a century of compound life:

Every week five or more special trains arrive at Johannesburg with hundreds of Africans going to work on the mines. Some have been there before; many are coming for the first time from the simple, pastoral life of the Reserves to the rush and noise of a big city, and to a strange machine-dominated existence in a highly organised industry. The train journey is the first unfamiliar experience; thereafter come the harsh compounds with their brick buildings and concrete bunks, the mass-produced, balanced diet, the shattering experience of being rushed to the bowels of the earth in a cage to work at a dangerous job. It is a big change from the small village community … to the anonymous vastness of a mining compound where he has a number instead of a name and where he hears the roar of mining machinery instead of the lowing of cattle on the hills.

From *The Peoples & Policies of South Africa* (1962) by Leo Marquard

❖

Gold mining reshaped Johannesburg's skyline.

Writer and historian AP Cartwright recalls a conversation with a 'compound manager who in his time had seen half-a-million mineworkers come and go'. There is a doubtfully romantic aspect to the compound manager's perception:

> To the old hands, this is like a club. They get away from the squabbles of the women and the domestic worries, and then, just as sailors do, they go home and are received as heroes. They love it.

From *The Gold Miners* (1962) by AP Cartwright

———— ❖ ————

In contrast to the black experience, opportunities for whites were unlimited, even for foreigners.

In the early diamond-mining days, one of the most colourful and unlikely figures to emerge as a fabulously rich mine-owner came to Kimberley from the East End of London in 1873, as a magician. His name was Barney Barnato. By 1888 he owned one of the mines. A year later he sold it to Rhodes for a staggering £5,3 million.

Another man who made it big was a Russian immigrant named Sammy Marks. He arrived in South Africa in 1868 at the age of 24 and made a modest living as a hawker. After amassing large profits at the diamond fields, he began buying up claims, became a wealthy mine-owner and, later, on the Witwatersrand, a powerful industrialist.

The rumbustious, wealthy, bawdy, poor, thriving city of Johannesburg grew from the mixed fortunes of the ranks of exploited workers, the growing white middle class of managers, shopkeepers and engineers, and the rich and influential Randlords and their successors who laid the foundation for the modern South African economy.

> What all these riches, hardships and migrations had in common was industrial capitalism – a revolution in the way human beings created wealth. In Britain, where the revolution happened first, it took more than a century – but in southern Africa it was telescoped into a few years following the discovery of diamonds and gold, as the small but wealthy elite grappled to impose industrial capitalism on a largely peasant society consisting mainly of subsistence farmers – Boer and African.

From *Reader's Digest Illustrated History of South Africa* (1994)

Industrial capitalism created an urbanised African community from which evolved a new kind of politics that would become a steadily more powerful counterpoint to the white world of the 20th century. It also strengthened Afrikaner 'republicanism' which, as Britain moved to grab control of the Witwatersrand gold fields at the end of the 1800s, inspired resistance that cost the British Empire dearly in battle.

———— ❖ ————

The last 10 years has been a decade of postscripts, and this is especially true of mining.

Former mineworkers' leader Cyril Ramaphosa – and chief political negotiator for the ANC in the ground-breaking talks leading to democracy in the early 1990s – left politics for the boardrooms of Johannesburg, where he made a name for himself as a multi-millionaire capitalist.

Mining hastened the emergence of industrial capitalism in South Africa.

Former activist and Robben Island prisoner Tokyo Sexwale was the first premier of Gauteng, home of the gold industry, and, after leaving politics for business, listed his multi-billion rand Mvelaphanda Resources mining group on the Stock Exchange in May 2002.

And the colonial-style hold over South Africa's mineral wealth by the big mining houses – most of which trace their roots to the exploitative operations of the early years – was ended, by consensus, through a far-reaching Mining Charter that cleared the way for African partnerships in the ownership of the multi-billion rand industry.

The significance of mining, and the Mining Charter, underscores a point made by Nelson Mandela that for all the exploitation that went into establishing the mining industry, its founders contributed to the development of modern South Africa.

Back in 1990, there was a richly symbolic link between the birth of industrial capitalism and what may be regarded as its inevitable consequence: it was at Cecil Rhodes's Cape Town mansion, *Groote Schuur*, built at the height of his power, that the ANC engaged in the first round of negotiations with the apartheid government that led to democracy in South Africa.

More recently, in a symbolic – but also a material – sense the Rhodes legacy came full circle. Cecil John Rhodes, selected in 2000 by Eurobusiness magazine as the greatest businessman of the 20th century, was linked by name with another giant of the century, and a man who represents the very opposite of the Rhodean vision of a civilising empire: Nelson Mandela. In February 2002, the Nelson Mandela Foundation joined forces with the powerful international Rhodes Trust – established by the mining magnate in 1903 – to consolidate the gains of democracy in South Africa. The partnership, Mandela said, 'is to signal the closing of the circle and the coming together of two strands in our history'.

Back in the 1890s, Rhodes was paramount, and the enlightened impulses of the Mandelas of southern Africa were banished to the fringes of colonial society.

Comrades of the boardroom, Cyril Ramaphosa (top) and Tokyo Sexwale.

Credit to
the Crown

Credit to the Crown

At 11 o'clock on the night of Sunday, 29 December, 1895, Sir Graham Bower was upstairs getting ready for bed when he heard a horse clatter up to the front door of his Cape Town home.

'I ran downstairs,' he later recalled, 'and opening the door myself saw Rhodes's butler on a horse. He told me that Mr Rhodes was anxious to speak to me at once. I went to *Groote Schuur*, which was about a mile distant. He was in his bedroom and in a very excited state. He told me that Jameson had entered the Transvaal with all his men but he had sent to stop him and things might yet come right.'

Of the three men – Bower, Leander Starr Jameson and Cecil John Rhodes – Bower had but a small, though costly, part to play in a public drama that was both scandalous at the time and damaging in the decades to come.

Things didn't come right, as Rhodes hoped they might in his anxious meeting with Graham Bower on that summer's night at the end of 1895. Not by a long shot.

But who were these men, and what was the anxiety about?

Bower was secretary to Britain's high commissioner Sir Hercules Robinson, London's representative in Cape Town.

Cecil Rhodes, prime minister of the Cape since 1890, was one of the wealthiest men in the world, and probably the most powerful man in southern Africa. His British South Africa Company had conquered for the Crown a vast territory to the north, covering today's Zimbabwe and Zambia.

And Leander 'Dr Jim' Starr Jameson, a medical doctor who had had a practice in Kimberley in the early diamond days, was a devotee of Rhodes and a keen imperialist.

At this moment – at the end of December 1895 – Jameson had just left Pitsani in the Bechuanaland Protectorate – taken over by Britain a decade before – and crossed the border into Paul Kruger's South African Republic. He had with him an armed force of 661 Mashonaland and Bechuanaland police and a number of volunteers, with eight maxims, two seven-pounder guns and one 12,5-pounder. They were off to 'invade' the Boer republic.

It wasn't much of an invasion force. And the whole idea of it, cooked up by Rhodes and Jameson with the knowledge of Colonial Secretary Joseph Chamberlain in London, turned out to be a feeble, bungling attempt in the name of the mighty British empire to wrest control of the richest gold mines in the world. They were driven by the big idea of the time: even reckless action was justified if it brought credit to the Crown.

———— ❖ ————

Rhodes's ambition had less to do with amassing personal wealth. He was not a flamboyant man, and liked to live plainly. But immensely capable though he was, his greatest flaw was that he believed the ends justified the means. His grand vision was of an expanding empire, wealthier – for the gold – and greater – for the new territories it could contain. He imagined Africa, from the Cape to Cairo, under a superior British influence that would, essentially, be good for everybody. It would be far better than an Africa under the Germans, Portuguese or French, who were also scrambling to grab chunks of the continent for themselves.

John X Merriman, who became prime minister of the Cape in the early 1900s, was not a fan of Rhodes.

'He is a pure product of the age, a capitalist politician,' Merriman once said,

> ... and has neither moral courage nor convictions, but he has the sort of curious power that Napoleon had of intrigue and of using men ... for his purpose which is self-aggrandisement under one high-sounding name or another.

Rhodes's own sense of his mission was unmistakably arrogant. 'I contend,' he once said of his imperialist ideal,

> that we are the finest race in the world, and that the more of the world we inhabit, the better it is for the human race. Just fancy, those parts that

Leading players (left to right): Paul Kruger, Sir Alfred Milner, Cecil John Rhodes.

are at present inhabited by the most despicable specimens of human beings, what an alteration there would be if they were brought under Anglo-Saxon influence.

In the mid-1890s, Paul Kruger was the biggest stumbling block to this 'alteration'.

❖

Paul Kruger, who was ultra-conservative to the point of seeming backward – supposedly even believing that the world is flat – was also shrewd and observant. Though confident enough as a leader, he drew to his government a number of men with skills he didn't have. One was a Cape lawyer named Jan Smuts – a future prime minister of a united South Africa – who returned from taking a law degree at Cambridge University to be Kruger's state attorney. He also encouraged assistance in building a rail link with Delagoa Bay, which gave his republic independent access to a seaport outside of British control.

But the vast, demanding metropolis of Johannesburg, both wealthy and seedy, that had arisen around the gold mines created new risks. And Kruger knew a threat when he saw one.

He had already had a taste of Britain's territorial ambitions when the Transvaal was annexed in 1877. At that time, Britain was keen to forge a confeder-ation of settler-dominated states in southern Africa. For three years the Boer republic protested and petitioned against it, and ultimately took up arms, scoring several victories and finally defeating the enemy at the battle of Majuba in February 1881.

But, having regained self-rule, Kruger's problems grew after the discovery of gold. Though the mines made his republic the richest territory in the region by far, they attracted vast sums in foreign investment, and huge numbers of foreign settlers, called Uitlanders. Between 1870 and 1891, the white population of southern Africa had shot up from 250 000 to 600 000, and the Witwatersrand had drawn a considerable concentration of them. Many of the newcomers – and much of the capital – were British, and Britain's interfering interest resumed.

At the head of a country of farmers – who had trekked north to escape interference in the first place – Kruger was anxious to limit the foreigners' influence in his territory. When he introduced measures – such as having to be resident in the republic for 14 years before being allowed to vote – to make it difficult for Uitlanders to exercise political rights and possibly take control, Rhodes and others saw their chance.

They hatched a plot to invade the Transvaal on the pretext of supporting a popular Uitlander uprising against Kruger's apparently unreasonable restrictions.

As Rhodes put it in a letter sent secretly to his co-conspirator, mining millionaire Alfred Beit, in August 1895:

Johannesburg is ready … [this is] the big idea which makes England dominant in Africa, in fact gives England the African continent.

While the plotters made their plans for Jameson's 'raid' from Bechuanaland, though, it turned out the Uitlanders were not particularly keen to rise up against Kruger. When it became clear to Rhodes that the raid should be called off, he tried desperately to stop Jameson's force.

The show is over ... Boer commandos riding through Johannesburg after stopping Jameson's force in its tracks.

It was at this point, near midnight on Sunday, 29 December, 1895, that he summoned Sir Graham Bower to tell him that Jameson had entered the Transvaal … and might yet be stopped.

But it was Kruger's forces who stopped Jameson. Two days later, as dawn broke, Jameson's men could see the mine dumps of Johannesburg, but they would not reach them or come anywhere near meeting their political objective. Harried by Transvaal commandos, the force was compelled to surrender. Jameson was led away in tears.

There was outrage, both in South Africa and Britain. Whatever the Uitlanders' grievances, Britain was not at war with the Transvaal and the raid was regarded as an invasion of friendly territory.

By agreement between the two states, Jameson and his senior officers were returned to England and tried under the Foreign Enlistment Act. They were imprisoned for various terms. Owing to ill-health, Jameson was released before serving his full 15-month sentence.

In Johannesburg, the leading members of the Reform Committee – the other plotters siding with Rhodes – were tried, too. Most were fined, and four sentenced to death, though the death sentence was later rescinded.

Rhodes escaped direct punishment, but his political career was brought to a sudden end. He was forced to resign as prime minister of the Cape colony and

also, though only temporarily, as head of the British South Africa Company. His imperial dream was in tatters.

Remarkably, Jameson emerged from the shame of failure to enter Cape politics, become prime minister, and earn a knighthood. When he died in 1917, he was held in such high esteem by Rhodesians that he was buried alongside Rhodes in the Matopos.

As for Sir Graham Bower, his selfless sense of duty cost him his career. In the inquiry that followed the raid, Bower refused to incriminate either Rhodes or his own boss, High Commissioner Sir Hercules Robinson. He later wrote: 'Since a scapegoat was wanted, I was willing to serve my country in that capacity.'

———— ❖ ————

The political cost of the raid extended far beyond the careers of individuals, though.

Writing in the mid-20th century, historian Elizabeth Longford noted that 50 years after the Jameson Raid, when it was imagined that all its evil effects would have burned themselves out, 'the most poisonous by-product' – racial conflict – burst into flames.

The new race war was to eclipse the earlier conflict between the two white races as the Anglo-Boer War eclipsed the Raid. Yet, but for the Raid, the Boer War and the settlements that

Colonial Secretary Joseph Chamberlain.

Ardent imperialist, Sir Alfred Milner.

followed, the colour question might have been solved peacefully and piecemeal.

From *Jameson's Raid* (1960) by Elizabeth Longford

Author Tabitha Jackson highlights in her book, *The Boer War* (1999), the uncannily ironic speech made by Joseph Chamberlain in the House of Commons in May 1896 to underscore his dissociation from the Jameson Raid.

'A war in South Africa,' he declared,

> *'would be one of the most serious wars that could possibly be waged. It would be in the nature of a civil war. It would be a long war, a bitter war, a costly war. ... It would leave behind it the embers of a strife which I believe generations would hardly be long enough to extinguish ... to go to war with President Kruger in order to force upon him reforms in the internal affairs of his state ... would have been a course of action as immoral as it would have been unwise.'*

Wise or not, the immediate consequences of the Jameson Raid were that, from 1896, first the Transvaal and then the Free State republic began to import arms on a huge scale, and anti-British sentiment went hand in hand with a rise in Afrikaner nationalism.

The defenders, the Boer republics, Jan Smuts later said, 'silently and grimly prepared for the inevitable'.

The inevitable, as Smuts saw it, began to crystallise with the appointment in 1897 of a new British high commissioner at Cape Town, Sir Alfred Milner. An ardent imperialist, he was all for a Britain-friendly, pro-capitalist government in the Transvaal. And when Kruger was re-elected for a fourth time in 1898, Milner began to see that the question of Uitlanders' political rights could be used to force a crisis. As British pressure mounted in 1899, Kruger offered concessions on political rights, but with conditions attached. Britain remained unsatisfied, and underlined this by sending 10 000 troops as reinforcements to South Africa. In late September, Kruger mobilised his forces, and President Marthinus Steyn of the Orange Free State followed suit in early October.

On 9 October, Kruger drew up an ultimatum to Britain that if it did not withdraw its troops from the borders of the Boer republics and send reinforcements home within 48 hours, it would be taken as a declaration of war.

When the ultimatum lapsed on 11 October, 1899, the forces of the embattled Boer republics squared up against the mighty British Empire.

Unconventional and outwardly unimpressive, the Boers proved to be adept guerrillas whose exploits severely tested the mighty British army.

'Now, for the first time in my life, I heard the sharp hiss of rifle-bullets about my ears, and for the first time I experienced the thrill of riding into action.' So wrote the young Deneys Reitz, son of the former Free State president Francis Reitz, of his first taste of battle on the outskirts of Dundee in the early days of the war in Natal.

> My previous ideas of a battle had been different, for there was almost nothing to see here. The soldiers were hidden, and, except for an occasional helmet and the spurts of dust flicked up around us, there was nothing. We reached the spruit we were making for with one man wounded, and leaving him and our horses in the bed below, we climbed the bank and were soon blazing away our first shots in war.

It was a mixed experience. The English troops finally surrendered. Reitz dashed up to see what there was to see.

> Officers and men were dressed in drab khaki uniforms, instead of the scarlet I had seen in England, and this somewhat disappointed me as it seemed to detract from the glamour of war; but worse still was the sight of the dead soldiers. These were the first men I had seen killed in anger, and their ashen faces and staring eyeballs came as a great shock, for I had pictured the dignity of death in battle, but I now saw that it was horrible to look upon.

Yet, young and impetuous as he was, Reitz admits he was

> too elated … at having taken part in our first success to be downcast for long, and I enjoyed the novelty of looking at the captured men and talking to such of them as were willing.

From *Commando* (1931) by Deneys Reitz

———— ❖ ————

As it wore on, it proved to be a nasty, costly, debilitating war, for the Boers, the British and everyone else in southern Africa. The English writer Rudyard Kipling said of the conflict that it taught Britain 'no end of a lesson'. A war the great power imagined would be over quickly – the phrase 'it will all be over by Christmas' became popular – dragged on for three years. And the force sent to beat the Boer republics into submission would eventually be the largest army sent abroad in British history.

Triumph seemed certain when this British column entered Pretoria … but the war was far from over.

British troops had to adapt to a harsh terrain, but also to a style of war they were not trained for.

❖

The war opened with five months of set-piece battles and the besieging by the Boers of Ladysmith in Natal and Kimberley and Mafeking (now Mafikeng) in the Cape. As the British forces moved to relieve the besieged towns, the Boers won impressive victories at Magersfontein on 11 December, 1899, Colenso four days later and at Spioenkop on 24 January, 1900. In the next two months, though, the tide turned. As huge British forces moved up to the Boer territories, chiefly from Durban and Cape Town, Kimberley was relieved on 15 February, Boer General P Cronje surrendered at Paardeberg with 4 000 men 12 days later, and Ladysmith was relieved on 1 March.

And, as the Boers retreated, the massed columns of British troops, cavalry, artillery and supplies pressed on to the Boer capitals. British commander Lord Roberts occupied Bloemfontein on 13 March and Pretoria fell to the British on 5 June. By September 1900, Roberts believed he had captured the prize and had both republics under his thumb.

One consequence was that many Boer commandos, or burghers, surrendered, believing the cause was lost, or not worth pursuing in battle.

A second consequence, though, was a fiercer period of fighting under the direction of daring and dynamic generals such as Christiaan de Wet, Koos de la Rey and Louis Botha, who ranged across the country making lightning raids on British columns and camps, and proving themselves an elusive enemy for a sluggish imperial army unsuited to such tactics.

'In this way,' war historian Fransjohan Pretorius

writes, 'the resistance of the Boer bitter-enders was to continue for almost two more years – what is known as the guerrilla phase of the war.'

Lord Kitchener, who replaced Roberts as the British commander-in-chief, adopted a new strategy. Pretorius sums up the essence of it:

Firstly, he continued Roberts's scorched earth policy. The Republics were deliberately and systematically devastated. Some towns and thousands of farmsteads were burnt or ravaged. This onslaught on Boer survival was backed up by the destruction of food supplies. Herds of livestock were wiped out and fields of maize and wheat were set alight.

Secondly, the concentration camp system was expanded, confining civilians, especially women and children, in camps. In Kitchener's view, this meant that burghers on commando would no longer be able to obtain food from women on the farms, and would, moreover, surrender in order to reunite their families. Blacks, too, were gathered in concentration camps, partly to deprive the commandos of yet another means of obtaining food. Thirdly, Kitchener launched his drives … a method of chasing and trapping commandos against lines of blockhouses constructed in a network across the entire war zone.

The British feared that intensified Boer incursions into the Cape colony might spark a rebellion among sympathisers there. But, in the long run, Pretorius says, the strategy was effective. On 31 May, 1902, after two weeks of talks, the majority of the 54 delegates

Insanitary conditions in concentration camps claimed the lives of thousands.

at Vereeniging decided to submit to Britain's terms for peace: the republics would be incorporated into the British Empire as Crown Colonies, with the promise of self-government later on. Only six of the 54 voted against.

———— ❖ ————

At the end of the conflict, 16 years after gold had been discovered on the Witwatersrand, Britain had gained control over the South African Republic and its huge underground wealth.

But it had cost the British more than 22 000 men (more than half died of disease) out of an army of 450 000, and an estimated £200 million.

The Boer forces totalling some 88 000 lost about 6 000 men in the field and several thousand more in the concentration camps.

About 27 900 Boer internees, mostly women and children, and between 14 000 and possibly as many as 20 000 Africans, died in the concentration camps. By the end of the war there were more than 115 000 Africans in the camps – former burgher employees or people from rural settlements whose food stocks the British believed were useful to the guerrillas. Few of the deaths of Africans on the battlefield were recorded, but between 10 000 and 30 000 were armed by the British alone, and thousands served with the burghers, though fewer as armed combatants than in the British forces.

———— ❖ ————

The naming of the war in the century since reveals much about the different ways in which it has been viewed and remembered.

The 'Anglo-Boer War' was the official name for the conflict for much of the 20th century, both in South Africa and elsewhere. It suggested this was a war between British soldiers and the citizens of the Boer republics – a white man's war.

The 'Second War of Independence' was the preferred name for the conflict among Afrikaner

Women and children became victims of Britain's desperation to defeat the Boers.

nationalists and, even today, the Afrikaner rightwing. For them, it defined the conflict as a fight for freedom.

But the name that has been increasingly accepted as a truer reflection is the 'South African War'. It came to the fore as apartheid declined and, with it, the dominant mythology that South Africa was and is a white man's world. It emerged from research that shed more light on the total impact of the war, showing that it affected, and involved, all South Africans to a greater degree than was ever recognised before.

❖

When the Anglo-Boer War began, the Boer Republics conscripted into their service, not only the men with their skills of driving the ox-wagon, but all their property – their oxen, wagons and even their 'touleiers'. Thus my father, then a youth of sixteen or seventeen, found himself in the Anglo-Boer War, first as a 'touleier' and later as an 'ox-driver'. His cousin was conscripted to serve with the Boer commandos. Historians have not yet adequately brought to the surface the untold sorrow and misery which the Anglo-Boer War meant to the indigenous population of South Africa. Families became scattered and were lost to one another, to say nothing of the material impoverishment which was meted out to them by both the Boers and the British. It became a repetition of the Difaqane (Mfecane) *experience.*

So wrote theologian Gabriel M Setiloane in *The Image of God Among the Sotho-Tswana* (1976).

Since the 1970s, much new research has made it plain just how comprehensively the whole population of southern Africa was drawn into what had always been thought of – and memorialised – as a war between the rival minority white groups.

Both British and Boer leaders suggested by their more formal statements that they did not want to involve blacks in the war, but went ahead and did so on a huge scale. They often fiercely criticised one another for arming blacks, and exchanged denials, but the fact is black people were as much a part of the conflict as white people, and not merely in the roles of spies, so-called *agterryers* (field assistants or lackeys) or waggon-drivers.

Writing in the early 1990s, historian Bill Nasson notes:

Many thousands of black men were armed and drawn into a conflict long mistaken as a white man's war.

The flurry of self-righteous accusations and counter-accusations between the British and Boer officers [about arming blacks] appeared to represent little more than a dialogue of the deaf.

But it went beyond that. It wasn't merely that blacks were being 'used' by the white forces, but, as Nasson argues, that they were making choices of their own, to fight or resist, to take sides and play an active role in the war to assert or defend their own interests.

Fellow-historian Nigel Worden notes that, for instance,

the Tswana in the northern Cape and western Transvaal attacked Boer cattle and encampments as well as assisting the British during the siege of Mafeking, and Zulus raided Boer territory which had previously been annexed from Zululand and aided the British in tracking down guerrillas. The Pedi under Sekhukhune did likewise in the hopes of regaining lands lost to the South African Republic.

In the Cape, in the face of grave risks, black communities made clear choices about where they stood in the war.

This is strikingly true of Abraham Esau.

He was a blacksmith in the Cape town of Calvinia, and a staunch supporter of Britain who urged coloureds to rally to the British flag.

When the Boers occupied Calvinia early in 1901, Esau was unbowed. He was arrested 'for having spoken against the Boers and having attempted to arm the natives', and sentenced to 25 lashes. Tied to a gum tree, he lost consciousness in the course of the whipping. In the weeks that followed he was publicly assaulted by the Boers on several occasions and, not long after, when the Boers were evacuating the town ahead of a British force, Esau, in leg irons, was tied between two horses, dragged out of town, and shot.

His story was handed down by word of mouth but was little known outside the district until 1991 and the publication of Bill Nasson's ground-breaking study of black involvement in the South African War at the Cape, *Abraham Esau's War, A Black South African War in the Cape, 1899–1902* (2002).

LEFT: Patriot Abraham Esau.

BELOW: Esau's slaying by the Boers provoked outrage.

THE MARTYRDOM OF ESAU !
(MURDERED BY THE INVADERS AT CALVINIA.)
JUSTICE INVOKED BY HUMANITY.

In Mafeking, Sol Plaatje, later one of the founders of the South African Native National Congress (it became the ANC) and South Africa's first black novelist, was a court interpreter attached to the British administration.

His account of an incident on 29 October, 1899 in the beleaguered town indicates that for all their objection to the British arming blacks, the Boers were not reluctant to shoot at them. The account also shows the literary dexterity, and ironic humour, of the young writer:

Mauser bullets were just like hail on the main road to our village. I had just left the fence when one flew close to my cap with a 'ping' – giving me such a fright as caused me to sit down on the footpath. Someone behind me exclaimed that I was nearly killed and I looked round to see who my sympathiser was. When I did so another screeched through his legs with a 'whiz-z-z-z' and dropped between the two of us. I continued on my journey in the company of this man, during which I heard a screech and tap behind my ear: it was a Mauser bullet and as there can be no question about a fellow's death when it enters his brain through the lobe, I knew at that moment that I had been transmitted from this temporary life on to eternity. I imagined I held a nickel bullet in my heart.

It was, he surmised, his soul imagining this. But it wasn't quite.

A few seconds elapsed after I found myself scanning the bullet between my finger and thumb, to realise it was but a horsefly.

From *Sol Plaatje: A Biography, Solomon Tshekisho Plaatje 1876–1932* (1984) by Brian Willan

While Plaatje, like Esau, and thousands of other blacks counted themselves on the British side, others were with the Boers, often enough without choosing, but also loyally, too.

Ruiter, the *agterryer* to Free State president Marthinus Steyn, saved the republican leader on the morning of 11 July, 1901, when the laager came under British attack. He quickly got the president onto a horse and made him flee in the right direction, and then hoodwinked the British officer that the disappearing rider was 'just an old boer'. He led the officer this way and that 'in search' of the elusive president, allowing Steyn to get away.

Solomon Tshekisho Plaatje described life in besieged Mafeking.

❖

There was no Truth and Reconciliation Commission to investigate the abuses of the war afterwards, but had there been one, it would have thrown an unforgiving light on both armed forces.

Boer general Gerhardus 'Manie' Maritz was responsible for one of the most notorious atrocities of the war at the Namaqualand Methodist mission station of Leliefontein. Maritz's commando called at Leliefontein in January 1902 and ordered the coloured inhabitants – who had sided with Britain – to cease supporting the Crown forces. An outraged Baster leader named Barnabas Links rejected the order and struck Maritz with a knobkerrie. The burghers opened fire on the crowd, mortally wounding Links and killing and wounding others. When armed Basters returned the fire, the burghers beat a hasty retreat, but were not unscathed. The commando was ambushed and lost 30 men. Two days later, Maritz returned with reinforcements and in the course of a battle that lasted two days, all but wiped out the settlement.

Deneys Reitz, operating with General Smuts in the Cape, rode into the town shortly after Maritz had left.

We found the place sacked and gutted, and among the rocks beyond the burned houses lay twenty or thirty dead Hottentots, still clutching their antiquated muzzle-loaders. ... To avenge the insult, he [had] returned the next morning with a stronger force and wiped out the settlement, which seemed to many of us a ruthless and unjustifiable act.

Smuts, Reitz believed, was 'displeased'.

Inhumanity was a feature of one of the key elements of British strategy: the scorching of farms, and the summary incarceration of black and white innocents in concentration camps where appallingly insanitary conditions cost thousands their lives. Disease was rife in these tent towns and care of the internees was often criminally negligent.

The gathering up of the women and children was heartlessly conducted. British officer Lieutenant Jack Wynn admitted:

I myself, if I am sent to a farm to see what is in it, and to get the women out, I never hesitate to burn the place before I leave, and only give the people five minutes to pack up and get into the wagon. I have no pity on them, no matter how they weep, they are far worse than the men.

Women often played a critical role as spies, as providers of food and refuge, and, though there were relatively few of them, as armed guerrillas.

❖

Typically of all wars, it fell mostly to women to care for the sick and the wounded. In the South African War, thousands upon thousands of women became victims, too, when they were herded into insanitary, ill-run concentration camps.

It was another woman, an Englishwoman, who highlighted the shame of the camps, and came to be revered by Afrikaners for her outspoken support and her practical assistance.

Emily Hobhouse was an anti-war campaigner who, on learning of the existence of the camps, made her way to South Africa and conducted a three-month tour of the dismally inadequate facilities in 1901. She returned to England to stir government and public sympathy for internees, and managed to extract some concessions from the government. Accused of being a Boer sympathiser, she was denied permission to return. When she did, later in 1901, on the pretext of visiting British refugees, she was not

Emily Hobhouse was tireless in her efforts on behalf of Boer women and children in British concentration camps.

As a young woman, Sarah Raal joined her brothers' commando in the conflict in the Free State. Anxious, often afraid, she nevertheless steeled herself to do her bit in the war against the 'oppressors':

Before we knew what had happened, the house was showered with bullets and we had to catch and saddle our horses under deadly fire. Commandant Nieuwoudt told me I could choose for myself whether I wanted to make a run for it or hide until the wounded had gone, after which they would return and provide cover to enable me to escape. ... But I wouldn't hear of it. ... So I told the men I wanted to ride with them, and that if I was shot and killed they should ask the English for my body, and take the money I still had on me and give it to my parents.

allowed to go ashore, and was soon forcibly transferred to a troop ship in Table Bay and deported under martial law.

The harrowing scenes she witnessed in the camps dispelled all doubt about the horror of the war. Typical of it is this account of a transit camp at the Springfontein railway siding in the bitter cold of May 1901.

> Called to a shelter to see a sick baby, Hobhouse found '[t]he mother sat on her little trunk with the child across her knee'.
>
> *She had nothing to give it and the child was sinking fast. I thought a few drops of brandy might save it but though I had the money, there was none to be had. I thought of the superintendent of the camp – a mile off – and sent a hasty message to ask him to let me have some for a sick child, but the reply was that his supplies were only for his camp. There was nothing to be done and we watched the child draw its last breath in reverent silence. The mother neither moved nor wept. It was her only child. Dry-eyed but deathly white, she sat there motionless looking not at the child but far, far away into depths of grief beyond all tears.*
>
> From *Emily Hobhouse – Boer War Letters* (1999) by Rykie van Reenen (editor)

But there is a telling postscript to the role of Emily Hobhouse. In the speech she wrote for the inauguration of the Women's Memorial in Bloemfontein in 1913 – she was too ill to deliver it herself – she reminded the Afrikaner people of the reason why they fought, and urged them to bear it in mind in the coming decades.

'Do not open your gates to the worst foes of freedom – tyranny and selfishness,' she urged. 'Are not these the withholding from others in your control the very liberties and rights which you have valued and won for yourselves?'

These two lines were cut out of later printings of the speech, and entirely ignored in the decades of Afrikaner nationalist politics that made apartheid infamous. (Though she died in England, Hobhouse's ashes are kept in a niche at the Bloemfontein memorial.)

❖

General Louis Botha, destined for political leadership.

The South African War itself was internationally infamous. Britain was the target of ridicule and vehement criticism in Europe and elsewhere, the subject of mocking cartoons and angry journalism.

There were other striking international associations with the war, though some would become evident only later.

Within a short distance of each other on the same battlefield in Natal in the early weeks of the war, two young men who would become giants in world affairs later played supporting roles in the drama of the conflict: Winston Churchill was a war correspondent (and, for a while, became a prisoner-of-war) and Mahatma Gandhi was a stretcher-bearer. Both would become leading statesmen.

A third figure in the same battle, who would become a statesman on a smaller scale, was General Louis Botha, first prime minister of the Union of South Africa. (General Jan Smuts, who fought elsewhere during the war – and famously carried a copy of the philosopher Immanuel Kant's *Critique of Pure Reason* in his saddlebag – was also a major world figure to emerge from the South African War. He later wrote the Covenant of the United Nations.)

The first military use of wireless telegraphy, developed by the father of modern radio, Marconi, was in the South African War, briefly in the vicinity of

De Aar, then on Royal Navy vessels based at Simon's Town.

The war was a 'landmark' event in the development of medical treatments, surgical techniques, the use of X-rays and other medical innovations, including organised military nursing, and it attracted leading British and European surgeons to hospitals in the field.

The relief of Mafeking (now Mafikeng) even introduced a new word into the English language: to 'maffick' is to 'celebrate wildly'. It arose from the action of the crowds in London on hearing the news that the siege of the town was over.

Cinema audiences saw the first moving images of war from this South African conflict, courtesy of some of the first forerunners of television journalism, William Dickson and Joseph Rosenthal.

And, not surprisingly, the field tactics and administration of the mighty British army were significantly revised on the strength of its frustrated dealings with the likes of guerrilla general Christiaan de Wet.

De Wet was a remarkable man whose exploits made a deep impression on another remarkable South African of a later time: Nelson Mandela admired him immensely, but not without qualification. He saw the general as a 'fearless, proud and shrewd' leader who 'demonstrated the courage and resourcefulness of the underdog', a figure who 'would have been one of my heroes had he been fighting for the rights of all South Africans, not just Afrikaners'.

❖

But it was naturally the impact of the war at home, in southern Africa, that was most telling.

Among the unlikely consequences was the introduction of scores of alien species of plants – such as kakiebos (taken from the word 'khaki', the colour of the uniforms of British soldiers) and cosmos – from South America, Australia, New Zealand and elsewhere. These alien plants – which have since cost the agricultural economy hundreds of millions of rands – were introduced through feed imported for the hundreds of thousands of horses and mules in service in the British army.

The popularity of soccer as a black sport arose out of contact during the war with British soldiers.

The mythology of Afrikaner nationalism drew heavily on the 'freedom fighters' of the war, and the victimisation of the women and children.

But, chiefly, it was the forging of a single –

unitary – state, and the moulding of whites-only politics of the 20th century (dominated in large measure by former Boer field commanders, generals Louis Botha, Jan Smuts and JBM Hertzog) that were the most significant consequences of the conflict.

In a nutshell, says Worden, 'the South African War and its aftermath marked the end of the protracted process of the conquest of South Africa by settler and imperial powers'.

❖

Black people had been misled into thinking that at least one of the reasons for Britain's aggression towards the Boer republics was their mistreatment of people who were not white, and the injustices of the Boer 'Native policy'.

In October 1899, Colonial Secretary Joseph Chamberlain declared:

> The treatment of the Natives [in the Transvaal] has been disgraceful; it has been brutal; it has been unworthy of a civilised Power.

High Commissioner Sir Alfred Milner had made similar comments. And early in 1900, the British prime minister Lord Salisbury himself said there was to be

> no doubt … that due precaution will be taken for the philanthropic and kindly and improving treatment of those countless indigenous races of whose destiny I fear we have been too forgetful.

It all looked very promising. And it convinced many influential black people that the path to a better life and more rights lay in engaging in formal politics.

The shift had begun earlier, after limited rights were given to Africans in the Cape under the 1853 constitution for the first legislature in the Colony, from 1854.

The sentiment is reflected in a poem from the 1870s by one of the early Xhosa poets, IWW Citashe:

> Your cattle are gone, my countrymen!
> Go rescue them! Go rescue them!
> Leave the breechloader alone
> And turn to the pen.
> Take paper and ink,
> For that is your shield.
> Your rights are going!
> So pick up your pen.
> Load it, load it with ink.

Sit on a chair.
Repair not to Hoho
But fire with your pen.

From *Vukani Bantu! The Beginnings of Black Protest Politics in*
South Africa to 1912 (1984) by André Odendaal

This poem appeared in a newspaper that was the
first significant forum for African opinion, *Isigidimi*
Sama Xhosa, published at the Lovedale Missionary
Press. (Launched as the *Kaffir Express* in 1870, it
changed its name and got its first black editor, Elijah
Makiwane, in 1876.)

African political associations began to emerge,
too. One of the first was the semi-political Native
Educational Association of 1879, followed in 1882
by an explicitly political organisation Imbumba Nyama
Yama. It didn't last long, but others began to spring
up, such as the South African Native Association and
the Thembu Association. None managed to generate
wide support.

But the emergence of political organisations and
the founding of black newspapers were significant
developments, and they were combined in a man who
proved to be an oustanding and influential political
figure, John Tengo Jabavu.

He had taken over the editorship of *Isigidimi Sama*
Xhosa in 1881 and had also served as the election
agent for a liberal white independent politician James
Rose Innes, canvassing black votes for Innes's
successful 1884 campaign. Innes helped Jabavu set
up his own newspaper, *Imvo Zabantsundu*, which
was the fore-runner of a number of black-controlled
newspapers throughout southern Africa at the turn
of the century.

Using *Imvo* as a platform, Jabavu began to
establish himself as a spokesman for black interests.

Through the 1880s and 1890s, Cape laws kept
raising the minimum requirements allowing blacks to
vote and these became the focus of black political
activities and protests. But a split came in 1898 when
Jabavu offered electoral support to Afrikaner Bond
leader JH Hofmeyr, who had made a speech in favour
of African voting rights.

Jabavu, an Mfengu, now faced opposition from a
new generation of Xhosa leaders who launched the
Izwi Labantu newspaper, edited by another key figure
of the time, AK Soga (whose mother, incidentally,

ABOVE RIGHT: Christiaan de Wet, admired even by his enemies.

RIGHT: John Tengo Jabavu, one among those who sought to bring a
black voice to public debate.

was Scottish), and formed the South African Native Congress.

By the end of the 1800s, political activity in the African community in the Cape – where 8 000 Africans were registered voters – was intensifying. Though blacks in Natal, the Free State and the Transvaal did not have the vote, political consciousness was growing there too, and new organisations were emerging.

Against this background, Britain's public statements on the Boers' injustice to the 'Natives' at the start of the South African War raised Africans' hopes about the political possibilities offered by a British victory: the prospect of a softening of discriminatory legislation.

❖

The writer Olive Schreiner observed in the first years of the 20th century:

> Wherever a Dutchman, an Englishman, a Jew and a native are superimposed, there is that common South African condition through which no dividing line can be drawn .... South African unity is not the dream of a visionary, it is not even the forecast of genius ... [but] a condition the practical necessity for which is daily and hourly forced upon us by the common needs of life: it is the only path open to us. For this unity all great men born in South Africa during the next century will be compelled directly or indirectly to labour; it is this unity which must precede the production of anything great and beautiful ... by our people as a whole. ... It is the attainment of this unity which constitutes the problem of South Africa: How from our political states and our discordant races, can a great, a healthy, a united, an organised nation be formed?

From *Thoughts on South Africa* (1992) by Olive Schreiner

The unity uppermost in the minds of the white peacemakers at the end of the South African War was the uniting of what were then often referred to as the white 'races', the English- and Afrikaans-speaking people who had faced one another in battle.

Almost 40 years after the peace, historian CW de Kiewiet summed it up in this way:

> Much of the hesitant and evasive conduct of British statesmanship in the generation before the Boer War could be attributed to the indecision of the British Government between its obligation to the natives and its obligation to the white communities. ... Now, the Boer War compelled a decision on native policy. In terms of the peace the British Government promised that no attempt would be made to alter the political status of the natives before self-government had been granted to the ex-Republics. In that epochal decision the British Government receded from its humanitarian position and enabled the Boer leaders to win a signal victory in the very peace negotiations which marked their military defeat.

From *A History of South Africa Social and Economic* (1941) by CW de Kiewiet

The price of conciliation with the Boers was the sacrifice of African rights.

❖

IN MEMORIAM

On Tuesday, 16 November, 1999, South Africa's democratic parliament remembered the South African War in a debate that said much about the war itself, and much about what had become of the country since.

Some regarded the reconciliatory spirit of debates such as this one as a token of the times, a keenness, above all else, to make up and be friends, without anyone giving enough attention to correcting the real or material consequences of the past.

In this, they echoed the anxieties that arose in the minds of many after the peace was signed at Veereniging in May 1902.

Back then, a South Africa united by statute alone staked its future on preserving unity among whites at the expense of blacks. A hundred years later, the demands of genuine national unity were no less challenging.

This is how the *Cape Argus* reported the parliamentary debate of November, 1999:

Ela Gandhi MP, whose famous grandfather, Mahatma Gandhi, was a stretcher-bearer in the South African War.

Just five years ago, when the last white Parliament met for its final sitting in the old House of Assembly, conservatives turned bitterly to the Treaty of Vereeniging that sealed the Boer defeat 100 years ago to define the 'capitulation' of the 1990s.

The imagery, then, reflected a deep-seated anger many feared would fester into a right-wing revolt.

Yesterday, the once unthinkably disparate democratic Parliament paid more lingering attention to the South African War of a century ago in a measured debate remarkable as much for the absence of animosity as the nearly unanimous sentiment across an otherwise sharply divided political spectrum.

In chiefly non-partisan terms, parliamentarians highlighted the unnecessary losses, the harmful bitterness, the unacknowledged suffering of so many, the distortions of history, the costs of the peace in establishing white privilege and black exclusion.

But the common strand had more to do with looking forward, extracting from a shared – black and Afrikaner – experience of national injustice a sense of working together against its recurrence.

It says a lot about the reach of the war, the freshness of its imprint, that so many parliamentarians spoke of it with the intimacy of survivors.

Many were intimate with survivors.

The family associations to emerge in the two-hour debate are themselves a fascinating link between the crucible of war 100 years ago, and the negotiated peace of today, drawn in the nick of time from the mounting revolution of the 1980s.

For ANC MP Ela Gandhi, the family link was her grandfather, Mahatma Gandhi, who, quite controversially, organised stretcher-bearer parties during the Natal campaign.

Water Affairs Minister Ronnie Kasrils' grandfather Nathan Kasrils, a Russian immigrant of the 1870s, fought for the Boers, earning praise from General Koos de la Rey as 'a good spy and sharpshooter'.

The Democratic Party's Tertius Delport and Andries Botha both drew on direct associations.

One of Mr Botha's grandmothers was in a concentration camp. The other, an Irish woman, was besieged in Kimberley … while her future husband, not yet known to her, was part of the besieging force.

Dr Delport's mother-in-law Hester de Bruyn was born in the concentration camp at Mafikeng on December 4, 1901.

For ANC MP Melanie Verwoerd, the link was an implacable grandmother so appalled at the concentration camp deaths that she vowed never to speak English, a promise she kept to her death.

In an impassioned speech, Inkatha Freedom Party MP Koos van der Merwe described the pitiless destruction of his grandmother's farmstead and contents; the furniture, clothes, photographs, family documents, a beloved antique organ.

'I stand here today,' he said, 'as a victim of a gross abuse of human rights.'

Though he was born 35 years after the war ended, he said, he took in the stories of his grandfathers, both combatants, 'like mother's milk'.

But if there was a lesson from the war, it was that life must go on; that for all the atrocities, 'it is finish and *klaar*, *phikile* . . . and we must put it behind us.'

Ms Gandhi warned against allowing remembering to become a reliving of history that would create ethnic division and hatred. It was the lessons that must be remembered.

In a thoughtful reflection, Ms Verwoerd cited the

philosopher Paul Ricoeur's injunction that 'remembering is a moral duty … a debt to victims'. But the risks of 'ethical remembrance' becoming 'ethnic remembrance' were clearly reflected in the expurgation of Boer heroine Emily Hobhouse's prophetic message to Afrikaners.

Her challenge at the 1913 inauguration of the Women's Memorial in Bloemfontein, expunged from later reprintings of the speech, was: 'Do not open your gates to the worst foes of freedom – tyranny and selfishness. Are not these the withholding from others in your control the very liberties and rights which you have valued and won for yourselves?'

It was the gathering impetus of tyranny and selfishness that lay behind Azapo MP Mosibudi Mangena's unequivocal view that 'Africans, coloureds and Indians have absolutely no business nor justification to commemorate the South African War'.

If we have any pride at all, we cannot commemorate our own conquest, humiliation, oppression and exploitation.

But New National Party leader Marthinus van Schalkwyk drew the essential parallel when he noted: 'The freedom struggle of black South Africans is in many respects … what the South African War is to Afrikaners. For the Afrikaner to be a constructive part of the new South Africa, is to understand and acknowledge that simple, but very powerful truth.'

He drew another parallel – that the disillusioned Afrikaner today 'is faced with exactly the same choice as 100 years ago'.

For a moment, as a murmur of interjections threatened to become a clamour, he risked being misunderstood before being heard, a common enough experience in politics.

But he went on: 'Do you drown in your own bitterness or do you say, here I am, I am what I am, I am committed to building this country and unlocking my talents, my education, my skills to build a successful country, not only for the children of my fellow South Africans, but also for my own children?'

It was an elusive wisdom just five – let alone 100 – years ago. – Special Writer.

Union spells division

Union spells division

Cape Town faded into the salty haze as the RMS *Briton* steamed north into the Atlantic swells, bound for Southampton, days away still. It was a balmy evening.

The high-ranking politicians bound for England to recommend – and just one to oppose – the new law that would create the Union of South Africa had a fine send-off.

But these were not balmy times.

The festive atmosphere at the ship's departing late on the afternoon of 15 June, 1909, the waving crowds, the band playing on the hurricane deck, the dignitaries gliding along the quay in their carriages and being wafted aboard with fawning courtesy, all this was the deceptive foreground to a bigger, graver picture.

On the face of it, South Africa was coming into its own. The war that had wrecked thousands of lives, destroyed scores of the farms of the interior and disrupted the agricultural trade and the new,

RMS Briton, the vessel that bore rival delegations to London.

lucrative mining industry, had ended seven years before. Economic reconstruction was gathering apace.

And in the place of the warring of the turn of the century was a new agreement to create a single united country of four provinces. The old enemies might still be political rivals in a new parliament, but they would be common citizens, and they would speak for the interests of one country. Or would they?

The unity, the common citizenship, the patriotism, were really just for whites. A limited franchise for people who were not white was preserved in the Cape, but existed nowhere else.

And the National Convention that had spent about seven months drawing up the constitution that would bring this single 'united' country into being as the Union of South Africa had, for the sake of peace among whites, effectively ignored the rights and interests of the black majority.

In June 1909, the draft South Africa Act had only to be approved by the British government to become law.

The efforts of black political organisations and a number of prominent white individuals intensified with the release of the National Convention's draft law in May.

At the Cape Town docks on the afternoon of June 15, one man boarding the Royal Mail Ship carried the hopes of Africans. He was William Schreiner, prime minister of the Cape from 1898 to 1900, brother of the outspoken novelist Olive Schreiner, and a liberal who believed the new constitution was a recipe for disaster.

The historian André Odendaal notes in *Vukani Bantu! The Beginnings of Black Protest Politics in South Africa to 1912* (1984) that Schreiner warned that 'to enshrine the denial of human rights in a constitution was a grave injustice which would "eventually react with evil effect" on white South Africans'.

His had not been a solo effort, and he would not act alone in London. Schreiner's advance departure was backed by, among others, Dr Abdullah Abdurahman's African Political Organisation, the South African Native Convention, the Orange River Colony Native Congress, the Transvaal Native Union and Transvaal Native Congress and John Tengo Jabavu's Cape Native Convention. Both Jabavu and Abdurahman, and others, would join him soon in London.

He also had the support of leading Cape politicians and prominent figures in the white community, including Archbishop William Carter; Dr JJ McClure, ex-Moderator of the South African Presbyterian Church; C Abercrombie Smith, Vice-Chancellor of the University of Cape Town; Sir Gordon Sprigg, another former Cape prime minister; Sir Bisset Berry, a former Speaker of the House of Assembly, and five past and present Cape parliamentarians.

So off across the sea went Schreiner on the RMS *Briton*, bearing the most far-sighted political thinking of the day. The message to the British government was plain: in the draft South Africa Act union spells division.

But theirs would be a mission of disappointment, and the opportunity truly to unite the country would be lost, at great cost in the years to come.

———— ❖ ————

Cecil Rhodes's death at his cottage in Muizenberg in March 1902 – two years before the death in exile in Switzerland of Paul Kruger, the man whose wiliness had foiled Rhodes's reckless vision for Africa – coincided with the beginning of the end of British control in South Africa.

The South African War created entirely new circumstances. It permeated every aspect of life in the early 1900s.

British high commissioner Alfred Milner and his carefully picked young administrators – derisively nicknamed the 'Kindergarten' – got down to work in returning South Africa to a state of productivity and usefulness.

The countryside was ravaged. Boers – 31 000 of whom had been exiled as prisoners of war, and 110 000 imprisoned in concentration camps – returned to farms that were often nothing more than charred shells. Crops and stock had been destroyed. By 1903, most had been re-established on their farms, and £19 million had been paid out in claims and grants to get agriculture back on its feet.

Still, resentment was widespread, worsened by Milner's determination to 'anglicise' South Africa, downplay the Dutch language and draw new British settlers.

Both strategies failed. New settlers did not come in droves, and his attempts to convert the Boers to English ways only spurred Afrikaner nationalism. As historian William Beinart has noted of the Afrikaner experience:

There is nothing so dangerous as people who feel they have been deeply wronged, and are blinded by their own sense of injustice.

On the economic front, Milner was keen to get reconstruction moving as quickly as possible. Getting gold production going was a priority. Black workers, scattered and ravaged by the war, were – in his estimation – proving too slow in returning to the mines. Many had also accumulated money during the hostilities and were withholding their labour.

So, at the urging of mine-owners, he turned elsewhere for a solution, securing the importation of

TOP: Visionary politician William Schreiner.

MIDDLE: Anglican Archbishop William Carter.

BOTTOM: Former Cape prime minister, Sir Gordon Sprigg.

Chinese workers to get the mines working more quickly.

His solution would prove controversial: whites in South Africa were afraid of the consequences of the arrival of yet another grouping not like them and, in Britain, there were accusations of slavery and abuse. Within six years, the Chinese were sent home.

But gold production was up, rising from £12,6 million in 1903 to £27,4 million in 1907.

Rugby dominated the headlines for a time in 1906: the national squad, led by the legendary Paul Roos, embarked on its first overseas tour, to Britain, and beat their opposition in all but two of 29 matches, winning two of the four Tests. It was on this occasion that the Springbok became the emblem of national rugby.

But grimmer headlines recorded the desperate rebellion by Zulu chief Bambatha against the government's hut tax. Troops were sent in and Bambatha and 500 of his supporters were killed. The uprising spread, and by the time it subsided some 3 000 Zulu had died. Armed resistance, the message was clear, would not be tolerated. It was the last major rural armed rebellion to occur in South Africa.

Rugby legend Paul Roos led the first Springbok team overseas.

The black elite, who had been led to believe the British victory would herald greater educational, property and civil rights for 'civilised Natives', soon found this was not to be. A critical moment for their future arose in 1905 with the appointment of the innocuously named South African Native Affairs Commission.

Chaired by Sir Godfrey Lagden, the commission set precedents that would take 90 years to undo. Its recommendations, based on the simple falsity that white people were of 'superior intellect' to black people and could thus not have a common system of government, laid the foundation for the formal separation of races and the creation of 'reserves' for black people to live in.

As the commission's findings and recommendations took form in the real world, political activity increased steadily.

The likes of AK Soga, editor of the *Izwi Labantu* newspaper, John Tengou Jabavu, editor of the *Imvo Zabantsundu* newspaper, and Solomon Tshekisho Plaatje, editor of the *Koranta ea Becoana* (*Bechuana*

Pale to a fault ... the South African Native Affairs Commission.

Gazette) were joined by scores of others whose opinions in the growing number of African newspapers gained them prominence and furthered the collective sense of grievance and will to action in the black community.

Historian André Odendaal notes:

Thus within a few years of the turn of the century the small politically conscious African educated class had everywhere mobilised themselves into political organisations ....

And African newspapers were the key to stimulating this interest and broadening the 'political horizons' of blacks.

Abdullah Abdurahman

Two particularly influential figures in the opposition to growing white political dominance and racism were Mahatma Gandhi, whose passive resistance campaigns in Natal and the Transvaal earned him time in jail but massive popular support, and Abdullah Abdurahman, the Scottish-trained doctor who was long-time leader of the Cape-based and predominantly coloured African Political Organisation. (It later changed its name to African People's Organisation.)

Charlotte Maxeke, a social worker and teacher and the first South African black woman to gain a university degree – a BSc – returned from the United States in 1903 to found the Bantu Women's League. It later became the African National Congress Women's League, and she became a significant figure in spearheading protests against discrimination.

While there was no sign from the British administration that black rights would get any attention, in 1907 the former Boer republics were granted self-government – as promised at the end of the South African War – and their white inhabitants held their first post-war elections.

Former Boer generals Louis Botha and Jan Smuts led their Het Volk (the people) party to power in the Transvaal, and another general, JBM Hertzog, led the Oranje Unie to power in the Orange River Colony (which reverted to the Orange Free State after Union).

In the same year, the Selborne

Charlotte Maxeke

Memorandum, drafted by Lord Selborne, Milner's successor as high commissioner, set out the desirability of creating a united South Africa.

Though it highlighted 'Native policy' as 'one of the most difficult problems facing white South Africa', it offered no suggestions as to how it should be resolved. But it was clear that unification would be dominated by white interests.

Fully aware of the threat posed by such developments, Odendaal says, 'African opinion became more vocal, organised and united in protest.'

———— ❖ ————

To think that such a meeting can be convened nine years after the first shot was fired in the bloody war between Boer and Briton! The character of this assembly guarantees the sincerity of the desire to unite South Africa.

So wrote Francois Malan on 12 October, 1908, nine years to the day after the first shot was fired at the start of the South African War in 1899. The assembly he describes was the National Convention, a gathering of white politicians from the Cape, Natal, the Orange River Colony and the Transvaal, whose task was to see whether national unity could be achieved under a single constitution.

Real business started the next day.

Malan reveals something of the underlying anxiety at the start of the meeting.

'The chairman called for resolutions. There was a long silence. One could almost hear the delegates think.'

Some sooner than others found their thoughts: the first two to speak were Cape prime minister John X Merriman and leading Transvaal delegate and former Boer general Jan Smuts.

Both warmly endorsed unification, with Smuts warning, Malan reports, that 'if we did not unite, serious difficulties would arise among the colonies'.

It was just two days later that the

first mention was made of the issue that from its inception made the Union of South Africa both flawed and embattled: Native policy.

And it was Malan himself who raised it. It was, Malan said, 'a consideration I will call the population difficulty'. And he spelled it out: 'We have two white races, the Natives, the coloured people and the Asiatics.' Elaborating on the 'difficulty', he went on:

> No man in this room will deny that it is necessary to place the Native policy in the hands of the Central Government .... When I [say this] I do not mean that violent changes should be introduced into the policy hitherto followed by the different Colonies. The change must be gradual, but the Central Government must from the commencement have the final veto.

From *Konvensie-Dagboek van FS Malan* (1951) by Johann Preller (editor)

This principle underpinned the steady erosion of black rights in the Cape and the consolidation of the exclusion of blacks elsewhere. The risk, raised later, was that to deal with black rights at this point would divide 'the Europeans' and that division would spoil the unification process.

Indeed, General Louis Botha warned that if any attempt was made to force the Native franchise of the Cape on the rest of the country he might 'just as well go home'.

The clearest indication of the primary focus of the National Convention on white interests – as they had been defined by the South African War – was the debate on language policy. Would South Africa have English as its official language, the language of the victors, or would both English and Dutch have equal status?

Both sides were eager to display generosity on this point, but the Transvaal and Orange River Colony left no doubt about just how serious the subject was. On the question of making both languages equal in practice, General Christiaan de Wet, for instance, said that '[i]f that were tampered with unification would seem to him impossible. Both races must be put on an equal footing.'

Eventually, unanimity prevailed. 'Truly this is a good sign,' Malan observed, adding tellingly: 'It was generally felt that the war with all its suffering had made this solution possible.'

Beyond the committee rooms of the convention (which, symbolically, met in Durban, Cape Town and Bloemfontein), feelings were less positive about this 'unity' process. But growing unity of purpose in black

Delegates to the National Convention represented what would become the four provinces of the Union, the Cape, Natal, the Transvaal and Orange Free State.

politics began to shift the emphasis from local or regional or provincial political organisations to the establishment of a national voice.

Thus, even before the National Convention's draft South Africa Act was released, opposition to it was broader and more consistent, and more united.

Jabavu organised a Cape Native Convention in April 1909, which declared that the introduction of a colour bar in the draft South Africa Act

is unjust ... is unprecedented in the annals of the British Empire ... and is calculated to ... disturb the harmony and happiness of the people of South Africa.

In Cape Town, Dr Abdurahman's African Political Organisation spearheaded protests and, significantly, used the terms 'Native' and 'coloured' interchangeably to indicate their sense that there was no difference between the political rights of the two groups.

William Schreiner, whose rallying cry was that 'Union without honour ... was the greatest danger any nation could incur', became the focus of much of the opposition.

His last-ditch attempt to have the draft law amended before it was sent to England ended in a vote in the Cape Parliament in early June of 69 votes

to two. Schreiner and another former prime minister, Sir Gordon Sprigg, then in his eighties, were the only dissenting voices.

The attention now switched to London.

There, Schreiner was joined by black and coloured leaders, including Dr Abdurahman, Jabavu, and Dr Walter Rubusana. They were supported in London by Mahatma Gandhi, John Dube, and three young aspirant lawyers, Richard Msimang, Alfred Mangena and Pixley Ka Isaka Seme, who would play a key role in the formation of the ANC.

In a Press statement, Schreiner underlined their goal:

... to try to get the blots removed from the Act, which makes it no Act of Union, but rather an Act of Separation between the minority and the majority of the people of South Africa.

But, as historian Nigel Worden concludes:

Political unity for the sake of economic growth was ... the British priority. Afrikaner nationalist sentiments needed to be accommodated provided they could be contained within a single economic and political structure.

In July 1909, William Schreiner, seated in the centre, was joined in London by leading coloured and African opponents of the Union constitution. They are, seated from left, John Tengo Jabavu, Abdullah Abdurahman, Walter Rubusana, Matt Fredericks, and, standing, Thomas Makipela, J Gerrans, Daniel Dwanya and D J Lenders.

Merriman, also in London, countered Schreiner's argument with the claim that 'agitation' would make things worse for blacks, adding: 'I think Mr Schreiner's present mission is one of the most unkind things ever done to the natives.'

Schreiner's final warning was that 'an easy downward step now taken may only be retraced, as it some day assuredly must be, with infinite labour, and at what cost?'

Britain would not listen.

Finally, on 19 August, the law was passed. On 31 May, 1910, South Africa would become a union, but a union divided. In September, in the first Union election, Louis Botha's South African Nationalist Party won 67 of the 121 seats of the new legislature, and he became prime minister.

Union was a victory for the Boer leaders: blacks would not have the vote, except in the Cape; and in the delimitation of constituencies, the rural vote would count for more, ensuring future Afrikaner political control.

———— ❖ ————

Within a year, the Union parliament enacted laws that widened the racial divide: the Black Labour Regulation Act made it an offence to break an employment contract; the Dutch Reformed Churches Union Act all but shut blacks out of the church, and the far-reaching Mines and Works Act consolidated job reservation for whites, confirming the status of blacks as cheap labour by putting a range of skilled jobs beyond their reach on the basis of 'competency'. Its forerunner was a British law in the Transvaal to limit the scope of Chinese workers in order to allay white fears.

In the same year, promoting 'South Africanism' among white people and furthering reconciliation between Afrikaner and English-speaker were among the goals of the formation of a new party, the South African Party, by Louis Botha and Jan Smuts.

It was a budding patriotism that would have been enhanced by the triumph of Potchefstroom policeman

TOP: Mythical Britannia seals the peace between former enemies by assenting to the Act of Union.

MIDDLE: Pixley Ka Isaka Seme, a leading figure at the launch of the South African Native National Congress, later renamed the African National Congress, in January 1912.

LEFT: African 'soldiers' served in the First World War against Germany, but without weapons.

Kenneth McArthur when he won the marathon gold medal in the Stockholm Olympics. Another close finisher was fellow South African Christopher Gitsham, who had never before competed in a marathon.

Yet, political division between English- and Afrikaans-speaking South Africans raised its head two years later in 1913 when former Boer general JBM Hertzog quit the Botha/Smuts South African Party to form the National Party. The new party was committed to Afrikaner interests and the avoidance of racial mixing of any kind.

The starker racial division now emerging prompted a more concerted African response. And when Pixley Ka Isaka Seme stood up to address a special four-day gathering in Bloemfontein on 8 January, 1912, he launched the organisation that struggled with difficulty to achieve it in the early years but grew to become the most powerful of all South African political parties of the 20th century.

The South African Native National Congress was the predecessor of the African National Congress that came to power, after a long struggle, in 1994.

Seme spoke in almost princely tones:

Chiefs of royal blood and gentlemen of our race, we have gathered here to consider and discuss a theme which my colleagues and I have decided to place before you. We have discovered that in the land of their birth, Africans are treated as hewers of wood and drawers of water.

The objectives, he told the 60 delegates, were to create 'national unity' among blacks and defend 'our rights and privileges'.

Despite the anguish of the post-war betrayal, the organisation was essentially moderate: it committed itself to keeping open a channel of communication with the government, to improving relations between white and black South Africans, and to maintaining a spirit of loyalty to the Crown. (Churchman, educationist and founder of the Zulu-language newspaper *Ilanga Lase Natal*, John Dube, was elected as the Congress's first president.)

If South Africa was standing on its own two feet as the Union, it still functioned very much within the ambit of Britain's world affairs.

And the outbreak of the First World War found South Africans drawn once more into a conflict shaped by interests elsewhere.

In the Afrikaner world, many were dead against South Africa's participation in the war. Some 11 000 of them – including former guerrilla leader Christiaan de Wet and several Union Defence Force officers – rose in rebellion against Louis Botha's decision to invade German South-West Africa on behalf of Britain. They were no match for Botha's government troops and the rebellion was soon crushed. De Wet and scores of others were fined or imprisoned, though sentences were generally lenient. For many Afrikaners, it reopened the wounds of the South African War.

But just how things had changed in South Africa is tellingly reflected in the destiny of the young Boer burgher Deneys Reitz, who had excitedly fired his first shots in battle against the British in a skirmish outside Dundee in Natal in 1899. In the war against Germany, he served in France, not merely on the side of the British Empire; he was an officer in command of Scots Fusiliers.

But where in the South African War Britain armed thousands of blacks to fight the good fight against the Boer republics, the First World War found them serving the Union of South Africa in France without arms.

At the outbreak of hostilities, Dr Walter Rubusana conveyed to Union Defence Minister Jan Smuts the South African Native National Congress's pledge of loyalty to the cause, promising not to criticise the government during the course of the conflict and offering to raise 5 000 troops to fight against German South-West Africa. The offer was turned down: Smuts argued this was a war among Europeans and the government did not want to involve people 'not of European descent' in the conflict.

It had no qualms, however, in using the services of no fewer than 83 000 Africans in non-combatant roles.

Nimrod Makanya, who watched his brothers going off to war in a Zulu labour contingent, wrote a song about the prospect of facing the Germans without guns:

It is very hard and difficult
To face the Germans without arms.
The government says we must go to France.
No man is bold enough to face the Germans
without arms.

From 'Lalela Zulu', *100 Zulu Lyrics* (1948) by Hugh Tracey

King George V praised the South African Native Labour Contingent for its contribution to the war effort, but none of these troops received a medal or ribbon, the customary form of recognition.

For many black people, the sense of unarmed help-lessness was tragically symbolised by the death of more than 600 men of the South African Native Labour Contingent in the sinking of the SS *Mendi* off the Isle of Wight on 21 February, 1917. The ship collided with another vessel, the SS *Darro,* in thick fog. In parliament less than a month later, Louis Botha praised the 'Native people' of South Africa for their efforts in the war. It was praise delivered to men of the Labour Contingent in Abbéville in France by no less a personage than King George V, who called them 'part of my great Armies which are fighting for the liberty and freedom of my subjects of all races and creeds throughout the Empire'.

Yet none of the black South African troops returning home after the war received the customary acknowledgement of a medal or a ribbon.

Some men who were not white were armed: coloured soldiers of the Cape Corps, a regiment dating back to the last days of Dutch rule at the Cape, are remembered as having fought with distinction when, in September 1918, they defeated Turks holding a key position in Palestine. Serving with General Allenby's forces, the Cape Corps men held the so-called Square Hill position on the road from Jerusalem to Nablus, despite heavy losses.

The white experience of the war has always been more prominently acknowledged.

South Africa, in fact, scored the first triumph of the conflict in July 1915 in securing the surrender of enemy forces in German South-West Africa.

But the event that most powerfully captures the First World War experience in France of many South Africans was the battle of Delville Wood in July 1916. Ordered to take the wood and hold it at all costs, 3 153 men of the South African Brigade stormed the position and held it for almost a week under a ferocious artillery bombardment and a counter-attack by enemy infantry. At the end of the battle, all but 755 men had been killed or wounded. In all, more than 12 400 South Africans died on active service in the so-called Great War.

The South African universe after the war was decisively shaped by a law passed in the year before the opening of hostilities: the 1913 Land Act.

Sol Plaatje wrote of its impact:

[A]waking on Friday morning, 20 June 1913, the South African native found himself, not actually a slave, but a pariah in the land of his birth.

Racial separateness in the regimental messrooms of the First World War was a token of how things were, and how things were going to be for most of the century.

The Act restricted the black majority's ownership rights to just seven percent of the country. It scheduled certain areas for exclusive black settlement – chiefly in Zululand, Transkei and Ciskei – and it prevented Africans from buying land anywhere outside these areas.

The first and most severe consequence was the eviction of hundreds of thousands of Africans from white-owned land.

The Act was the basis of the development of the reserves, or Bantustans, and the decades of forced removals, and mounting rural deprivation. And it was used to justify the system of racial segregation and inequality.

Ten years later, the 1923 Native (Urban Areas) Act was passed to control the lives of blacks in urban areas, force them into 'locations', make them carry passes, and provide for those not needed to work in towns and cities to be sent back to the Reserves.

African resistance and protest continued. Grievances were even raised by a South African Native National Congress delegation to the Treaty of Versailles talks that followed the First World War.

Pariahs in the land of their birth ... the fate of most African rural communities.

❖

White South Africa was well on its way to entrenching inequality on the basis that it was good for them, and good for black people too.

'In the first place, I wish to draw your attention to the composition of the population. In round figures we can fix it at 2 000 000 whites against 6 000 000 natives,' Nationalist leader JBM Hertzog told supporters at a meeting in Malmesbury in May 1926:

> Next to the European, the native stands as an 8-year-old child to a man of great experience – a child in religion, a child in moral conviction; without art and without science; with the most primitive needs, and the most elementary knowledge to provide for those needs. If ever a race had a need of guidance and protection from another people with which it is placed in contact, then it is the native in his contact with the white man.

From *20th Century South Africa, source material on South African history* (1984) by José Druker

Smuts, who became prime minister in 1919 after the death of Louis Botha – and who made headlines two years later by sending in the army to quell the 1922 Rand Revolt of white miners brutally – was defeated in 1924 by the National Party under Hertzog, together with the white Labour Party under Colonel Frederick Cresswell. Together they formed the so-called Pact government.

Soldier, politician and statesman Jan Smuts.

Hertzog would continue to rule the roost for the next 15 years, steadily promoting Afrikaner nationalism and introducing laws to deepen racial division and entrench the disadvantage of black South Africans.

The colour bar – limiting jobs that blacks could apply for – was extended by the 1926 Mines and Works Amendment Act. The first Immorality Act and the Native Administration Act – which 'retribalised' African government and law – were introduced in 1927. There were others.

In 1924, Afrikaans, as opposed to Dutch, was given official recognition, and the new South African flag was introduced three years later.

Oppression of blacks and the promotion of Afrikaner nationalism went hand in hand. But opposition was stiffening, too.

The Communist Party of South Africa (it later became the South African Communist Party) was founded in Cape Town in 1921. Though at the start it was entirely white, it began to 'Africanise' from 1924. And, tapping into widespread rural discontent among blacks, the Industrial and Commercial Workers' Union formed in 1919 by a Nyasalander named Clements Kadalie stirred massive protests through the 1920s.

In the first two decades of the century, women began to emerge as significant agents in opposing discrimination and exploitation.

Charlotte Maxeke, a key figure in the formation of the Bantu Women's League in 1918, led demonstrations by women in the Orange Free State five years earlier, in September 1913, against government attempts to impose passes on women. It was the first time passes were burned in protest.

In January 1914, black and coloured women in the Orange Free State launched a petition against passes, and in 1918 the Bantu Women's League sent a delegation to Prime Minister Louis Botha to reinforce their position.

In Johannesburg, a former Mine Workers' Union typist named Mary Fitzgerald came to prominence as a vigorous campaigner for women's rights. She became Johannesburg's first female city councillor, in 1921, and took part in the Rand Revolt in the next year.

Yet, the opposition – including that of the ANC – seemed too moderate and accommodating to check the steady rise of white nationalism. It was given a further boost by the world-wide economic slump, the Great Depression, triggered by the Wall Street collapse of 1929. The impoverishment of thousands of whites in the countryside, the towns and the cities, heightened Afrikaner disenchantment.

In the face of difficult economic conditions, the National Party under Hertzog and the South African Party under Smuts formed the United Party in 1934 under the slogan 'South Africa First'. Many Nationalists, however, led by a young Cape politician

– a journalist and former *dominee* – DF Malan rejected the Fusion coalition and formed the 'purified' National Party.

Black organisations made a new bid for unified action: in 1935, more than 400 delegates from a variety of organisations – including Jabavu, Seme and leaders of the Communist Party, the African People's Organisation and the South African Indian Congress – met, in Bloemfontein again, to the form the All African Convention.

But, as historian Worden notes, its

tactics of petition and moderate reformism differed little from earlier methods and it met with as little response from the government as the South African Native National Congress in 1912.

Events in Europe in the 1930s had their echoes in South Africa. The rise of Nazism, and the spread of anti-Semitism under Adolf Hitler in Germany, prompted scores of Jews to seek refuge elsewhere in the world.

In South Africa, immigration laws were steadily tightened to restrict the influx of these desperate escapees from Hitler. The last vessel to bring refugees, the steamship *Stuttgart*, beat a fresh ban by a few days when it docked at Cape Town on 27 October, 1936. On the quay, the 600 bewildered Jews were confronted by a mob of anti-Semitic protesters whose leader was a young Stellenbosch academic who would make his mark, and pay for it, in time to come. His name was Hendrik Verwoerd.

For black South Africans, however, 1936 would be remembered grimly as the year of the successor to the 1913 Land Act, the Native Trust and Land Act. The new law would be the basis of massed forced removals in the decades to come.

And, in the same year, Cape Africans were removed from the common voters' roll by the Representation of Natives Act. A year later, the Native Laws Amendment Act tightened control on the influx of Africans to urban areas.

Unionist Clements Kadalie.

With Hitler's invasion of Poland on 1 September, 1939, Britain issued an ultimatum, and declared war on Germany two days later.

What was South Africa to do? For the second time in less than three decades, white South Africa's divided sentiments over Britain threatened a political crisis.

Some South Africans had been openly admiring of Hitler's economic programme, his infectious nationalism and his anti-Semitism. No less a figure than South Africa's defence minister Oswald Pirow had even visited the Nazi demagogue in Berlin in the 1930s.

Half the South African cabinet was in favour of neutrality, including Prime Minister Hertzog.

But his deputy, Smuts, had no doubt that South Africa had to join Britain in standing up to fascism in Europe and, on 4 September, he put a motion to parliament in favour of entering the war. It was carried by 13 votes. Hertzog resigned, and Smuts became prime minister, declaring war on Germany on 6 September.

During the next six years, 386 000 men and women volunteers served, many with great distinction, in land, sea and air forces, and in every theatre of the war from the Far East to North Africa, the Atlantic to the Indian and Pacific oceans, from the Mediterranean to the North Sea, from Europe to the Middle East. Nearly 9 000 South Africans were killed in action.

On the home front, the war years threw up fresh challenges.

Radical Afrikaners formed the pro-Nazi *Ossewa Brandwag* in 1939, organised terror groups and sabotage against army targets during the war, and whipped up nationalist sentiment.

Among them was a young man named Balthazar John Vorster who, in 1941, was interned – detained without trial, as he would later see it – at Koffiefontein for the duration of the war. He later became a prominent Nationalist, a minister of justice and ultimately president.

But more radical groupings began to emerge in black politics, too.

Anton Lembede, Oliver Tambo and Walter Sisulu were among the key figures in the founding of the ANC Youth League

When the government relaxed influx control regulations to make it easier for blacks to move to the cities and fill jobs left by whites who had gone off to fight, the South African Communist Party and others became vigorously involved in unionising blacks.

New organisations emerged. One was the influential African National Congress Youth League under Africanist Anton Lembede in 1943. Prominent members were two young Johannesburg lawyers, Nelson Mandela and Oliver Tambo, and a young trade unionist, Walter Sisulu. They would soon exert a strong and more radical influence on the middle-class, moderate ANC.

Another more radical organisation to emerge in 1943 was the Non-European Unity League, which urged 'non-collaboration' and boycott as strategies to block or disable structures of segregation, such as councils.

———— ❖ ————

The end of the war in 1945 found the country grappling ever more strenuously with the single most pressing issue that the National Convention had failed to deal with in 1909: colour policy.

In August 1946, it was the turn of black miners to flex their muscle. The African Mineworkers' Union, which the Communists had helped to establish during the war, launched what became the biggest strike since the Rand Revolt of 1922, involving more than 60 000 workers. It wakened white South Africa's sense of the political power of black labour. The police and army were deployed, in some cases to drive miners back underground to work. Twelve miners died and more than a thousand were injured.

The strike galvanised the unionists, Communists, and the ANC to rethink their strategies and to develop a broad-based movement to oppose segregation.

In the same year, Smuts had the satisfaction of signing the charter of the newly formed United Nations on behalf of South Africa and, a year later, he hosted the two-month Royal visit by King George VI, Queen Elizabeth and the two princesses, Elizabeth (later queen) and Margaret. (On one occasion during the tour the Royal Family was entertained by a 15-year-old singer making her first – but not her last – solo performance. She was none other than Miriam Makeba.)

But the key focus of public life in the post-war years was the work of two rival commissions set up to look into the question of race policy.

At the close of the 1946 parliamentary session, Smuts had appointed Judge Henry Fagan to report on the pass laws, the position of Africans in the urban areas and industry, and the issue of migrant labour. The report rejected complete segregation as 'totally impracticable'. The government's failure to act on this finding was a lost opportunity.

DF Malan's National Party's response was to commission similar research, and the Sauer Report

DF Malan's 'purified' National Party, formed in the mid-1930s, took power after the Second World War.

Nelson Mandela in the late 1940s.

that emerged said the opposite: complete separation would secure the interests of whites and ensure the development of Africans in their own areas.

The Sauer Report, which introduced to the world the term 'apartheid' for the first time, set the agenda for the elections of May 1948. Smuts, counting unwisely on his international stature and the loyalty of soldiers who had served under his overall command in the war, was confident of retaining his hold on the country. He was wrong.

DF Malan presented a characteristically unsmiling face to the world when he emerged from his Stellenbosch home late on the afternoon of 27 May, 1948. It was odd, really, because it was the stern former dominee's moment of triumph. The cheers of disbelieving supporters confirmed it.

It was almost a whole day after the closing of the polls in a general election that changed the South African political landscape for decades.

'Today,' Malan declared dourly,

South Africa belongs to us once more. For the first time since Union [1910] South Africa is our own. May God grant that it will always remain our own.

Afrikaner nationalism had won the day. Though Malan and his alliance partner Nicolaas Havenga's Afrikaner Party had won more seats, they did not win a major-

ity of the votes: their 443 719 votes were 181 000 less than the 624 500 won by their opponents.

But even Jan Smuts lost his seat in Standerton. The slim margin of 224 votes was no consolation. It was a bitter blow.

Crude political sloganeering had proved decisive for the Nationalists.

The election, as Nelson Mandela recalls in his autobiography, *Long Walk to Freedom*, 'was fought on the twin slogans of *"Die kaffir op sy plek"* (the nigger in his place) and *"Die koelies uit die land"* (the coolies out of the country)'. It was callous and inelegant, and it worked.

It is clear from a debate in the House of Assembly in September 1948, just months after the Nationalist victory, that Smuts was not exactly a progressive thinker when it came to race, but that his somewhat kindly, gentle-seeming – and, to blacks, no doubt patronising – views paled, for whites, against the vigorous no-nonsense approach of the Nationalists.

Sparring with Malan in the debate, Smuts said at one point: 'We have always stood and we stand for social and residential separation in this country, and for the avoidance of all racial mixture.'

To which Malan shot back: 'Is that your apartheid?'

Smuts conceded that 'there is a great deal about apartheid that is common to all parties', but went on to say:

We see no reason to change the political rights, small as they are, of the Native people and the

Coloured people of this country. The small position they have in the parliament of this country, let them keep … let them have their say here too.

He stood for gradual change.

To increasing numbers of white voters, it just seemed too wishy-washy.

Smuts, a venerable, able and famous man, had found himself tangled in the web of increasingly difficult and bitter race politics, a web he had had a hand in weaving when the National Convention decided in 1909 to defer the question of 'Native policy' to the future for the sake of white unity.

———— ❖ ————

The presence of DF Malan still looms large in 21st-century Stellenbosch, but it's a presence that has been symbolically neutralised.

This was strikingly, but unassumingly, achieved when the ANC held its 51st national conference in 2002 not just in the town of Stellenbosch, but in a hall named after DF Malan himself.

'That the ANC is meeting here today,' President Thabo Mbeki told delegates,

sends out a powerful message to all our people and the peoples of the world. That message says that the people of South Africa have made a common determination that our country belongs to all who live in it, black and white.

It says that the people of South Africa, black and white, are committed to living up to the pledge they made to themselves, to refuse to be enslaved by the divisions and antagonisms of the past.

It was a matter of celebration that the people gathered in the hall, in peace and freedom and as compatriots, were 'the descendants of Sarah Baartmann and Simon van der Stel, the products of the struggle in which Moses Kotane and DF Malan engaged'.

The symbolism of the moment was all the more powerful for the fact that just months before the conference the ANC had entered into a cooperative agreement with Malan's successors, the New National Party under Marthinus van Schalkwyk.

Whatever the problems that beset South Africans 92 years after the flawed Union came into being in 1910, unity based on constitutional equality was an unremarkable fact of life in 2002.

Decades after DF Malan's Nationalists came to power and entrenched apartheid, the African National Congress chose the Stellenbosch hall named after him as the venue for its 51st national conference.

The ✦ Star

CITY
LATE

RICH

ESTABLISHED 1887 — JOHANNESBURG, FRIDAY, MAY 28, 1948 — PRICE 2d.

. Malan Summoned To Form Cab

NATION OF UNITED PARTY CABINET ACCEPTED

AL SMUTS ASKED TO CARRY ON ADMINISTRATION UNTIL NEW MINISTRY IS FORMED

ONALIST GROUP SECURES ALL WORKING MAJORITY

By Our Political Correspondent

HOW TIDE TURNED AGAINST UNITED PARTY

ATIONALIST AND AFRIKANER PARTIES MAJORITY OF 15 SEATS TO BE ANNOUNCED

ASONS FOR U.P. DEFEAT

MR. B. J. SCHOEMAN'S ANALYSIS

DR. MALAN EXPECTED IN PRETORIA ON TUESDAY

DIFFICULTIES FOR H.N.P. IN SENATE

From Our Correspondent
CAPE TOWN, Friday.

TERMS OF ACT

U.P. ON RAND PREPARING FOR NEW PHASE OF POLITICAL STRUGGLE

FIGURES SHOW MAJORITY OF POPULATION SUPPORTED GEN. SMUTS AND LABOUR

SURPRISE AT ELECTION RESULT GENERAL

Hewers
of wood,
drawers of
water

HOW THE PROVINCES CAST THEIR VOTES

DR. MALAN SPENDS BUSY DAY

REQUESTS IN LONDON FOR PHOTOGRAPHS OF DR. MALAN

It's the little things that count...

ARAB REACTION TO SANCTIONS

SECRETARY FOR JUSTICE

chapter nine

Hewers of wood, drawers of water

DF Malan's 1948 victory brought deepening change. But you had to be an ass, one cartoonist suggested, to choose the Hitlerian option of conservative Afrikaner nationalism.

The meeting had gone on all night, and there was a chill in the air when the two men emerged at dawn.

It was the end of May and the icy cold of the Johannesburg winter was already upon the city.

The weather was of little consequence to them as they made their way down the street, mulling over strategies, ideas. But their conversation came to an abrupt end when they reached a newspaper stand. The headlines caught them completely unawares: the Nationalists had beaten Jan Smuts at the polls. It was unthinkable.

It was also deeply significant to these two young men. Both lawyers, they naturally took a professional interest in the news of the day. But parallel with their interest in the law was a commitment to politics, to political change.

The unthinkable victory of DF Malan intensified that commitment.

And from that day on, the destinies of Nelson Mandela and Oliver Tambo would be inextricably bound up with the electoral fortunes of the Afrikaner nationalists.

Many years later, when the Nationalists had come and gone, Mandela would remember that morning vividly. 'The victory was a shock,' he recalls in *Long Walk to Freedom*.

> The United Party and General Smuts had beaten the Nazis, and surely they would defeat the National Party. On election day, I attended a meeting in Johannesburg with Oliver Tambo and several others. We barely discussed the question of a Nationalist government because we did not expect one.

Then, having been up all night and pausing now at the newspaper stand confronting the truth in the day's lead story, Mandela was 'stunned and dismayed'.

But Tambo, his partner in law, had a different view. 'I like this,' Mandela remembers him saying. And Mandela was confused. Why would he like it? And Tambo explained: 'Now we will know exactly who our enemies are and where we stand.'

It was a turning point, politically, socially and economically. It drew the battle lines between the enemies, as Tambo rightly saw it.

The vision of Malan's government, and that of succeeding governments, was imagined 36 years before when Pixley Ka Isaka Seme stood to address delegates at the ANC's founding conference in 1912. Africans, Seme said then, were being treated as serfs – as the Israelites had treated the Gibeonites, according to the book of Joshua in the Bible – good for little more than cutting wood and carrying water.

From May 1948, Seme's biblical metaphor became the virtual objective of government. By means of policy, law and decree, the single-minded Nationalists would attempt to construct a state and a society in which, they dreamed, most blacks would be nothing more than hewers of wood, drawers of water.

There is a lovely road that runs from Ixopo into the hills. These hills are grass-covered and rolling, and they are lovely beyond any singing of it.

So begins one of the most influential stories of the first years of post-war Nationalist rule in South Africa.

These opening lines of the novel *Cry, The Beloved Country* by Alan Paton, first published in 1948 and reprinted many times in the years that followed, are deceptively pretty. What the book really describes is the bewilderment, despair and brutalisation of urbanising black society under the pressure of white fear and prejudice. It was a warning of sorts of the mounting social disintegration that was already occurring across South Africa, and which would intensify.

It influenced people in South Africa and around the world into viewing the country differently. But while virtually every enlightened white household in the Nationalist state had a well-thumbed copy of the book, it became clear to the new generation of young black leaders that sympathetic attitudes among a liberal minority of whites were not, and would never be, enough.

Paton's book ends on a note of hopelessness, or at least of almost hopeless uncertainty:

But when that dawn will come, of our emancipation, from the fear of bondage and the bondage of fear, why, that is a secret.

It wasn't a secret in the usual sense. But it felt like one.

The unexpected election win of DF Malan's Nationalists ended the era of more moderate Afrikaner leaders such as Jan Smuts, whose race policies were no doubt patronising and illiberal, but not deliberately vindictive or nasty. Smuts, who was deeply disappointed, though still widely admired, died two years later.

And on the strength of promising that they were guided by a policy of 'preserving and safe-guarding the White race', the Nationalists were to remain in power for just a month short of 46 years.

The *Broederbond* (fellowship of brothers), a secret Afrikaner organisation that had emerged in the early decades of the century, came into its own once the Nationalists took power.

Broeders in the civil service and the armed forces, in the teaching corps and in the professions, were committed to advancing the interests of an 'Afrikanerdom' that was defined by the exclusion of others, of English-speakers and anyone who was not white.

The broeders had been dead against the conciliatory theme of Smuts and Botha's politics, the emphasis on building a shared sense of South Africanhood among Afrikaans- and English-speaking people.

In 1945, Smuts had tried to break their power, ordering civil servants who were members of the secret organisation to resign, or face dismissal. A little more than 1 000 resigned. Two were dismissed. One of them, Wentzel du Plessis, had the satisfaction of taking Smuts's Standerton seat from him in the 1948 election.

From May 1948, the 'affirmative action' of the

Partners in law, Oliver Tambo and Nelson Mandela, who were destined to become giants in black politics.

time – though it wasn't called that – was vigorously applied and the *Broederbond* was the pool from which the Nationalists drew recruits for top government posts. And through the *Broederbond*, the government reached deep into civil society to consolidate its national mission.

The cohesion of Afrikaner nationalism was vital to the government in its first years in power.

The men who ran the armed services, government departments and big state corporations such as the railways were soon *Broederbond*

JG Strijdom succeeded DF Malan in the early 1950s.

appointees. They became increasingly powerful in business, too, especially through institutions that were formed in the years before the Second World War with the express goal of establishing an independent Afrikaner stake in the economy. Among them were the insurance corporation Santam, the life assurance company Sanlam, the winegrowers' cooperative, KWV, and the Volkskas bank.

But the most dramatic and cynical use of loyal Nationalists was in the removal of coloureds from the voters' roll of the Cape.

Most coloureds had voted for Smuts in 1948 and Malan wanted them rendered powerless as soon as possible. It took a while. There was a constitutional hitch: a two-thirds majority in a joint sitting of both houses of the Union parliament – the Senate and the House of Assembly – was needed to change their electoral status. Malan tried a different tack: having a law passed in each house separately, but by a simple majority, 50 percent plus one. However, four coloured voters – a van driver and a bricklayer from Woodstock, a trade union worker and a businessman – challenged this in the courts, and the Appellate Division of the Supreme Court, the highest court in the land, ruled unanimously in their favour. The government tried again, this time introducing a law to create a committee of MPs capable of overruling the Appellate Division. The same four voters went to court again, and won again.

It was now 1954, and Malan's successor JG Strijdom adopted a cynical new strategy. He introduced a law raising to 11 the number of judges required to assess the validity of government legislation. He appointed five new Appeal Court judges,

ensuring that the sentiment of the Bench was pro-Nationalist. To make doubly sure of success, he 'packed' the Senate, enlarging it from 48 to 89 seats. Most of the new members were Nationalists.

This time, in the face of the secret, powerful workings of the *Broederbond* and the cunning determination of the Nationalists over six years, the Cape's 45 000 coloured voters were stripped of their franchise in 1956. It made clear to many of them that their true interests lay in joining forces with black South Africans.

By 1954, the legal framework of post-war apartheid was already fastidiously complex. Because the common law – drawn from the law of ancient Rome, and of Holland and England – was and remains colour-blind, every element of discrimination introduced by the Nationalists had to be carefully codified in new laws.

So-called 'petty' apartheid was well established … whites-only trains, park benches, beaches, post office entrances, cinemas, restaurants and so on. It was the apartheid of 'separate amenities'. Wherever people worked or played, racial separateness was laid down by law.

But there was more.

Nationalists who prided themselves on self-righteous Christian piety had no difficulty devising brutal laws that denied human love. A year after coming to power, they passed the Prohibition of Mixed Marriages Act. It speaks for itself. It split families, and further entrenched racial division. A year later, a supplementary law prohibiting sex between people of different races – expanding a law from 1927 – became known as the Immorality Act. Scores of suicides and decades of heartache were among its results.

And in 1950 they introduced the law that would 'make sense' of all apartheid measures – the Population Registration Act. This statute defined

Petty apartheid was not petty so much as degrading, preserving white privilege while denying access to everything from beaches and buses to restaurants and hotels to those who were not white.

people as either white, Indian, Asian, black or coloured, along with various other categories, including Cape Malay, Cape Coloured, Griqua, Chinese, Other Asiatic and Other Coloured.

Arbitrary tests were often used to decide which category people fitted into: the notorious 'pencil test' was frequently used to decide doubtful cases. A pencil was pushed into an applicant's hair. If it stuck in the hair, it signified *kroes* or frizzy hair and the person was deemed to be coloured or African. If the pencil fell out, it signified straight hair, which usually meant classification as coloured or white.

The combination of these three laws on skin colour, marriage and sex carved society into arbitrary sectors, crossing the boundaries of which was a punishable offence.

The Population Registration Act had tragic consequences. People could appeal to have their race classification changed, and 100 000 did when the law was passed. Attempts at 'passing for white' were often motivated by the desire to keep jobs or higher wages that would be lost with reclassification. Some were 'downgraded' and lost their jobs or had to move home, some had their marriages torn apart, families were cut down the middle. The profound consequences of these callous divisions remain today.

'European' superiority was a fiction fondly nurtured by the young PW Botha.

Vigorously reinforcing the social divisions created by laws proscribing personal relationships, the Group Areas Act of 1950 carved up the geography of towns and cities, declaring areas 'white' or 'black' or 'coloured' or 'Asian'. It determined where people of different races could live, work or do business. Over the next three decades, hundreds of thousands of people would lose their homes, often their livelihood, and their sense of belonging through this hated law.

Consolidating the Group Areas idea, the 1955 Native (Urban Areas) Amendment Act introduced tougher 'influx control', with regulations to limit the movement of blacks from country to town – denying by decree the international phenomenon of urbanisation that has characterised the development of modern human society – or from any part of the country to another.

One of the purposes of the Group Areas Act, as much as influx control, was to assure poor whites special treatment: they were increasingly given sole occupation of areas they had, until the law was applied, shared with people of the same class, but who happened to be black or coloured. In this way, all classes of white people began to 'understand' that they were superior to all people of other skin colours. Most whites eventually regarded this as a division of nature. It was just how the world worked.

❖

As recently as 1990, FW de Klerk's reforming parliament was given a breakdown of the number of racial reclassifications during the previous year. It is bizarre that there was a law in modern times that, as Hansard, the official record of parliament shows, enabled people to change from 'White to Cape Coloured; Cape Coloured to White; Cape Coloured to Chinese; White to Chinese; White to Malay; Malay to White; White to Indian; Malay to Chinese; Indian to Cape Coloured; Cape Coloured to Indian; Indian to Malay; Malay to Indian; Other Asian to Cape Coloured; Black to Cape Coloured; Cape Coloured to Black; Black to Other Asian; Black to Indian; Black to Griqua; Cape Coloured to Malay; Chinese to Cape Coloured; Indian to White; Malay to Cape Coloured; Cape Coloured to Griqua; and Cape Coloured to Other Asian'.

In all, the House of Assembly was told in March 1990, there had been 1 229 successful reclassifications in the preceding 12 months. One hundred and six applications had been turned down. It is difficult to imagine on what logical grounds they failed.

Among the young MPs to drum home this fallacy of white superiority in the 1950s was PW Botha, who was later feared, and ridiculed, as the finger-wagging state president of the embattled, repressive Nationalists of the 1980s. The hardline former party organiser told the House of Assembly in August 1953:

We must accept that the non-European in South Africa in his level of civilisation is hundreds of years behind the European, and he can only insist on the same privileges and rights as those enjoyed by the European in South Africa today when he reaches that stage that the white man has reached.

From *Apartheid, The Lighter Side* (1990) by Ben Maclennan

Adam Small's play, *Kanna hy kô hystoe*, conveys the simple and heartless rationale of the Group Areas Act:

TOEFIE: Hulle't die hyse in die Kaap in afgebriek.
SKOEN: Kos hulle't biesagheite gebou daar, toe skyf hulle al die mense yt.
(TOEFIE: They've demolished the houses in the Cape (District Six).
SKOEN: Because they've built businesses there, so they've move all the people out.)

From *Kanna hy kô hystoe, 'n drama* (1980) by Adam Small

Having made a determined start on constructing its racially fragmented society and landscape, the National Party moved quickly to keep a lid on political opposition to its grand plan.

The initial target was Communism. Communists had during the war years gained much ground in unionising black workers who had streamed to the towns and cities to occupy jobs vacated by white men who had gone off to fight the Germans. The Communist Party of South Africa had also, since the 1920s, played a key role in building a non-racial tradition among the forces opposed to racism and exploitation. The broad front of opposition faced by Malan's Nationalists was certainly emboldened by the hard work and convictions of the Communists.

In 1950, when a May Day general strike, in which

18 people were shot dead by police, demonstrated the new spirit of unity of the apartheid opposition, the government cracked down. The Suppression of Communism Act outlawed the Communist Party (which strategically dissolved itself beforehand, going underground as the South African Communist Party).

But the law went much further in allowing the government to define as Communist virtually any individual or organisation hostile to the state, or intent on 'bringing about any political, industrial, social or economic change' by unlawful acts or omissions. It was a legal sledgehammer.

Yet, as repressive measures increased – such as the carrying of reference books (the new version of the pass) by all black people, men and women, and influx control, both introduced in 1952 – so opposition grew, too.

Repression escalated: tougher penalties and deterrents, such as the 1953 Public Safety Act, to allow for the declaration of a state of emergency, and, in the same year, laws to make passive resistance, and strikes by black workers, illegal.

Reducing the scope of future generations of black people to assert their rights or fulfil their aspirations in life was another goal the Nationalists set them-

From its earliest days in power, the National Party provoked resistance and protest.

STOP MALAN TERROR: PROTEST NOW! WITH SWART'S GESTAPO BILLS— NO CONCENTRATION CAMPS NO MARTIAL LAW

Saki Macozoma, activist, senior ANC executive member, former managing director of Transnet and a captain of industry, most recently as chief executive officer of New Africa Investment Limited, started his schooling in East London in the 1960s. In the 1980s, he recalled the conditions imposed on black teachers by a 'Bantu Education' system deliberately intended to undermine the intellectual development of Africans:

> As kids we soon discovered that 'the mistress' had a problem keeping track of the attendance of the 80-odd Sub A pupils that were in her class. Nobody missed us. So we went to the rubbish dump where we helped ourselves to any edibles that were thrown away and sniffed glue to make the whole thing even more interesting.

He had an advantage, he remembered. He could already read and write. But it didn't make any difference: the class was so big the teacher was not even aware of his ability, '... and the rubbish dump was beckoning'.

Macozoma added: 'With hindsight I now see that apartheid can make even an early start count against one.'

From 'History and History Teaching in Apartheid South Africa' by Melanie Walker in *History from South Africa, Alternative Visions and Practices* (1991) by Joshua Brown, Patrick Manning, Karin Shapiro, Jon Wiener, Belinda Bozzoli and Peter Delius (editors)

selves. Job reservation – limiting the jobs blacks could do – had already been well established in the early decades of the century. Now, the post-war Nationalists focused their attention on black schooling.

The primary aim of the 1953 Bantu Education Act was to limit the tuition of black children to an inferior curriculum sufficient merely to serve the white economy. It created the foundation for mass education for the first time, geared to imparting low-level skills to meet the requirements of post-war industry. It shifted responsibility for black schools away from provincial education authorities to the Department of Native Affairs. And it all but ended independent schooling for blacks, extensively reducing the role of mission schools, which had been so influential in producing articulate, confident black leaders since the late 1800s.

Yet, there was a contradiction at the core of mass black schooling, as historian William Beinart points out:

> A striking feature of the new system was the increase in overall education provision for Africans from about 800 000 school places in 1953 to 1 800 000 in 1963; numbers expanded even more rapidly afterwards.

HF Verwoerd, acknowledged as the architect of 'grand apartheid'.

Though there was 'gross underfunding, inadequate teacher training and very many pupils did not get beyond the first four years of schooling, the proportion of students at secondary level gradually rose'. The quality of education and the funding were 'inadequate', '[b]ut the consequences of Bantu Education and more widespread literacy were to be far less predictable than either its planners or its opponents expected'.

❖

Late in 1950, at the urging of the young PW Botha, DF Malan promoted one of his new senators, Dr Hendrik Verwoerd, to head the new Department of Native Affairs. It was a critical appointment.

Verwoerd, a Dutchman by birth, was a fiercely loyal convert to South African nationalism. (His thesis in psychology at Stellenbosch University in the 1920s was the first to be written in Afrikaans.) He was a professor of sociology at the university in the 1930s before being selected by the Nationalists in 1935 to edit a new pro-Nationalist newspaper, *Die Transvaler*. Becoming a senator when Malan came to power, Verwoerd excelled himself as a party theoretician, setting out in cold, painstaking detail the deeply flawed but – to growing numbers of whites – appealing idea of complete racial separation.

He was never put off by the contradiction between the needs of white farmers and industrialists for cheap, readily available black labour and the pipe dream of towns and cities and the white-dominated countryside emptied of black people.

In a phased way, he argued, whites could gradually take over black jobs, and blacks could be shipped off to the reserves to run their own affairs.

Verwoerd went to great lengths to promote 'tribalism' – strong chiefs, though always under his department's control, and a return to traditional authority structures. In this way he hoped to justify the bantustans and counter the influence of liberal and left-wing ideas spreading among urban Africans.

It was contrary to the steady shift in black politics from the turn of the century, but the Nationalists were determined to make it 'work'.

One of Verwoerd's most important tools was the Bantu Education Act. His explanation of it was shameless:

> There is no place for [the 'Bantu'] in the European community above the level of certain forms of labour. ... What is the use of teaching the Bantu child mathematics when it cannot use it in practice?

(He hoped to deepen the disadvantage four years later with the Extension of Universities Act, which closed existing English-language universities to blacks and allowed for the establishment of 'ethnic colleges' on a tribal basis in black rural areas.)

In addition, Verwoerd introduced legislation to limit black politics to 'tribal' authorities in the reserves. Again, his logic was simple: living together 'will inevitably cause growing resistance and resentment' among whites and blacks. 'The only possible way out is that both sides accept development apart from each other.'

So was laid the foundation for 'separate development', and the despairing decades of the balkanisation of South Africa into bantustans, or 'independent states' as they eventually pretended to become.

It was Verwoerd's 'final solution'. South Africa would, he calculated, have no African citizens at all.

Intellectuals helped to reinforce the idea, too. The Stellenbosch-based South African Bureau for Racial Affairs provided apparently serious-minded substance to it, believing that separate development was the

key to the survival of Africa's white tribe.

That 60 percent of Africans lived in 'white areas' did not upset the logic of the Nationalists. If they wanted rights, blacks would find them in 'their home areas'. And the 'home areas' for 70 percent of the population accounted for no more than 13 percent of the country. In the next two decades, 3,5 million people would be uprooted from their homes.

Engineering separateness contradicted a fundamental truth about South Africa:

The strongest impulses in South African society are towards national integration. Hence the tremendous barriers of laws that apartheid must erect to divide people.

From *For Their Triumphs and For Their Tears, Women in Apartheid South Africa* (1978) by Hilda Bernstein

It was Malan's successor who made clear exactly what this was about. JG Strijdom said:

Call it paramountcy, baasskap or what you will, it is still domination. I am being as blunt as I can. I am making no excuses. Either the white man dominates, or the black takes over.

He boasted that it was the Nationalists' own laws alone that made

the white man ... baas in South Africa. ... To suggest that the white man can maintain leadership purely on the grounds of his greater competency is unrealistic. The greater competency of the white man can never weigh against numbers if natives and Europeans enjoy equal voting rights.

From *Apartheid, A History* (1986) by Brian Lapping

❖

'They are by nature a cheerful race,' National Party MP MC de Wet Nel was moved to tell the House of Assembly in May 1950. 'If you make their souls happy they are a dancing, singing, happy race.'

De Wet Nel's 'they' were the black people of South Africa, but he was quite wrong about 'them'. 'They' had other ideas.

Initially, the Nationalist victory in 1948 seemed largely irrelevant to many black leaders. Albert Luthuli, elected leader of the ANC in 1952, acknowledged:

It did not seem of much importance whether the whites gave us more Smuts or switched to Malan. Our lot had grown steadily worse, and no election seemed likely to alter the direction in which we were being forced.

But Tambo was right when he told Mandela that the election result would indicate more clearly 'who our enemies are and where we stand'.

And, as oppression intensified, it had – for the Nationalists – the unintended consequence of 'awakening the mass of Africans to political awareness, goading us finally out of our resigned endurance', as Luthuli put it.

Academic and leading political figure ZK Matthews emphasised the need for unity under the ANC:

The claims of the African people will ... not be heeded until we are organised into a fighting unit instead of the disgruntled rabble which we tend to be today.

Black politics had begun to move away from moderation during the war years. This was signalled by two organisations formed in 1943: the ANC Youth League under Africanist Anton Lembede (whose prominent members included Nelson Mandela, Oliver Tambo and Walter Sisulu) and the Non-European Unity League.

After Malan's victory, more forceful views came to the fore. The Youth League's 1949 Programme of Action was accepted by new ANC leader James Moroka, and 'marked a decisive break with the conciliatory policies of the previous decades', according to historian Nigel Worden. It called for 'national freedom' and recommended civil disobedience, boycotts and strikes as weapons.

But there were still differences of opinion in the ANC on whether it should work with other organisations and races – such as the Communists, or

ANC leader Albert Luthuli.

coloured and Indian groupings – or stick to a strictly Africanist approach.

Mandela, an acknowledged firebrand when he was elected national president of the Youth League in 1951, was initially opposed to working with the Communists and others, believing the political challenges associated with race were for Africans to settle on their own.

But Moroka, and his successor, Luthuli, believed in the virtue of united action among all apartheid's opponents. Mandela – elected as Luthuli's deputy in 1952 – and others came round to this way of thinking.

This set the stage for the Defiance Campaign and other forms of mass action. The Campaign for the Repeal of Discriminatory Legislation – popularly called the Defiance Campaign – was planned jointly by the ANC and the South African Indian Congress in 1951. It was launched on Freedom Day, 26 June, the next year. It was timed to extend protests in the Cape and elsewhere against white South Africa's celebration on 6 April, 1952 of the 300th anniversary of Jan van Riebeeck's arrival at the Cape.

Malan's government warned the ANC leaders to reconsider the campaign, threatening to 'use the full machinery at its disposal to quell any disturbances'. But the ANC was not to be deterred. As white South Africans celebrated the climax of the Van Riebeeck celebrations in early April, 50 000 people gathered at Freedom Square in Fordsburg to hear James Moroka warn that 'whites ... cannot escape the fact that whatever page they turn in the history of South Africa they find it red with the blood of the fallen, with ill-will and insecurity'.

The Defiance Campaign was on.

The idea was that volunteers would deliberately break discriminatory laws and have themselves arrested. Mandela himself was the volunteer-in-chief, and he witnessed with satisfaction the widening of resistance. 'We welcome true-hearted volunteers from all walks of life without consideration of colour, race or creed,' he said of the campaign. 'The unity of Africans, Indians and Coloured people has now become a living reality.'

The campaign was eventually ended by a combination of factors – outbreaks of violence persuaded the organisers to call it off, but it was also weakened by the government's banning and imprisoning leaders, and introducing legislation to forbid civil disobedience. More than 7 500 volunteers were arrested in the course of the campaign.

The campaign gave the government the excuse it needed to introduce tougher legislation to curb opposition, and it brought more whites into the fold in the 1953 election. Scores of leading ANC and other opposition figures, including Luthuli, were banned or restricted.

But the campaign established the power of non-

Luthuli's predecessor, James Moroka.

violent mass action, and enhanced the scale of the ANC as a political organisation: between 1951 and 1953, ANC branches increased from 14 to 87, and its paid-up membership rose from 7 000 to 100 000.

Opposition gained an international dimension when, in September 1952, the Indian government moved in the United Nations that South Africa's race policies be debated by the General Assembly. The UN decided to set up a commission on apartheid, signalling the beginning of a long period of mounting international pressure on South Africa's minority white regime.

Mass action against apartheid gained steadily wider support as people recognised that their oppression was being entrenched.

Row upon row of soulless houses formed the dormitory towns – locations, as they were called, and located almost always on the fringes of cities – where urban Africans were compelled to live.

The Defiance Campaign did little to deflect the Nationalists from demonstrating just how they would advance the interests of whites over blacks.

In 1954, the Native Resettlement Act cleared the way for the destruction of a Johannesburg suburb the government could not tolerate. Sophiatown, initially developed by a land speculator as a white suburb in the last years of the 1800s, had, by the 1950s, become an oddity in South Africa, a city enclave where blacks owned property and, for many of them, lived life to the full.

Once called the 'Chicago of South Africa', Sophiatown was – rather like District Six in Cape Town – run-down and seedy and poor in part, but lively and cosmopolitan, a bohemian district that attracted and inspired writers and poets, musicians, entertainers, journalists and politicians.

At Sophiatown's Odin Cinema, or at shebeens such as 'Aunt Babe's', 'The House on Telegraph Hill' or 'The Back of the Moon', homegrown talents forged the infectious rhythms and melodies of indigenous jazz and dance that had all the glamour and zest of American popular culture but with a distinctive African character.

The kwela and mbaqanga sounds, and the energetic tsaba-tsaba dance, expressed the vibrant, liberating quality of Sophiatown.

Yet, from February 1955, on the pretext of slum clearance, the forced removals began. There were spirited protests – and spirited protesters such as

'Valid housing for the urban Bantu' was the bleak conceptual framework within which post-Second World War planners designed the sprawling townships built under apartheid.

Jane Dakile recalls the moment, at 5.30 am on Thursday, 10 November, 1958, when officials came to force her family out:

Before we had even opened the door, I just heard the hammer on the pillar of the verandah ... a big sound that made me wonder if I was dying. That sound went right into my heart and I shall never forget it. ... We had to take everything and throw it outside. Imagine taking your washing just as it is, a chair just as it is. ... I felt such pity for my husband ... because he had built that house with his ... bare hands. That house was our one and only little kingdom. We had our freedom there in Sophiatown and that day I felt we were losing our rights ... my friends in the yard and that old spirit of the people I lived with.

From *Reader's Digest Illustrated History of South Africa* (1994)

And still I wander among the ruins trying to find one or two of the shebeens that Dr Verwoerd has overlooked. But I do not like the dead-eyes with which some of these ghost houses stare back at me.

From *The Will to Die* (1972) by Can Themba

Meadowlands was a significant step in the 'grand apartheid' plan to fortify the segregated city. A large strip of land now separated the 'white city' from the black locations. But if apartheid's social engineers thought they would crush the vitality and creative resourcefulness of black culture by removing Sophiatown's black residents to Meadowlands, they were mistaken. ... Over the years [the neighbourhoods] bonded to form well-knit, supportive communities. Burial societies, cooperative savings clubs – known as 'stokvels' – women's charity groups, choirs and dance, theatre and music clubs all flourished throughout the apartheid years. The members of the Soweto String Quartet, to name just one well-known group, were born and bred in Meadowlands.

From *The world that made Mandela, A Heritage Trail, 70 sites of significance* (2000) by Luli Callinicos

former nurse Maggie Resha, who later rose to prominence in the exiled ANC.

But more than 60 000 people were eventually moved to Meadowlands in the emerging complex of Soweto. Later the bulldozers would come in and flatten the place. Soon, the government would build a new suburb for whites on the rubble, and provocatively name it Triomf (triumph).

In time, as more venues were denied to them, many of the leading performers – the giants of South African music – left the country to pursue their careers abroad. Among them were Miriam Makeba, Hugh Masekela, Dollar Brand (Abdullah Ibrahim) and Letta Mbulu.

Meanwhile, Sophiatown became a symbol of waste and loss.

Syncopation city: For three decades from the 1930s, the West Rand suburb of Sophiatown was the heart and soul of a vibrant, innovative urban African culture, the birthplace of new sounds, new rhythms, new dance steps; the home of poets and writers and gangsters; a poor, sometimes dangerous, but always exciting community whose spiritedness, in the 1950s, was jarringly out of sync with apartheid. The Nationalists were determined to change the tune for good. They razed Sophiatown and gloatingly called it Triomf.

ABOVE: Home-grown sounds, such as kwela, suffused Sophiatown life, drawing the best musicians into the making of unique blends of American and African music. It was infectious fun, while it lasted.

BELOW: It was a poor town, but it was home to people who had no desire to live anywhere else. Eventually, their desires didn't count: the trucks came, their belongings were loaded up, and they were made to live a new life that had the outward look of uniform oppression.

Anglican priest Trevor Huddleston was an unusual white person in the 1950s. He lived with blacks, in Sophiatown. It gave him a view of life in the South Africa of the time that few other white people had, and that few chose to have. It made him a fierce and lifelong opponent of white nationalism.

I do not weep for the destruction of the material which was Sophiatown. At least two thirds of it would have had to be destroyed in any scheme for the renewing of that area which we always dreamed might come to pass. I do not weep, either, simply because what I have known and greatly loved is no more. Nor do I condemn Meadowlands as a place to live. It has a pretty name. It is a pleasant site. And if you are used to locations, I suppose it bears comparison with any other. At least it is just as dull. But I weep because the Western Area Removal Scheme, and the uprooting of sixty thousand people, is being carried out with the connivance of the Christian conscience of Johannesburg. I weep because in spite of all we have tried to do, we have failed so utterly to uphold principle against prejudice, the rights of persons against the claims of power.

From *Naught for Your Comfort* (1956) by Trevor Huddleston

'We will not move ...' the people said, but the authorities were always implacable.

Black political activity in the 1950s became more sharply focused on upholding principle against prejudice, and asserting the rights of the people against the claims of power.

This was dramatically illustrated by the 1956 pass protest march on the Union Buildings in Pretoria by 20 000 women, organised jointly by the ANC Women's league and the Federation of South African Women, and led by former unionist Masedibe Lilian Ngoyi. 'We are women from every party of South Africa,' they said in their petition to the Prime Minister.

We are women of every race, we come from the cities and towns, from the reserves and the villages. We come as women united in our purpose to save African women from the degradation of passes.

It was clear that the victims of apartheid were not waiting helplessly and impassively for a saviour.

At an athletics track near Soweto, thousands of black, coloured, Indian and white people from all parts of the country came together on 26 June, 1955, to decide what their future would be. It would, first and foremost, be a future of freedom.

This was the Congress of the People at Kliptown. And the document the people endorsed there was the Freedom Charter. This would, broadly, be the road map for the long years of struggle ahead, and form the core of the new Constitution of a democratic South Africa in 1996.

The idea of a people's vision for the future was first suggested by Fort Hare academic and influential

Outspoken priest Trevor Huddleston was synonymous with Sophiatown. He remained devoted to the struggle for justice and democracy in South Africa for the rest of his life.

Freedom, the Federation of South African Women asserted, was no abstract notion, but meant 'homes, food, jobs ... and real education for all'. Stressing these demands at a meeting in the 1950s is Lilian Ngoyi (standing).

ANC thinker ZK Matthews in 1953, and for two years scores of volunteers fanned out through the country to ask people in villages and townships, in factories and farms, at sports clubs and churches, what it was they wanted for their future. The culmination of this process was the assembly of 2 884 delegates representing the ANC, the South African Congress of Trade Unions, the South African Indian Congress, the South African Congress of Democrats and the South African Coloured People's Organisation, at Kliptown in June 1955.

Placards carried by some of the audience of about 7 000 people expressed the people's desires: Votes for all; Down with Bantu Education; We want better houses; Equal work for equal pay; Down with passes; Freedom of speech; Freedom for All.

The Charter asserted rights to equality without distinction of colour, race, sex or belief within a democratic state based on a universal franchise.

The opening lines of the preamble to the Charter, drafted primarily by Lionel 'Rusty' Bernstein, read:

We, the people of South Africa, declare for all our country and the world to know ... [t]hat South Africa belongs to all who live in it, black and white, and that no government can justly claim authority unless it is based on the will of the people.

Mandela, who was banned at the time, attended secretly, watching proceedings from behind the fence of a neighbouring house.

The police were watching, too, and eventually could tolerate this freedom business no more: wielding Sten guns, they waded into the crowds and began taking down names and confiscating documents.

The first people's parliament began to break up, but it had done its work.

For years to come, it gave to the struggle against apartheid the resounding slogan: The People Shall Govern.

Luthuli said of the congress that 'nothing in the history of the liberatory movement of South Africa quite caught the popular imagination as this did, not even the Defiance Campaign. Even remote rural areas were aware of the significance of what was going on.'

The formation of the South African Congress of Trade Unions in 1955 as an alliance partner to the ANC further emphasised the movement's shift to mass participation.

❖

Delegates from around the country brought their demands to the Congress of the People at Kliptown in 1955. This historic gathering endorsed the Freedom Charter that remained the guiding document of the struggle for more than 35 years.

The show of unity and purpose at Kliptown inflamed the Nationalists, who had been painstakingly assembling a case which they hoped would shatter it.

The government's lawyers were convinced the Congress of the People provided them with more than sufficient evidence of a plot to overthrow the government.

So, at dawn on 5 December, 1956, police swooped on more than 100 households around the country, arresting what *Drum* magazine journalist Anthony Sampson described as 'South Africa's real opposition'.

In all, 156 people were arrested and charged. It was the beginning of one of the longest and most futile of political trials in South Africa. Among the accused were Albert Luthuli, ZK Matthews, Nelson Mandela, Walter Sisulu, Oliver Tambo, Helen Joseph, Communists Ruth First and her husband Joe Slovo, and Ahmed Kathrada. There were 105 blacks, 23 whites, 21 Indians and seven coloureds.

A Treason Trial Defence Fund was established in South Africa and in London. It was the forerunner of the Defence and Aid Fund which, for the next three

decades, would play a key role in assisting the struggle against apartheid.

By the time the trial ended in 1961, charges had been dropped against all but 30 of the 156. And the judges found that even against these individuals the state had failed to prove its case. All were acquitted.

Mandela, who commended the three trial judges as individuals who stood by the rule of law, recalls:

After more than four years in court and dozens of prosecutors, thousands of documents and tens of thousands of pages of testimony, the state had failed in its mission. The verdict was an embarrassment to the government, both at home and abroad. Yet the result only made the state more bitter towards us. The lesson they took away was not that we had legitimate grievances, but that they needed to be far more ruthless.

From *Long Walk to Freedom* (1994) by Nelson Mandela

Verwoerd, who became prime minister in 1958 on the death of JG Strijdom, remained as committed as ever to his vision of 'grand apartheid'. In a lengthy, complex speech to parliament in 1959 he set out his elaborate vision of independent black states in the reserve territories which would leave the bulk of South Africa to whites and justify the exclusion of blacks from national life. 'Like Italians working as miners outside Italy,' Verwoerd once reasoned, '[blacks] will have no political rights outside the homelands; their position will be that of honoured guests.'

There might, for the Nationalists, have been a glimmer of hope in 1959 that their opposition was breaking up a little when 300 members of the ANC broke away under Robert Sobukwe to form the Pan Africanist Congress (PAC).

From as early as the Congress of the People in 1955, Africanists were unhappy with the ANC going along with the idea that South Africa belonged to all, white and black, since this failed to take stock of centuries of colonial dispossession by whites. They were also opposed to joining forces with whites, coloureds and Indians, and the alliance with communists. Differences came to a head in November 1958 at a meeting in Orlando, where the Africanists were ejected. In April the next year the PAC was formed. It believed in the primacy of African interests rather than multi-racial equality.

Opposition was being felt abroad, too. In London, Freedom Day – 26 June – marked the launch of the Anti-Apartheid Movement. At home, both the PAC and the ANC announced plans for a new round of protests, this time against the pass system.

❖

The year 1960 was a turning point. It started inauspiciously for Verwoerd when British prime minister Harold Macmillan visited the country and warned the Nationalists that an irresistible 'wind of change' was blowing through Africa.

The gathering shift to independence in Africa had begun three years before, in Ghana, and would continue through the 1960s as former colonies gained self-rule. Against this background, South Africa was the glaring exception.

In the month after Macmillan's cautionary speech, Verwoerd's police earned South Africa shocking headlines for an event that radically altered the

TOP: In all, 156 people were charged in the Treason Trial, but it was a four-year fiasco for the government: the state had no case.

ABOVE: Robert Sobukwe, who formed the Pan Africanist Congress in 1959.

Britain – now fast loosening its colonial grip on Africa – did not see eye to eye with what South Africa was up to, as Macmillan told a joint sitting of the Senate and House of Assembly:

> ... [I]t is our earnest desire to give South Africa our support and encouragement, but I hope you won't mind my saying frankly that there are some aspects of your policies which make it impossible for us to do this without being false to our own deep convictions ... We ought, as friends, to face together, without seeking to apportion credit or blame, the fact that ... this difference of outlook lies between us.
>
> From *Apartheid, A History* (1986) by Brian Lapping

But Verwoerd was stubbornly unmoved, as Macmillan discovered. He recalled a meeting with the South African prime minister at this time:

> *I had long discussions with Dr Verwoerd ... and it was only during these days that I began to realise to the full extent the degree of obstinacy, amounting really to fanaticism, which he brought to the consideration of his policies. Even in small matters he had pressed apartheid to its extreme. In a country where there is at least the advantage of being able to enlist African staff, he refused to have a single African in his house. An old and rather incompetent Dutch butler looked after us. The Prime Minister, with his quiet voice, would expound his views without any gesture or emotion. At first I mistook this calm and measured tone for a willingness to enter into sincere discussion. However, I had the unusual experience of soon noticing that nothing one could say could have the smallest effect upon this determined man.*
>
> From *Apartheid, A History* (1986) by Brian Lapping

nature of the country's political battle.

The ANC had decided to hold an anti-pass protest on the last day of March in 1960. A week later, the PAC held its first conference and decided to launch its own anti-pass campaign, but 10 days before the ANC's protest.

Heeding the call, about 5 000 protesters gathered on 21 March at the police station at Sharpeville, the new township at Vereeniging, intent on having themselves arrested. Their motto was 'No bail, no defence, no fine'.

The government ordered Sabre jets to fly low over the crowds at Sharpeville and other police stations. In some places, the protesters took fright and fled. But not at Sharpeville.

The bewildered police brought in reinforcements. Then, in the early afternoon, as the crowd still waited determinedly at the perimeter fence, a scuffle near one of the gates caused the mass of people to surge forward out of curiosity. Without warning, the police opened fire. When the firing stopped, 69 people lay dead, and more than 200 were injured. Most of the victims were shot in the back.

The reaction, nationally and internationally, was immediate. Violence flared at Langa in Cape Town. As conditions deteriorated, Verwoerd reacted harshly: at the end of March he declared a state of emergency. Under its regulations, no fewer than 18 000 people were detained. And he hastily passed laws to ban the ANC and the PAC.

———— ❖ ————

Some whites, including influential Afrikaner intellectuals, began to wonder if the time had not come for a change of approach, a softening of apartheid, but Verwoerd put paid to the idea. 'The government,' he said, 'sees no reason to depart from the policy of separate development.'

And to further underline his confidence, he went ahead with plans at the end of 1960 to ask white voters in a referendum whether the Union should become a republic: 52 percent voted Yes. In May the next year, after telling an increasingly critical Commonwealth that South Africa was pulling out of the family of former British colonies, the country became a republic.

Was all of white society indifferent, and uninterested in trying to uphold principle over prejudice?

A flaring of white resistance earlier in the 1950s focused on the disenfranchisement of coloured voters in the Cape.

The War Veterans' Torch Commando, drawing

Sixty-nine people were shot dead at Sharpeville in March 1960, a massacre that decisively altered relations between the government and its black opponents.

mainly on Smuts's United Party supporters, took to the streets with massed torchlight rallies in Cape Town, Johannesburg and Port Elizabeth to protest against the threat to the Constitution posed by the Nationalists' tactics. It was led by a Second World War fighter pilot, Group Captain Adolf 'Sailor' Malan. At its height in 1952, the campaign was supported by some 250 000 ex-servicemen. But it was weakened by failing to take a clear position on African rights and declining to allow coloured ex-servicemen to join its ranks.

The Black Sash, a white women's group formed in the 1950s at the time of the constitutional protests, later switched its attention to passes, influx control and forced removals. It remained a dogged opponent of the Nationalists. Nelson Mandela called the Black Sash 'the conscience of white South Africa'.

The Liberal Party, opposed to apartheid and communism and in favour of a non-racial franchise, was formed in 1953 – a leading member was the writer Alan Paton – but never won a seat in parliament, and disbanded in 1968 when the government passed the Prohibition of Political Interference Act, which prohibited multi-racial parties. Its members did more than most South Africans to develop genuine bonds across the racial divide.

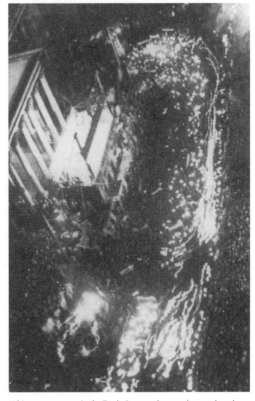

White war veterans in the Torch Commando staged massed torchlight rallies to protest against the government's determination to strip coloureds in the Cape of the vote.

Redoubtable Helen Suzman, the admired and effective Progressive Party MP in parliament. For her first 13 years she was the lone Progressive.

Suzman. She was successful in spotlighting government excesses and abuses of human rights, but her solitary presence illustrated the complacency of most whites. The Progressives, later the Progressive Federal Party, became the Official Opposition in parliament in 1977.

There was, almost certainly, a false sense of security across white society.

Apartheid did not seriously disrupt the economy, and white living standards increased steadily. White workers benefited from job reservation, foreign investment attracted by cheap labour boosted the prosperity of the largely English-speaking business class, and gold production expanded markedly. South Africa thrived on the global capitalist boom of the 1960s.

White people lived well in secure, pretty suburbs. Seaside holidays and vacations away from home became popular and commonplace. The birth rate dropped as the white population became more urban and wealthier. Car ownership almost doubled every decade between 1940 and 1960. An Americanised consumer culture took root. Historian William Beinart notes that cars and consumer spending reshaped South African shopping, and that the new consumerism brought with it new cultural influences.

The United Party remained an ineffectual opposition under Sir De Villiers Graaff until its disbandment in 1977, and the breakaway Progressive Party – formed by 12 liberal UP MPs in 1959 – was a small, if significant, voice. It stood for a qualified non-racial franchise.

For 13 years – from 1962 to 1974 – its sole MP was the admirably effective and outspoken Helen

These things are satirically but tellingly illustrated - as Beinart points out - in the hit song 'Ag pleez Deddy' by Jeremy Taylor from the 1960s show *Wait a Minim*. The following are the last two verses, and the chorus:

Ag pleez Deddy won't you take us off to Durban
It's only eight hours in the Chevrolet
There's spans of sea and sand and sun and fishes in the aquarium
That's a lekker place for a holiday.

Ag sies Deddy if we can't go off to bioscope
Or go off to Durban life's a hang of a bore,
If you won't take us to the zoo then what the heck else can we do
But go on out and moera all the outjies next door.

Popcorn chewing gum peanuts and bubble gum
Icecream candyfloss and eskimo-pie
Ag Deddy how we miss acid-drops and liquoris
Pepsicola gingerbeer and Canada-dry.

From *The Magic Tree: South African stories in verse* (1989) by Guy Butler and Jeff Opland (editors)

When, in 1962, historian Leo Marquard revised his book *The Peoples & Policies of South Africa* – first published 10 years before, in 1952 – he was able to look back on and assess a decisive decade. He decided that

> Most South Africans have so far evaded the real issue, either by advocating a total territorial separation which is not practicable, or by dreaming of an equally impracticable perpetual trusteeship of Europeans over Africans. Both policies are born of the false hope of being able to retain absolute political control, and neither has any real value except to catch European votes.
>
> To the African, the Coloured, and the Asian alike, both policies are totally unacceptable on a long-term view.
>
> Since neither these nor the Europeans have any other homeland, there is only one alternative to an increasing antagonism – that is co-operation.
>
> When the Europeans in South Africa can at last bring themselves to realise this, they will be on the way to solving their major problem. ... Until South Africa has seen her own problem clearly and has begun to ask the right question, her policies will be rejected by the world and by Africa; and, within her own borders, white authority will extend only as far as physical force can operate.

From *The Peoples & Policies of South Africa* (1962) by Leo Marquard

Indeed, while most white people were enjoying life, politically, they were becoming increasingly isolated from the outside world, and from the lives of Africans. Historian Beinart writes:

> Most whites were unable to see black South Africans during this critical period in the country's history. Homelands, passes, group areas, social amnesia, and powerful ideologies put them out of sight, literally and metaphorically. Whites believed they knew 'their' Africans, and this justified their system against attacks from ignorant outsiders. Many of them came across Africans only as servants and workers.

From *Twentieth-Century South Africa* (2001) by William Beinart

In January 1962, in the first of her solo 13 years in parliament, Helen Suzman described the rarity of confident realism:

> I am ... the only person in this House apparently who belongs to a party that does not have to indulge in swart gevaar [black menace] tactics ....
> It seems to me that my party is the only party in this country [apart from the unrepresented Liberal Party] which does not shake with fear at the implications of accepting South Africa as what it is, and that ... is a multi-racial country.

From *Helen Suzman's Solo Years* (1991) by Phyllis Lewsen (editor)

However, novelist Barbara Trapido – who left South Africa in 1963 but 'returned' to her homeland in her sixties in an autobiographical fiction, *Frankie and Stankie*, in 2003 – suggested in an interview that the accident of birth had much to do with how whites grew up, and lived, under apartheid:

> It's most curious to me how people from abroad assume that if they had grown up in [South Africa under apartheid] they would have been war heroes. I don't think we did accept things, but not because I was ... more intellectually or morally superior through the accident of growing up with parents who didn't share the local racial views. What I was trying to put across [in *Frankie and Stankie*] was that people just get on with their ordinary little lives, and often that's ignored in literature about places that are living through hard times. People carry on living, having fun with their friends, getting married, going to birthday parties, buying new shoes, and the victims of oppression do it as well.

From *The Guardian* May 2003, in an interview with Libby Brooks

———— ❖ ————

Certainly, what most white people failed to recognise – ironically, given the history of Afrikaner resistance to what was perceived as British oppression half-a-century earlier – was that banning the liberation movements simply pushed them underground and made them more radical.

A key figure in this would be Nelson Mandela.

Justice Minister John Vorster, detained without trial as an internee during the Second World War, had no qualms about using detention against black opponents.

mission – Mandela and others began to formulate plans for armed resistance.

Just a week after Albert Luthuli's return from being awarded the Nobel Peace Prize in Oslo in December 1961, the ANC's newly formed armed wing, Umkhonto we'Sizwe, made its presence felt in the first of a series of bomb blasts in a campaign that continued for 18 months.

> A leaflet announcing the formation of Umkhonto we'Sizwe:
>
> *The time comes in the life of any nation when there remain only two choices: submit or fight. That time has now come to South Africa. We shall not submit and we have no choice but to hit back by all means within our power in defence of our people, our future and our freedom …*

The express objective initially was sabotage, and strict instructions were given to operatives to avoid killing or injuring people.

To the Nationalists, bombs were bombs and, under newly appointed justice minister, Balthazar John Vorster, a former *Ossewa Brandwag* tough man, police tactics became more brutal. Mandela noted that there was no evidence during the Treason Trial of torture by police to extract information. That changed after 1960. And, after the humiliation of the failure of the Treason Trial, police had built up a huge network of paid informers.

Their big prize was the 'black pimpernel', Nelson Mandela, who had elected to become an 'outlaw in my own land'. In 1962, he travelled outside the country, visiting various African states – and receiving some military training in Algeria – and London to raise support for the ANC's new armed wing, and to explain the liberation movement's shift in strategy.

Shortly after his return, he was driving to Natal to brief Luthuli when, after a tip-off from an informer, police stopped his car near Howick in Natal and arrested him. He had been on the run for more than a year.

Charged with inciting people to strike and with leaving the country without a passport, he was found guilty and sentenced to five years in prison. It was the heaviest sentence yet imposed for a political offence.

After his acquittal in the Treason Trial, he went underground before the authorities could detain him. His partner in Johannesburg's first black law firm, Oliver Tambo, said of him later:

> *Of all that group of young men, Mandela and his close friend and co-leader Walter Sisulu were perhaps the fastest to get to grips with the harsh realities of the African struggle against the most powerful adversary in Africa.*

In June 1961, Mandela issued a statement while on the run that defined the way of the future:

I have chosen this course … to live as an outlaw in my own land … I shall fight the government side by side with you, inch by inch and mile by mile, until victory is won … Only through hardship, sacrifice and militant action can freedom be won. The struggle is my life. I will continue fighting for freedom until the end of my days.

From *The world that made Mandela, A Heritage Trail, 70 sites of significance* (2000) by Luli Callinicos

As the ANC and the PAC moved to establish themselves in exile – Oliver Tambo, sent abroad shortly before the banning, led the ANC's international

Nelson Mandela and Walter Sisulu engaged in discussion as prisoners on Robben Island.

While he was in prison, Vorster's forces scored the coup of the decade. On 11 July, 1963, they swooped on a rural retreat in Rivonia outside Johannesburg called Lilliesleaf Farm. It was the underground headquarters of the ANC, and the arrests of people such as Walter Sisulu, Andrew Mlangeni, new Umkhonto we'Sizwe commander Wilton Mkwayi, Ahmed Kathrada, Govan Mbeki, Dennis Goldberg and Rusty Bernstein were spectacular. Mandela joined them as Accused Number One.

At the time, scores of key ANC and Communist Party people managed to get out of the country and, in the years to come, help to sustain the struggle from abroad.

The Rivonia Trial sharpened the world's criticism of South Africa, but the government was smug about having nabbed what it regarded as its most dangerous opponents.

Though Mandela and the other accused had prepared themselves for the death penalty, the trial ended on 12 June, 1964, with their being sentenced to life imprisonment.

Probably the most famous political statement in 20th-century South African history was uttered near the end of the Rivonia Trial by Mandela. It came at the end of his five-hour statement, which he read from the dock. The final passage, which he and his legal team had agonised over, he knew off by heart. He raised his eyes to Judge Quartus de Wet and said:

During my lifetime I have dedicated my life to this struggle of the African people. I have fought against white domination, I have fought against black domination. I have cherished the ideal of a democratic and free society in which all persons live together in harmony and with equal opportunities. It is an ideal which I hope to live for, and to see realised. But, My Lord, if needs be, it is an ideal for which I am prepared to die.

RAND
Daily Mail

AND GET YOUR SHARE TRULY EXCEPTIONAL BARGAINS OUR JULY SALE

JOHANNESBURG, SATURDAY, JULY 13, 1963. Price 3 cents.

Security swoop on Rand sparks huge investigation

UBVERSION: END NEAF

rests give ow clues— lice chief

PRETORIA REPORTER

...est of six Whites and 12 non-
...s, including the former secretary
...anned African National Congress,
...usulu, in Johannesburg yesterday,
...jor breakthrough in the elimina-
...subversive organisations. General
...Commissioner of Police said in
...last night.

...It one following big raids that will
...been held by the end of next Decem-
...year... He said that many of
...yesterday were the outcropping
...investigations during the past

...confirmed what we suspected all the time.
...would not have been able to get away,
...General Keevy said.

TALL POLE'S
THREE-MAN POLICE GUARD AT GATE
SIX POLICEMEN AND POLICE CARS
POLICEMAN
GARAGE

Dramatic news greeted readers on the morning of Saturday, 13 July, 1963: 'Security swoop on Rand sparks huge investigation.' Lilliesleaf Farm in Rivonia was the clandestine headquarters of the ANC's underground operation, and the target of the devastating police raid. But the authorities were misguided if they thought 'subversion' was really at an end.

It was not death but a long imprisonment that awaited him.

'There I had time just to sit for hours and think,' Mandela remembered of his days on Robben Island. And it was an immensely thoughtful, remarkably unembittered and towering international figure who eventually emerged from apartheid's prison cells 27 years later.

But the 'long, lonely wasted years' for prisoner 466/64 and the scores of others held there were difficult to bear. They were years of hard labour, abuse, psychological deprivation, fear, longing. Yet they were also years of fortitude, courage, unfailing conviction. The dream of realising their ideal never faded.

The Rivonia trialists were flown to the island from Pretoria, leaving under cover of darkness in a Dakota. It was well into the morning by the time the plane began its descent over the Cape Peninsula. 'Soon, we could see the little matchbox houses of the Cape Flats,' Mandela recalls, 'the gleaming towers of downtown … and out in Table Bay, in the dark blue waters of the Atlantic, we could make out the misty outline of Robben Island.'

PAGE **182**

The ANC leader later acknowledged that in the Sixties the movement had had false hopes that, especially with the tide of independence sweeping through Africa, South Africa would be a non-racial democracy by the 1970s. It was not to be. Still, the Nationalists' Alcatraz, which the government confidently believed would break the spirit and the organisational capacity of the struggle against apartheid, served only to strengthen the resolve and commitment of the prisoners and provide an international beacon for a steadily growing campaign against what came to be called the 'Pretoria regime'.

Esteemed advocate and leading Communist Bram Fischer, in disguise, moments after being arrested. The man on the left is a policeman.

❖

In 1963, the United Nations called for a voluntary embargo on arms sales to South Africa. The international community's position stiffened a year later when the UN recommended that complete economic sanctions were the only feasible means of ending apartheid.

In the same year, South Africa was excluded from the Tokyo Olympics for refusing to allow mixed-race teams. Sanctions and sports boycotts would intensify.

At home, despite an economic dip immediately after Sharpeville, the 1960s was a decade of unprecedented prosperity. Though this benefited whites mostly, black unemployment also remained relatively low.

Verwoerd got his grand scheme of black independent states off the ground with the Transkei Self-Government Act, which in 1963 made the Transkei semi-autonomous under former minor chief Kaizer Matanzima.

At the same time, repression was intensive. The banning of the liberation movements, the imprisoning of many of its key leaders, and the flight into exile of others significantly reduced visible resistance to apartheid.

A shock to many Afrikaners came early in 1966 when Bram Fischer, Queen's Counsel, president of the Johannesburg Bar and son of the former attorney-general of the Free State, was revealed to have been a leading Communist for years and a staunch supporter of the 'revolutionary' idea of a democratic South Africa.

Fischer had once earned glowing attention from Ouma Steyn, wife of the former Free State president Marthinus Steyn. 'I know,' she said in a message to him when he turned 21, 'that Bram Fischer is going to play an honourable role in the history of South Africa.' Now he was rejected as a traitor.

He was also Mandela's advocate in the Rivonia Trial. When his turn came, having been arrested as a

HF Verwoerd was a commanding presence in the National Party, and the principal thinker behind the idea of 'grand apartheid'.

fugitive, Fischer mounted his own eloquent defence. On 9 May, 1966, he was sentenced to life imprisonment. He died a prisoner on 8 May, 1975.

In a powerful and prophetic statement, Fischer told the court:

> If today there is an appearance of calm, it is a false appearance induced entirely by … oppression. The police state does not create calm or induce any genuine acceptance of a hated policy. All it can achieve is a short-term period of quiet and long-term hatred.

Nelson Mandela later said of Fischer:

> As an Afrikaner whose conscience forced him to reject his own heritage and be ostracised by his own people, he showed a level of courage and sacrifice that was in a class by itself. I fought only against injustice, not my own people.

If Nationalists were shocked by the 'treason' of Bram Fischer, another horrifying shock was to follow later in the year.

———— ❖ ————

The bells were still ringing in parliament early on the afternoon of 6 September, 1966, summoning MPs to their benches, when a man only recently employed as a messenger made his way into the House of Assembly and approached the prime minister. Hendrik Verwoerd had just taken his seat.

'I could not make out what the man was up to,' one eyewitness, a Hansard reporter, Johann Theron, recalled. But it soon became perfectly clear.

> He bent over Dr Verwoerd and raised his right hand high in the air … grasping a sheath knife. With his left hand he plucked off the sheath and plunged the knife downwards. Dr Verwoerd fell back in his seat and remained sitting upright for a moment or two before slumping forward over the bench.

Demitrios Tsafendas plunged his knife three more times into the mortally wounded prime minister's body before being dragged to the floor and disarmed by enraged MPs. The country was shocked. The heart of apartheid power had been invaded.

The grave fear among Nationalists was that Verwoerd had died at the hands of a politically inspired assassin, that his death had been plotted. Tsafendas, born half-Greek, half-African, in colonial Mozambique, did indeed harbour deep political resentment at the policies pursued with such cold logic by Verwoerd, but there was also no doubt that he was mentally disturbed. He claimed that a worm in his stomach had made him do it.

But the death of Verwoerd did little to change the Verwoerdian concept of an apartheid state maintained by force if necessary. By 1966, Macmillan's wind of change was barely a breeze in the streets and towns of white South Africa.

It was clear the country was not going to be easily divided in two, with a secure and prosperous white minority in one privileged social and political category served by a docile, self-governing black majority, forever content to be hewers of wood and drawers of water, in another.

Yet repression kept the illusion alive.

Whites did not feel the need seriously to rethink their future. They believed, if anything, that there was no reason for alarm. The prime minister's murderer was, after all, just a madman acting on an impulse of lunacy. There was a worm in his stomach. And, after all, the leaders of the attempted black/Communist 'revolution' were behind bars.

Yet, just how clearly Verwoerd's brutal experiment was creating the conditions for escalating conflict would be demonstrated in the next 20 years.

———— ❖ ————

A little more than a year after taking office as president of a democratic South Africa, Nelson Mandela set off on a curious excursion to visit a 94-year-old woman living in a small, drab dorp more or less in the middle of the country. Some felt the trip was foolhardy, but, typically, Madiba showed he had no difficulty making up his own mind about that. So it was, in August 1995, that the President trekked to Orania to have tea with Betsie Verwoerd, widow of the architect of 'grand apartheid' and the man

Furthering reconciliation between the races, and particularly between blacks and Afrikaners, was Nelson Mandela's main reason for visiting the whites-only enclave of Orania to have tea with HF Verwoerd's ageing widow, Betsie, in 1995.

whose government had jailed him and his comrades. Orania was a symbol of everything Mandela had opposed all his life: it was a 'private', whites-only town owned and occupied by right-wing Afrikaners who utterly rejected democracy and the ANC.

His going for tea with Mrs Verwoerd said much about Nelson Mandela's generosity, but also his enthusiasm for reconciliation, for helping the former white oppressors to overcome their fear and embrace a democratic future. Many had been convinced by then, even if Betsie Verwoerd was not one of them.

At that time, Mandela was no stranger to the Verwoerd family. In Stellenbosch in 1991 he had met the assassinated prime minister's grandson, Wilhelm, and his wife Melanie, both philosophers, and both thoughtful Afrikaners who, within a year, had joined the ANC.

It split the family deeply, which Wilhelm regretted. 'But,' he said then,

> *there comes a time when you have to do what you believe is right. I hope they come to understand that this is not a betrayal – I am just trying to help to find a way for us to live together in this society.*

It was on the strength of this way of thinking that the name Verwoerd appeared once more in the records of parliament. At 27, Melanie Verwoerd became the youngest woman ever to become an MP when she took her place on the ANC benches after the 1994 election.

Later appointed South Africa's ambassador to Dublin, she urged Afrikaners in the first year of democracy to engage in the new society: 'Instead of being a threatened minority we must see ourselves as part of an exciting majority.'

The history of the Verwoerds – much like that of the Fischers – reflects, perhaps, an important lesson about South Africa: to lump all Afrikaners into a single negative racist stereotype was and is as good as lumping all blacks into a single negative racial stereotype. It also possibly reflects the often overlooked idea that what had pitted black South Africans and Afrikaner nationalists against each other for so long was that they shared a passionate sense of belonging in Africa.

From the late Sixties, this common, almost earthy, commitment would cost many more lives before proving itself to be the solid foundation of a settlement first imagined by the 'people's parliament' that met at a dusty athletics track in Kliptown in the winter of 1955.

Armed and dangerous

Armed and dangerous

It is the same for everybody. Blood is blood. So it was, poet Sipho Sepamla reasoned in his verse, 'Da Same, Da Same', in the 1970s:

sometime you wanna know how I meaning for
is simples
when da nail of da t'orn tree
scratch little bit little bit of da skin
I doesn't care of say black
I doesn't care of say white
I doesn't care of say India
I doesn't care of say kleeling
I mean for sure da skin
only one t'ing come for sure
and da one t'ing for sure is red blood
dats for sure da same, da same
for avarybudy.

From *A World of Their Own, Southern African Poets of the Seventies* (1976) by Stephen Gray (editor)

———— ❖ ————

It is difficult to imagine the anguish of Mannie Kaufman, who lost his son Robert to internal bleeding after a road accident in August 1973. Robert might have been saved had the right ambulance been sent to take him to hospital. 'Rightness', here, was a matter of law.

Mr Kaufman explained to the *Sunday Times* that the chief ambulance officer had told him that 'someone had telephoned the department to say that "two boys" had been injured in an accident. They assumed from the reference to "boys" that the caller meant Africans, not youths, so an African ambulance was despatched. It was only later that the department was informed that the "boys" were white.' At the accident scene, a traffic officer had refused to allow the 'black' ambulance crew to treat Robert Kaufman. That's what the regulations said. Only later was the boy taken to hospital in a 'white' ambulance, and there he died of internal bleeding.

This sad and absurd incident is described in a book compiled in 1990 under the easily misjudged title, *Apartheid, The Lighter Side*, by journalist Ben Maclennan. Some of the milder lunacy of apartheid is funny in a comically ridiculous way. But

Maclennan's title for this anthology of statements in parliament, in the press, in public speeches and, though it's hard to believe, in academic papers, was deliberately ironic. It reflects, really, a madness made ordinary by a thoughtlessly brutal system.

In a brief foreword, playwright Athol Fugard wonders if there 'has … ever been a society where the dominant political philosophy, aided and abetted by the dominant Christian theology, has led seemingly rational men and women into [such] mind-boggling and logic-defying lunacies' as those catalogued in the book. And, he adds, 'what makes it even more astounding is the all-pervasive nature of this madness'.

By the time Hendrik Verwoerd was stabbed to death in parliament in 1966, the idea that all people were fundamentally the same was so deeply contradicted at every level of public life that it was possible – as the Kaufman family found – even for the intended beneficiaries of race privilege to suffer the ultimate consequences of its idiocy.

It is from Maclennan's anthology that we learn that even bird-watching had to be segregated: Senator Jan de Klerk (father of FW de Klerk, who later unbanned the ANC and released Nelson Mandela from prison) was minister of education, arts and science when he wrote to the South African Bird Watchers Society in May 1964 to remind it to confirm officially that it had barred membership to people who were not white.

Maclennan also reminds us that there was more to the drama of South Africa's first heart transplant in 1967 than was known at the time.

International acclaim was heaped on the young surgeon Chris Barnard – and, by extension, South Africa's medical expertise – when he became the first doctor in the world successfully to perform a heart transplant on 3 December, 1967. The heart of a 25-year-old woman who was killed in an accident was implanted into middle-aged Louis Washkansky. Though Washkansky died 18 days later, the operation was a celebrated surgical breakthrough.

Yet, in an extraordinary sequel 20 years later, Barnard revealed in 1987 that his famous operation could have been conducted two weeks earlier when the first donor had become available. But the first potential donor was black.

Barnard insisted patients of all races were treated equally in his heart unit at Groote Schuur Hospital, but because of the risk that a black donor for the first heart operation 'might be misinterpreted by the political critics of South Africa ... I agreed that both recipient and donor should be Caucasian'.

If it was controversy that worried the young heart surgeon, there were deeper 'medical' concerns at the time about the mixing of races.

A year after Barnard's breakthrough, no less a person than the Dean of Medicine at the University of Stellenbosch, Professor FD du Toit van Zyl, found it possible to tell a graduation ceremony at the University of the Western Cape of the duty of coloureds in combating 'genetic dangers'. 'I refer,' he explained,

> to the dangers of inter-mixing with genetically bound heredity and cultural characteristics which differ so much from those of your nation that there is a danger of bringing degeneration upon your people. I refer specifically to inter-mixing with the Bantu.

It was a confident and dangerous foolishness that was no better expressed than in the statement Verwoerd made to the newspapers in October 1960. 'I never,' he said, 'have the nagging doubt of wondering whether perhaps I am wrong.'

Millions knew he was wrong, but they were systematically silenced, or remained silent.

In a far-sighted speech to the Indian Ratepayers' Association in Durban in the early 1960s, Communist thinker Jack Simons advised:

> If we are to build a democracy for all, we must begin now to put our principles into practice, and not wait until liberation comes. For if we put off working for unity and achieving it, then liberation will find us disunited and unable to create a free society for all.

Such counter-arguments were intolerable to the Nationalists. Within a few years, Simons, like so many others of similar reasonableness, was forced into exile, where he remained until 1990.

Heart surgeon Chris Barnard describing his first heart transplant operation to the Press. What was not revealed at the time was that race was a determining factor in choosing donor organs.

Liberal opinions were regarded as radical and dangerous, and actively rejected by most of the very people who, then, could have made a difference by peaceful means, at the ballot box: white support for the system that suited them grew.

For many white people, perhaps especially young people growing up in the late 1960s, their way of life seemed unexceptional, familiar, habitual. Their South African reality was as ordinary as life could get. Being white was naturally different from being black and that was just how the world worked.

The purer concept of whiteness was underlined by the shift from the terminology of 'Europeans' and 'Non-Europeans' to that of 'Whites' and 'Non-Whites'. But white consciousness had its sharper, radical opposite in an emerging black consciousness among the steadily growing body of black students.

So, as the barriers were raised at every turn to deny the common humanity of South Africans, resistance to them rose, too. It became an increasingly embattled society, full of fear, full of anger, armed and dangerous.

❖

An airline passenger travelling over Johannesburg's northern suburbs in the late 1960s could not have failed to notice scores of bright blue squares, ovals and rectangles dotting the spacious gardens of the homes hundreds of metres below him. The sight of so many swimming pools moved one observer [South African writer and Oxford academic RW Johnson], to comment: 'At some point around 1970 white South Africans overtook Californians as the single most affluent group in the world.'

However, had the plane swung towards Cape Town, a different sight would have greeted our traveller: south of the city, frequently hidden beneath a blanket of smog from thousands of wood stoves, lay Johannesburg's south-western townships (Soweto); ignored, silent, quiescent, smouldering. In a land of stark contrasts, this must surely have been the starkest of all.

From *Reader's Digest Illustrated History of South Africa* (1994)

Such sharp differences in the lives and lifestyles of South Africans were true of every part of the country. In the Cape, the breaking up of the city into racial blocks under the Group Areas Act produced a starker landscape, too. The lasting symbol of the process was the destruction of District Six from 1966.

Like Sophiatown in Johannesburg in the first half of the 20th century, District Six was Cape Town's distinctively vibrant, bohemian quarter. Much of it was run-down, crime-ridden and unsanitary. But it was lively and colourful, and culturally rich. District

Six, people knew, had a soul. It was occupied mostly by coloured people, and it was on the doorstep of the Mother City. Under the pretext of 'slum clearance', the government moved in, shipped some 60 000 people out to the lifeless, windblown Cape Flats – far from their places of work – and bulldozed everything but for a few mosques and churches. It has remained since a shameful scar on Cape Town's cityscape.

The narrator of Richard Rive's novel 'Buckingham Palace', District Six describes returning to the destroyed suburb:

I walked up to the District clambering over broken bricks and half-flattened foundations of houses once inhabited by people. And the ghosts of the past swirled around me in the growing dusk. I walked along what had been Hanover Street with a few left-over houses standing self-consciously on both sides. They resembled broken teeth with craters in between where the raw gums showed. I turned up into Tennant Street and then walked along what had been Caledon Street. From that corner to St Mark's Church every building and landmark had been flattened: Handler's Drapery Store, Bernstein's Bottle Store; Buckingham Palace, Seven Steps. Only the church on Clifton Hill stood in stony defiance overlooking the destruction. I stood where the entrance to 207 had been, where the house had stood in which I was born and … raised. From there I could look over the desolate landscape to the dazzling lights of Cape Town … the neon signs, the brightly lit shops. In my darkening landscape individual buildings stood out in neglected silhouette … with the desolate winds and ghosts of the past moaning around them.

From 'Buckingham Palace', District Six (1986) by Richard Rive

❖

District Six was, not unlike Sophiatown, a bustling community. It had its seemier side, but it was a vibrant home to people who had grown up in the shadow of Table Mountain. That changed when the government's bulldozers moved in, razing everything but a few churches and mosques.

As far as the prime minister was concerned, some coloured people at least were quite happy with the elaborate business of separate development. It's with what seems now to be almost child-like simplicity that John Vorster recalls in journalist John D'Oliviera's biography of him, *John Vorster – The man* (1977), a 'lovely chat' with coloured stall-holders he had befriended on the Grand Parade in Cape Town. He was already premier when he had gone down to the Parade on his own one day to pay a visit to an old couple he had often had tea with on his visits there. 'I went to the Stokes' stall and we had tea sitting on boxes – those were the only seats. I had a lovely chat to Mr and Mrs Stokes about this and that.' They were joined by a coloured minister who, it turned out, 'wanted to talk to me about separate development and how he saw it'. Vorster was gratified to learn that this man thought it was a good idea, that he was 'proud to go to a post office and talk to a postmaster who was one of his own people', proud to patronise a garage owned by one of his own people, and proud to 'go to a good-class restaurant

run by one of his own people'.

Vorster did not evidently appreciate that in the late Sixties, not least because of his own activities as a brutally efficient Minister of Justice, South Africans – white as much as black – did not feel free to speak their minds about politics.

Whites especially had no wish to upset the status quo since South Africa had every appearance of being a success story: the economic growth rate in the 1960s averaged six percent a year; foreign investment valued at R3 billion in 1963 rose to R7 billion by 1972, with vast sums pouring in from new investors in Europe; imports and exports rose by more than 100%.

English-speaking opponents of the Nationalists were increasingly won over by the economic successes. This was evident in the 1966 election, when the NP gained 21 seats from the Opposition – the biggest gain since 1953 – securing 126 of the 170 seats in the House of Assembly.

But the stark contrasts, the huge disparity in the share of wealth, and the injustice of a privileged

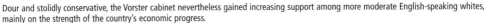

Dour and stolidly conservative, the Vorster cabinet nevertheless gained increasing support among more moderate English-speaking whites, mainly on the strength of the country's economic progress.

minority living off the backs of an exploited majority, could only really be maintained by force in one form or another.

In 1967, the Defence Amendment Act made military service compulsory for all white males. Defence spending rocketed during the 1960s, from US$63 million at the time of Sharpeville to more than US$1 billion by the early Seventies.

Also in 1967, the Terrorism Act was extended, defining terrorism as anything likely to threaten law and order. It conferred unlimited powers of arrest, indefinite detention and trials without jury, and transferred the burden of proof to the accused. Terrorism was equated with treason and so it incurred the death penalty.

Even the government-supporting newspaper, *Die Beeld*, noted that 'the police will now have a free hand to act without legal restraints'.

The Act had only one real opponent in parliament: Helen Suzman.

In a House of Assembly debate in June of the next year, Suzman hit the nail on the head when she said that while

a lot of people pay lip service to this ideal of separate development ... the vast majority ... in fact simply want the maintenance of the status quo. And that is, to put it quite bluntly, the maintenance of vast reservoirs of cheap black labour for the benefit of white employers in this country and the maintenance of white domination. That is all they want.

It was at this time, to Suzman's lasting credit, that improvements began to occur in the lives of a group of people white South Africa did not want to think too much about at all. Suzman's first visit to Robben Island as an MP in 1967 was a turning point for the likes of Mandela, Sisulu and the other Rivonia trialists; and also for increasing numbers of other political prisoners, including Neville Alexander, who was jailed on the island for 10 years in 1964 for his part in an organisation called the National Liberation Front.

In his *Robben Island Dossier* 1964–1974 (1994), Alexander notes that until about 1967 the nature of imprisonment on the island was not just punitive in the sense of prisoners being locked away there, but retributive and often sadistically harsh. Assaults and psychological abuse were common.

It is telling that Suzman was the only individual MP to bother to visit the island, to listen to prisoners' complaints and to take them up with the authorities.

It is perhaps little wonder. Just across the bay, in Cape Town, few people wanted to be seen getting involved in what was increasingly a dangerous kind of politics, the politics of real opposition.

Vorster, a keen and very able chess player, brought all his strategic acumen to bear on the political threats to the state he headed. In 1969 he appointed his old *Ossewa Brandwag* pal and fellow internee at Koffie-fontein, General Hendrik van den Bergh, to head a new branch of special police. The Bureau of State Security (Boss), which took over military intelligence, too, would report directly to the prime minister and would draw increasingly large sums in secret funding.

This went hand in hand with an extension of the Official Secrets Act to cover all information relating to munitions, police and military matters. There was even a prohibition on evidence in any court relating to matters of state or public security.

Simultaneously with these developments, censorship increased sharply. Throughout the Seventies, the authorities were banning an average of 700 books a year. Some of them were out-and-out pornography, but the main targets were political writings the government did not want its black opponents to be inspired by. In one ridiculous case after another, even works of international literary importance were declared undesirable. Notoriously enough, the Publications Control Board, which was established in 1963, went as far as banning the children's classic, *Black Beauty*, the story of a young girl and her horse, because of its name.

Equally absurdly, a magazine carrying a picture of a black man hugging a white woman in Greenwich Village in New York was banned in 1972 because the Publications Control Board was afraid it might 'encourage young readers to follow its example'. It comes almost as a surprise that the ban was over-turned by a Supreme Court judge who said the reasoning behind it was 'far-fetched'.

The mostly free flow of popular music – the protest songs of Bob Dylan and others, and the exuberance of the likes of Jimi Hendrix – kept many young people tuned in to the counter-culture of the Sixties, but the stifling of ideas helped to isolate society from the critical thinking of the outside world. The closing of the South African mind was compounded by mounting pressure overseas to isolate the apartheid state in sport, diplomacy, culture and trade.

When Albert Luthuli died in 1967, Oliver Tambo,

in exile, became the president of the ANC and began building networks of support and solidarity that by the 1980s became a formidable international opposition to apartheid.

The ANC's armed wing, Umkhonto we'Sizwe, demonstrated its potential in 1967 when it joined the Zimbabwe African People's Union forces in a combined raid into what was then still called Rhodesia.

Just two years before, Rhodesia had made a unilateral declaration of independence when the country's 250 000 whites – about five percent of the population – under President Ian Smith defied the British government and bucked the trend of independence in Africa. They had decided to go it alone, intent on holding out, they fondly believed, for a thousand years.

———— ❖ ————

White South Africa may have had similar fantasies, but it was becoming clearer that, internationally, apartheid was not going to get an easy ride.

Vorster was widely admired among voters. A 'national' opinion survey early in 1968 showed that 82 percent of white adults of both language groups and all classes rated his performance as 'excellent'. A higher number, 92 percent, of Afrikaners thought he was doing excellently.

But white South Africans were being made to recognise that, however highly they thought of themselves, it wasn't enough. And it was sport initially – the cricket and rugby that are still national obsessions – that brought it home to them.

The Basil D'Oliviera affair of 1968 was a case in point. D'Oliviera, a celebrated all-rounder who learned his stuff in the narrow streets of the predominantly coloured quarter of the Bokaap in Cape Town, was at this time playing for the English county Worcestershire. The county player had earlier made such a good impression in the Lancashire League – he had also recently scored a century against Australia at the Oval – that he was selected for a national squad bound for South Africa. This was a problem, and it blew up into a major controversy: the government refused D'Oliviera entry to the country of his birth. The MCC (Marylebone Cricket Club) tried a different tack, offering to take the former Cape player out of the team but proposing to bring him to South Africa as a correspondent for *The News of the World* newspaper. This still didn't satisfy the government.

Cape Town-born cricket star Basil D'Oliviera was selected for the English side bound for South Africa in 1968. That he was not white prompted the Vorster government to refuse him entry into the country of his birth.

Vorster thundered that South Africa

cannot allow those organisations, individuals and newspapers to make political capital out of such relations or to use certain people or sportsmen as pawns in their game to bedevil relations, to create incidents and to undermine our way of life …

The team, he claimed, were not cricketers but 'troublemakers for South Africa's separate development policies'. The MCC cancelled the tour.

In 1969, the Springboks under Dawie de Villiers flew to Britain for a tour of the British Isles and encountered stiff opposition off the field when anti-apartheid protesters turned out in force, besieging stadiums and tossing smoke bombs on to the field at some matches. Thousands of British police had to be deployed to protect the visitors. Rugger fans loved them, but the tide of anti-apartheid sentiment was growing.

———— ❖ ————

As the Seventies dawned, the National Party (NP) crowed in parliament about a 'dynamic third decade' of NP rule being in the offing. But all it turned out to be was a waste – and mostly a waste of lives.

The ludicrous nature of petty apartheid was illustrated in a special survey by the *Sunday Tribune* which highlighted, among other things, the bar on coloured hospital nurses from tending to white patients in a country in which black nursemaids bathed and fed white babies; an Indian cancer specialist being barred from teaching white students; a black nuclear physicist being offered a homelands teaching job at R55 a month.

The Pietermaritzburg Philharmonia Society lost a government grant because it refused to stop playing to coloured audiences. International singing star Eartha Kitt was barred from performing in the Bloemfontein city hall.

Among the penalties imposed upon South Africa was the International Olympic Committee's decision to withdraw the country's recognition for the Munich Olympics in 1972.

It was around this time that South Africa joined the United States, Britain and France as the Western world's only producers of enriched uranium, a key ingredient in the manufacture of nuclear weapons. Under the strictest secrecy in the ensuing years, South Africa did develop a nuclear weapons capability. But weapons were essentially ineffective against the rising anger of the black majority.

A telling development in black politics was the formation in 1969 of the South African Students' Organisation under Natal University medical student Steve Bantu Biko.

Biko had started out as an active member of the white-dominated but liberal National Union of South African Students, which, in the late 1960s when some of its leaders had been banned, had begun to soften its political stance under the influence of conservative members. Biko and other black students were dissatisfied and began considering forming an all-black student movement to better express their politics and their demands. At the heart of the new movement was the idea of 'black consciousness', a positive statement of identity that made no reference to whiteness or the white world as an ideal or an aspiration. It meant liberating blacks from an imposed slave mentality. 'The most potent weapon in the hands of the aggressor,' Biko once wrote, 'is the mind of the oppressed.'

Steve Bantu Biko, whose success in propagating black consciousness ideas cost him his life at the hands of callous security policemen, became a potent symbol of revolt.

Writing in the 1970s, Thenjiwe Mtintso – she was a journalist then, but rose to prominence in ANC structures in the Eighties and Nineties – discussed the meaning of black consciousness:

Whatever we do in this country, be it on the economic, social or political level, it has to be by blacks, for blacks, period. It doesn't matter how well-meaning white people may be … they can never deliver me from the hands of the Nationalists … whatever they do, they must try to work within their own community and concentrate on liberating their counterparts. I'll be doing the same thing in the black community.

From *The Role of Women in the Struggle Against Apartheid* (1980), a United Nations report

Black consciousness was an increasingly popular concept among young black people, and many organisations sprang up to express and promote it. They gained an umbrella body in 1972 with the establishment of the Black People's Convention. Though black consciousness never succeeded in galvanising mass support in the rural areas or among workers – the key to mass political action – it was a popular force among students and young urban blacks.

In the mid-1970s, in an essay written secretly on Robben Island, Nelson Mandela reflected on the significance of the Black Consciousness Movement (BCM). There's an almost disapproving, fatherly tone to Mandela's comments. He wrote that 'like all emotional slogans, "Black is Beautiful" has lost its original appeal', and argued that the BCM 'must now come up with something fresh and concrete to gain the initiative'.

By and large, he believed that

in spite of all its weaknesses and mistakes, the BCM attracted able and serious-minded young people who acquitted themselves well, appreciated the value of unity, and whose main efforts were directed to this goal. Realists among them accepted that the enemy would not be defeated by fiery speeches, mass campaigns, bare fists, stones and petrol bombs, and that only through a disciplined freedom army, under a unified command, using modern weapons and backed by a united population, will the laurels be ours.

The government was less certain about the 'weaknesses and mistakes' of the new brand of black politics and banned and restricted its leading figures in the hope of erasing threatening ideas from the black mind.

In a prescient warning in parliament in 1973 – in which she condemned 'in the strongest possible terms' the latest banning of black consciousness leaders without trial -- Helen Suzman told the Nationalists they could never succeed in defeating blacks politically.

This government is so used to the fatalistic submission of blacks to policies that have been imposed on them, up to now, that it is completely unaware of the fact that young black South Africans, the younger generation of blacks, are simply not prepared to take its suppressive policies lying down any longer. It can ban leaders, and others will rise up in their place, because the government itself spawned an indestructible black nationalism which all of us are going to live to regret and which is, after all, only a by-product of white nationalism.

It became clear within a few years just how little of Suzman's warning had been heeded by the government.

———— ❖ ————

In an atmosphere of increasing world isolation, John Vorster embarked, in the first half of the 1970s, on a process of détente (peace-making) in Africa. It was, ironically, one of his security police chief General Van den Bergh's tasks to set up lines of communication with black Africa's leaders. Vorster's intention was to build some trust at least among his African neighbours. Malawi's Hastings Banda was the first to be wooed. These efforts had intensified by 1974, when Vorster visited Liberia, delegations from the Ivory Coast and Central African Repubic visited South Africa and, in probably the most important encounter, Vorster met Zambian president Kenneth Kaunda in a railway carriage on the Victoria Falls bridge.

The South African prime minister was flattered to encounter Zambians holding up placards with slogans such as 'Vorster is a Statesman', and he seemed to get on well with Kaunda. He recalled later:

When we came out of the coach, I asked him: 'Mr President, when last were you in Rhodesia?' He said he could not remember, but he thought it was in 1961 or 1962. So I said to him: 'Let's go and look at the place.'
He replied: 'Okay, with you I will go anywhere.' So off we went to the Rhodesian side to the great consternation of the security men. We got into a car – I don't know whose car it was, but I rather think it was Ian Smith's car – and we drove off with assorted security men rushing behind.

They ended up in another railway coach at the Victoria Falls station, where, for an hour, the two men chatted and were served tea by South African Railways general manager, Kobus Loubser. Kaunda, Vorster thought, 'seemed to be enjoying himself enormously'.

Both men were set on trying to resolve the impasse in Rhodesia, to get Ian Smith to begin negotiating with his opponents. It didn't work. But the Rhodesia difficulty was soon eclipsed in the aftermath of an event in Europe that would drastically reshape relations in southern Africa for the next decade and more.

It was in 1974 that the Portuguese dictatorship of Marcello Caetano was toppled in a military coup. The new leaders moved swiftly to ditch the state's costly colonies, Angola and Mozambique. In both countries, the Portuguese had long been fighting to stave off freedom fighters, the MPLA in Angola and Frelimo in Mozambique. The military knew these were wars it could not win.

Dates were set for the independence of the two colonies: June 1975 for Mozambique and November 1975 for Angola.

In Mozambique's case, South Africa's response came as a surprise to many: it opted, initially, for friendly relations – and much economic cooperation – with Samora Machel's Marxist Frelimo government in exchange for a promise that Mozambique would not allow itself to be used by anti-South African guerrillas.

The situation in Angola was more complicated, mainly because there were at least three liberation movements, each in conflict with the other. And the main one, the Marxist MPLA, was distrusted by other African leaders, such as Vorster's new-found friend, Kenneth Kaunda, as well as by the Western powers.

South Africa became caught up in a complex round of political jockeying between the United States and France, both of whom foresaw strategic and trade opportunities for themselves in the region. Both had made offers of arms to Pretoria as an inducement to act.

But Vorster's government misjudged the situation when, a month before the due date for Angolan independence, it drove an armed column across the border, aided by Angolan nationals under Unita and the FNLA. It was called 'Operation Zulu'. The column got within 12 kilometres of Luanda, only to pull back in the face of stiff resistance from newly arrived Cuban troops, backed by heavy Soviet artillery.

The commander of Operation Zulu requested reinforcements from Pretoria, but Vorster was beginning to have second thoughts. South Africa was not ready for a war, nor did it want intensified international

TOP: Vorster cherished the idea of building diplomatic bridges in Africa to bolster South Africa's status and deflect criticism of apartheid. His meeting with Zambian President Kenneth Kaunda provided some ground for optimism.

RIGHT: A South African soldier on patrol on 'the Border', the popular term for the war zone along the Angola border. Conflict in the region intensified after Operation Zulu, a South African military incursion into Angola intended to secure a friendly post-independence government in Luanda.

ABOVE AND LEFT: Police lay into student protesters in central Cape Town, eventually pursuing them into St George's Cathedral.

RIGHT: What started out as a peaceful protest against the use of Afrikaans in Soweto schools became a national uprising that eventually delivered thousands of young cadres into the armed struggle.

condemnation. Despite pleas from Zambia and Zaire to keep up the pressure on the dominant Marxist MPLA forces, Vorster decided to withdraw. He was confirmed in this view when the United States Senate – which had not, it now turned out, been consulted on the exercise in the first place – halted any further aid to anti-MPLA forces in Angola.

The South African forces began to withdraw in January 1976. A month later the Organisation of African Unity recognised the MPLA as the government of Angola.

As the *Reader's Digest Illustrated History of South Africa* (1994) describes it,

> [the] whole exercise had cost Pretoria dearly: the détente policy with Africa was up in smoke, the military had lost face, there was a large communist presence on the doorstep and France had been lost as a supplier of weapons.

Worst of all, there was no chance in an atmosphere of suspicion and fear to strike the sort of deal South Africa had gained with Machel's Frelimo government in Mozambique.

South-West Africa now became an armed frontier, under steadily deepening South African military occupation.

❖

On the home front, a gathering force of young white opposition to apartheid was developing on university campuses, though it would be the rebellion of black scholars that would stir the public's and the world's imagination in the 1970s.

An infamous baton charge by police of white students protesting in central Cape Town in 1972 made headlines when overzealous constables followed the demonstrators into the sanctuary of St George's Cathedral.

There were some sideshows, too.

In 1973, at a meeting in a garage in the Transvaal town of Heidelberg, Eugene Terre'Blanche and six

like-minded colleagues launched the ultra-right wing Afrikaner Weerstandsbeweging. By 1980 he was popularising the idea of a '*blanke volkstaat*' (white national state) with a spitting rhetoric that matched the outfit's Nazi-style regalia.

And there was heartening news for white South Africans in 1974 when a beautiful 19-year-old Afrikaans girl, Anneline Kriel, won the Miss World title. But it did not signal any thawing of international attitudes to apartheid.

In the same year, the Nationalists were steering towards another crisis.

Had they heeded Suzman's 1973 warning about the irrepressibility of black opposition, they might have thought twice about a decree at the beginning of 1975 that Afrikaans be used equally with English as the medium of tuition for all subjects at black schools. The government was warned, through Progressive Reform Party MP René de Villiers, by the director of the South African Institute of Race Relations, Fred van Wyk, that its policy was causing 'very serious' tension in Soweto.

Deputy minister of Bantu administration and development, and of Bantu education, Andries Treurnicht, was unperturbed. 'I am not aware of any real problem,' he responded in May 1976.

By 25 May, six schools were boycotting classes. The government merely threatened to close the schools down and expel the boycotters.

A second warning was sent to the government on 11 June, but again Treurnicht dismissed it. Soweto's schoolchildren, though, were not to be dismissed. Afrikaans, they said, was a 'tribal language', the language of 'pass laws, permits and police'. They would not tolerate it.

It was a well-kept secret. Student leaders, conscious of the risk of worried parents hearing of their plans, or, worse, impimpis (police informers), succeeded in keeping arrangements for the massed protest under wraps.

It came as a complete surprise to everyone else. Children went off dutifully to school on Wednesday, 16 June, a cold, sunny Transvaal morning. The march was to start at 7 am. By 6 am, hundreds of pupils had already gathered at pre-arranged assembly points. Some were handed hastily made placards – 'Down with Afrikaans' and 'To Hell with Bantu Education' were among the slogans. At 7 am on the dot, the first group of chanting marchers set off towards Orlando.

Police moved to try to stop them. Student leaders told the crowds to be 'cool and calm' and not taunt the police.

Almost immediately, they were confronted by a large force of policemen. It was not long after 9 am that a tear-gas canister was lobbed into the crowd, and then a single shot fired. There was panic, stones were thrown, more shots fired. And then, out of the crowd, there emerged a huddle of children, one of them carrying a 13-year-old boy, covered in blood. His name was Hector Petersen. Within hours, his death in Soweto on 16 June, 1976, became an international symbol of apartheid repression. Anger and violence spread together through the townships of the Witwatersrand and beyond.

In little more than a week, 176 people, mostly schoolchildren, had been killed. Scores of government buildings and beer halls were burned to the ground, and cars and buses torched.

This eyewitness account by an unnamed *Star* newspaper journalist gives some idea of what it was like in Soweto on the day:

> *Yesterday was the most terrifying day of my life as I was caught between the crossfire of police bullets and stones from enraged students on the rampage. A rock hit me on the shoulder as I ran behind police lines after they had opened fire on the demonstrators. More and more stones came crashing down. Then I turned back to join the pupils and about the same time the police opened fire directly on us. It is terrifying to watch a gun being aimed at you. If I lay on the ground, the pupils would have trampled over me.*

From *The Star* newspaper 17 June, 1976

Phydian Matsepe of Orlando High School recalled his part in the day's events:

> *The soldiers surrounded us and we threw stones at them. Then they started shooting, so we burnt the municipal offices and any building that belonged to the government – even cars. Unfortunately we ended up injuring innocent people.*

From *Recollected 25 years later: Soweto 16 June 1976* (2001) by Elsabé Brink, Gandhi Malungane, Steve Lebelo, Dumisani Ntshangase and Sue Krige (editors)

Student teacher Sue Krige had spent the morning of 16 June teaching a class of boys at an elite private school all about the storming of the Bastille in revolutionary France. She heard about the uprising during her lunch break in the staffroom and phoned her history lecturer, Peter Kallaway, who urged her to join a student protest.

> *On the afternoon of 16 June I remember standing [in a protest] on Jan Smuts Avenue with hundreds of other students ... [where] students from the Rand Afrikaans University pelted us with eggs and tomatoes, and motorists swore at us as they drove past.*

From *Recollected 25 years later: Soweto 16 June 1976* (2001) by Elsabé Brink, Gandhi Malungane, Steve Lebelo, Dumisani Ntshangase and Sue Krige (editors)

The government's misguided and hard-hearted view was exemplified by justice minister Jimmy Kruger, who said in a snap debate in parliament on 17 June that there was more to the revolt than a language dispute: 'My first task is to free South Africa from thugs in the streets of Soweto and elsewhere.'

And minister of Bantu administration and development, and of Bantu education, MC Botha said:

> *The alleged aversion to Afrikaans as medium can hardly be the only reason for the demonstrations.*

From *The Argus* newspaper 18 June, 1976

❖

Television – which the Nationalists had long resisted, fearing it would undermine the moral fibre of South Africa – was eventually permitted from early 1976 ... just in time to beam into white living rooms the graphic and disturbing images of revolt and repression from Soweto.

Equally, fondly nurtured stereotypes were challenged on the box, too. This was perhaps especially true when black South African golfer Vincent Tshabalala won the French Open.

No government explanation would ever temper the impact of this iconic photograph of 13-year-old Hector Petersen, shot dead by police on the first day of the Soweto uprising.

But it was the images of violence, and the possibilities of revolt, that were so graphically and immediately imprinted on the national mind.

This underscored Helen Suzman's warning three years before that the government had become 'so used to the fatalistic submission of blacks to policies that have been imposed on them' that it was completely unprepared for the anger and the idealism of the black consciousness-inspired young people of the 1970s.

The imprisonment and banning of the leadership of the national liberation movements gave white South Africa a false sense of security. Nelson Mandela and other ANC leaders were safely incarcerated on Robben Island, and PAC leader Robert Sobukwe – having been jailed on the island for six years – was banished to Kimberley, under house arrest, for life. (He died two years after Soweto, in 1978.)

It was clear, in 1976, that the convictions that had underpinned the campaigns of the 1950s had been reinvigorated among a new generation of activists who were turning the country's thousands of schools into a new arena of struggle.

Looking back, oral historian Gandhi Malungane confirms the sense of idealism of the time, but hints at a fuller story that few accounts of the uprising succeeded in conveying:

For some years after 16 June 1976 I found myself confused about my participation in the event. There was criticism and condemnation from various people – politicians, academics, clerics, to name a few – of all colours. I did not know the significance of what I had taken part in or whether it was seen as good or bad. My instincts, however, kept insisting (and still do today) that my participation had been worthwhile. ... I experienced the start of the uprising at Nghungunyane and witnessed many killings and burnings at various places around Chiawelo which I have never come across in any books I have read about the events. For that reason I felt that there might be many people like myself ... who experienced it differently from those who are mentioned in the many books about June 1976. ... I have often heard people talking about their experiences of the most essential day in the history of South Africa. Some had bad memories ... whereas some recall good things. To some it carries a mixture of both bad and good memories. One good example is the two women in Dhlamini One and Two. To them 16 June 1976 meant a lifetime of confinement in wheelchairs. The family of the woman who was killed in Chiawelo bottlestore is no exception to those who have haunting memories.

From *Recollected 25 years later: Soweto 16 June 1976* (2001) by Elsabé Brink, Gandhi Malungane, Steve Lebelo, Dumisani Ntshangase and Sue Krige

Historian Elsabé Brink reflects on the story of one of the victims of police action during the revolt:

Having heard the story of Abe Lebelo who died tragically on 4 August 1976 in an alley in Diepkloof ... I would like to contribute in a small way to honouring the memory of a very brave young man. When he left home on that day to join the march, he knew that the police would be waiting for them, and that he would be courting danger. He had had six weeks' worth of personal experience of what the police had done and what they were capable of doing. Yet he still chose to march. He died, not accidentally as a bystander who happened to be in the line of fire, but as a young activist who believed in what he was doing and was fully aware of the consequences. He is a person I would have liked to meet.

From *Recollected 25 years later: Soweto 16 June 1976* (2001) by Elsabé Brink, Gandhi Malungane, Steve Lebelo, Dumisani Ntshangase and Sue Krige (editors)

Abe Lebelo's brother, Steve, describes the story of 16 June, 1976 as being 'very close to my heart'. The costs were high. He remembers that his family 'was made to believe that Abe's death was not all in vain' ... but that 'we were never the same again':

Until Abe was killed, I was not particularly involved with the events of 16 June, 1976. Then I seemed to perceive his death as a challenge to me to pursue his goal. My mother tried to persuade me to distance myself from the struggle. ... I refused, thinking then it was an act of political commitment. I think differently now. Twenty-five years later, I realise I could have chosen to remain uninvolved and would not be considered less of 'a man'. I often think that had I not been as involved as I was, I could have made or done other things more worthwhile than I ultimately have.

From *Recollected 25 years later: Soweto 16 June 1976* (2001) by Elsabé Brink, Gandhi Malungane, Steve Lebelo, Dumisani Ntshangase and Sue Krige (editors)

The protests sparked by the Soweto uprising spread to more than 200 towns and cities over the next 15 months, renewing a sense among black people of the power of mass action. The campaign for the international isolation of South Africa intensified, and thousands of young black people fled across the borders to swell the ranks of the liberation movements.

Thousands were detained, and the struggle gained thousands of new supporters, increasingly among young whites.

This was true of a young Durban man named Raymond Suttner who endured torture and imprisonment as a result of his role in the struggle:

> In 1975 I was a young, very idealistic revolutionary, and I was prepared to die for my beliefs. I felt a strong connection with all those who had gone before me, and with all those who had faced similar tortures; and I felt a responsibility to the traditions of our liberation movement. That is what gave me strength. That is what made my resistance possible. And that is why I did not simply succumb to torture or lapse into despair.
>
> Writing this now, 24 years after my arrest, I don't seem as single-minded as I was back then. I now tend to see myself as having been rather naive. All the same, it remains true that single-mindedness was the weapon that got me through.

From *Inside Apartheid's Prison, Notes and letters of struggle* (2001) by Raymond Suttner

'Nkosi Sikelel' iAfrika' was popular as a freedom song, and was often used by white supporters of the struggle to underscore their commitment to opposing apartheid.

In the weeks after the start of the Soweto uprising, young people sustained the protest, which spread throughout the country.

Business leaders sat up and took note of the intensifying struggle, too. At the height of the unrest, Harry

Business magnates Harry Oppenheimer of Anglo American, left, and Anton Rupert of the Rembrandt group, with former judge Jan Steyn at the launch of the Urban Foundation. Steyn became the foundation's first chief executive.

Oppenheimer of Anglo-American and Anton Rupert of the Rembrandt group – the giants of English and Afrikaans business respectively – met in London to discuss ways to convince the government of the importance of developing a black middle class, in part as a buffer against radical politics, of socialism.

Thus, in March 1977, the Urban Foundation was born to promote opportunities for Africans in education and home-ownership and economic development.

Though many blacks distrusted it at first, the Foundation became an important pressure group in shifting government thinking towards accepting the permanence and importance of stable African communities in towns and cities.

Unsettling contemporary politics began to reach the bedside table in white, especially Afrikaner, households in the 1970s with the appearance of novels by André Brink, including *An Instant in the Wind, A Dry White Season* and *Rumours of Rain*.

The following exchange between two of the characters in *Rumours of Rain*, Cambridge University business graduate Charlie Mofokeng and establishment Afrikaner Martin Mynhardt – the narrator, and the figure through whom Brink explores the tense and dangerous divide between white and black South Africans – would have caused disquiet at least among many readers:

Charlie Mofokeng: *'Of course I hold you responsible. You and every other White in this country.'*

'Now you're being unreasonable, Charlie. I inherited this situation exactly as you did. Neither of us can be blamed for what our forefathers did.'

'That's not what I'm blaming you for. What gets me is that history didn't teach you anything at all.'

'My history provided me with the means to survive in this land!'

'That's what you think. All your history taught you was a mistrust of others. You never learned to share anything or to live with others. If things got difficult you loaded your waggon and trekked away. Otherwise you took aim over the Bible and killed whatever came in your way. Out in the open you formed a laager. And when you wanted more land you took it. With or without the pretext of a "contract".'

Some time later, in a different conversation, the theme recurs:

'It's a matter of survival, Charlie. I'm not trying to defend the methods of history. But what else could my people have done to survive?'

'Do you expect me to approve of survival achieved at the expense of others?'

'You're just generalising as usual, Charlie.'

'Jesus, Martin: your people started as pioneers. I respect them for it. But that you still haven't shaken off the frontier mentality – that's the rub.'

From *Rumours of Rain* (1994) by André Brink

Many other writers had explored South African politics in radical or literary vein, but no current Afrikaans writer had reflected in a popular, accessible story the personal and public ramifications of contemporary events with quite the same impact.

The government didn't like it. *A Dry White Season*, for instance, was banned because, the authorities claimed, it endangered national order by portraying the security police in a less than positive light.

More black literary voices came to the fore, too. In 1975 Miriam Tlali became the first black South African woman to have a novel published with her debut book, *Muriel at the Metropolitan*. Three years later, a new magazine, *Staffrider*, created a forum for the emerging angry voices in poetry and prose.

Typical in sentiment of much of the work *Staffrider* published was the poem 'burning log' by Charles Mungoshi:

i am
a burning log
my history being reduced
to ashes
what i remember
of yesterday
is the ashy taste
of defeat
my hope
for tomorrow
is the fire.

From *Ten Years of* Staffrider *1978-1988* (1988) by Andries Oliphant and Ivan Vladislavić (editors)

Within a year of the Soweto uprising, the first groups of insurgents of the class of '76 began returning to the country, armed with AK-47 assault rifles, limpet mines and hand grenades.

The establishment of guerrilla bases and liberation movement cells closer to home took South Africa's armed forces, fighter jets and special forces, and its undercover assassins, into neighbouring countries that now offered the armed wings of the liberation movements a springboard for attacks on home targets.

And, from the mid-1970s, the long military occupation of South-West Africa became a defining experience for many young white men that had its parallels in the bitter experience of young Americans in Vietnam. In the end, it proved as futile and as wasteful.

❖

'By the time I went to Orlando West High School,' the young accused told the Pretoria Supreme Court in 1978, 'I was already beginning to question the injustice of the society … and to ask why nothing was being done to change it.'

This young man, a guerrilla of the class of '76, was caught on his return to the country on an armed mission. His name was Mosima Gabriel 'Tokyo' Sexwale, who would later become a key ANC leader, premier of Gauteng after 1994, and a captain of the boardroom from the late 1990s. The questions raised in his mind in the 1970s became pressing in many young minds across the country at that time.

To live up to the answers came, often, at great personal cost, but contributed to a significant and increasingly non-racial solidarity.

This was true of the son of a South African Navy officer, who, in the 1970s, was a lecturer in philosophy and politics, and a member of the South African Communist Party. Jeremy Cronin was arrested in 1976 under the Terrorism Act for doing underground work for the ANC, tried and jailed for seven years. While he was in prison, his wife died unexpectedly. He was denied permission to attend her funeral. The spirit of solidarity that impelled him and others is crisply captured in a poem he wrote in this period:

Motho ke Motho ka Batho Babang
(A person is a person because of other people)

> By holding my mirror out of the window I see
> Clear to the end of the passage.
> There's a person down there.
> A prisoner polishing a doorhandle.
> In the mirror I see him see
> My face in the mirror,
> I see the fingertips of his free hand
> Bunch together, as if to make
> An object the size of a badge
> Which travels up to his forehead
> The place of an imaginary cap
> (This means: A warder)
> Two fingers are extended in a vee
> And wiggle like two antennae.
> (He's being watched.)
> A finger of his free hand makes a watch-hand's arc
> On the wrist of his polishing arm without
> Disrupting the slow-slow rhythm of his work.
> (Later. Maybe, later, we can speak.)
> Hey! Wat maak jy daar?

> – a voice from around the corner.
> No. Just polishing baas.
> He turns his back to me, now watch
> His free hand, the talkative one,
> Slips quietly behind
> – Strength brother, it says,
> In my mirror,
> A black fist.

From *Inside* (1983) by Jeremy Cronin

———— ❖ ————

Vorster had no doubt about the necessity of drastic action to defend the state.

He reflected without rancour on his own experience as a detainee – he was interned without trial during the Second World War for his activities with the anti-British *Ossewa Brandwag* – but was irritated by the apologies made to him after the war by the Smuts government.

'If you have got to do it,' he said of detention,

> do it, but don't apologise for doing it. … In other words, if they genuinely saw me as a threat to the state and, according to their lights, saw the need to lock me up, I would have respected them for it.

Thus, he had no qualms about using detention without trial on his own opponents:

> If I see a man or a woman as a threat to the state and if there are valid reasons for not bringing that person to trial, then I must take them out of circulation one way or another.

He also insisted that he 'never hesitated to take action' (against the police) if detainees were not treated 'properly'.

But Vorster's certainties, as minister of justice in the 1960s, that humane treatment was observed, and ruthless cops rooted out, were patently not applicable to the late 1970s when he was prime minister.

———— ❖ ————

Just how ruthless the authorities were prepared to be to preserve the system emerged with bitter tragedy in 1977, when the security police arrested Steve Biko, who had been eluding them for a year.

Biko was caught at a roadblock outside Grahamstown on 18 August, 1977, and held under section 6 of the Terrorism Act, which allowed for indefinite detention. Police said he was a danger because he was on his way to Cape Town to distribute pamphlets 'inciting blacks to cause riots'.

What followed brought shame and scandal to the South African government, the police, the medical doctors who examined Biko at various points – and on the society that allowed such things to happen.

After a night in a police cell in Grahamstown, Biko was taken to Port Elizabeth, where he was held, naked, in various cells. On 6 September, still naked but now also in leg irons, he was taken to police headquarters in Port Elizabeth and interrogated by five security police officers.

This was the beginning of the end for Biko. The autopsy revealed the cause of his death had been a blow or blows to the head, forceful enough to have knocked him unconscious. Police insisted he had bumped his head against a wall in a scuffle. They later admitted in the Truth and Reconciliation Commission that Biko had been rammed against a wall.

As his condition worsened, three doctors visited Biko and made up false diagnoses, apparently entering into a conspiracy with the police to cover likely causes of the prisoner's condition. Finally, when the police were urged to take a clearly gravely ill Biko to hospital, they dumped him naked in the back of a police Landrover and drove 1 628 kilometres to Pretoria to have him admitted.

There, as the family's lawyer Sydney Kentridge described it during a highly charged inquest, Biko 'died a miserable and lonely death on a mat on the stone floor of a prison cell'.

In a statement that shocked the world, justice minister Jimmy Kruger said of Biko's death: 'I am not glad and I am not sorry about Mr Biko ... He leaves me cold.'

The immediate consequence of his death, and the banning of black consciousness leaders and organisations in October 1977 – including the shutting down of the *World* newspaper – was the

In the middle of nowhere, often, the subjects of forced removals would find themselves having to manage with the barest resources.

imposition of a mandatory arms embargo on South Africa by the UN Security Council.

Biko was the 45th person to die in police custody since detention without trial had first been introduced in 1963. He was not to be the last. Five years later, prominent labour leader Dr Neil Aggett was found hanging in his cell after being held in solitary confinement, deprived of sleep and subjected to 60 hours of non-stop interrogation.

———— ❖ ————

Embattled as it was, the government was determined to try to relieve some of the pressure by showing it meant to carry through its promises of independent governance for the tribal states it had turned the bantustans into.

Between 1976 and 1981, 'independence' was granted to Transkei, Bophuthatswana, Venda and Ciskei. 'Citizens' of these states – recognised only by South Africa – lost their South African nationality. It was both naive and deceptive.

The *Reader's Digest Illustrated History of South Africa* notes that 'an estimated 3.5-million people ... were forced to move in one of the most ambitious and widespread examples of social engineering in recent history'.

By the early 1980s, the government was dressing this policy up as part of the creation of 'national states' where people could live with 'full independence' and economic opportunities. But it just never got off the ground. Political opposition to it was complemented by its economic unviability: even with expensive incentive schemes to promote the relocation of industry to the homelands, there were never enough jobs.

On the other hand, South Africa's growing industrial economy needed increasing numbers of workers near at hand, in the cities.

Chief Mangosuthu Buthelezi, the strongman of KwaZulu, who resisted independence but opted for a degree of self-rule.

Mangosuthu Buthelezi, who collaborated to the extent of opting for a measure of self-rule in KwaZulu, resisted independence. He said in 1980 that Inkatha had gained the full support of the Zulu people 'on the basis of rejecting independence. ... I think our people realise that they can only maximise their rights in the labour market if they remain South Africans, if they don't just become vassals of South Africa'.

The same was not true of the Ciskei, as *Rand Daily Mail* labour correspondent Riaan de Villiers discovered on his first visit there:

> For the first time in my life, after a visit to the Ciskei, I have understood what the homelands mean in terms of economics. It's just God-awful. The leftwing phrase that homelands are labour reservoirs is absolutely true. The Ciskei is a tiny piece of land, with blacks crammed into it, with the highest population density in South Africa, twice as high as the Transkei – 129 people per square kilometre. The place is a vast ghetto. The subsistence agriculture theory is a myth. Under dry land conditions, one man can't feed himself for a year from one hectare. Forty-nine percent of the Ciskei is over-grazed with cattle and goats.
>
> Those people are crammed in there and they can't get out. The only way a man can get out is if he is recruited as a contract worker. The government is bringing in more people all the time, into resettlement camps. I saw those places ... they have moved 100 000 people in a decade ... you drive through desolate countryside and come to a settlement of tens of thousands of people, a township without a town. There's nothing, no visible means of life support.

From *South Africa Speaks* (1981) by Jill Johnson (editor)

But there were those who supported the move to so-called independence. Lucas Mangope of Bophuthatswana said in an SABC-TV interview:

> Well, nationhood is one of those things that even if we do not like we cannot wish away because it is in the nature of man to want to belong to a nation, and we in Bophuthatswana are no exception. Independence has enhanced the self-esteem of the people, it has created self-reliance ... People feel, with the responsibility that independence brings, that they have a role to play.

Transkei's leader Kaiser Matanzima commented in 1980:

> To be free makes you able to do things you would not do while you were not free. ... Years of independence have meant to us a spirit of self-determination.

The government spent many millions of rands on trying to make the homelands succeed. Part of this was an attempt to draw industry to the rural areas through expensive incentives. Yet, as Helen Suzman noted soberly:

> It is no good spending R36 000 creating a job in a remote homeland when the same job can be created for R9 000 in the existing metropolitan areas. That's not economic.

The *Oxford History of South Africa* has the following to say about the homelands policy:

> The charge against [the policy of homeland independence] was that in the white man's territory, comprising 87 percent of the country's land surface and containing seven-twelfths of the total African population, the African had no political rights worth mentioning and no voice whatever in the central legislature. In other words ... the white man was in absolute and undisputed control. ... This was the position in spite of the fact that the role of the African in the economic life of the country continued to grow in importance.

From the *Oxford History of South Africa, Volume II* (1971) by Monica Wilson and Leonard Thompson (editors)

❖

Industrial development in the cities intensified demand for labour, but influx control impeded urbanisation. Desperate for jobs, the rural poor streamed to the urban centres only to be harried by officials and frustrated by outdated regulations.

The homelands were a costly social, political and economic failure, and urbanisation continued despite the best efforts of the bureaucracy to regulate it at 'acceptable' levels.

The pressure of poverty in the homelands was so great that people streamed defiantly to the cities to try to find jobs, just to survive. Settlements grew in 'white' South Africa. The Western Cape, for example, drew hundreds of thousands of people from the Ciskei and Transkei.

Under government policies, Africans could live and work in 'white' urban areas only if they had so-called 'section 10 rights'. These were available only to people who had been born in an urban area, or had worked for one employer for 10 years, or were children under 18 of a person with such rights.

But the colour-bar on jobs, which had long provided job security for white blue-collar workers, and Afrikaners especially, became, from the late Sixties, economically counter-productive. The rapid and large-scale improvement in the fortunes of whites, and a falling white birth rate, meant there were not enough of them to fill jobs in factories and on the mines. Employers began to rely increasingly on black workers, despite the law.

Yet, as the 1970s wore on and the rather desperate effort to make the 'independent states' work persisted, even the *Afrikaanse Sakekamer* (chamber of business) in Cape Town urged the government to act to preserve the idea of separate development (as apartheid was now routinely called), and of the so-called coloured-labour preference policy in the Western Cape, a policy that attempted to give coloureds first choice over blacks for jobs.

In the winter of 1977, the summary destruction of the settlement of Modderdam demonstrated just how serious the Nationalists were in clearing 'illegal' black residents from white areas. Over a few days, the 10 000 people who had lived at Modderdam were scattered – some to other settlements in the region, some to the Eastern Cape. It shook even right-wing theology students from Stellenbosch University, who wrote in a letter to *Die Burger* newspaper: 'God forgive us, because we know not what we have done.' A 1977 *Sunday Tribune* report described the scene at a Cape Town squatter camp:

An eye-smarting hell of teargas and snarling dogs, of laughing officials and policemen, of homeless families crouched pitifully with their meagre possessions beside the road.

Government policy aimed at reversing migration to the urban areas succeeded only in intensifying anger, resentment and a spirit of protest in the heart of the urban areas white South Africans believed belonged to them.

In February 1977, the minister of community development, SMJ Steyn, told the House of Assembly that the media was being untruthful in its reports on the destruction of informal settlements. His 'evidence' speaks for itself.

Last night's Argus *said: 'An evicted mother ...' – that is, of course, their method of plucking at the heart strings – 'looks up from bathing her son as a bulldozer demolishes their tin shanty at Kraaifontein today.' I have studied the photograph from all angles; I consulted the experts about this, but I am still looking for the 'bulldozer'. There is no bulldozer. What is shown in the photograph is an excavator.*

From *Apartheid, The Lighter Side* (1990) by Ben Maclennan

The image of the evicted mother, the infant, the devastation, conveys something of the larger picture of the plight and the courage of women.

The South African narrative is dominated in most tellings of it by the voices of men: it was man's work – the mythology has it – to tame the wilderness; it was man's work to fight, to conquer, to defend communities or to avenge aggression, and it was men, more often than not, who charted the course of events, who made the crucial decisions and who devised the policies that determined how all of society lived. If women were saddled with the problems, men, it might be thought, had the solutions or could be counted on to find them.

Yet, this conception overlooks or underplays the significance of the actions of women – particularly in the 20th century – in the struggle for justice, and in managing the consequences of it.

As a report to the World Conference of the United Nations Decade for Women in Copenhagen in July 1980 put it:

Women in South Africa, since the turn of the century, have emerged as the primary catalysts for protests against, and as challengers of, the apartheid regime. ... Although there is no doubt that the overt leadership has been dominated by men, the seemingly unacknowledged and informal segment of society controlled by women has been the key to many of the most significant mass movements in modern South African history. It is only in the very recent past that the crucial role played by women in raising basic issues, organising and involving the masses has become more widely recognised.

From *The Role of Women in the Struggle Against Apartheid* (1980)

Hilda Bernstein argued that the personal struggles of black women particularly were inseparable from the broader struggle against apartheid:

Black women cannot change the immediate conditions of their lives without fighting against restrictions on, for example, free movement or access to education, both of which are controlled by apartheid laws. To fight male domination they need to fight the basis on which bantustans are established. ... To maintain family life, they must enter the field as protagonists against migratory labour and the pass laws.

From *For their Triumphs and for their Tears, Women in Apartheid South Africa* (1978) by Hilda Bernstein

The importance of women in the struggle was recognised by former ANC president Albert Luthuli when he said:

Among us Africans, the weight of resistance has been greatly increased in the last few years by the emergence of our women. It may even be true that, had the women hung back, resistance would still have been faltering and uncertain. ... The demonstration [by women, against passes, in 1956] made a great impact, and gave strong impetus. ... Furthermore, women of all races have had far less hesitation than men in making common cause about things basic to them.

From *The Role of Women in the Struggle Against Apartheid* (1980)

Like most of the tireless women campaigners in the struggle for justice in South Africa, Helen Joseph endured years of police persecution.

Women's involvement spanned every sphere of society, from church groups to liberation movements. But it was in the trade union movement that women first rose to positions of importance.

The leader of the 1956 march, Masedibe Lilian Ngoyi, for instance, had been a union organiser and was a former secretary of the Garment Workers' Union.

Helen Joseph, another courageous and tireless campaigner throughout the struggle years, had also been a member of the Garment Workers' Union. A founder member of the ANC's white ally, the Congress of Democrats, she was one of the key figures at the Congress of the People at Kliptown in 1955 which framed the Freedom Charter. She endured years of police persecution, but remained unbowed. There was a joke in the 1970s that said much about her public reputation. A National Party politician was addressing a meeting of supporters: 'We have the finest army in the world,' he told them, 'the finest navy, the finest airforce ... what do we have to be afraid of?' To which a lone voice from the back of the hall responded: 'Helen Joseph!'

Ray Alexander Simons, who had joined the underground communist movement in her native Latvia at the age of 13, came to South Africa in 1929 just short of three years later and, within days, joined the Communist Party and plunged herself into organising black workers. She was active in union affairs in many different trades, but the union with which her name became synonymous was the increasingly militant Food and Canning Workers' Union. With Helen Joseph, Lilian Ngoyi and Florence Mkhize, she helped found the Federation of South African Women.

Women made their mark in local politics, too. Among them was Cissie Gool – born in Cape Town in 1897 – who, following in the footsteps of her prominent politician father Dr Abdullah Abdurahman, founded the National Liberation League in 1936. From 1938 to 1951, she represented District Six on the Cape Town City Council. She played a leading role in the Non-European Front in the 1940s and, later, in the Franchise Action Council, forerunner of the South African Coloured People's Organisation.

The quiet determination and apparently inexhaustible energy of countless women campaigners, who never sought the limelight but devoted their lives to the struggle, are exemplified by the likes of Albertina Sisulu, wife of Rivonia trialist Walter Sisulu, unionist Frances Baard, activist Maggie Resha and Black Sash veteran Mary Burton.

Domestic service defined and constrained the lives of millions of women in the 20th century. It was, for them, a vital source of income, as well as the basis of enduring, often abusive, but also intimate bonds with white families. In many cases, 'maids' or 'servants' – as they were generally called – grew to love the children in their care through the long hours and years of domestic duty, only to watch their own families disintegrating under the uncaring pressures of a society founded on discrimination, abuse and disadvantage. Being forced to live apart from their husbands, domestic workers often struggled to maintain their marriages. In a telling reflection on her interviews with domestic workers in the early Eighties, Suzanne Gordon writes:

The interviewee reviewed ... her life: looked back upon the striving, the decisions taken; puzzled over the complexities, dwelt on the regrets or the occasional triumphs; sometimes chuckled over escapades. ... Bitterness was surprisingly infrequent and there appeared to be an almost heroic acceptance of the forces behind the march of events. ... [I]t often seemed that there dawned a recognition of the almost epic quality of the struggle, of the hardships confronted if not always overcome.

From *A Talent for Tomorrow, Life Stories of South Africa's Servants* (1985) by Suzanne Gordon

Ellen Kuzwayo

Albertina Sisulu

Mary Burton

Ray Alexander

Maggie Resha

Determination, courage and selflessness are among the qualities of the women who rose to prominence in the decades-long campaign against apartheid.

Florence Mkhize

Frances Baard

Cissie Gool

❖

If the Nationalists were indifferent to the plight of women – or oblivious to their potence as agents of change – they were, by the late 1970s, beginning to feel the squeeze.

But in its eagerness to win the argument, the public relations war, about separate development, the government became a victim of its own arrogance and grandiosity.

By then, secret funding running to millions of rands was being used by the Department of Information in clandestine business and media deals to try to sell the apartheid message better. Covert projects included launching the *Citizen* newspaper and buying into newspapers and other media, including publishers, around the world. And money was also spent on influencing foreign politicians.

Eventually, though, details began to leak out, and it wasn't long before the cover was blown. It became known as the 'Information Scandal'.

As the story unfolded, and more secret spending was uncovered, the Prime Minister himself became vulnerable. Vorster elected to resign, claiming health reasons … though he immediately became State President, then largely a figurehead position.

A fierce party tussle for leadership of the NP, and thus for the position of Prime Minister, pushed PW Botha to the fore. He immediately appointed a commission of inquiry under Judge Rudolph Erasmus, whose findings damned information minister (and

Transvaal leader of the NP) Connie Mulder and Vorster. Both resigned.

Botha, who was minister of defence and Cape leader of the party, had a reputation as a hawk, a conservative, who would be tough on opponents. It was a reputation he more than lived up to. He changed the order of battle for the defence of apartheid. It would involve limited reforms – partly urged by *Broederbonders* commanding Afrikaner corporates such as Sanlam – coupled with boosting compliant homeland leaders, destabilising neighbouring states that were friendly to the liberation movements, and sinister, often clandestine, security projects. Petty apartheid measures, such as race barriers at restaurants, theatres and cinemas were relaxed.

It was a 'Total Strategy' to confront a 'Total Onslaught'. Botha hoped to remove grievances that could be used by radical opponents to stir opposition, and to consolidate a black middle class, while maintaining a firm grip on political control. This 'Total Strategy' would cost South Africa, and the so-called 'frontline states' of southern Africa, a great deal in the next decade.

❖

Cheap black labour had long been the mainstay of white well-being and wealth, and of good returns for international investors. It was a pattern established in the early days of diamond and gold mining in Kimberley and Johannesburg in the last decades of the 19th century.

In the early 1970s, black and white wages began to narrow for the first time.

But when, in 1973, the Organisation of Petroleum Exporting Countries closed ranks and hiked prices, there was a world-wide energy crisis, and economic recession. The gold price dropped and inflation increased.

After a decade of improvements, the economic setbacks were felt acutely by workers, and scores of wildcat strikes involving up to 200 000 workers occurred in Natal, various parts of the Rand and the Eastern Cape.

Black unions were not recognised at this stage, and black worker grievances could not be resolved through the industrial relations arrangements that enabled more orderly negotiations. Through the 1970s, employers began to urge the government to consider including Africans in the industrial relations process, chiefly in the interests of productivity and foreign investment.

So it was that two commissions were appointed towards the end of the 1970s to look into labour questions, with far-reaching and unforeseen consequences.

The Wiehahn Commission under Professor Nic Wiehahn convinced parliament in 1979 to extend labour legislation to African workers. It was a reform that in the next six years gave immense political leverage to hundreds of thousands of black union members, who used it to press for both workplace and socio-political rights. This was especially so after the formation of the half-a-million strong Congress of South African Trade Unions in 1985.

The second commission under Dr Piet Riekert recommended more freedom of movement and choice of workplace for black workers. This eventually resulted in the scrapping of the pass laws in the mid-1980s.

———— ❖ ————

Even so, the Nationalists' hope for some breathing space, some recognition, at the start of the 1980s was a vain one. The pressure just mounted all the more.

The tide of change in the region was brought home to white South Africa when Zimbabwe became independent in March 1980 under a black president, Robert Mugabe.

At home, the Free Mandela Campaign was launched by Bishop Desmond Tutu, general secretary of the South African Council of Churches, on 10 March, 1980 – a month and a decade before the ANC leader was eventually released.

Botha pressed on with his complicated and controversial reform process, spelled out in a 12-point plan the previous year. The key elements were security, gradual change, a new Constitution, recognition of the rights of ethnics groups, the removal of 'unnecessary discrimination' and the creation of a 'constellation of southern African states'.

Reform took a step forward in 1980 when the Senate was abolished and replaced with a President's Council comprising nominated white, coloured and Indian – but no black – representatives whose task it was to investigate a new form of government to match the Nationalists' limited reform initiative.

A decade before Nelson Mandela's release, hundreds of thousands of people around the world rallied behind the Free Mandela Campaign, launched by Bishop Desmond Tutu, then general secretary of the South African Council of Churches.

Blacks were divided on how to respond to Botha's thinking.

In 1979, Mangosuthu Buthelezi told an Inkatha rally in Soweto that 'only political cowards refuse seats at negotiating tables'.

The riposte from writer and publisher Mothobi Mutloatse reflected the liberation view: 'I see no hope in talking. Our views are known now, so they need not be reiterated.'

ANC guerrillas underlined the message in an attack on the Sasol fuel complex at Sasolburg. The destruction of eight fuel tanks sent a huge pall of black smoke rising hundreds of metres into the sky. It was a menacing image for the Botha administration.

Internationally, there was no let-up in the pressure.

The Springboks embarked on what proved to be their last and most troubled tour for years, to New Zealand, in 1981. Violent clashes with protesters – and a sustained flour-bomb assault on players in the final game by a light aircraft that flew back and forth across the field – left South Africa in no doubt that the door was closing on participation in world sport.

At home, the South African Council on Sport (Sacos) conducted a very effective campaign around the slogan 'No normal sport in an abnormal society'. At a time when white South Africa wanted desperately to be friends on the playing field – though to have the ballot box all to itself – the Sacos campaign hit home.

Sanctions stiffened in 1981, too. Though the Botha administration removed nearly 800 discriminatory provisions from legislation, major Western powers supported the drawing up of a blacklist of 'collaborators' with the regime – including sportsmen, entertainers, film companies and businesses involved in military projects.

Journalist, writer and activist Ruth First – wife of leading Communist Joe Slovo – was killed by a South African letter bomb in Maputo in 1982.

———— ❖ ————

By the early Eighties, thousands of young and old South Africans were living in exile, some by choice, some by force of circumstance, and in vastly different environments and conditions, from military camps in southern Africa, to university campuses in Europe or America, dingy flats in London or Berlin to pleasant homes in Toronto or Paris.

For some, life was secure, for others, perilous. For all of them there were difficulties.

It is an experience that is captured in all its varied forms in a remarkable book of memories called *The Rift, The Exile Experience of South Africans* by Hilda Bernstein. Bernstein, a writer who left after being banned and prevented from publishing anything at home, notes that no one really knows how many South Africans went into exile between the 1950s and 1990, but it was possibly somewhere between 30 000 and 60 000:

Over a span of more than thirty years many of the most politically conscious, the most able and gifted people in all fields and of all races, left their own country. Lost, therefore, were the doctors, the teachers, the organisers, the

diplomats, the politicians, the leaders who had so much to contribute to South Africa, but were denied that right by apartheid. Lost, too, the careers of many fine writers, painters and musicians, because life in exile removes the artist's inspiration.

From *The Rift, The Exile Experience of South Africans* (1994) by Hilda Bernstein

For many, the exile experience was one of loneliness, loss, alienation, guilt, disorientation, of alcoholism, breakdown and mental collapse, or of death in solitary isolation from friends and family, but also in violence, not least at the hands of death squads sent to track down 'enemies of the state' beyond South Africa's borders.

Under the 'Total Strategy' regime of PW Botha, activist and author Ruth First – wife of leading Communist and ANC strategist Joe Slovo – was killed in 1982 by a letter bomb sent to her office at the Centre for African Studies at Maputo's Eduardo Mondlane University by South Africa's sinister agents. A car bomb in Mbabane in Swaziland killed the ANC representative there, Petrus Nzima, and his wife Jabu. Many more would die in much the same way.

In a more overt attack, the South African Defence Force 'hit' 12 targets in the Lesotho capital of Maseru in the same year, killing 41 'political' refugees. Among the dead were women and children.

In London, South African agents were arrested after a break-in at the ANC's offices in the British capital, but they fled to South Africa while awaiting trial.

———— ❖ ————

From the 1990s, the *Oxford English Dictionary*, the international benchmark of the dominant language of the 20th century, immortalised the mounting *broedertwis* (struggle between brothers) that had been developing in Afrikaner politics from the mid-1970s.

The words 'verligte' and 'verkrampte' – which came to signify the two, enlightened and conservative, streams of thought in the ruling party about how best to secure the survival of Africa's white tribe – were officially absorbed into the ever-broadening

Diehard verkrampte politician Andries Treurnicht, right, broke away from the Nationalists in 1982 and formed the right-wing Conservative Party.

vocabulary of world English.

You couldn't talk about white politics in South Africa without resorting to the terms 'verligte' and 'verkrampte'. Afrikanerdom, the once unified core of white nationalism, was disintegrating as a politically cohesive force.

The final crisis for the conservatives was publication of the details of the new constitution, recommended by the President's Council, to give coloureds and Indians qualified political rights in a three-chamber parliament.

Led by Andries Treurnicht, 15 rebel MPs left the National Party and formed a new party on Botha's right, the Conservative Party. It favoured old-style apartheid.

———— ❖ ————

The poet Sepamla's notion that 'for sure now dis heart go-go da same/dats for meaning to say/one man no diflent to anader' was eventually beginning to register among increasing numbers of whites at the beginning of the 1980s, the last decade of Nationalist rule.

But the dawning truth that racism simply had no rational basis was a complicated truth to accept. And even those whites who didn't accept it found that clinging to racism for whatever security they thought it offered was becoming increasingly difficult, too.

For the reformists, the problem was how to untangle the mess without making a bigger mess. Every reforming step the government thought would be gratefully welcomed by the oppressed as a gesture of goodwill or an improvement in their lives seemed only to infuriate black South Africans all the more.

Botha's complex and ultimately insufficient tinkering simply made it worse.

Sally Motlana, wife of the outspoken chairman of the Soweto Committee of Ten, Dr Ntatho Motlana, expressed it crisply:

We don't want our chains made more comfortable. We want them removed.

From *South Africa Speaks* (1981) by Jill Johnson (editor)

———— ❖ ————

State President PW Botha, centre, and his defence minister, General Magnus Malan, left, presided over 'defence' forces that, in the Eighties, were seen as the agents of aggression.

In the more than two decades since the armed and dangerous 1970s, supporters of apartheid just seemed to vanish.

They didn't really disappear, though some still thought life was better under apartheid. But no one would openly defend that past, or claim ownership of the racist system of government. For many, guilt or fear or shame prevented them from owning up to supporting apartheid. But disowning it was made easier by the fact that the once mighty white National Party rapidly gained favour among many of its former victims.

Even before Nelson Mandela came to power in 1994, the Nationalists who once thronged to Vorster and PW Botha's racist flag had reinvented themselves, and succeeded in attracting significant support from people they once oppressed.

Many coloureds – distrusting the ANC's long association with Communists, or fearing they would be sidelined in political rivalry between whites and blacks, or as a result of a new majoritarian nation-alism – became indispensable to the survival of the new Nationalists.

If it was ironic, it was also a token of the defeat of apartheid itself.

Equally, however, some black commentators argued that too little had changed for any defeat to be honestly celebrated.

Reflecting in 2003 on the events of the 1970s, and especially the 'heroic' revolt of Soweto which had the appearance at least of a revolutionary event, journalist Sandile Memela asked bluntly:

What the hell has June 16 achieved for the African majority? The tree of liberation, watered by the blood of so-called martyrs, has not borne any fruit to be enjoyed by the African majority. Instead, Africans who had been in the vanguard of the struggle, are still trapped in an unchanged global economic apartheid framework that protects the privileged lifestyle of the white minority.

And in a letter to the *Sunday World* newspaper, the Congress of South African Students complained that Youth Day – 16 June – 'is being turned into an official alcohol drinking day for young people'.

There is, on the other hand, an argument that only genuinely free people decide for themselves just how they will spend their Youth Day holiday, or feel free to express whatever controversial opinion they have of their history.

Or, for that matter, choose to vote for the party that once oppressed them.

As Botha tried desperately in the early 1980s to justify white rule while staving off the crisis it had created, it was a freedom that often seemed remote and unimaginable, that had still to be fought for.

Storming
the fortress

[chapter eleven]
Storming the fortress

'The Purple Shall Govern' ... the graffiti by which protesters snubbed their noses at the government after the police sprayed a demonstration with purple dye.

As the water cannon swivelled atop the armoured vehicle, a lurid purple dye spewed out over the protesters. The place was a mess.

The police manning the water cannon didn't care much about the mess. What they wanted, and what they achieved to an extent, was to mark the demonstrators with a dye that would impregnate clothes and skin – and take days to wash off – so that they could easily be identified, and detained if necessary. And be deterred from protesting again any time soon.

It must have seemed a good, even a clever, strategy. But the battle was being waged at every level, and psychologically the struggle turned a tactical ploy by the authorities into a devastating propaganda coup.

Within hours of the police spraying the demonstrators in central Cape Town in the second half of 1989, the struggle hit back. Borrowing from the Freedom Charter's resounding demand, The People Shall Govern, graffiti began appearing all over town. It said, simply: 'The Purple Shall Govern.'

Fortress apartheid, under siege now for years, was looking shaky. Nothing the police apparatus could throw at the protesters would put them off. Increasing numbers of angry South Africans were uniting behind a concerted and irrepressible campaign. It was among the biggest international news stories of the decade: the people were storming the fortress.

Back in 1930, Roy Campbell provided a forewarning of sorts in his poem, 'The Serf', a part of which reads:

> *But as the turf divides*
> *I see in the slow progress of his strides*
> *Over the toppled clods and falling flowers,*
> *The timeless, surly patience of the serf*
> *That moves the nearest to the naked earth*
> *And ploughs down palaces, and thrones, and towers.*

From *Selected Poems* (1981) by Roy Campbell

It was not a rural peasantry that was rising up, nationally, to challenge the regime: but with every passing year more of the people the Nationalists had wanted to turn into 'serfs' were willing to demonstrate at sometimes unthinkable personal cost the failure of racialism as a basis for ordering society.

> *Change in this country can come from two directions – from the black majority or from the people who have the actual political power, the Afrikaner Establishment.*
>
> So writer André Brink speculated in an interview at the start of the 1980s.
>
> *If it comes from the black majority, exclusively, it will have to be violent. There is a possibility of it coming through the Afrikaner Establishment. The situation has eased up through the expectations created, through the fact that for the first time in thirty years the necessity for change, the word change, is mentioned, is no longer taboo.*
>
> He added that, while he was 'totally cynical' about PW Botha,
>
> *he has introduced the possibility of change and that may carry him or other people further. Once a certain historical momentum is created I don't think it can be stopped.*
>
> From *South Africa Speaks* (1981) by Jill Johnson (editor)

The battle lines that the young Oliver Tambo foresaw back in 1948 had not been starker than they were in the early 1980s, with both the black majority and the Afrikaner Establishment, as Brink saw it, determined to control, and fashion, change in South Africa. And the efforts of both sides, each working furiously against the other, ensured that an unstoppable historical momentum was at work.

❖

PW Botha once famously proclaimed that apartheid was a word to be rejected because it was inaccurate: 'Good neighbourliness … describes our policy in South Africa much better.'

But it wasn't as simple as that. Typical of the government's complicated gobbledygook at the start of the 1980s was this 'explanation' from the president of his 'reforms': 'The acceptance of vertical differentiation with the built-in principle of self-determination must apply on as many levels as possible.'

The 'good neighbourliness', the 'vertical differentiation', the 'principle of self-determination', these were all euphemisms for a pretending reform that would ensure power remained in white hands.

Confusing legalistic complexity was the hallmark of the tricameral Constitution of 1983.

The objective of the Republic of South Africa Constitution Act, said minister of constitutional affairs Chris Heunis, was to 'accommodate the coloured people and Indians without detracting from the self-determination of the whites'. The problem, as historian William Beinart summarises it, was that 'it seemed to offer little more than a new language of white command'.

There would be three chambers of parliament, one for each of the three 'race' groups. And the business of government would be divided into 'general affairs' which applied to all three groups – and included defence, foreign affairs, justice, police and transport – and 'own affairs', which applied only to each group on its own and covered education, culture, health, community development and local government. Coloured and Indian MPs could pass their own 'own affairs' laws, but 'general affairs' laws needed approval in all three chambers.

Expensive duplication of effort was common. Under the tricameral system, the budgetary process of 25 legislative stages increased dramatically to 87 stages.

Where there was no agreement on a 'general affairs' Bill, the law was sent on to the President's Council, 35 of whose members were appointed by the three 'own affairs' chambers, and 25 – including 10 Opposition representatives – were appointed directly by the state president.

Under his new constitution, President Botha was the all-powerful figurehead and executive head of government, as well as being commander-in-chief of the South African Defence Force.

Without doubt, the new Constitution changed the parliamentary political scene markedly: for the first time since Union in 1910, which had given South Africa an all-white legislature, MPs who were not white were given seats, and a say in running the show.

But the fundamental flaw of the Union Constitution

Colour-coded democracy, but not for blacks: the tricameral parliament was welcomed by some moderates as a step in the right direction, but mostly rejected as a wasteful and insufficient reform. Here, South Africa's first racially mixed electoral college meets in the old House of Assembly to elect executive State President PW Botha.

– the exclusion of the majority – was repeated these 74 years later in the tricameral blueprint.

Limited recognition, however, was given to urban blacks in the hope of pacifying resentment, and gaining the support of the emerging African middle class: they could elect semi-autonomous local authorities in the townships.

Just as in the early 1900s, the whole package was fiercely challenged, but this time what became known as the extra-parliamentary opposition was broader, angrier and more defiant.

Ironically, as Brian Lapping points out in his book, *Apartheid, A History* (1986), these 'innovations meant that [the government] could hardly ban political campaigning. It had created the legal space for its opponents to manoeuvre.'

———— ❖ ————

Late on the afternoon of 20 May, 1983, a 60 kilogram bomb placed in a stolen car parked outside the South African Air Force headquarters in central Pretoria was prematurely detonated, killing at least 16 people, nine of them whites, and injuring 188.

The dying and wounded were scattered over the streets and pavements. Cars blazed. It ranked as the country's worst 'terror' attack to date. White South Africans were stunned.

In a revenge raid that night, the Air Force launched attacks on targets in the Mozambican capital of Maputo, claiming they were ANC bases. Mozambique said five of its nationals and one South African refugee were the victims.

The frightening evidence of the penetrating reach of the armed struggle – coupled with the strident old-style apartheid stance of the Conservatives on the National Party's right – made it easier for moderate English-speaking South Africans, who once opposed the Nats, to back Botha's government.

But Botha wanted to be sure of his support. Though the new constitution had become law at the end of August, he called a referendum in early November to test white opinion.

The poster campaigns of the main opposing camps – the verligtes and the verkramptes – cryptically reflect the reasoning of white society: 'I'm here to stay … Yes', and 'Don't be a Yes-man, have guts … No'.

But there was another category of No voters, to

Yes and No: most whites backed the limited extension of political rights to coloureds and Indians, and the exclusion, again, of the black majority.

the left of the government. Among them were Frederik van Zyl Slabbert, leader of the Official Opposition, the Progressive Federal Party, and Harry Oppenheimer, chairman of the giant Anglo American Corporation and one of the country's most influential businessmen. Africans, they warned, would bitterly resent a new constitutional set-up that would exclude them again.

However, many other business leaders, and many, though not all, of the avowedly anti-apartheid mainstream newspapers, urged people to support the new constitution as a step in the right direction.

On the day, whites turned out in force: of the high turnout of 76 percent in the referendum on 2 November, 66 percent – more than 1,3 million – voted Yes.

Many of them thought the new constitution was a positive and reasonable shift away from politics that were clearly leading to trouble.

But, as Van Zyl Slabbert argued in the late Seventies, it was deceptive reasoning.

I was struck by the realisation of how ignorant the average white was of the fact that the relatives of those who were committed to the armed struggle, to violence, were living in our midst, working in our kitchens, gardens and factories and how futile it was for the government to convince blacks that we were the subjects of some foreign 'total onslaught'. In fact, such a propaganda effort simply served to wrap whites into a tighter cocoon of ignorance and make them less prepared to meet the challenges that lay ahead.

From *The Last White Parliament* (1986) by Frederik van Zyl Slabbert

———— ❖ ————

The challenges were brought home forcefully in late 1983 with the formation of a coalition of opposition forces inspired by the rhetoric and politics of the liberation struggle. In fact there were two, one reflecting the political sentiments of those who drew on the Freedom Charter of 1955 and sided with the ANC, and those who, rejecting the Charter's non-acceptance of racial groupings, threw in their lot with the black consciousness thinking of Steve Biko. (There was a period of violent clashes between the two.)

The black consciousness front was the first off the ground. The left-wing revolutionary National Forum

Government opposition was broadened and emboldened by the launch of the United Democratic Front in the Cape in 1983.

was launched by the Azanian People's Organisation (Azapo) and other groups, including the socialist Cape Action League, at a meeting at Hammanskraal near Pretoria in June 1983. It never gained the popular support of the second coalition, which came into being at a rally at Mitchells Plain on 20 August, 1983.

Between 6 000 and 15 000 people packed into the Rocklands civic centre, and a marquee alongside,

to launch the United Democratic Front (UDF), an alliance that by 1984 had the support of some 600 civic and student organisations and unions and an estimated membership of three million.

Its core demand was expressed to a roar of approval by one of its most prominent founding leaders, Allan Boesak, who at the time was president of the World Alliance of Reformed Churches, when he

Before she became a politician, Helen Zille was a journalist. She described the UDF launch in *Frontline* magazine:

> Some packed the central hall beyond capacity, like a fat man trying to squeeze into a pair of toddler's shorts. … Scores of people, squeezed out of standing room, had moved upwards, finding perches on the beams and ledges near the enormous suspension lights of the modern civic centre. [The caretaker insisted they move, and organisers appealed to them to do so. They didn't budge.] Then someone explained it like this: the struggle, he said, would demand many sacrifices from them, the first of which was to

> get down from the beams and rafters. It worked. Slowly, people began to clamber down. … And the final word on the subject came from a voice that said: 'Kom nou van the beams af sodat ons kan beginne history to maak.' (Come down from the beams now so that we start making history.)

From *Frontline* October, 1983

The mood, Zille wrote, was

> summed up by an elderly woman as she boarded one of the 70 buses that would drive through the night to take people back to various corners of South Africa: 'We will have something to talk about for years.'

said the thrust of the UDF could be summed up in three words: 'all, here and now. … We want all our rights, we want them here and we want them now.'

Earlier in 1983, Allan Boesak had expressed in a speech to the Indian Congress in Johannesburg what was wrong with working for change 'within the system', which is what coloured and Indian parties angling for seats in the new parliament were intent on doing:

Working within the system for whatever reason contaminates you. It wears down your defences. It whets your appetite for power … And what you call 'compromise' for the sake of politics is in fact selling out your principles, your ideals and the future of your children … Churches, civic organisations, trade unions, student organisations and sports bodies should unite on this issue, pool our resources, inform the people of the fraud that is about to be perpetrated in their name, and expose those plans for what they are.

He had set out the agenda for the growing extra-parliamentary opposition that was within months created and nurtured by the UDF. And at the launch of the Front, he underlined the single most important truth about the emergence of modern South Africa when he said:

The time has come for white people in this country to realise that their destiny is inextricably bound with ours … They will never be free as long as they have to lie awake at night worrying whether a black government will one day do to them as they are doing to us.

❖

PW Botha was the first Nationalist leader who was not a lawyer, a cleric or an academic. He had dropped out of university in 1936 to become a party organiser, and the National Party was his life. None of his critics expected him to have any vision that took stock of anything beyond the narrow ambitions of the party.

Stirring orator and controversial cleric Allan Boesak.

Yet there was some irony in the fact that – as André Brink noted – it was PW who made the word 'change' acceptable. He started out in what seemed a promising frame of mind, alarming the conservatives in his own party by saying in effect precisely what Boesak later expressed, that white South Africa had to 'adapt [or] die'.

We are moving in a changing world, we must adapt otherwise we shall die … The moment you start oppressing people … they fight back … We must acknowledge people's rights and … make ourselves free by giving to others in a spirit of justice what we demand for ourselves … A white monopoly of power is untenable in the Africa of today … A meaningful division of power is needed between all race groups … Apartheid is a recipe for permanent conflict.

From *Apartheid, A History* (1986) by Brian Lapping

Oppressive governments, however, are always at their weakest when, in the piecemeal way they think assures them the initiative, they begin to ease the pressure, to retreat.

And as the Nationalists opened more space for political expression among people who were not white – through the tricameral parliament, for instance, and through the recognition of black unions – the oppressed filled it in vigorous and unanticipated ways. The social landscape was changing, too: urbanisation increased dramatically in the 1980s – Durban and Cape Town drew hundreds of thousands of new residents in just a few years, with the Cape Peninsula's new township Khayelitsha mushrooming by the month. At the same time, unions were growing steadily, and school pupils and university students were more united and organised than ever before.

The anger, but also the political conviction, of young people was a critical element of the struggle of the 1980s, as it had been a decade before when, without waiting for guidance or direction from the liberation movements, the students of Soweto had launched what became a national uprising.

In the Eighties, the idealism of the struggle for justice and democracy among school pupils and students dramatically broadened the front in the 'war' on apartheid, and drew many thousands of young South Africans into the firing line.

Without doubt, the first sitting of the tricameral parliament on 3 September, 1984 was a new experience for South Africans. Only about 30 percent of registered coloured voters, and 20 percent of Indians, cast ballots. Allan Hendrikse's Labour Party won the House of Representatives, or coloured, election, and the House of Delegates, or Indian house, was led by Amichand Rajbansi's National People's Party. The success of the stayaway arose in good measure from an established tradition of non-collaboration that had its roots in the early decades of the 20th century.

Some time after activist Eddie Daniels had emerged from his 15 years on Robben Island, he took up teaching. It brought home to him the extraordinary contrasts in the lives of young South Africans. His first taste of teaching was at a school in Milnerton in the mid-1980s, where

[t]he first thing that struck me ... was the acres of green grass that made up the sports complex. They also had tennis courts and I saw [the headmaster] teaching some girls golf. It was quite pleasant teaching there.

From 1985, he began teaching at Garlandale High, which was caught up in the political turmoil of the time:

In the past politics had been the terrain of adults only but, since the Soweto uprising ... the picture had rapidly changed. By 1985, schoolchildren from standard six upward were actively involved. ... The children were well organised and extremely brave in spite of the State of Emergency [declared in July 1985] ... Children were beaten, imprisoned and killed. One of the most notorious

incidents was the 'Trojan Horse Killings', when a group of policemen hid inside crates on the back of a government railways truck [and, when children began stoning it] popped up ... and opened fire indiscriminately with automatic rifles. Three children died. ...

From *There and Back, Robben Island 1964–1979* (2002) by Eddie Daniels

Daniels notes that the 'student uprising' continued for years, 'resulting in many students losing out on their schoolwork and failing their examinations'. This gave rise to the term, the 'lost generation'. He adds:

This term is often used in a dismissive and contemptuous manner, which is extremely unfair to ... children ... [who] helped to bring the apartheid government to its knees that much sooner. ... Many of them, because of their bravery and commitment to the cause of freedom, became casualties of the struggle against oppression.

Nevertheless, for many Nationalists, mingling with people of oppressed communities made them more intimate with the folly of apartheid.

One can imagine even the most dogged supporter of the Population Registration Act being struck by the irrationality of it when the Labour Party's Griqualand West MP Ishmail Essop explained in a debate in February 1988 how a fellow MP, Egyptian-born Mrs Soheir Hoosen, the United Democratic Party representative for Tafelberg, was classified coloured, while he himself was classified Cape Malay, two of his brothers were classified coloured, another white, two of his sisters coloured and another Indian.

But it was not to be a peaceable time in which truths could dawn gradually.

Beyond the precincts of the new, much enlarged legislature, protest burst into violence.

As Van Zyl Slabbert had warned during the referendum, the tricameral system was 'so defective and ill-conceived' that it would 'set back the process of reform for at least a decade'.

And 'the smouldering fuse of African bitterness at being excluded from any say in the running of the country,' the *Reader's Digest Illustrated History of South Africa* (1994) recalls, 'ignited an explosion of violence comparable to that of the darkest days of June 1976'.

In the townships, local council elections drew a pitiful turnout. Only between two and three percent of those eligible to vote did so, and in many seats candidates did not dare stand. Opposition was brutal. Brian Lapping writes in *Apartheid, A History* (1986):

> On 3 September 1984 the newly elected deputy mayor of Sharpeville was hacked to death on his front doorstep. The same day in Sharpeville, two blacks were burned to death trapped in their cars, four people were strangled behind a plundered garage, a man burned to death in a liquor store, many buildings and cars were set on fire. The official tally for Sharpeville, September 1984, was 26 dead. With comparable killings in nearby Sebokeng, it marked a new phase in South African history; the moment when blacks turned their anger against fellow blacks they regarded as collaborators with the white government.

The violence spread.

The cycle of insurrection and repression based around schools, universities, factories and townships that had begun in 1976 rose to a crescendo between late 1984 and early 1986. This marked the turning point for the apartheid state. Some groups identifying with the UDF took a more militant path. The ANC itself was becoming the focus of opposition forces, and demands for Nelson Mandela's release from prison became a central unifying call in the external anti-apartheid movements and at home.

From *Twentieth-Century South Africa* (2001) by William Beinart

South Africa's relations with the world were changing significantly.

Close to home, PW Botha gained credit in some quarters for pulling off an agreement with his socialist neighbours in Mozambique which seemed to show an ability to do business diplomatically with black Africa.

The Nkomati Accord he signed with Samora Machel was a non-aggression pact: in return for

Friendly relations with Mozambique – the intended objective of the Nkomati Accord signed by PW Botha and Samora Machel – did not last long.

Moments of drama during the United Democratic Front's mass rally in Soweto at the weekend. Left: Nobel laureate Bishop Desmond Tutu holds the Peace Prize medal up to the crowd, saying: "Take it, it's yours." Right: Zinzi Mandela, daughter of Nelson, brings her father's message from jail: "I cannot sell my birthright, nor the birthright of the people to be free." Pictures by Juda Ngwenya.

First unban the ANC — Mandela

This is the full text of Nelson Mandela's response to the conditional offer of freedom made in Parliament by the State President, Mr P W Botha. It was read by his daughter Zinzi.

"On Friday my mother and our attorney saw my father at Pollsmoor Prison to obtain his answer to Botha's offer of conditional release.

"The prison authorities attempted to stop this statement being made but he would have none of this and made it clear that he would make the statement to you, the people.

"Strangers like Bethell from England and Professor Dash from the United States have in recent weeks been authorised by Pretoria to see my father without restriction yet Pretoria cannot allow you, the people, to hear what he has to say directly. He should be here himself to tell you what he thinks of this statement by Botha. He is not allowed to do so. My mother who also heard his words is also not allowed to speak to you today.

"My father and his comrades at Pollsmoor Prison send their greetings to you, the freedom-loving people of this, our tragic land in the full confidence that you will carry on the struggle for freedom.

"He, with his comrades at Pollsmoor Prison, sends his very warmest greetings to Bishop Tutu. Bishop Tutu has made it clear to the world that the Nobel Peace Prize belongs to you, who are the people. We salute him.

"My father and his comrades at Pollsmoor Prison are grateful to the United Democratic Front, who without hesitation made this venue available to them so that they could speak to you today.

"My father and his comrades wish to make this statement to you, the people, first. They are clear that they are accountable to you and to you alone. And that you should hear their views directly and not through others.

"My father speaks not only for himself and for his comrades at Pollsmoor Prison but he hopes he also speaks for all those in jail for their opposition to apartheid, for all those who are banished, for all those who are in exile, for all those who suffer under apartheid, for all those who are opponents of apartheid and for all those who are

Rejection hits UK headlines
The Star Bureau

LONDON — Nelson Mandela's rejection of President Botha's offer of conditional release is prominently reported in most Fleet Street newspapers today.

The Daily Telegraph, makes it front-page news under the headline, "Mandela rejects lure of freedom". The Times publishes a front-page photograph of Bishop Desmond Tutu with Mandela's daughter, Zindzi, and The Guardian places the same photograph on an inside page.

The statement was also featured on radio and television.

Several correspondents note that Mandela appeared to leave open the possibility of negotiations with the Government.

puppets who have claimed to speak for you. They have made this claim, both here and abroad. They are of no consequence. My father and his colleagues will not be like them.

"My father says: 'I am a member of the African National Congress. I have always been a member of the African National Congress and I will remain a member of the African National Congress until the day I die. Oliver Tambo is much more than a brother to me. He is my greatest friend and comrade for nearly 50 years. If there is any one amongst you who cherishes my freedom, Oliver Tambo cherishes it more and I know that he would give his life to see me free. There is no difference between his views and mine.'

"My father says: 'I am surprised at the conditions that the Government wants to impose on me. I am not a violent man. My colleagues and I wrote in 1952 to Malan asking for a round-table conference to find a solution to the problems of our country but that was ignored.

'When Strijdom was in power, we made the same offer. Again it was ignored. When Verwoerd was in power we asked for a national convention for all the people in South Africa to decide on their

'It was only then when all other forms of resistance were no longer open to us that we turned to armed struggle.

'Let Botha show that he is different to Malan, Strijdom and Verwoerd.

'Let him renounce violence.

'Let him say that he will dismantle apartheid.

'Let him unban the people's organisation, the African National Congress.

'Let him free all who have been imprisoned, banished or exiled for their opposition to apartheid.

'Let him guarantee free political activity so that the people may decide who will govern them.

'I cherish my own freedom dearly but I care even more for your freedom. Too many have died since I went to prison. Too many have suffered for the love of freedom. I owe it to their widows, to their orphans, to their mothers and to their fathers who have grieved and wept for them. Not only I have suffered during these long, lonely, wasted years.

'I am not less life-loving than you are. But I cannot sell my birthright, nor am I prepared to sell the birthright of the people to be free. I am in prison as the representative of the people and of your organisation, the African National Congress, which was banned. What freedom am I being offered while the organisation of the people remains banned? What freedom am I being offered when I may be arrested on a pass offence? What freedom am I being offered to live my life as a family with my dear wife who remains in banishment in Brandfort? What freedom am I being offered when I must ask for permission to live in an urban area? What freedom am I being offered when I need a stamp in my pass to seek work? What freedom am I being offered when my very South African citizenship is not respected?

'Only free men can negotiate. Prisoners cannot enter into contracts. Herman Toivo Ja Toivo, when freed, never gave any undertaking, nor was he called upon to do so.'

"My father says: 'I cannot and will not give any undertaking at a time when I and you the people are not free. Your freedom and

'I cherish my own freedom but I care even more for your freedom' ... Zindzi Mandela reads her father's words to a rapt audience at a UDF rally in Soweto.

Mozambique's expelling the ANC and thus stopping guerrilla attacks into South Africa from that quarter, South Africa undertook to stop helping the Renamo rebel movement that was intent on frustrating Frelimo policies. All evidence suggested that South Africa failed to keep to its side of the bargain.

Elsewhere on the international front, opposition was mounting.

Where South Africa had once been regarded as a good bet economically, with investors being prepared to overlook internal policies for the sake of good profits and cheap labour, this changed markedly in the 1980s. The rise of militant unions, the under-performance of the economy and its weakness in competing internationally, the fall of the gold price and rising inflation all had an impact.

Politically, South Africa was becoming a dicey bet, too. Beinart writes:

In the cold-war era, the US and Western European governments tended to judge the ANC as revolutionary, and avoid it. A rapidly growing South Africa was seen, although increasingly uneasily, as a good investment and a bastion against communism. But anti-apartheid forces in these countries were able to claim some of the moral high ground. Boycott campaigns involving such varied targets as Outspan oranges, Cape fruit, cultural exchanges, and the arms trade met with some success. As in the case of the anti-slavery campaigns over 150 years earlier, it became increasingly difficult to justify apartheid in Western countries.

It became all the more so when the then Bishop-elect of Johannesburg and general secretary of the South African Council of Churches, Desmond Tutu, was awarded the Nobel Peace Prize. He, perhaps more

Sanctions campaigns abroad gained increasing popular support.

than any other single individual, personified the commitment of black South Africa to bringing economic hardship on themselves through sanctions in order to overcome the far greater hardship of living under apartheid. And as a consequence of the government's detention of thousands of opposition figures, clerics such as Tutu and Boesak – who were not so easily shut up – became potent, outspoken and internationally recognised symbols of the struggle.

Though Botha had allies in Britain's Conservative prime minister Margaret Thatcher and US Republican president Ronald Reagan, the campaign for the economic isolation of apartheid South Africa ranged powerfully across every social and business activity in every corner of the world. To overcome it, through whatever so-called 'sanctions-busting' tactics could be devised, began to cost South Africa a steadily increasing premium.

The year 1985 was probably the most decisive of the decade, for both obvious and not-so-obvious reasons.

In 1976, Mandela had been made an offer he'd found easy to refuse: his sentence would be dramatically reduced if he would agree to recognise the independence of Transkei and retire there in what the Nationalists fantasised would be political obscurity.

In January 1985, it was PW Botha's turn – there had been other similar overtures – to make an easily rebutted offer: the president said in parliament he would free Mandela if the ANC leader 'unconditionally rejected violence as a political instrument'.

It was a signal moment for Mandela. His reply, read in public by his daughter Zindzi in February, was the first time in more than 20 years that South Africans

White resistance to apartheid gained ground in the Eighties with the formation of the End Conscription Campaign.

Political tension mounted in the Eighties when South African Defence Force troops were deployed in the townships to counter resistance to the government.

were able legally to hear his words. This is, in part, what he said:

> I am surprised at the conditions that the government wants to impose on me. I am not a violent man. ... It was only ... when all other forms of resistance were no longer open to us, that we turned to armed struggle. Let Botha show that he is different to Malan, Strijdom and Verwoerd. Let him renounce violence. Let him say that he will dismantle apartheid. Let him unban the people's organisation, the African National Congress. Let him free all who have been imprisoned, banished or exiled for their opposition to apartheid. Let him guarantee free political activity so that people may decide who will govern them.
>
> I cherish my freedom dearly, but I care even more for your freedom. Too many have died since I went to prison. Too many have suffered for the love of freedom. ... Not only I have suffered during these long, lonely, wasted years. I am not less life-loving than you are. But I cannot sell my birthright, nor am I prepared to sell the birthright of the people to be free. ... Only free men can negotiate. Prisoners cannot enter into contracts ... I cannot and will not give any undertaking at a time when I and you, the people, are not free. Your freedom and mine cannot be separated. I will return.
>
> From *Long Walk to Freedom* (1994) by Nelson Mandela

If the government had hoped to gain the initiative – or some relief from continuing violent revolt – the hope was shattered on the anniversary of the Sharpeville massacre of 1960.

A huge anniversary march in Uitenhage's Langa township was heading towards the white suburbs to attend a funeral when they were confronted by police in armoured Casspirs. When the marchers showed no sign of stopping, the police opened fire with live rounds, killing 20 of them.

Condemnation from within South Africa and from abroad was sharp and swift. While the government appointed a judge to investigate what had gone wrong, it showed no sign of easing up in quelling what had become a national revolt.

Troops had first been deployed in townships in October 1984, and many thousands more were now deployed routinely in an effort to help police impose public order.

When journalist Ralph Rabie reinvented himself as the outspoken and irreverent singer-songwriter Johannes Kerkorrel – even his assumed surname, 'church organ', was a satirical barb – young, progressive Afrikaners found lyrics that spoke for them, too. The song *'Sit dit af'* outraged deferential conservatives:

> Die ander dag toe voel ek lam,
> Ek wou 'n klein bietjie ontspan,
> En 'n boer maak 'n plan
> Ek sit my TV set toe aan,
> Jy sal nie glo wat ek sien,
> Op my TV screen.
> Dit was 'n nare gesig,
> Dit het my heeltemal ontwrig,
> Dit was 'n moerse klug,
> Dit was PW se gesig,
> En langs hom staan Oom Pik, ja,
> O, ek dog ek gaan verstik.
> Sit dit af sit dit af
> Sit dit af sit dit af
> Want dis 'n helse straf.
> Ek stap kombuis toe kry 'n bier,
> Ek skakel oor na TV 4,
> O my God wat het ons hier,
> Wat my TV set ontsier,
> Is daar nerens om toe te vlug,
> Van daai man se mooi gesig,
> Met sy vinger in die lug,
> Gaan hy my lewe net ontstig,
> En die program hang in the lug
> Sien jy net PW se gesig
> Ek vat jou nou 'n wed
> Al die bure het Mnet.
> O, ek sê jou dis finaal
> Voor julle my kom haal
> En ek met my verstand
> In die gestig beland.
> As daar iets wat my kwel,
> Is dit my TV stel.
> From *Eet Kreef* (2002), Shifty Music

This dramatic shift in the use of conscripted civilian whites against black citizens – who could not by any stretch of the imagination have been regarded as an external enemy of the country – led to mounting disquiet among young white men.

Out of this grew the End Conscription Campaign – which was banned in 1988 – and, in London, the Committee on South African War Resistance. For the first time, the South African Defence Force was being actively opposed by some among the hundreds of thousands of young conscripts on whom it depended to maintain its occupation of Namibia, and to strike fear into the townships.

An unnamed conscript describes in a letter published in the journal of the Committee on South African War Resistance in London what for many became an intolerable experience:

I had never previously gone into a black township. I would like to have gone there as a friend, but because I was called up for township duty, I went in wearing a uniform that was obviously hated by those people. I saw how the other side lived. After a while I started to understand what rent boycotts and school unrest were all about. I certainly would pay no rent for such pigsties as they are forced to live in, and I would have revolted even more as a teenager if I had been forced to go to school in the shadow of casspirs and shotguns. I really resent the fact that I had been part of that kind of maintenance of law and order.

From *Resister, Journal of the Committee on South African War Resistance* October–November, 1986

While the End Conscription Campaign was a predominantly English-speaking initiative, even among young Afrikaners PW Botha's South Africa was becoming increasingly indefensible and repugnant.

The emergence of so-called Alternative Afrikaners – spearheaded by deliberately 'subversive' singer-song writers, helped shatter the stereotype of Afrikaans-speaking whites as conservative and racist, or as unquestioning supporters of apartheid. Although David Kramer's song *'Hoekom blaf die honde by die hekke van paradise?'* (Why are the dogs barking at the gates of paradise?) was not an overtly political lyric, the title captures the unsettling quality of questions among young Afrikaners about the soured dream of a white *Vaderland*. Kramer began to find his songs were being banned from the national broadcaster, the SABC.

Official disapproval was earned by other Alternative voices, the likes of Johannes Kerkorrel, Koos Kombuis and James Phillips.

In the James Phillips song, 'Shot Down in the Street', listeners were confronted with a discomforting idea which, until the 1980s, would not have registered in the homegrown popular culture of Afrikanerdom:

I'm a white boy who looked at his life gathered in his hands
And saw it was all due to the sweat of some other man
That one who got shot down in the street.

From http://www.gypsy.co.za (2003)

The publishing of 'alternative' media in the Eighties – feisty, critical papers such as *Saamstaan, South, Work in Progress* and the *Weekly Mail* – had its Afrikaans equivalent in the *Vrye Weekblad*.

These were not insignificant developments for the ANC, monitoring developments at home from a now extensive international network from its main base in Lusaka, and more than 30 missions around the world.

Some 16 years before, at its first consultative conference – the Morogoro Conference in Tanzania in 1969 – the ANC had agreed in principle to open its doors to whites. But it was only at the second consultative conference at Kabwe in Zambia in 1985 that it voted on the issue, endorsing open membership overwhelmingly.

One of the key tactical goals to emerge from Kabwe was to strengthen white support, and to challenge whites to decide where they stood. As the Kabwe communique put it: 'It is becoming more necessary than ever for whites to make it clear on which side of the battle lines they stand.'

It was a challenge well understood by Eastern Cape activist Molly Blackburn, whose awakening consciousness in the early 1980s propelled her transformation from an anonymous Port Elizabeth estate agent into a courageous political figure. In the four years before she died in a car accident in 1986, Blackburn devoted all her energy to fighting apartheid. At a gathering in 1984, she explained why it was important to her:

We should not dwell on the hatreds and sufferings of the past, but should put all our energies into looking into and working towards the future. The time is past when whites can think that the events in the townships do not concern them – whether it be the toilets in Red Location, whether it be the school boycotts or the unequal education opportunities, whether it be influx control or the so-called residential rights.

From *Frontline* February, 1987, in a profile by Bill Krige

❖

The battle lines became more clearly defined in another sense with the formation of the giant trade union alliance, the Congress of South African Trade Unions (Cosatu) – representing some 30 non-racial unions and about half a million workers. Huge stayaways headed by Cosatu – and similar campaigns at hundreds of schools led by the Congress of South African Students – demonstrated the power of concerted mass action, which the government felt compelled to respond to with ever more repressive action.

In July 1985, Botha announced a state of emergency in 36 magisterial districts. It was the first time since the Sharpeville revolt in 1960 that the government had resorted to such measures. They didn't help. Violence continued, and spread.

Against this background, however, speculation had been mounting for months – partly sponsored by pointed hints to diplomats from foreign minister Pik Botha – that the president was to make a major policy announcement in a speech to the annual National Party conference in Durban in August. There was hope that a significant change of political direction was in the offing.

In the build-up to what everybody was now expecting would be the big day, when Botha would lead South Africans across their Rubicon – the expression comes from Julius Caesar's irrevocable step in crossing the Rubicon River in 49 BC to march against Pompey, and signifies the crossing of a figurative boundary – possibly to a negotiated settlement of sorts, other developments seemed to make him rethink his ideas.

Historian Nigel Worden sums up the scene in the mid-1980s:

The resistance of the mid-1980s destroyed utterly the 'total strategy' tactics of the Botha government. Tricameralism and African urban councils had been firmly rejected by the demand for 'People's Power'. The campaign to win hearts and minds was in tatters, with thousands in detention and an occupying army in the townships. ... With the collapse of total strategy, the government seemed bankrupted of ideas, relying on internal repression and international bravado.

From *The Making of Modern South Africa, Conquest, Segregation and Apartheid* (1994) by Nigel Worden

The spirit of the time, the place, was captured in one of the seminal fictions of the period, JM Coetzee's Booker Prize-winning novel *Life and Times of Michael K.* The narrative closes with the resourceful itinerant Michael K making his way in a near-apocalyptic landscape:

And if the old man climbed out of the cart and stretched himself ... and looked at where the pump had been that the soldiers had blown up so that nothing should be left standing, and complained, saying 'What are we going to do about water?', he, Michael K, would produce a teaspoon from his pocket, a teaspoon and a long roll of string. He would clear the rubble from the mouth of the shaft, he would bend the handle of the teaspoon in a loop and tie the string to it, he would lower it down the shaft deep into the earth, and when he brought it up there would be water in the bowl of the spoon; and in that way, he would say, one can live.

From *Life and Times of Michael K* (1985) by JM Coetzee

South Africa used its armed forces – and surrogate forces nurtured to destabilise the region – to strike at 'the enemy' in neighbouring countries.

One was that the white right appeared to be making gains among the electorate, putting the fear of God into people about the implications of any further 'reforms'. The other was economic.

South Africa had become steadily more dependent on big loans from overseas banks to maintain the high living standards of the white community and keep the economy growing to absorb the steady increase in young black job-seekers entering the labour market each year. For years, the international banks had turned a deaf ear to anti-apartheid protesters, but, as Brian Lapping writes, they 'changed sides' in 1985:

> The large New York bank, Chase Manhattan, influenced by students, churches and charities that had withdrawn deposits rather than have them invested in South Africa, refused to renew a major South African loan.

This happened just before the Durban meeting.

When PW Botha stood to address his Natal audience – and, because of the extensive international pre-publicity, a global audience of some 300 million expectant television viewers – he wagged his finger at the world and warned: 'Don't push us too far.' He added:

> I am not prepared to lead white South Africans and other minority groups on a road to abdication and suicide. Destroy white South

> Africa and our influence, and this country will drift into faction, strife, chaos and poverty.

The reaction was quick and devastating. Within 10 days, the rand plunged against the US dollar and other international banks followed in Chase Manhattan's tracks. After being long committed to avoiding meddling in politics, bankers were now demanding more decisive reforms to ensure safer investments.

The government took the unprecedented step of closing the Johannesburg Stock Exchange for a week so that it could try to persuade the banks to reconsider. They wouldn't, and Finance Minister Barend du Plessis was left with no choice but to announce a four-month freeze on foreign debt repayments. It heightened the international squeeze on the country.

Economically, the country was weakening: there was mass unemployment and high inflation. Between December 1984 and December 1985, inflation was at 18,4 percent, the highest it had been in 66 years.

Protests, often over bread-and-butter issues such as bus-fare increases, spread to the rural areas. Bantustan administrations were also targeted. Throughout the country, violence worsened.

What was more, rejection of the government was not limited just to voteless blacks. Businessmen who at the start of the Eighties had backed the Nationalists' reform agenda were now sharply critical of it.

Within a month of PW Botha's disastrous performance in Durban, Anglo American's Gavin Relly led a powerful delegation to Lusaka for the first talks of their kind between South African business and the banned African National Congress. The ANC delegation was led by Oliver Tambo. Relly called the meeting 'useful' and suggested cryptically that if it were followed up, it 'might lead to some fruitful conclusions'.

Scores of other white South Africans – students, writers, professionals – began to make pilgrimages to the north to the meet the once-feared 'revolutionaries' of the exiled ANC.

---------- ❖ ----------

But perhaps the most significant event of 1985 – and it was less an event than a notion – was an idea in the mind of the man who would symbolically, but in many practical ways, too, lead South Africa to democracy: Nelson Mandela decided, on his own, that it was time to talk.

On the face of it, it contradicted his statement earlier in the year that '[o]nly free men can negotiate … [p]risoners cannot enter into contracts'. Of course, he wasn't about to enter into any contract. And it was also true that he had the stronger hand. Though he was the prisoner, the initiative was his to show the way.

It was after a prostate operation outside prison that Mandela was lodged in a separate cell from his Rivonia colleagues, Walter Sisulu, Ahmed Kathrada and Raymond Mhlaba, at Pollsmoor. It gave him, he later wrote, the liberty to think through, and act on, something that had been on his mind for some time: to 'begin discussions with the government'.

Mandela's dramatic, but secret, decision was not known outside, and would not yield any immediate changes or benefits for the country for a long time.

As 1986 dawned, South Africans remained embattled.

Margaret Thatcher in London and Ronald Reagan in Washington were defiant in trying to resist Commonwealth, European and United States sanctions on South Africa. They were intent on pursuing a policy of 'constructive engagement' with the Botha government.

A Commonwealth diplomatic initiative – the Commonwealth Eminent Persons Group – was the kind of compromise Thatcher favoured. The idea was that it would try to shift the parties in South Africa towards negotiations. Ultimately, the Botha government was not interested: the delegation was still in the country when South Africa launched raids on supposed ANC bases in Harare, Lusaka and Gaborone, and the initiative collapsed.

Despite the Reagan/Thatcher opposition, sanctions mounted: by the mid-1980s, Europe, the Commonwealth and the United States were behind a comprehensive package that included an oil embargo, limits on military and nuclear cooperation, restricted investment, certain diplomatic sanctions and bans on the imports of gold coins, arms, iron, steel and coal.

We had been engaged in the armed struggle for more than two decades. … It was clear to me that a military victory was a distant if not impossible dream. It simply did not make sense for both sides to lose thousands if not millions of lives in a conflict that was unnecessary. They [the government] must have known this as well. It was time to talk.

From *Long Walk to Freedom* (1994) by Nelson Mandela

It was highly sensitive, he realised. Each side 'regarded discussions as a sign of weakness and betrayal'. Equally, pondering these things in his 'splendid isolation', Mandela recognised that while the decision to talk to the government 'should only have been made in Lusaka …

someone from our side needed to take the first step'. And with this extraordinary conviction, Mandela opened the dialogue that would dramatically alter the country.

I chose to tell no one what I was about to do. Not my colleagues upstairs (in Pollsmoor, Sisulu, Kathrada and Mhlaba), nor those in Lusaka. … I knew that my colleagues upstairs would condemn my proposal, and that would kill the initiative even before it was born. There are times when a leader must move out ahead of his flock, go off in a new direction, confident that he is leading his people the right way.

From *Long Walk to Freedom* (1994) by Nelson Mandela

Frederik van Zyl Slabbert, who resigned from parliament, but remained actively engaged in the political debate.

Oil embargoes became especially costly. Until 1979, South Africa got all its oil trouble-free from Iran. But with the fall of the Shah, that supply dried up. Through sanctions-busting deals – that by 1986 had cost the country US$25 billion – oil still reached the country, but the supply was often so constricted that at one point in the 1980s PW Botha admitted the country had enough oil reserves for just one week.

From late 1985, the banks' refusal to grant new loans, or 'roll over' old loans, began to have a dramatic effect: influential multinationals began to quit the country.

Some 500 transnational corporations withdrew from the country, including giants such as IBM, General Motors, General Electric and Coca-Cola.

In October 1986, the US Congress overrode Reagan to approve the Comprehensive Anti-Apartheid Act.

The psychological blow of sanctions was possibly toughest in the sports sphere. By the late Eighties, South Africa was banned from 90 percent of world sport.

Writing in *The Legacy of Apartheid* (1994), published by *The Guardian* newspaper in London, Joseph Hanlon notes:

The realisation in South Africa that support from … Reagan and Thatcher was not enough and that further isolation was inevitable, was a sharp blow to the morale of white … business people. It demonstrated that business could not remain above politics, and shifted many business leaders into the reform camp.

While maintaining repression to contain the threat from 'radical' elements, the government attempted to win support from moderates with several important reforms in 1986: the central business districts of main towns and cities were opened to trading by people of all races; hotels and restaurants were freed of having to get permission to allow black patrons; the Influx Control Act was repealed, and a new law gave blacks rights to freehold property in townships.

But it was also a time of massive repression. Historian William Beinart records that

in the first eight months of the 1985 emergency, 8 000 people were detained and 22 000 charged with offences arising from protests. In the year from June 1986 – when a new emergency was imposed after the first had been briefly lifted – a further 26 000 people were detained.

None of this dealt with the central issue, summed up in February 1986 by journalist Percy Qoboza, who wrote:

Talking and negotiating with the ANC and the PAC has become something the government cannot duck any longer. They may take all the refugees they want out of Lesotho, Botswana or Swaziland, but they will not defuse those bombs. The problem is not in those countries, but right here inside our borders.

The sterility of white politics, the seeming pointlessness of it, was forcefully underscored when Frederik van Zyl Slabbert, the outspoken leader of the liberal opposition, the Progressive Federal Party (PFP), announced his resignation from parliament. He was followed within the week by fellow PFP MP Alex Boraine.

Four days before he resigned, Van Zyl Slabbert told parliament that there were naturally 'uncertainties' involved in his suggestion that free democratic politics was the only way forward, but that 'if the government continues acting the way they are acting now, there will be no uncertainties … conflict, siege and escalating violence are inevitable'. He and Boraine soon established what became an influential and widely respected organisation, the Institute for a Democratic Alternative in South Africa (Idasa).

Looking back, Boraine recalled:

We had no real plans for an alternative course of action, simply an awareness that genuine negoti-

ation politics could not emerge from a parliament dominated by whites, and we wanted to make that point as starkly as we could.

From *A Country Unmasked, Inside South Africa's Truth and Reconciliation Commission* (2000) by Alex Boraine

Neither of the two men believed South Africa was anywhere near ready for 'negotiation politics', but were convinced someone had to make a start.

———— ❖ ————

Francis was already a street child at 15. And his brief comments about why in *Malunde, The Street Children of Hillbrow* (1990) say a lot about township conditions in the late 1980s: 'I am here because of all the fighting in the townships. I don't like all the violence. When it is quiet I will go back.'

Boraine was right about just how unready South Africa was for negotiation politics in 1986.

The country was into its second round of emergency restrictions, though this time they were tougher. Added to all the other conditions was a near blanket ban on reporting. The *Weekly Mail* went as far as publishing reports with blank spaces to indicate how little they could legally report – and the government then banned the 'publication' of blank spaces.

Much of the censorship was self-imposed by editors and journalists who did little to test the limits of what was possible, or who simply ignored

important events. And, as Van Zyl Slabbert recalls in his book, *The Last White Parliament* (1986), newspaper owners were not guiltless: the shutting down of the politically outspoken *Rand Daily Mail*, he writes, 'was directly attributable to corporate indifference and atrocious management'. He adds:

> If you wish to test racial or communal insulation in South Africa, take a black newspaper for a week and compare its contents to that of a white newspaper. You read about two different worlds. The *Rand Daily Mail tried to bridge that gap. Its passing reinforces our ignorance.*

Many whites were ignorant of – and indifferent to – the appalling conditions in townships living in fear … of police, of informers, of the army, of the excesses of young, radical 'Comrades', and of the conservative vigilantes who rose up to challenge them.

By this time, many townships were virtually ungovernable – which was in line with an ANC tactical directive. Street committees emerged to run local affairs. In some areas these were effective, democratically run organisations. But less fortunate communities were dictated to by young, ruthless, ideologically inspired Comrades who delivered summary justice against 'offenders' (anyone who disagreed with them, or who they declared were siding with the 'enemy'), who were often brutally punished or killed. The idea of 'semi-liberated zones' was sometimes tragically ironic.

The 15-year-old street child, Francis, describes his drawing of a township scene:

> My school is here, but you can't see it because it is broken up. Here is a 'hippo' [armoured vehicle] of the army. These are the tyres. The people took them and burnt a man. They put the tyre round his neck and poured on petrol. They burnt him to death. He suffered while he burnt; he cried and screamed. I do not know why they burnt him. These people here are schoolchildren running away from the police. This one is a policeman with a sjambok. Here is a policeman hitting a child who threw a stone at him.

From *Malunde, The Street Children of Hillbrow* (1990) by Jill Swart

Victoria Mxenge

And the more conservative men who emerged to confront the Comrades, forming vigilante groups such as the 'witdoeke' (white scarves) of the Cape townships, so named because they identified themselves by binding their heads with white scarves, were soon exploited by the police.

In Natal, the political division between the UDF and its allies in Cosatu, and Inkatha, and the union it established in 1986, Uwusa, led to protracted violence, which was also readily exploited by the security forces as a means of dividing black communities.

The petrol-soaked tyre, placed round a bound victim's neck and set alight was called a 'necklace', an awful term for something that was never pretty, nor was meant to be. Necklace victims were usually people who were merely suspected of being police informers. Nobody ever bothered to establish any proof. The bitter rivalry of the township conflicts did not allow the time or the scope for niceties. It was a problem, a contradiction, for a 'struggle' which proclaimed its ideals as being justice, freedom and democracy for all.

As Beinart writes:

While the [exiled] ANC called for ungovernability, it was not able to establish formal internal organi- sation, and a number of Congress and UDF members were uneasy with the excesses of the Comrades. … Some UDF militants justified violence, yet the movement had to be careful not to make itself even more vulnerable to state retaliation by openly espousing armed struggle. Zwelake Sisulu, son of the imprisoned Walter and later editor of the UDF-oriented New Nation weekly, publicly criticised the meting-out of punishments by youths in the name of people's power. … In Alexandra, Johannesburg, activists recognised by 1986 that some rebels were not only 'ungovernable to the enemy', but 'ungovernable to their own organisa- tions'. These tensions were to leave a difficult legacy for the liberation movements when they came to government.

One of the most notorious public statements on the use of the necklace was made by Winnie Mandela at a rally at Munsieville in April 1986. The time for 'speeches and debate has come to an end', she said. It was the year of the

liberation of the oppressed masses of this country. … We have no guns – we have only stones, boxes of matches, and petrol. Together, hand in hand, with our boxes of matches and our necklaces we shall liberate this country.

Winnie Mandela's incendiary tone expressed the bitter anger of communities that bore the brunt of appalling violence.

It is no better illustrated than by the fate of another prominent woman of the struggle, Victoria Mxenge. A trained nurse and midwife from the Eastern Cape, she had settled in Natal with her husband, popular ANC civil rights lawyer Griffiths Mxenge. Victoria followed him into law, and into working for the struggle. In 1981, the year she was admitted as an attorney, Griffiths Mxenge was murdered by the police. He was taken to a cycle stadium in Umlazi and stabbed 40 times. (The three policemen convicted of his murder in 1997 were granted amnesty by the Truth and Reconciliation Commission later that year.)

After his death, Victoria rose to prominence in the legal world when she began representing and assisting young people and students who had been detained and ill-treated by the security police. She was also a member of the legal team which defended the United Democratic Front and the Natal Indian Congress in a treason trial in this period.

But, just four years after her husband's killing, Victoria Mxenge was shot and axed to death at her home, in front of her children. Her killers were never found.

———— ❖ ————

Writing in the mid-Eighties, Mark Uhlig cites the often-made claim that MK – which, at that time, was estimated to have between 6 000 and 10 000 fighters in training in Angola and Eastern Bloc countries – was 'one of the least successful liberation movements'.

'This record of military ineffectiveness,' Uhlig wrote,

> is due largely to the ANC's own self-imposed limitations on violence against civilians. For many years, ANC leaders have taken pride in their organisation's refusal to engage in careless or indiscriminate violence aimed at sowing terror in the white population. 'If we wanted to, we could hit buses, trains and shopping centres,' said one ANC official. 'But we are not terrorists. We are not fighting a race war. It is precisely against that kind of racial definition that we are doing this.' ... Principles aside, the ANC's poor record of military accomplishment may also be seen as a significant reflection of the strength of the South African Defence Force and the enormous difficulties that face any effort to weaken the white government by direct military means.

From *Apartheid in Crisis* (1986) by Mark Uhlig

Just how chillingly formidable the government's forces had become by the late 1980s began to emerge with the revelation of the existence of a National Security Management System that deliberated on, among other things, the 'elimi-nation' of key activists. Allied to it were police hit squads and agents of the so-called Civil Cooperation Bureau (CCB), which undertook missions ranging from scaring people to killing them in cold blood.

It was in the first months of FW de Klerk's presidency that the CCB first came to light, but it was years before anything like the truth began to emerge.

Pumla Gobodo-Madikizela, who served on the Truth and Reconciliation Commission in the 1990s, sums up the state's violent reach in the 1980s:

> State-orchestrated violence escalated during the 1980s, when covert operations units were established in the security police and defence departments, which ran a network of police informants (black and white), murder squads, and scientists skilled in the art of biological warfare. South Africa saw an increase in widespread torture by security police, the disappearance of political activists, mass killings, and the mysterious deaths of detainees and others, which usually occurred under direct instruction from, or with the full knowledge of, police generals. Most of the police 'investigations' of these incidents were simply cover-up operations. At the same time, the police were given immense powers and immunity, with many laws on the books that protected them from prosecution for the human rights abuses that they committed.

From *A Human Being Died That Night, A Story of Forgiveness* (2003) by Pumla Gobodo-Madikizela

---

In contrast to the involvement of thousands of township Comrades and residents in daily conflicts, the ANC's own armed wing, Umkhonto we'Sizwe (MK), had a relatively low profile – given its numbers and the resources spent on them. The TRC report at the end of the 1990s found that MK ended up killing fewer security force members than civilians. Nelson Mandela later wrote that, at the beginning of the negotiation phase, the armed struggle was potent as a 'rhetorical device', because it was 'a sign that we were actively fighting the enemy'. He added: 'As a result, it had a popularity out of proportion to what it had achieved on the ground.'

❖

South African agents also became adept at infiltrating the ANC, and the internal anxieties and insecurities within the movement had appalling consequences for people suspected of being turncoats.

There was an ANC camp in Angola, 15 kilometres from the town of Quibaxe, north of Luanda, that was grimly named after the Johannesburg prison, popularly known among its black inmates as 'No 4'. The camp was called Quatro, Portuguese for 'four'. It was not a good place to end up in during the 1980s.

Quatro was, officially – according to the ANC

security department that ran it – a 'rehabilitation' centre. To dissenters who found themselves imprisoned there, it was a hell of abuse and despair.

Like every army engaged in war, MK had constantly to keep a watch out for infiltrators, turncoats and spies. It also had its fair share of mutineers, who were unhappy about conditions in the training camps in Angola and the treatment meted out to them by their seniors.

But the torture and summary executions that are associated with Quatro from the mid-1980s presented a liberation movement fighting for democracy in South Africa with a challenge some believe it did not adequately confront and resolve at the time.

In 1992, the global human rights watchdog Amnesty International issued a damning report on the abuse, torture and execution of prisoners in ANC camps in Angola, Tanzania, Uganda and Zambia during the 1980s. It said most of the victims were genuine members of the movement who were punished over grievances or differences of opinion on policy. Amnesty International said:

This pattern of gross abuse was allowed to go on unchecked for many years, not only by the ANC's leadership in exile, but also by the governments of the Frontline states.

In the early 1990s, at the time the ANC was developing the idea of a truth commission, senior member Pallo Jordan – himself a victim, once, of the movement's overzealous security department – cautioned against making a distinction between 'regime torture' and 'ANC torture'.

By 1987, as historian Nigel Worden sees it, South Africa had reached a 'stalemate'. Politics was bogged down in violence, society was riven with mistrust, the economy was slowing, sanctions were biting hard. White society was feeling more embattled, black society angrier.

In the May 1987 general election, the government found itself, for the first time since 1948, standing to the left of the Official Opposition after Andries Treurnicht's Conservative Party had eroded PW Botha's Nationalist power base.

But other developments – some public, some private – pointed the way to the future.

Midway through 1986, Mandela's lone decision to open dialogue with the government took a significant step forward when, still in his prison clothes, he was driven at short notice from Pollsmoor prison to the suburban residence of justice minister Kobie Coetsee.

Mandela remembered that

Coetsee greeted me warmly and we settled down on comfortable chairs in his lounge. He apologised that I had not had a chance to change out of my prison clothes. I spent three hours in conversation with him and was struck by his sophistication and willingness to listen.

The process of getting some kind of talks going was slow, but it had begun.

Talks of a different kind made headlines in 1987.

Van Zyl Slabbert and Boraine ironically infuriated PW Botha by taking a group of more than 50 mainly Afrikaans-speaking business, academic and professional people to Dakar in Senegal for what turned out to be important ice-breaking discussions with the ANC in exile.

Botha condemned them as 'political terrorists', but Van Zyl Slabbert said of the debates in Dakar that they were 'some of the toughest I have heard in a long time', though it was clear that both sides were in broad agreement on the need for a non-racial democracy in South Africa.

Boraine said of the meeting:

Our initiative arose out of a deep concern for our country, which is so hopelessly divided and a victim of escalating violence. At present there exists a stalemate. … The state cannot govern without a state of emergency … and the black majority cannot overthrow the state by force. … It is quite clear the ANC is the largest single party in South Africa, but they are banned. … We have been criticised that in meeting with them we have given the ANC credibility. The simple answer is, of course, that we met with them because they have credibility, have been in existence for 75 years and their real base of support is not in Lusaka or in London but in South Africa.

From *A Country Unmasked, Inside South Africa's Truth and Reconciliation Commission* (2000) by Alex Boraine

---

It was in May 1988 that Mandela first sat down with the 'secret working group' of top government officials put together by Kobie Coetsee. They met in the 'posh' officers' club at Pollsmoor and though the first meeting was 'quite stiff', Mandela recalls, 'in subsequent sessions we were able to talk more freely and directly'. The group met virtually every week for a few months, and less regularly after that. The question of the armed struggle and violence was the key issue to start with. Then it moved 'from a philosophical question to a practical one':

> [They] pointed out [that] the National Party had repeatedly stated that it would not negotiate with any organisation that advocated violence: therefore, how could it suddenly announce talks with the ANC without losing its credibility? In order for us to begin talks, they said, the ANC must make some compromise so that the government would not lose face with its own people. It was a fair point and one that I could well understand, but I would not offer them a way out. 'Gentlemen,' I said, 'it is not my job to resolve your dilemma for you.' I simply told them that they must tell their people that there could be no peace and no solution to the situation in South Africa without sitting down with the ANC. 'People will understand,' I said.

From *Long Walk to Freedom* (1994) by Nelson Mandela

It was also in 1988 that Soviet premier Mikhail Gorbachev called for a 'new world order', and recon-firmed his commitment to '*glasnost*' (transparency) and '*perestroika* ' (reform). Ronald Reagan, who in the previous year had met Gorbachev to agree on reducing the superpowers' nuclear arsenals, visited Moscow. The Cold War thaw had set in. Within another year, Berliners would break down the dreaded symbol of the Iron Curtain, the Berlin Wall, and the 'Communist threat' – so long exploited by successive South African administrations – would lose its potence. This would have a significant bearing on South Africa.

Of more immediate importance was Nelson Mandela's move to a comfortable house in the prison grounds of Victor Verster prison, among the vineyards in the pretty Franschhoek valley. It heightened public and international excitement about the prospect of his release.

Ahmed Kathrada, one of Mandela's closest friends, a fellow Rivonia trialist and long-time prison companion, was dead against Madiba's talking to the government. But he eventually came round to seeing the wisdom of it. Looking back in 2003, he said:

> The fact is that he had foreseen the moment, the possibilities, and must have known others had not. And so, understanding what it meant – not for him, or not him alone, but the people – he acted alone. It was the masterstroke of a visionary, and it changed everything.

From *Nelson Mandela: From Freedom to the Future, Tributes and Speeches* (2003) by Kader Asmal, David Chidester & Wilmot James (editors)

Mandela's primary goal at this point, however, was to see PW Botha himself. He kept pressing Coetsee to organise it.

———— ❖ ————

It was a smaller event – a neurological accident in the brain of PW Botha, causing him to suffer a mild stroke – in January 1989 that had a more immediate impact on the South African political landscape, and on Mandela's plans for a presidential get-together.

In the next seven months, PW resigned first as party leader, and – after a scrappy and unseemly fight with his own party – as state president. Nationalists recognised that the country was in a crisis that the *Groot Krokodil* ('big crocodile', as PW was mockingly nicknamed) could no longer manage.

Against the continuing revolt throughout South Africa, and the dramatic developments in Europe, Botha's 'Total Onslaught/Total Strategy' mindset was increasingly seen as being out of step and out of date.

Botha himself reflected this in his almost petulant resignation speech, on television, in August 1989:

PW Botha

It is evident that after all these years of my best efforts for the National Party and for the government of this country, I am being ignored by ministers serving in my cabinet. I consequently have no choice but to announce my resignation.

By the time he left office, PW Botha had, in many ways, vastly changed the country he had become the leader of a little more than a decade before.

Just a month before resigning, Botha finally met Mandela, the man who was his enemy, his very opposite in every apartheid sense, and the man he had eyed suspiciously for decades across the tragic divide of South African politics.

Mandela recalls the encounter:

From the opposite side of his grand office, PW Botha walked towards me. He had planned his march perfectly, for we met exactly halfway. He had his hand out and was smiling broadly, and in fact from that very first moment, he completely disarmed me. He was unfailingly courteous, deferential and friendly. … The meeting was not even half an hour long, and was friendly and breezy until the end. [The only 'tense' moment in the meeting was when Mandela asked him to release all political prisoners, including himself, unconditionally, and Botha said he 'was afraid he could not do that'.]

While the meeting was not a break-through in terms of negotiations, it was in another sense. Mr Botha had long talked about the need to cross the Rubicon, but he never did it himself until that morning at Tuynhuys. Now, I felt, there was no turning back.

From *Long Walk to Freedom* (1994) by Nelson Mandela

In the election later in the year the Nationalists lost to opponents on both the left and the right, and it was clear that, under the new president, FW de Klerk, the government would have to come up with a bolder, more convincing initiative.

Mandela, certainly, believed De Klerk 'represented a genuine departure from his predecessor'.

Out on the streets, there was more hope, but still much animosity and mistrust, and a determination to

Toleration of organised mass protest was a feature of the period of transition.

sustain the struggle.

As a result of restrictions placed on the UDF, Cosatu and other political groupings, there emerged a new massed front, which drew together a wide range of anti-apartheid forces. It was called the Mass Democratic Movement, and in August 1989, 12 days before PW Botha's resignation, it launched a campaign of defiance against apartheid.

In the run-up to the 6 September elections, protests were met with stiff police resistance, but immediately after the ballot the new government eased up and gave permission for a mammoth march of thousands of people through central Cape Town. Others followed elsewhere in the country.

After a decade of virtual civil war, it was an extraordinary event. The political climate began to change quickly.

In October, De Klerk released the remaining Rivonia prisoners and others: Walter Sisulu, Ahmed Kathrada, Andrew Mlangeni, Raymond Mhlaba, Elias Motsoaledi, Jeff Masemola, Wilton Mkwayi and Oscar Mpetha.

In November, beaches were opened to all people forthwith, and plans were made to drop the Separate Amenities Act soon.

De Klerk recalls in his autobiography, *The Last Trek, A New Beginning* (1998), that he also moved 'to dismantle the powerful structures that the securocrats had developed under PW Botha', including the National Security Management System. He acknowledged later that his 'ability to dent the long-established cultures [in the army and the police] was limited'.

In December 1989, a month later, Mandela and De Klerk met at *Tuynhuys*.

De Klerk remembers:

'So this,' I thought to myself, 'is Nelson Mandela.' This was the man who during his twenty-seven years of imprisonment had become a global icon of the struggle against apartheid. Like a grain of sand trapped in an oyster, Mandela had been a continuous and growing irritation to previous governments. ... He was taller than I anticipated, slightly stooped by his seventy-one years. The first impressions he conveyed were of dignity, courtesy and self-confidence. He also had the ability to radiate unusual warmth and charm – when he chose to. ... During most of the meeting, each of us cautiously sized up the other. ... I allowed him to do most of the talking and took his measure while he spoke. I think we both reached more or less the same conclusions: that it would be possible for us to do business with each other.

From *The Last Trek, A New Beginning* (1998) by FW de Klerk

Mandela remembers:

From the first I noticed that Mr De Klerk listened to what I had to say. This was a novel experience. National Party leaders generally heard what they wanted to hear in discussions with black leaders, but Mr De Klerk seemed to be making a real attempt to listen and understand. ... I was able to write to our people in Lusaka that Mr De Klerk seemed to represent a true departure from the National Party politicians of the past. Mr De Klerk, I said, echoing Mrs Thatcher's famous description of Mr Gorbachev, was a man we could do business with.

From *Long Walk to Freedom* (1994) by Nelson Mandela

The two men agreed to meet again soon and discuss, then, Mandela's release.

❖

After 1994, everybody got so used to, and pleased about, celebrating the achievements of the struggle that only a few risked making a critical assessment of the mistakes.

The advent of democracy was, after all, an unthinkable settlement between warring sides who did not in the end find it necessary to settle who the winner was in a contest of arms. It had been heading that way, but a bloody showdown was averted. There was much to praise in the way it had all turned out, that the struggle had produced a democratic order.

So it was almost jarring when it was suggested that the struggle itself had made costly errors, especially in its last decisive decade.

What it came down to was this question: did the end justify the means? Was everything done in the name of the struggle justified by the outcome, the defeat of apartheid?

It is the kind of question that can be applied often in South African history to show failures and lapses of judgement and costly mistakes. It applies to 19th-century British governor Sir George Grey in his handling of the cattle killing in the 1850s; to Cecil Rhodes and his imperial ambitions in the closing years of the 1800s; to the British generals who packed men, women and children into unsanitary concentration camps during the South African War; to the politicians who united South Africa in 1910 at the expense of majority rights; to Nationalists who came to power in 1948 and consolidated white privilege through a system of government that was eventually declared a crime against humanity.

In every case, there was a view that the end justified the means, that – to put it in its crudest form – you could try to achieve good things by doing questionable or false things.

And the Eighties produced just such difficult questions.

Historian William Beinart writes that the 'erosion of state authority [in the 1980s] was attended by increasing civil disorder and crime. This uncomfortable interregnum bequeathed a difficult legacy to its successor.' In a speech in 2003, educationist Brian O'Connell, rector of the University of the Western Cape, went much further. Focusing on the fervour that went with the rejection of conventional schooling in favour of so-called People's Education, he said:

Whatever else we may have got right in struggle during the 1970s, 1980s and early 1990s, as we tried to understand our oppression in order to liberate ourselves ... we were wrong with respect to knowledge, and the consequences of our errors haunt us still today.

We [failed to oppose] those who would reduce all relationships to power relationships. We failed to perceive that our People's Education project ... was reduced to a project that promised new knowledge and magical ways of acquiring it simply through political and ideological action.

The road back from such 'anti-intellectualism, conceptual sloppiness and triumphalist arrogance' was a steep one:

As true disciples, we suspended our intellectual scrutiny, and driven by our need to transform our society and create a new order, we assailed the very structures that held the promise of our transformation.

Filled with misguided passion, we all but destroyed our reconstruction and infrastructure. We assailed authority relations in families and schools and many higher education institutions – including the authority of knowledge – as comprehensively as the apartheid state had done, and we are now faced with the challenge of reconstructing these social organs.

In the hard 1980s, such thinking would have amounted almost to treachery.

———— ❖ ————

Yet O'Connell's – and other critics' – frankness about South Africa's recent past actually confirms in an easily overlooked sense the achievements of the negotiated settlement. It was then, for the first time in more than three centuries, that South Africans gained the constitutionally guaranteed scope to speak their minds.

A culture of questions – which is almost always unpopular among those in power, or wanting to be – had, from the 1990s, begun to replace a culture of answers. The long decades of accepting the world as the armed or the powerful said it must be, made way for freer thinking about how it could be.

End of the beginning

End of the beginning

From sunrise the air carried the heat of summer. In the clear, still sky a police helicopter clattered back and forth, holding the grid of central Cape Town under its roving supervision.

FW de Klerk did the unthinkable – for a Nationalist – by unbanning the liberation movements and declaring his willingness to negotiate an end to white rule.

Hundreds upon hundreds of protesters were streaming to Greenmarket Square from the station and the bus and taxi terminus at the Grand Parade, not vengefully, not at a run, but with purposeful confidence. Marshals in armbands directed the flow along routes sealed off by traffic police. These days, protests were formally, if perhaps grudgingly, permitted. Office workers leaned out of their windows to watch. Soon the square and the streets feeding into it were packed. It was a surging mass of colour. Banners in the green, black and gold of the still-banned ANC and the blazing red of its struggle

partners in the unions and the South African Communist Party swayed defiantly above the crowd. Freedom songs and mantra-like chants filled the air.

It was an unequivocal protest, a mass demand from the people to the national legislature – just a few blocks away – where the new president, FW de Klerk, would, within a few hours, deliver his first opening of parliament address. Parliament's first day of work was, and still is, the occasion for the national leader to set out the political intentions of the executive. The events of the preceding months, the sudden decline of PW Botha's hawkish presidency, the softer reformist line of his successor, the new rhetoric of change, all these things heightened the sense of anticipation on this February morning. The country waited.

Friday, 2 February, 1990, however, was possibly the most remarkable day in the history of white minority rule for being the moment at which the inevitability of its own failure was openly admitted. Things had been changing rapidly in recent months, but nothing signalled it quite as surely as the start of the second session of the ninth Republican parliament.

When De Klerk unbanned the ANC, the PAC and the South African Communist Party; announced that Nelson Mandela would soon be released unconditionally; lifted emergency restrictions on organisations such as the UDF and Cosatu; released scores of political prisoners; lifted media restrictions, and declared that the time had come to create a 'totally new and just dispensation' based on equality, the scope and nature of national politics changed for good.

By the admission of the government itself, the days of white rule were numbered. The imminent end of more than three centuries of colonial, settler and minority control over the bitterly fought-over southern region of Africa was certain. It was, in this sense, the beginning of the end.

But in the instant that FW de Klerk conceded,

and the organisations that represented the majority of South Africans openly entered the political debate, the focus shifted squarely to a barely imaginable future. In this sense, 2 February, 1990 was the end of the beginning.

―――― ❖ ――――

He hadn't even told his wife all that he was going to say, though at the last minute De Klerk gave Marike a graphic indication of what it would mean. After arriving at parliament in the presidential motorcade, while he and Marike stood on the steps of the great hall to take the national salute, De Klerk turned to her. It was just minutes before going in to begin his ground-breaking address. 'After today,' he confided, 'South Africa will never again be the same.'

The president remembered later that he woke that morning 'with a sense of destiny'. 'I knew that my speech would usher in a new era. I felt like an athlete in the starting blocks waiting for the crack of the starter's pistol.' But he was also tense.

Despite our careful planning I still could not be sure of the success of our initiative. The test would be the reaction of the media, the leaders whom we wanted to involve in negotiations, the international community and the public.

If it was dramatic effect De Klerk was intent on achieving – in South Africa, and in a world community waiting with bated breath for a clearer sign of hope – there's no doubt he achieved it. He knew that 'the eyes of the world were more intensely focused on South Africa on 2 February 1990 than at any time before in our history'.

He had, for months, been talking of fundamental change. But the record, with the Nationalists, often suggested that words could not be taken to have a plain meaning. Vorster had spoken of change, so had PW Botha. So what version of 'change' would FW's be, people wondered?

His 2 February speech arguably restored the word to its plainest meaning. Without 'drastic change', he warned, there would be nothing but 'growing violence, tension and conflict'. It was time to talk openly and freely about reshaping the character of the South African state.

The agenda is open and the overall aims to which we are aspiring should be acceptable to all reasonable South Africans. Among other things those aims include a new, democratic constitution; universal franchise; no domination; equality before an independent judiciary; the protection of minorities as well as of individual rights; freedom of religion; a sound economy based on proven economic principles and private enterprise; and dynamic programmes directed at better education, health services, housing and social conditions for all.

The first two items on the list were what mattered: a democratic constitution; a universal franchise. It would mean nothing less than the undoing of South Africa's long, defining history of political inequality. But it would not be quickly, or easily, or even painlessly, achieved.

Reaction to the speech was immediate and acclamatory. Archbishop Desmond Tutu declared that De Klerk 'has taken my breath away'. Newspaper headlines such as 'South Africa and the World Rejoice' and 'South Africa breaks through the political sound barrier' were typical. It was, Nelson Mandela later wrote, 'a breathtaking moment, for in one sweeping action [De Klerk] had virtually normalised the situation in South Africa. Our world had changed overnight.'

The lone voice of despair and outrage was that of the white right. Conservative Party leader Dr Andries Treurnicht declared De Klerk's speech – probably accurately – as 'the most revolutionary speech I have ever listened to in this parliament during the last 19 years'. Unbanning the ANC, the PAC and the Communist Party was 'absolutely outrageous', an act that had 'awakened the tiger in the Afrikaner'.

'Now the closet communists may come out into the open,' Treurnicht fumed impotently.

Now we can be openly taunted with ANC-Communist T-shirts. … Now Joe Slovo can come and open his office in Adderley Street, Cape Town. … And now … they can shout in the streets: 'Viva Comrade De Klerk!' I am shocked by this.

In the jubilation that greeted the release of Nelson Mandela after his 27 years in prison, South Africans seemed to fling off the restraints separateness had imposed.

Many conservative Afrikaners were, too. But the bulk of white South Africans, though some were anxious, were relieved that the long-ignored core issue of national life was being confronted openly at last.

By the standards of more than four decades of Nationalist rule, De Klerk's speech was revolutionary.

In Lusaka, and elsewhere in the ANC's extensive international network, the announcements in Cape Town came as a complete surprise. There were disputes between those who believed it was a genuine opportunity for dialogue and those who suspected it might be a ruse, and between those who thought it was time to engage in peace talks and those who took it as a sign of a weakening state against which a final military assault would surely prove decisive.

Even on Robben Island, prisoners huddled around radios to listen. Among them was Tokyo Sexwale, who admitted years later – when he shared a platform at a speaking engagement with De Klerk himself – that he was uncertain just how genuine the last white president really was about negotiating a future based on equality.

Throughout the country, though, people were exuberant. Scores packed into cars and taxis and cruised central city streets, hooters blaring and ANC flags fluttering from the windows.

Foreign governments applauded the speech. There were messages of congratulation – a wholly new experience for the arch-pariah state of the modern world – from US president George Bush, British prime minister Margaret Thatcher, French president Francois Mitterand, Zambian president Kenneth Kaunda, UN secretary general Xavier Perez de Cuellar and many others.

Now the focus was on the man who, more than any other, would symbolise the national transformation: the release of prisoner 466/64, jailed since June 1964, was expected within days.

De Klerk, in fact, acknowledges that

I had no illusions why the world media had focused their attention on Cape Town: they had not done so to hear me speak, but to witness the release of Nelson Mandela.

'You could almost say that for practical purposes he has been set free. He must just reside [in prison] a

With fists raised in triumph, Nelson Mandela and his wife Winnie walk from the gates of Victor Verster prison, a historic moment heralded by the bold headline of the Sunday Times of that morning, 11 February, 1990.

little longer.'

This apparently nonsensical way of describing the fate of Nelson Mandela early in February 1990 by Stoffel van der Merwe, who was then education minister in De Klerk's cabinet, hinted at the government's curious relationship with its most important and influential prisoner. The fact was, the place and time of Madiba's imminent release was not just up to the government. The man himself had to be consulted about when and how he wished to be freed, and it was Mandela who asked to delay the moment.

The risks were great, he perceived. If not handled well, his liberation could degenerate into a fiasco. He didn't want to be rushed into it.

The government was nervous about it, too. When, on the evening of 9 February, De Klerk met Mandela to discuss his release, it was clear each side would have to compromise. Mandela wanted a week's delay, and to walk free from his prison near Fransch-hoek. The government wanted to release him in two days' time, in Johannesburg. As Mandela recalled: 'It was a tense moment and, at the time, neither of us saw any irony in a prisoner asking not to be released and his jailer attempting to release him.' In the end,

they compromised, agreeing on 11 February, with Mandela completing his long walk to freedom on foot. That settled, De Klerk poured two whiskies, though Mandela confesses he only pretended to drink his because 'such spirits are too strong for me'. Details were announced by De Klerk at a hastily summoned international news conference on the afternoon of Saturday, 10 February.

On Sunday morning, there was a buzz of activity at Mandela's prison cottage. True to form, Madiba made a point of saying goodbye to some of his jailers, one of whom he confessed he would miss. These were men, he wrote, who 'reinforced my belief in the essential humanity even of those who had kept me behind bars ....'

Later, Madiba emerged into a very different world from the one he had been taken from in 1964. He remembers that when a television crew 'thrust a long, dark and furry object [a microphone] at me, I recoiled slightly, wondering if it were some newfangled weapon developed while I was in prison'. Few individuals had been the focus of global attention on quite the scale that Nelson Mandela found himself to be as he left his prison life behind him that day.

A rapt, worldwide audience of millions listened to the first words spoken by a free Mandela in 27 years. He addressed an entranced crowd of thousands from the balcony of the Cape Town city hall:

Friends, comrades and fellow South Africans, I greet you all in the name of peace, democracy and freedom for all.' With these words Mandela began his speech from the balcony at the Cape Town city hall that overlooks the historic Grand Parade, openly resuming his place in public life after a forced absence of 27 years. The crowd of thousands that had waited in the broiling sun for hours cheered, whistled and applauded as Mandela worked his way through acknowledgements to individuals and organisations whose efforts during the long struggle had led to this moment. He praised the ANC's struggle partners, the unions and the communists. He acknowledged the role played by students, liberals and the churches. He also made a point of singling out FW Klerk as 'a man of integrity' who 'has gone further than any other Nationalist President in taking real steps to normalise the situation.

But the speech demonstrated clearly – in case anyone was deluded into thinking his imprisonment had softened Madiba's resolve – that the ANC was sticking to its guns … figuratively, but literally as well:

Our resort to the armed struggle in 1960 … was a purely defensive action against the violence of apartheid. The factors which necessitated the armed struggle still exist today. We have no option but to continue. We express the hope that a climate conducive to a negotiated settlement would be created soon so that there may no longer be the need for the armed struggle. … Our struggle has reached a decisive moment. We call on our people to seize this moment so that a process towards democracy is rapid and uninterrupted. We have waited too long for our freedom. We can wait no longer. Now is the time to intensify the struggle on all fronts.

Historian William Beinart writes:

Mandela's slow walk to freedom, followed by a cavalcade of cars, was an emotional moment, a televised event of religious intensity – the raising of a man from another world who seemed to carry the promise of salvation.

It was an extraordinary moment for the man himself:

As I finally walked through those gates to enter a car on the other side, I felt – even at the age of seventy-one – that my life was beginning anew. My ten thousand days of imprisonment were at last over.

——— ❖ ———

One man who was disappointed in the speech (and there were surely many who were anxious about it) was FW de Klerk: 'Mandela failed completely to rise to the occasion,' he believed.

'Instead of calling for peace and reconciliation,' he wrote later, 'he recommitted the ANC to armed struggle. … Instead of allaying fears regarding the ANC's links with international Communism, he stressed his solidarity with the South African Communist Party.' … Instead of calling for a common effort to rebuild the economy and create a better life for all, he called on the international community 'to continue the campaign to isolate the apartheid regime'.

Mandela himself remembers a telegram from a Cape Town housewife, in the mound of messages of congratulation from heads of state and scores of others from around the world, which said that she was 'very glad that you are free, and that you are back among your friends and family, but your speech yesterday was very boring'.

❖

Whether his speech was boring, disappointing, defiant or inspiring, there was no turning back. The question was, what now? A start had been made, but few foresaw, then, the extremely difficult and horrifyingly violent phase the country was about to enter.

In the first weeks after De Klerk's speech and Mandela's release, there was much euphoria and, probably, much naivety. Many journalists predicted, for instance, that there would be a new constitution by the end of the year and a black government installed soon thereafter. Apartheid would be over, peace would reign, sanctions would end, and everybody would get on with their lives.

But such predictions overlooked the truth that the contest of the streets, the struggle itself, was, far from ending, merely being transferred to formal politics, and would intensify. What's more, the forces ranged against one another were, by the nature of the history of the conflict, uneven, mutually distrustful and ill-prepared or even poorly equipped for the demands of a negotiation era thrust on them more suddenly than they had ever anticipated it would be.

A big challenge for the Nationalists was how to manage an extensive and ideologically inspired security machinery whose very reason for being – aggressively combating the liberation movements – had been overturned at the stroke of a pen.

For the ANC, being clearly the symbolic representative of the overwhelming majority of South Africans was no compensation for its almost total lack of organisational structure on the ground, or the fact that many thousands of its core people were still in jail or in exile.

A sobering reality was that the armed struggle remained in force. It was a headache, in a way, for both sides: the ANC had to be sure that negotiations were for real before pulling back its fighters. And the government had to be sure it could manage the potential threat without spoiling the conditions for dialogue. At the same time it had to prove to its white constituency – which still had the power of the vote – that the risks of lifting all barriers to normal politics were worth it.

Champion of the moment ... Nelson Mandela, free at last, is presented to the people from a balcony at the Cape Town City Hall by Archbishop Desmond Tutu.

Arch imperialist Cecil Rhodes's Groote Schuur estate in Cape Town was the venue of the first formal meeting between ANC and government delegations led by Nelson Mandela and FW de Klerk.

As Mandela made clear in his speech on 11 February, there were 'further steps' he expected from the government 'before negotiations on the basic demands of our people can begin'.

In this, he – or his speech-writers, for the speech was not Mandela's own – was guided by the Harare Declaration of the previous year.

❖

The opening talks in Cape Town in May 1990 between ANC and government delegations took months to yield substantial progress on real negotiations. The first inclusive negotiating forum, the Convention for a Democratic South Africa (Codesa) was launched only in December 1991, a year and seven months later. That eventually broke down in 1992, and was followed in 1993 by a new talks process, the Multi-Party Negotiating Forum, which

In July 1989, the ANC and its partners in the union federation Cosatu and the UDF had met in Zimbabwe to set out a revised blueprint for a future South Africa. It was called the Harare Declaration and was endorsed by the Organisation of African Unity (OAU) and the United Nations. At the heart of it was political and legal equality in a democratic, non-racial state, governed by a Bill of Rights and driven by an economy that promoted the well-being of all South Africans. It seems ordinary now, but at the time many thought it an inconceivable

pipedream, or a dangerous fantasy. The Harare Declaration set out five conditions that had to be met before negotiations on this future state could begin. They were:
- the unconditional release of all political detainees and prisoners;
- the lifting of bans and restrictions on organisations and people;
- the removal of troops from the townships;
- the end of the state of emergency, and
- the ending of all political trials.

had more success, eventually sealing the political settlement in November that year. A transitional Constitution was adopted in December 1993, and the first democratic elections – out of which emerged the Constituent Assembly that wrote the final Constitution – were held in April 1994.

And this whole period of essentially hopeful dialogue was accompanied by appalling, widespread violence. This was not foreseen in the early months of 1990.

Two weeks after his release, Mandela flew to Lusaka to the meet the movement's national executive committee, in part to convince them that he had not gone soft, or made any secret deals with the government. He was also elected deputy president of the movement, second in command to his old friend Oliver Tambo. He then travelled extensively through Africa, going on to Sweden – to visit Tambo – and to London, to attend, among other things, a huge concert in his honour at the famous Wembley stadium.

Back home, the talks process was developing, but shakily.

The initial plan for a meeting on 11 April was scuppered by the ANC over the death of eight protesters from a crowd of 50 000 demonstrating against local council rents in Sebokeng. The process was saved only after a meeting between De Klerk and Mandela. It was a pattern that would repeat itself often in the next four years.

As De Klerk recalls: 'As he [Mandela] and I would often have to do throughout the long negotiating process, we had to resolve this first deadlock ourselves.' The De Klerk–Mandela relationship became increasingly difficult – mainly over the question of violence, and each man's belief that the other wasn't doing enough to stop it – yet they always managed to find common ground and preserve the idea of a settlement won in the boardroom rather than on the battlefield.

By May, the two sides were ready for their first formal discussion, which focused on the obstacles to full negotiations. Primarily, these related to freeing political prisoners; granting immunity from prosecution to ANC members in the country and to exiles; lifting emergency regulations, and reviewing security legislation.

The Groote Schuur Minute, the joint statement the two sides issued after the three-day talks, was a step forward, but the substance would depend on the details still to be hammered out by a working group.

In terms of the minute, the two sides agreed that:
– they would establish a working group to define political offences in order to release political prisoners and grant immunity from prosecution to exiles;
– they would maintain 'efficient' lines of communication the better to curb violence and intimidation;
– the government would give temporary immunity to key exiles to allow them to return to South Africa and help get the negotiations ball rolling, and
– the government would review existing security legislation to make 'normal and free' political activity possible, and 'work towards' lifting the state of emergency.

Forming the working group and committing themselves to sustaining dialogue were the meeting's most significant results.

In the first week in June, De Klerk lifted the state of emergency everywhere in South Africa except in Natal (where violence was intensifying), meeting one more Harare Declaration demand.

Within less than a month, the ANC proved its strategic mettle by unilaterally suspending the armed struggle. The idea was that of leading Communist thinker Joe Slovo, the person white South Africans had learned to detest and fear as the 'mastermind' of the armed 'onslaught' of the Seventies and Eighties. The silver-haired, jovial Slovo – who tickled the public by sporting red socks on his arrival home from exile – would prove himself a master of compromise at the most crucial stage of negotiations later. In 1990, hardliners in the ANC weren't initially convinced that suspending the armed struggle at this point was wise, but Slovo and Mandela convinced them. It was the precursor to the next meeting with the government, this time in Pretoria, on 6 August.

In combining the suspension of the armed struggle with the setting of target dates for the release of political prisoners, and amnesty for crimes committed with political objectives, the Pretoria Minute was a breakthrough.

Again, though, it was at the time viewed with an

Joe Slovo, leading Communist and mastermind of the armed struggle during the 1980s, in a township street that, out of defiant loyalty to the struggle, was unofficially named after him.

optimism that misjudged or underestimated the fierceness and complexity of the political contest.

❖

Early in 1990, *Die Burger* newspaper reported that words such as 'Kleurling', 'meid' and 'kaffer' – deemed to be 'racially offensive' – were to be eliminated from the Word List and Spelling Rules of the Afrikaans language, a new edition of which, revised after 25 years, was to be published later in the year. The chairman of the commission responsible for its publication, Professor FF Odendaal, said the intention was to counteract the use of such words.

Such intended generosity reflected a widely felt keenness to show good faith, to ease the suspicion and mistrust that years of apartheid had embedded in the national psyche. For a long time still, society, the way people lived, would be full of contradictions.

The Nationalists recognised that one of the most glaring of these was the party itself. It was time, they decided, that its members, too, became 'new' South Africans. And so, on 19 October, 1990, the party that was for so long synonymous with white exclusivity opened its doors to all races. Though De Klerk later regretted it did not change its name – it became merely the New National Party (NNP) – it was a historic shift. But it had less to do with new South African bonhomie than with the hard realities of political competition: if they were to survive, Nationalists knew they would have to reinvent themselves. And while the NNP did not gain many African voters, it succeeded in drawing significant numbers of coloured and Indian supporters, many of whom were anxious about the implications of majoritarian politics which proclaimed a commitment to meeting the needs of a mass African majority.

❖

Right across the political landscape, aggression more than adaptation to new conditions was the order of the day.

A negotiated settlement of some form was almost everybody's declared objective, but the real conditions and real pressures seemed often to undermine it.

For the next three years, movement towards a settlement was repeatedly interrupted or threatened by violence that claimed an average of more than 10 lives a day, a death rate higher than in the Eighties.

In summary, writes historian Robert Ross, '[t]he history of South Africa between February 1990 and April 1994 was chaotic and bloody, though not as bloody as it might have been'.

He makes the point that, apart from the liberal Democratic Party, 'all groups involved in the process of negotiations coupled the use of force to their bargaining'.

All the 'armed' parties, including the government, found it difficult to control their supporters, or were accused by the others of failing to do so. In the government's case, the difficulty lay in being sure it fully controlled the police and army in whose ranks many believed was a 'third force' intent on wrecking the negotiations by stirring up trouble, chiefly between Mangosuthu Buthelezi's powerful Inkatha movement and the ANC and its allies, mostly in Natal and on the Witwatersrand. There were instances where police openly sided with Inkatha. And in one of the absurdest measures of the time, the government excluded 'cultural weapons' – such as 'tribal' spears and knobkieries – from otherwise strict bans on displaying weaponry in public.

All too often, South Africans' hopes for a future free of conflict were tempered by grief. The negotiation era of the early 1990s was among the bloodiest periods of the country's recent history.

These factors, and the conditions of life of millions of people, wrote Reuters journalist Rich Mkhondo, created a recipe for a 'deadly brew':

Millions of blacks are caught in a spiral of landlessness, homelessness, unemployment and poverty. Add to that a clash between modern political structures and traditional tribal ones. Mix in a struggle for hegemony in the region between major political players. Stir in the security forces in all their guises. ... Add faceless, apparently trained killers such as the 'third force'. ... Sprinkle all that with ancient and recent political and social grudges and you get a deadly brew.

From *Reader's Digest Illustrated History of South Africa* (1994)

In the second half of 1990, heavily armed gangs boarded commuter trains in the Johannesburg area and shot and stabbed passengers at random in a campaign of terror that by March 1994 had claimed the lives of more than 600 people and injured more than 1 400.

Claims, counter-claims and denials from all sides hinted at hidden agendas. Mistrust and fear were widespread. The very idea of a negotiated settlement see-sawed between impossible hope and dashed dream.

The ANC leadership was strongly criticised by young supporters for going ahead in preparing the ground for a deal with the government while the killings continued. ANC prisoners went on strike to back demands that they be released immediately.

And though Mandela remained convinced that everything possible must be done to sustain movement towards a negotiated settlement, he became deeply suspicious of the commitment of the government to resolving violence. This, he wrote later, stemmed in part from personal experience. In July 1990, the ANC 'received information' that Inkatha hostel-dwellers were planning a raid on ANC members in Sebokeng on 22 July. Through its attorneys, the ANC alerted the minister of law and order, the commissioner of

Once a member of the ANC Youth League, Mangosuthu Buthelezi emerged in the 1990s as a determined political opponent of the majority party.

police and the regional commissioner. On the day, an Inkatha rally was held, after which 'Inkatha members, escorted by police vehicles, entered Sebokeng in broad daylight … [and] went on a rampage, murdering approximately thirty people in a dreadful and grisly attack'.

> I requested a meeting with Mr De Klerk the following day. When I saw him, I angrily demanded an explanation. … He had no reply to what I said. I asked De Klerk to furnish me with an explanation, and he never did.

De Klerk, on the other hand, became increasingly doubtful about the ANC's commitment to peaceful negotiation. He was certain that violence – and claims about the government's role in it – was being used to exert political pressure on the government, to force concessions in bad faith.

This, he felt, was particularly true of Operation Vula, 'a major ANC plot [unearthed by police, who made a number of arrests] … to infiltrate key operatives into South Africa … to organise an underground network

to prepare for revolution'. It was, De Klerk argued, contrary to the Groote Schuur Minute. Mandela told him he knew nothing of Operation Vula. After making enquiries, Mandela assured him that he had been misled by police, and that the operation was 'moribund'. A year later, De Klerk says, Mandela praised Operation Vula members for their work in the intervening period, and 'boasted' about the infiltration of personnel and weapons into the country. Tensions mounted.

———— ❖ ————

The Inkatha–ANC rivalry – often portrayed then by government spokesmen and many journalists as tribal conflict or black-on-black violence – had complicated beginnings.

Buthelezi, an active ANC Youth League member in his early years, had become prominent in the Seventies as the political head of the KwaZulu territory, eventually becoming its chief minister. He founded the Inkatha National Cultural Liberation Movement in 1975 at the instigation of the ANC in the hope that, as the *Reader's Digest Illustrated History of South Africa* (1994) describes it, 'Buthelezi would keep the flame of resistance alive in the region'. He refused to accept independence and consistently backed the idea of a non-racial, multi-party democracy. In this, he helped to weaken a key element of National Party policy, separate political representation in the independent homelands. Inkatha grew increasingly powerful and, with Buthelezi's strong stance against the armed struggle and against sanctions, came to be seen as a more moderate and important alternative to the ANC. This was strengthened in the 1980s when Inkatha helped to quell student unrest and formed its own union federation, the United Workers' Union of South Africa in opposition to Cosatu. Labour formed a key political constituency which, in the absence of an Inkatha-aligned movement, was being drawn into the pro-sanctions ANC camp. By the Nineties, Inkatha was virtually synonymous with the 'Zulu nation' and drew on the authority of the Zulu monarchy and the mythology of national pride that went with it. By now, Buthelezi had political ambitions of his own.

But Inkatha's role in the evolving politics of negotiation – the movement became a political party, the Inkatha Freedom Party (IFP), in 1991 – was complicated by its links with the government. The government appeared to have begun to think in terms of an alliance with the mostly Zulu party against the liberation movements. But the revelation of secret links that were being fostered – and paid for with taxpayers' money – had the opposite effect.

This was given credence by the confirmation in 1991 of secret government funding for the training of armed Inkatha units from the late 1980s. De Klerk, angered that this had continued without his knowledge after 2 February, 1990, demoted Minister of Defence Magnus Malan and Minister of Law and Order Adriaan Vlok. He speculated later:

> The possibility can not be discounted that … some elements in our security forces were reluctant to dismantle their clandestine capabilities or to abandon people that they had come to regard as their allies.

Throughout the four years of the negotiation initiatives, the government tried to convince the world that it was intent on getting to the bottom of the violence, and to claims that its forces were involved. Various investigations, including two separate commissions under members of the judiciary, Judges Louis Harms and Richard Goldstone, did much to shed light on the murky world of dirty tricks and death squads – such as the top-secret South African Defence Force outfit innocuously named the Civil Cooperation Bureau. As a consequence, there were purges of senior officers in the army and the police in 1992 and 1994.

But suspicions remained, and violence continued. De Klerk admitted later:

> In retrospect, it is clear that the truth was not established by the Harms Commission and that we failed at that stage to get to the root of the totally unacceptable covert activities in which some elements of the security forces were involved.

As for relations between the ANC and Inkatha, two summit meetings between Mandela and Buthelezi in the first quarter of 1991 did nothing to stop the violence. Mandela complained that 'as far as I could tell, Inkatha never made any effort to implement the accord [on conduct between the two parties]', adding pointedly, 'and there were also violations on our side'.

A National Peace Accord in September – signed by 24 organisations, including the ANC, the NP and Inkatha – also failed to stop the killings.

Those who were for peace applauded these efforts, but it was evident that those for violence were unmoved.

❖

As the government moved to honour its commitments to 'levelling the playing field' – terminology that was common in this period as shorthand for the hugely uneven terms on which parties to the talks were competing – thousands of prisoners were released from early in 1991, and the process of granting immunity from prosecution to exiles got under way.

De Klerk's government also abolished the keystones of apartheid with the repealing of laws that for decades had shaped the landscape and the mind of South Africa. But the scrapping of the Population Registration Act, the Group Areas Act, various Land Acts – and amendments to scores of other laws governing everything from merchant shipping and marriage to unemployment insurance and national parks – now seemed merely a technical element of the larger exercise of transformation, which had still not got off the ground.

The UDF disbanded to concentrate on building the organisation of the ANC, and the movement held its first national conference on home soil since its banning in 1960. Mandela was elected president, his long-time friend and confidant Walter Sisulu, deputy president.

Perhaps the most significant elevation was that of Cyril Ramaphosa, the former mineworkers' leader who had, since the early 1980s, gained a formidable reputation as a negotiator. Sebastian Mallaby notes in *After Apartheid* (1993), that 'Ramaphosa's instincts were a world away from the blanket calls for no compromise that came from some quarters in the ANC'. He had learned, Mallaby writes, that compromise had yielded real gains. Within six months, Ramaphosa would begin to show his mettle.

❖

Finally, at the very end of the year, on 22 December, 1991, most of the country's political parties signed the Declaration of Intent that launched the Convention for a Democratic South Africa (Codesa) talks.

In this, they committed themselves to a multi-party democracy in a unitary state. Some parties were absent: the Conservatives refused to participate until the idea of a white homeland was accepted; the PAC stayed away, claiming parties other than the ANC and the NNP would be expected merely to initial a deal between the two big players, and the IFP

ABOVE: South African-trained General Bantu Holomisa (right), the last leader of an independent Transkei, threw in his lot with the ANC.

LEFT: Codesa, the Convention for a Democratic South Africa, gave South Africans hope that a negotiated settlement was possible. Clockwise from top left: Dwarfed by a symbolic drape, FW de Klerk addresses delegates; leading negotiators Nationalist Roelf Meyer and the ANC's Cyril Ramaphosa discuss the day's agenda; struggle heroes Joe Slovo and Chris Hani; television lights cast a gleam over a plenary session; ANC delegate Gill Marcus; and Nelson Mandela at the microphone.

pulled out after failing to get additional delegations for the Zulu king and for the KwaZulu administration.

Still, Codesa created five working groups to begin to sort out the main areas of dispute: principles for a new constitution; arrangements for an interim government; the future of the homelands, and the setting of target dates for the change to democracy.

It would not be plain sailing.

By 1992, political pressures on both the main parties – the NNP and the ANC – were high and mounting. It was now two years since the promise of a sunnier future based on equality had seemed to be in the offing.

The outlook was more promising than it had been a year earlier, but De Klerk now found his right-wing opposition growing alarmingly. This was underscored on 19 February, 1992, when the NNP failed to hold the parliamentary seat of Potchefstroom in a bruising by-election battle with the Conservative Party. But De Klerk had a trick up his sleeve which gave the whole negotiation process a shot in the arm: dismissing Conservative demands for a general election to test what it believed were dramatic shifts in white sentiment, he called a referendum on the negotiation process itself. The right didn't stand a chance.

Whites were asked simply: 'Do you support the continuation of the reform process which the State President began on 2 February 1990 and which is aimed at a new constitution through negotiation?' Though the ANC had deep reservations about endorsing exclusive white political rights, it called on whites to vote Yes. The poll on 17 March was a Yes-vote landslide. Optimism soared.

It was reinforced by South Africa's return to the Olympic fold at the Barcelona Games after a long, enforced absence.

But at the second meeting of Codesa in May, talks broke down over disputes about majority rule, power sharing and the question of regional powers. The ANC and its allies were furious, and soon announced plans for a 'rolling mass action' campaign to intensify pressure on the government. Their fury was heightened on 18 June when South Africa awoke to news of an appalling massacre of men, women and children in the Slovo informal settlement at Boipatong by a group of 200 Inkatha supporters from the nearby KwaMadala hostel.

Visiting the area the next day, a visibly shaken Mandela said: 'I am convinced we are not dealing with human beings but animals. … I have never seen such cruelty.' He levelled his anger at President De Klerk, the NNP and the IFP.

The ensuing protest campaign, which included a mass stayaway involving millions of workers over two days in early August, also focused attention on the discredited homelands where, as ANC supporters saw it, puppet regimes were still clinging on to power.

The campaign had tragic consequences: on 7 September, a march on the Ciskei leader Brigadier Oupa Gqozo's capital of Bisho ended in bloody turmoil when Ciskei soldiers opened fire on defiant ANC marchers, killing 29 and injuring about 200. The action brought condemnation on the Ciskei, but the ANC was also exposed to harsh criticism for what many perceived as irresponsible recklessness.

The ongoing violence spread gloom and despair.

There were to be more horrors yet. Both the ANC and the NNP recognised that the conflict was wasteful and pointless, and that it was time to reinvigorate the talks process. Mandela and De Klerk agreed to hold a summit meeting.

The preparations for it pushed to the fore two men who epitomised the struggle for a settlement: flinty former union negotiator Cyril Ramaphosa and the Nationalists' almost boyish and unassuming Roelf

As violence intensified, the patience of the people was tested to the limit, and tense confrontations were common.

Meyer. Both were trained in law, but were, super-ficially at least, poles apart politically. They were, one journalist said, 'the most unlikely Tweedledum and Tweedledee of negotiations'. But it was a partnership that worked.

Meyer once explained that their interaction was based less on friendship than on 'a good working relationship', one so effective that 'we could say not only that we could resolve problems, but that there was not a problem we could not resolve'. And so it turned out to be.

In 19 days in September 1992, the two men hammered out an agreement that their principals came together to sign on 26 September. This Record of Understanding paved the way for the next round of talks in the Multi-Party Negotiating Forum, successor to Codesa.

Behind-the-scenes negotiations continued into the first months of 1993, with the two main parties making good progress towards agreement, but no sooner had representatives of 26 parties resumed talks at the World Trade Centre after an 11-month break than tragedy struck again.

On the morning of Saturday, 10 April, Polish immigrant Janusz Waluz drove to the Boksburg home of South African Communist Party general secretary

Journalist Shaun Johnson, writing in the *Star* newspaper in December 1992, reflected on the fearful mood of the Christmas season:

This year we will be staying at home while foreigners are staying away. We are frightened; ours has become a truly frightening homeland in the past 12 months. We are also poorer and expecting to become more so, and there is a wholly non-racial sense of uncertainty and fearfulness about what the new year will bring. Everywhere the crustacean mentality is on display: tuck into your hard shell, make yourself small and inconspicuous, scuttle rather than swagger, protect what you have and take no chances. I suppose this indicates that we are still a logical people. Caution is a rational response to what has transpired in our country since Codesa I.

From *Strange Days Indeed, Tales from the old, and the nearly new South Africa* (1993) by Shaun Johnson

Chris Hani, one of the most widely respected and easily misjudged of the ANC's freedom fighters, was committed to negotiation.

Chris Hani, waited for the widely respected former MK commander to return from buying the newspapers at his local shop, and gunned him down.

The murder sent a shock wave through the country. Waluz, whose car registration was noted by Hani's Afrikaner neighbour Retha Harmse, was soon caught, and he and his partner in the assassination, senior Conservative Party member Clive Derby-Lewis, were arrested and convicted in due course.

But, more immediately, turmoil ensued. Talks were suspended, the foreign exchange rate and the share market slumped, and violent protests – with looting, stoning, petrol bombings and the torching of trains and private cars – occurred in Cape Town, Port Elizabeth, Durban and Pietermaritzburg.

Mandela appealed for calm, and parties that might otherwise have returned to open conflict over the death of Hani resumed discussions on the national future.

It was notable that, right across society, the idea that even the most difficult issues could be settled by debate gained ground. It was an idea exemplified by the discussions at the World Trade Centre in Kempton Park, the venue of the talks.

In June Eugene Terre'Blanche's neo-Nazi *Afrikaner Weerstandsbeweging* (Afrikaner Resistance Movement) and a new umbrella grouping, the *Afrikaner Volksfront* (Afrikaner People's Front) stormed the World Trade Centre in a costly but mainly petulant protest, smashing computers and daubing slogans on the walls. It was a futile gesture: a month later, the Negotiating Forum announced the date of the first democratic election – 27 April, 1994.

The key to clearing the way for agreement on a future democracy was Joe Slovo's compromise proposal of a 'sunset' clause to allow for a government of national unity until 2000, and to secure government employees' jobs for 10 years after the installation of the new government.

❖

Most South Africans were sick and tired of violence, and were feeling their way into a new kind of society. Conditions had changed to the point where the national 'will' was ready for a new accommodation.

> *South Africans began to discover that they had some things in common. Many people were familiar with more than one language – thus providing the scope for cultural fluidity. As black people were drawn into the core political processes, English increasingly became the shared language of national politics. The media, especially some television [channels], began to reflect black aspirations and also to promote a more inclusive South African identity. While television is drawn to images of violence and unobtainable luxury, it also has enormous power to project shared symbols and new roles. Christianity still provided a potent language, so that conciliators such as Archbishop Desmond Tutu could draw on a widely understood code of prayer, biblical reference and forgiveness. For an increasing number of people the aisles of the new cathedrals, the supermarkets … gave access to a common society of consumption.*
>
> From *Twentieth-Century South Africa* (2001) by William Beinart

The clearing of apartheid's barriers began to change the way people lived – or some people anyway.

Foreign Minister Pik Botha hosted a cocktail party when his new neighbours moved in. And though the experience of the Mashabas of Heatherdale, north of Pretoria, was starkly different from those of some black families who found themselves ostracised or even threatened when they moved into former 'white' areas, the *Reader's Digest Illustrated History of South Africa* (1994) notes that, especially in high-income suburbs, 'the gentle influx of new black faces caused hardly a stir'.

Bewildered parishioners survey the shattered pews and blood stains after the attack at the St James Church in Cape Town during a Sunday evening service in 1993.

Of course, racism – and fear of one another – was still a daily reality for many South Africans. But the big change, the constitutional turnaround, was only months away now.

There was still much tension and violence.

A series of PAC armed wing (Azanian People's Liberation Army) attacks on farms, hotels and restaurants in the Eastern Cape, and the shocking grenade and rifle assault, during a Sunday evening service, at the St James Church in suburban Cape Town in July 1993, underlined the risks posed to the transition in South Africa from groups that felt excluded, or had excluded themselves, from the talks process. Though the PAC actually condemned the 1993 attacks, it was only early in 1994 that its leader Clarence Makwetu announced the movement's suspension of the armed struggle.

In September, Mandela told the UN General Assembly in New York that it was time all remaining sanctions were lifted. The UN responded immediately, and, in November, US President Bill Clinton signed the South Africa Democratic Transition Support Act, which reversed sanctions and pledged assistance.

After a bad few years, the economy began to pick up in 1993: the growth rate moved back into a positive 1,2 percent; the gold price recovered; international investors, encouraged by the announcement of an election date, began to show fresh interest in South Africa; and, in a new departure, representatives of business, labour and government formed the National Economic Forum to develop consensus on growth and redevelopment.

In October, Mandela and De Klerk were jointly awarded the Nobel Peace Prize.

———— ❖ ————

The decade that ended in November 1993 had claimed the lives of some 20 000 South Africans. Now, at last, a deal was about to be struck.

The 'last mile to freedom', as Negotiating Council chairman Mr Justice Ismael Mohammed described it, was reached early on the morning of 18 November when all the parties to the negotiations agreed on an interim Constitution that would, at once, decisively redefine, but also preserve, much in the society at the southern tip of Africa.

At once rivals and partners of sorts, Nelson Mandela and
FW de Klerk had a complex, difficult relationship, and a vital role
in sustaining negotiations.

On 22 November, the tricameral parliament gathered
for its penultimate sitting to ratify the interim constitution and usher in an all-party Transitional Executive
Council (TEC)

'Importantly,' historian Robert Ross writes, 'this
meant that the transition from apartheid to
democracy was achieved with constitutional conti-
nuity. … The country's laws might be changed; the
supremacy of its law maintained.'

Both the main parties had shifted towards each
other to reach the settlement: the NNP ditched its
insistence on special minority rights and opposition
to an elected constituent assembly, and the ANC
accepted private property and a free market
economy based on growth. They drew their
supporters with them into a parliament that was at
one on the fundamentals of the 'new South Africa'.

Problems remained in the first hectic months of 1994
since, as most parties were getting their election
campaigns off the ground, the right wing, some
homelands, and Inkatha were still out in the cold.

Homeland administrations in Bophuthatswana
and Ciskei had thrown in their lot with the right-
wing Freedom Alliance grouping, which was determined to resist the move to democracy. But, in
January, Ciskei broke ranks and signed up with the
TEC. In March, after a violent convulsion,
Bophuthatswana was placed under TEC control.

On the strength of a clause in the interim
Constitution that future negotiations could be held
on a white 'volkstaat' (homeland) if the election
results showed there was 'substantial support' for it,
former South African Defence Force chief, General
Constand Viljoen also broke away from the Freedom
Alliance, forming a new grouping, the Freedom
Front, and decided to contest the election.

But the biggest headache was Inkatha. Buthelezi
held out to the very end. The country was on tenter-
hooks. Just a week before the election in April, a
summit between De Klerk, Mandela and Buthelezi
resolved the impasse. The terms that brought the IFP
(Inkatha Freedom Party in were recognition of the
Kingdom of KwaZulu, and the protection of the institution of the Zulu monarch, his status and his constitutional role.

Parliament was hastily summoned on 25 April to
amend the interim constitution accordingly. Special
votes were cast the very next day. The last-minute
breakthrough was a nightmare for the Independent
Electoral Commission, which had already had ballot
papers printed, excluding the IFP. Stickers with the
party's name and logo, and a colour picture of its leader
now had to be stuck on to 80 million ballot papers.

The country De Klerk presided over at the beginning of 1990 was a country in crisis. The tricameral system had proved a wasteful and costly failure. Revolt was fierce, violent, widespread and seemingly unstoppable. Homelands were poor, corrupt and absorbing vast sums without contributing to political stability. The political argument that a gradually reforming, 'responsible' South Africa was standing alone and heroically against a global Marxist threat had – especially after the fall of communism in the late 1980s – lost its rationale. South Africa's armed forces had suffered a defeat in the conflict in Angola, and the country had submitted to pressure to accept a negotiated solution to the future of Namibia. Namibian independence became a reality with democratic elections there in 1989. Economically, South Africa was limping, with the value of the rand having dropped to unprecedented levels. As the *Reader's Digest Illustrated History of South Africa* (1994) sums it up, foreign debt repayments were a huge burden on the treasury, unemployment was rising, foreign companies were leaving, and sanctions were biting. Skilled South Africans were leaving in droves to settle elsewhere at a cost to the economy of billions of rands, and the sub-standard education system was not producing enough skilled people, not even artisans, to meet mining and industry needs.

Novelist Olive Schreiner understood the inevitability of national unity.

Facing all these difficulties, it was not possible for South Africa to avoid significant change.

Still, FW de Klerk was widely recognised as having been courageous in confronting the challenge as boldly as he did, and at such obvious, immediate, political cost.

Back in February 1990, there was undue optimism about the pace of the transition. By the time the negotiations were completed four years later, and thousands had died or been maimed in violence that welled from apparently depthless anger and fear, the most popular way of viewing the change – in South Africa and abroad – was that it was nothing short of a miracle.

Yet, as many have argued, there was something fundamentally inevitable about it.

At the end of the day, no South African community could seriously contemplate going it alone.

The result of the talks in 1993 uncannily matched the conclusion drawn by novelist Olive Schreiner at the beginning of the century, when she argued that the unity of all South Africans of whatever background was 'not the dream of a visionary' or 'the forecast of genius' but a condition forced on the country 'by the common needs of life'. It was, Schreiner wrote, 'the only path open to us', and a unity 'which must precede the production of anything great and beautiful ... by our people as a whole ....'

A free state

A free state

Two women on an errand stopped in their car at the traffic lights at the corner of Bree and Von Wielligh streets in central Johannesburg on 24 April 1994.

It was a Sunday, mercifully. There were some people about, but not the usual crowds.

At the wheel of the car was Susan Keane, a 37-year-old 'new' South African, as such people were admiringly called then, who was looking forward to the likelihood of taking her place on the ANC benches in what was to be the Pretoria/Witwatersrand/Vereeniging provincial legislature, forerunner of the Gauteng parliament. A day away, the elections to usher in a democratic order would decide her new role in life.

In the passenger seat was ANC regional executive member Joan Fubbs. The two women were on their way to the party's regional office at the nearby Lancet Hall, where there was a flurry of pre-election activity, as there was at the party's national headquarters in Shell House, two blocks away.

Just as the lights changed to green, there was a blinding flash ahead of them as the blast of a car bomb tore into the surrounding buildings and gouged a waist-deep crater in the tar. Smoke and dust billowed into the air, and glass and shattered concrete littered the street.

'Drive on,' Fubbs urged Keane. Fubbs was dazed, but unhurt. Susan Keane, bleeding from the nose, was not so lucky. All she could say was: 'I can't drive.' They were her last words. She managed to get out of the car, but died in Fubbs's arms.

Tragically, Susan Keane's death was one among more than 20 in a series of bomb blasts that was the old South Africa's last, pointless convulsion on the eve of a new era.

❖

'We are going to vote,' Archbishop Desmond Tutu told a special service at St George's Cathedral in Cape Town the next day, 'and the elections are going to be free and fair, and so there to all those ghastly creatures who are trying to subvert us.'

The bombing campaign was the horror everyone had feared: South Africa's first democratic elections would be blown sky-high by a final, violent assault from the right wing. Or people would be so afraid they wouldn't dare cast their ballots, and the whole exercise would be thrown in doubt. This was perhaps the intention of the five *Afrikaner Weerstandsbeweging* members who, two years later, were jailed for 26 years each for the terror campaign.

But when the bombs went off, South Africa was already a changed country. In their minds, millions of people woke up on 26 April – the first day of voting, for the sick and other special voters – with a quiet, unflinching determination to carry through what tens of thousands had died for, been jailed for, and struggled for. Nothing would deter them from making South Africa a free state.

❖

Serpentine queues, some stretching for kilometres, showed that, despite the bombs of the past few days, the country's democratic resolve was in good shape. There was plenty of patience and spirits were high. By the time they voted, many had waited for hours. Most had waited a lifetime.

RIGHT: 'By the time they voted, many had waited for hours. Most had waited a lifetime.' The queues of patient, determined voters testified to the democratic resolve of South Africans.

BELOW: Susan Keane, a victim of the last bloody convulsion of the old South Africa.

It was, often, truly a long walk to freedom, but voters, many of them casting the first ballot of their lives, proved it was worth the wait.

'You're ready, we're ready, let's do it,' was the Independent Electoral Commission's promise, and it proved a tough one to live up to. The man who led the exercise, Judge Johann Kriegler, had been told it would be impossible to organise an election on this scale in under a year, and that ideally, it would take two years. His commission, with 200 000 hastily employed staff, pulled it off in just four months.

In the absence of a voters' roll, they weren't even sure how many voters there were, but worked on a 'guesstimate' of 22,7 million. More than 80 million ballot papers were printed, and some nine thousand polling stations set up across the country, some in areas so remote they couldn't be reached by road.

Inevitably, problems arose. Ballot papers ran out in some places, other polling stations failed to open. There were long delays, and voting hours had to be extended.

At Mier, a village on the edge of the Kalahari Desert, Oom Daantjie Snyders, it was reported, took no chances. Alarmed by television news footage of seemingly unending queues around the country, he decided to wait until the second day of voting before making his way to the polling booth. 'I didn't want to vote on Wednesday,' he explained, 'because I wanted to avoid the rush.' It was an undue precaution: when he'd cast his vote, it brought the grand total for Mier to 10.

Across the country, in Umtata, on the other hand, 50 000 voters waited for many hours to cast their votes.

In chilly, wet weather in the Cape, queues formed early, and grew, some extending for kilometres. There were those who got up as early as two o'clock in the morning to be sure of avoiding a long wait. It often turned out to be a long wait anyway.

Some people, word had it, bought in supplies of tinned food, bottled water and candles, fearing that the world as they knew it would change so radically the minute a black government took over that electricity and water supplies would be cut, and shops would run out of food … or it would be too dangerous to go shopping even if they didn't. But all this was probably more of an urban legend than a phenomenon. It was true that for many people, conditioned for so long into thinking democracy was implausible, it must have come as a surprise that everyone really could have the same political rights, and exercise them together, without the sky falling on their heads.

The vast majority, of all classes and all colours, showed they had no difficulty grasping the idea of democracy. For all the complexity of political science, even the illiterate understood what it meant to have a vote and use it.

At 93, Miriam Mqomboti of Gugulethu could hardly believe she had finally been given a chance to choose the government of her country.

I am very happy this day has come. I never thought it could happen here. I came to Cape Town from Transkei when I was 18 and after this long time, I thought I would never be able to vote.

From the *Reader's Digest Illustrated History of South Africa* (1994)

It was with a sense of history, but also with strategic wisdom, that Nelson Mandela made his way to Natal to vote on 27 April, the second of four days of voting.

'I chose to vote in Natal to show the people of that divided province that there was no danger in going to the polls,' he wrote afterwards. 'I voted at Ohlange High School in Inanda, a green hilly township just north of Durban, for it was there that John Dube, the first president of the ANC, was buried. This African patriot had helped found the organisation in 1912, and casting my vote near his graveside brought history full circle, for the mission he began eighty-two years before was about to be achieved.'

From *Long Walk to Freedom* (1994) by Nelson Mandela

Scholar and writer Njabulo Ndebele remembered his moment of making history like this:

When the voting moment came, it was fast and disarmingly simple, but profoundly intense. I trembled as I unfolded my ballot paper. … I was aware of the terrible fear of making a mistake. … I began to look for my face. My one and only face. Other faces were a blur as I looked for the one face that embodied all my hopes and, easing my trembling hand, I drew my X with the greatest care in the world. And it was done. When I proceeded to cast the provincial vote, I was already a seasoned voter.

From *South Africa 27 April 1994, an authors' diary* (1994) compiled by André Brink

There were, of course, those who did not vote, who did not trust the settlement, and suspected that the transition was a transition in inverted commas. One among these was Azanian People's Liberation Army commander Letlapa Mphahlele, who, on 27 April,

1994, was still on the run, in Lesotho. He later wrote with an indifference tinged with disdain:

Across the border, South Africa held its first non-racial elections. The ANC won by a big margin, and ANC president Nelson Mandela became the president of the Republic. Mandela didn't declare a general amnesty, thus ignoring many freedom fighters who were still in prison, in exile or operating underground.

From *Child of this soil, My life as a freedom fighter* (2002) by Letlapa Mphahlele

Albie Sachs, who lost his right arm in a Maputu car bomb blast set off by South African agents in the 1980s, and who would soon become a judge of the Constitutional Court, used his left hand – 'which writes just as well as my right one used to do' – to make his mark. It reminded him of the last time he had been handed a ballot slip:

[It was] in 1966 when I was in my second detention, in solitary confinement in Roeland Street jail, recovering from torture by sleep deprivation, with a double padlock on my cell-door, and Captain Rossouw of the Security Police holding his hand between the bars of the window with a voting slip in it, and telling me: Advocate Sachs, it's a democratic country and you can vote, and I answering: Captain Rossouw, no thank you, I would rather not.

From *South Africa 27 April 1994, an authors' diary* (1994) compiled by André Brink

Journalist and activist Gavin Evans kept tabs on the voting in Sebokeng.

For the three days of the election I returned to the townships of the East Rand and watched hundreds of thousands of people waiting with a patience of 342 years to vote for the first time in their lives. … Eventually, by late in the second day. … [they] were on their way to the front of a slowly moving line, and I watched with delight as they emerged beaming from the polling station after placing all their memories of the past and all their hopes of the future in that ballot box.

From *Dancing Shoes is Dead, A tale of fighting men in South Africa* (2002) by Gavin Evans

Joyful camaraderie animated the crowd that gathered in Pretoria to witness the inauguration of Nelson Mandela as the first president of democratic South Africa.

British Labour Party MP, South African-born Peter Hain – detested by white South Africa in the 1970s for the success of his anti-South African sport campaigning in Britain – was an election observer. Among the things he witnessed on 27 April was his driver, Desmond Khoza, casting the first vote of a lifetime:

He waited anxiously to have his hand stamped. Then, as he put his ballot paper in the box, he turned to catch my eye, smiling, part triumphant, part astonished – before leaving the polling station with a broad grin and punching the air in excitement. Hardly able to accept that in middle-age, he had actually voted for the first time in his life, he had been worried in case his ballot paper might be snatched away at the last minute.

From *Sing the Beloved Country, The struggle for the New South Africa* (1996) by Peter Hain

South Africa's Nobel Prize-winning writer Nadine Gordimer was reminded of the significance of the X as a marker of identity:

The first signature of the illiterate is the X. Before that there was only the thumb-print, the skin impression of the powerless. I realised this with something like awe when [monitoring proceedings at a polling booth] I encountered black people who could not read or write. ... The day has been captured for me by the men and women who couldn't read or write, but underwrote it, at last, with their kind of signature.

From *South Africa 27 April 1994, an authors' diary* (1994) compiled by André Brink

❖

It took days to count the almost 20 million votes. The process was complicated in some cases by mix-ups with ballot boxes, and a strike by vote counters for more pay. There were also computer problems and disputes between parties. But, finally, early in the afternoon of 6 May, Judge Kriegler declared the result: a 'substantially free and fair' election had delivered the national will.

Of the 28 competing parties, only seven won enough votes to earn seats in the new 400-seat parliament.

Nelson Mandela's ANC won 252 seats, with 62,5 percent of the vote.

FW de Klerk's National Party came in next, winning 82 seats (20,4 percent). On the strength of support among coloureds, the Nationalists won a majority in the Western Cape.

Mangosuthu Buthelezi's Inkatha Freedom Party (IFP) was third with 43 seats (10,5 percent). The party was dominant in KwaZulu-Natal. Another last-minute contestant, General Constand Viljoen's Freedom Front (FF), came fourth with nine seats (2,2 percent).

The Democratic Party (DP) won seven seats (1,73 percent), the Pan Africanist Congress (PAC) five (1,25 percent), and the remaining two went to the African Christian Democratic Party (ACDP) (0,5 percent).

It was a proud moment for Mandela, one he described as 'a joyous night for the human spirit'. Typically, he deferred the honour to South Africans themselves:

To the people of South Africa ... [t]his is your victory too. ... You have shown such a calm, patient determination to reclaim this country as your own.

Flying the new colours ... a South African National Defence Force helicopter trails the national flag in a symbolic fly-past at Nelson Mandela's inauguration as president.

The ANC's 82-year struggle against white domination was at an end – in the political sphere, anyway.

When it was all over, an exhausted Judge Kriegler commented:

We said at the start it was a mission impossible, and we were just too dumb to realise it. But you know what? It worked.

The election introduced a very different form of political representation from the one South Africa had had until then. Under the old system, parties put up candidates to compete for votes in constituencies, and won or lost power on the number of constituencies, rather than votes, gained. Because the number of votes in each constituency differed widely, it meant,

for instance, that one party could gain more votes than another yet fail to gain as many constituencies. While the primary benefit of constituency politics meant elected representatives were directly accountable to voters in a constituency, the system was flawed in failing to match the preference of voters nationally.

Under the new system of proportional representation, parties won or lost seats on the basis of their national support. While this system created a legislature that more accurately reflected voter sentiment across the country, it effectively enhanced the power of parties, whose prerogative it was to fill seats from candidate lists, and widened the distance between elector and elected.

Flanked by his first deputy FW de Klerk, Marike de Klerk and Chief Justice Michael Corbett, Nelson Mandela formally assumes office as president.

There was not a hint of hesitation in the transfer of the loyalty of apartheid's once-feared military apparatus from minority white regime to Mandela's black majority government. It was symbolically affirmed by the thundering flypast of fighter jets, and helicopters trailing the new flag, in the course of an at once solemn and celebratory inauguration of the new president at the Union Buildings on 10 May.

The day before, in Cape Town, Mandela was officially sworn in as an MP, a necessary precursor to his becoming president. It was a remarkable blend of ancient ways … the august restraint of parliamentary procedure combined with – for the first time in South Africa – the animated performance of Tembu *imbongi* (praise singer), Sthembile Mlangeni.

On 24 May, Mandela was back in parliament to deliver his first 'state of the nation' address in which he spelled out in broad outline the key initial objectives of his government. His vision was to create a 'people-centred society'.

My government's commitment to create a people-centred society of liberty binds us to the pursuit of the goals of freedom from want, freedom from hunger, freedom from deprivation, freedom from ignorance, freedom from suppression and freedom from fear. These freedoms are fundamental to the guarantee of human dignity. They will therefore constitute part of the centrepiece of what this govern-ment will seek to achieve, the focal point on which our attention will be continuously focused.

———— ❖ ————

Securing freedoms that guarantee human dignity will be the new government's primary focus, Nelson Mandela tells a rapt parliament in his first address as president.

It was an almost delirious moment, the first taste of freedom. But beyond this moment was a sobering challenge. Archbishop Tutu encapsulated it in the final passage of the book, *The Legacy of Apartheid*, published by *The Guardian* newspaper in London in 1994:

> The hard slog of turning freedom into reality has started in earnest, of trying to meet the justified but unrealistically high expectations of those who for so long have been deliberately deprived and systematically oppressed.

In form, the new administration of South Africa was very different from the old. Democratic institutions at national, provincial and local levels – though local elections took place only later – reflected the divergent interests and opinions of the wealthy and the poor, the men and the women, from a rainbow spectrum of political thinking.

It was an achievement in itself. But what the new institutions confronted was the awesome task of overcoming an extensive legacy of dispossession, conflict and disadvantage.

Deep-rooted poverty, backlogs in housing, health, education and basic services, and a high degree of racial polarisation and mistrust, defined South Africa in 1994 as a 'deeply divided society whose integrity will have to be ensured by the real, if fragile, bonds of interdependence and a sense of shared fate', as professor of southern African studies at the University of Cape Town, David Welsh, defined it at the time. 'Legitimate government,' he wrote, 'is a necessary, though not sufficient, condition for tackling these challenges with some hope of success.'

———— ❖ ————

A flood of pledges of billions of rands in aid from abroad – from the United States, Britain, the European Community and Australia, among others – accompanied South Africa's re-entry into the world arena as a confident, fresh-faced democracy led by a sparkly eyed and revered veteran.

In a matter of months, the country rejoined the Commonwealth after an absence of more than 30 years; took up the seat at the United Nations (UN) it had not occupied for more than 20 years; became the 53rd member of the Organisation of African Unity, and joined the Non-Aligned Movement.

The UN lifted the last remaining embargo, on arms.

Diplomatic relations widened dramatically, with scores of new agreements being entered into with countries as diverse as Cuba, Burkina Faso, Kuwait and Mongolia. The 'special relationship' with Israel was ended.

In the course of Mandela's presidency, an impressive list of world luminaries, royalty, and political and religious leaders, called at the southern tip of Africa. Among them were Queen Elizabeth II and her daughter-in-law Princess Diana, Pope John Paul II, Mother Theresa, British prime minister Tony Blair, United States president Bill Clinton – the first US president to visit South Africa; Iranian president Akbar Hashemi Rafsanjani; Palestinian Liberation Organisation leader Yasser Arafat; the Dalai Lama, and the black American Muslim leader Louis Farrakhan.

These visits underscored the world acclaim South Africa had earned for itself, but also the immense regard in which Mandela himself was held.

The substance of his international stature was strikingly illustrated in the first half of 1999, towards the end of his tenure, when he and his director-general, Jakes Gerwel, pulled off what had long been regarded as a mission impossible. They managed to persuade Libyan leader Muammar Gadaffi to hand over for trial the terror suspects in the downing of an American 747 airliner – it had exploded in mid-air – over Lockerbie in Scotland in 1988. Was there any other world figure capable of succeeding in such a delicate intervention? It's doubtful.

South Africans relished their new-found pride.

It was heightened by successes in international sport, something the country had been denied – or had denied itself – for years.

In quick succession, South Africa won the Rugby World Cup in 1995 and Bafana Bafana won the Africa Cup of Nations early in 1996. Later in the year, Penny Heyns and Josiah Thugwane won gold medals at the Atlanta Olympics. The happy racial symmetry was accidental, but potent.

And, for the first time, the South African flag, the new one – which earned some mostly affectionate ribbing for its resemblance to Y-front underpants when it was first used in April 1994, but became a popular bumper sticker anyway – was planted on Mount Everest in 1996.

The country was, you could say, on a high.

ABOVE LEFT: Springbok captain Francois Pienaar and his team's irreplaceable cheerleader Nelson Mandela at the triumphant conclusion of the Rugby World Cup final at Ellis Park.

ABOVE RIGHT: President Mandela and Deputy President De Klerk, left, join Bafana Bafana skipper Neil Tovey in celebrating the national team's victory in the 1996 Africa Cup of Nations final. With them are minister of sport Steve Tshwete, on Tovey's left, and president of the Confederation of African Football, Issa Hayatou, right.

Poet and journalist Sandile Dikeni captured the different kind of 1994 festive season spirit in a newspaper column:

Some of us are becoming normal. We wear suits and go to cocktail parties and speak without saying comrade. ... And now, oozing with feelings of goodwill we shall not declare another Black Christmas. Only a normal merry Christmas and a prosperous New Year. Take it easy – the RDP and affirmative action will reach you soon. God, I feel so normal. I think I am gonna qualify to go to heaven.

From *Soul Fire, Writing the Transition* (2002) by Sandile Dikeni

❖

Under Mandela's custodianship, the government of national unity sought to pull all of South Africa into the project of nation-building. Reconciliation, Mandela believed, was the key, and he used every opportunity to talk about it, and demonstrate it.

Among the most memorable gestures by the grand old man of South Africa were his donning the No 6 rugby jersey to join skipper Francois Pienaar on the field after the South African rugby squad had scored its way to victory in the 1995 World Cup tournament;

his excursion to Orania to have tea with Betsie Verwoerd, widow of the Nationalist prime minister regarded as the architect of 'grand apartheid' (whose assassin, Dimitrio Tsafendas, was released from prison to a mental asylum in 1994), and his convivial meeting with Rivonia Trial prosecutor Percy Yutar.

There were scores of other generous and gracious efforts to bridge the chasms of distrust, fear and ignorance between South Africans. Some wondered if it was not too cloying, too generous: whites had benefited so much, and now they were being soothed. Enough already, detractors felt.

But it was more than just bonhomie.

Commentator and former politician Frederik van Zyl Slabbert explored the significance of the Madiba factor in his contribution to *Nelson Mandela, From Freedom to the Future, Tributes and Speeches* (2003) edited by Kader Asmal, David Chidester and Wilmot James. He wrote that

I was completely disarmed by him and felt immediately that I would like to do anything to help him achieve his vision for South Africa. This must have been the most common response to the person of Mandela immediately after his release, and even today. His personality, as it became more and more revealed in his actions after his release, was an indispensable element in the unfolding process of reconciliation in South Africa.

But there was no real or implied capitulation in it, Van Zyl Slabbert believed:

Mandela was not going to reconcile at any cost. … [he] epitomises the willingness to compromise without sacrificing principle. … I have no doubt that history will record that the final accolades for the success of our transition will go to Nelson Mandela. … Through his example, he made a critical mass of South Africans want to make the new South Africa work.

It was clear Mandela was under no illusions about the material imbalances in society that a change of political guard would not, on its own, redress. But he argued that redressing them would require a unity of purpose, and reconciliation was essential to that.

The genesis of his own reconciliatory spirit had much to do with his time on Robben Island.

The island had long been a troubling Alcatraz in the South African mind, but it was only after 1994 that society as a whole could – or was encouraged to – gain better insights into the importance, and sometimes the contradictions, of the island experience.

It became a much-visited shrine, and considerable resources were – sometimes controversially – poured into making it an affirming, but also a profitable, destination for visitors.

Mandela's biographer Anthony Sampson, who had known Madiba well in the 1950s, noted at the end of the Mandela presidency how struck he had been by the importance of his prison years in forging the more 'thoughtful and interesting' leader that emerged in 1990. Mandela himself described how it was

during those long and lonely years that my hunger for the freedom of my own people became a hunger for the freedom of all people, black and white. I knew as well as I knew anything that the oppressor must be liberated just as surely as the oppressed.

From *Long Walk to Freedom* (1994) by Nelson Mandela

It was a place of epiphany, of life-altering experience, for many others who rose to prominence after 1994, within and outside politics.

Among them were Anglican priest Njongonkulu Ndungane, who became the new Archbishop of Cape Town at the departure of Desmond Tutu; Methodist cleric and former leader of the PAC Bishop Mmutlanyane Stanley Mogoba, and Constitutional Court Judge Dikgang Moseneke. They, and others, displayed the extraordinary tolerance of their former jailers that was Mandela's hallmark.

It was the discovery of a common humanity, often, that seemed to make the island experience a vital one for South Africa's future.

Mosioua Patrick Lekota, who became premier of the Free State after 1994 and, latterly, minister of defence, recalled:

The warders were primed to see us as terrorists, Communists and devils. … But these … people … eventually wanted to understand why we were there. It was tremendously refreshing and inspiring to see these ordinary people appreciating our cause. This experience led to my belief that South Africa had a promising future.

From *voices from ROBBEN ISLAND* (1994) compiled and photographed by Jürgen Schadeberg

But could that future promise be codified, affirmed, in law?

Achieving this went to the heart of democratic South Africa, and one of the keys to it was the inauguration in February 1995 of the Constitutional Court as the ultimate guardian of the Constitution and the rights enshrined in it.

At that time the country was still being governed under the interim Constitution hammered out at the Kempton Park talks. For two years from 1994, parallel with the government's efforts to refocus public spending and begin fixing a broken country, a Constitutional Assembly busied itself with drafting the final Constitution.

In the interim, though, the highest court got to work. A meaningful indication of the country's constitutional ethos was the court's confirmation of the abolition of the death penalty in the year of its inauguration.

Many South Africans were opposed to this. An escalation of violent crime in the 1990s turned people against the liberal view that the execution of criminals was murder by another name. At the beginning of 1996, crime figures showed the country was the most violent in the world outside a war zone, and that 15 percent of South Africans' disposable income was spent on security. In 1997,

Chief ANC negotiator Cyril Ramaphosa and his New National Party counterpart Roelf Meyer, who forged a special relationship.

All Constitutions seek to articulate, with differing degrees of intensity and detail, the shared aspirations of a nation; the values which bind its people and which discipline its government and its national institutions; the basic premises upon which judicial, legislative and executive power is to be wielded; the constitutional limits and the conditions upon which that power is to be exercised; the national ethos which defines and regulates that exercise; and the moral and ethical direction which the nation has identified for its future.

From South African Law Reports, I Mahomed in *S v Makwanyane and another* (1995)

The court was a defining element of the new way.

President of the Constitutional Court, Judge Arthur Chaskalson, acknowledged that it would be reasonable to 'assume that ... the majority of South Africans agree that the death sentence should be imposed in extreme cases of murder', but argued that '[t]he question ... is not what the majority believe a proper sentence for murder should be [but] ... whether the constitution allows the sentence'.

Drawing attention to the truer significance of the judgment, the judge added:

The very reason for establishing a new legal order ... was to protect the rights of minorities. Those who are entitled to claim this protection include social outcasts and marginalised people. It is only if there is a willingness to protect the worst and weakest among us that all of us can be secure that our own rights will be protected.

In the Constitutional Assembly, it was the nitty-gritty detail of touchy subjects such as education, property and labour relations that, towards the end of the two years of tough negotiations, led almost to deadlock. The Nationalists wanted special protections, the ANC said these weren't necessary, that the Bill of Rights assured sufficient protection for everybody, and that anything in addition would or could get in the way of necessary transformation.

As in the Kempton Park talks three years earlier, it was the 'special relationship' between chief ANC negotiator Cyril Ramaphosa and his Nationalist counterpart Roelf Meyer that proved decisive. That,

nearly 25 000 murders were committed – 70 a day. As much as R70 million was stolen in heists in 1997.

The rise in crime was a consequence, in part, of policing that, in the last years of apartheid, was so keenly focused on combating political 'threats' that significant changes in organised crime were overlooked. The emergence of an increasingly sophisticated criminal economy, a network that spanned all of southern Africa, and beyond, was generating a demand for goods such as top-of-the-range cars, often used in lieu of payment. Hijackers, especially in Johannesburg, obliged. The lucrative, high-stakes drug trade flourished.

The police had been sapped of their vitality by the onerous task of curbing political dissent, and it had cost them public trust, too. They were also underresourced.

Against this background, the abolition of capital punishment was not popular, but it was, and remains, a defining value of the new constitutional state.

Chief Justice Ismail Mahomed, a member of the Constitutional Court, wrote in his famous judgment reaffirming the ending of executions:

and a gentle warning from President Mandela that if the other parties failed to find agreement, the ANC – which had a 'mandate to transform the country' – 'will write its own constitution'. An eleventh-hour agreement between the two main parties in the early hours of 8 May settled the matter, and the DP and PAC went along with it.

It was opposed by the ACDP, and the FF abstained. The IFP maintained its boycott of the process to the bitter end.

The historic redefinition of South Africanness achieved by a document that annulled centuries of inequity was marked and celebrated by Deputy President Thabo Mbeki in his memorable and much-quoted 'I am an African' speech. Asserting his claim, and the claim of all South Africans, to being proudly African in equality, he said:

> The constitution whose adoption we celebrate constitutes an unequivocal statement that we refuse to accept that our Africanness shall be defined by our race, colour, gender or historical origins. … This thing that we have done today, in this small corner of a great continent that has contributed so decisively to the evolution of humanity says that Africa reaffirms that she is continuing her rise from the ashes.

Once parliament had voted – 421 to 2, with 10 abstentions – the 'birth certificate of the rainbow nation', as Ramaphosa called it, was referred to the Constitutional Court for certification.

The result came as a surprise to many.

The court proved its mettle on 6 September by rejecting the draft because, among other things, powers allocated to provinces were less than or inferior to the powers agreed to in the pre-1994 negotiated settlement, and there was a lack of adequate protection for the impartiality and independence of the key institutions of the Public Protector and the Auditor-General.

The court's rigorous examination of the draft, and its rejection of it for these flaws, was seen not as a crisis but as an important landmark on South Africa's path to constitutionalism. Parliament fixed it, and it was duly signed into law.

Reflecting on the Constitution in an address in 2001, one of the judges of the court, Justice Kate O'Regan, said:

> [T]he Constitution affirms that we have responded to our history of racial exclusion, injustice, and oppression with a bright and shining vision of a different society based on equity, justice and freedom for all. But the Constitution is not a description of our society as it exists, that requires nothing of us but the maintenance of the status quo. On the contrary, it is a Constitution that compels transformation.

From *Spirit of the Nation, Reflections on South Africa's Educational Ethos* (2002) by Kader Asmal and Wilmot James (editors)

———— ❖ ————

The institutional framework that would define the values of the new South Africa, and compel transformation, were beginning to take shape.

The more strongly protected offices of the Public Protector and Auditor-General were complemented by a Human Rights Commission and a Gender Commission. A Commission on the Restitution of Land Rights had been formed in November 1994.

Though the Human Rights and Gender commissions were strapped for cash, and complained that they were limited in their scope as a result, both made telling contributions in cases they took on. Between December 1996 and November 1997, the Human Rights Commission received 2 200 complaints. Among its successes was winning equal provision of medical benefits for female members of the South African National Defence Force, and it won many cases against institutions guilty of racist practices. It mounted a big campaign against xenophobia – fear or hatred of outsiders – to counter the ill-treatment of African immigrants and refugees drawn to the south by the opportunities and hope of a free South Africa.

A High Court judge, Willem Heath, was appointed in 1997 to head a commission to investigate fraud and track down stolen money. He claimed to have saved, or reclaimed, millions of rands.

The bywords in politics were openness and accountability. Committee meetings of parliament that under the old regime were closed affairs were now opened to public scrutiny and participation. Though it sometimes hampered or slowed projects or new laws, public consultation became the norm.

Members of Parliament had to declare financial and business interests and gifts. Those who fell foul of the rules were publicly exposed.

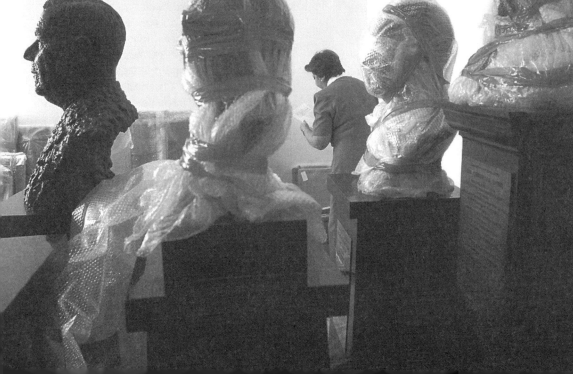

A conscious effort was made to ensure that marginalised people – not least women – were better represented in parliament and other public bodies. There was a commitment to recognising the country's 11 official languages, though it was eroded in part by cost considerations and the habit, or convenience, of simply using English.

There was no shortage of controversy and dispute. The new commissions, like all institutions in South Africa, straddled a deeply divided society, and from opposite sides of the fault lines of race and class and history they were judged to have succeeded or failed on different terms. Throughout, though, the culture of public life was being overhauled.

In 1996, the ambitious, and often controversial, Truth and Reconciliation Commission (TRC) began its painful examination of the human rights abuses committed in the name of preserving apartheid, and of fighting it. The challenge was explained by then minister of justice Dullah Omar when he said in 1994:

If the wounds of the past are to be healed, if a multiplicity of legal actions are to be avoided, if future human rights violations are to be avoided and indeed if we are to successfully initiate the building of a human rights culture, then disclosure of the truth and its acknowledgement are essential. We cannot forgive on behalf of victims, nor do we have the moral right to do so. … The fundamental issue for all South Africans is therefore to come to terms with our past on the only moral basis possible, namely that the truth be told and that the truth be acknowledged.

It was an attempt, the commission's co-chairman Archbishop Tutu said, to heal the wounds of the past by exposing the cause and the nature of the injuries.

As is evident from Chapter 15, it was an important,

Minister of justice Dullah Omar.

but difficult, objective for South Africans to reach. Some wanted vengeance, some wanted silence, others wanted biblical justice … an eye for an eye.

The TRC succeeded in erasing much deceit about the past.

On the other hand, there was some indication in 1996 that young South Africans were less inclined to dwell on the past and were focused more on a hopeful future. A Youth Day rally in Cape Town on 16 June, to commemorate the 20th anniversary of the Soweto uprising, drew an audience of only 350 young people where, 10 years before, such gatherings were rallying points for thousands of angry youngsters.

Non-racialism was becoming more of a reality for many, as schools and other institutions became increasingly integrated, and part of the freedom of the new South Africa was freedom from the conflict of the past. It was natural, perhaps, that after the intensively political and violent atmosphere of the 1980s and early 1990s, many found relief in a normality that had more to do with hanging out, socialising, going to the movies.

The gathering impetus of 'normality' was arguably present in the departure from political life into business of some who had been key players in the transition. Among them was Cyril Ramaphosa, who joined New Africa Investment Ltd, better known as Nail, as executive chairman.

The receding past was by no means forgotten, though. Wide support was given to the government's project of expunging the offensiveness of a racist history by changing the names of places and facilities that were intolerable tokens of it. Typical examples were the renaming of the Hendrik Verwoerd Dam the Gariep Dam, after the Khoekhoe name for the Orange River, and the renaming of the village of Kaffir River as Tierpoort. Buildings, too, were given new names: Shell House, the ANC's headquarters in Johannesburg, became Luthuli House, after former ANC leader Albert Luthuli. The administrative block opposite parliament, once called the HF Verwoerd building, became, simply, 120 Plein Street.

New names for some provinces – such as Gauteng, Mpumalanga and Limpopo – also signalled the desire

ABOVE LEFT: At many schools, racial integration gathered pace. The process was not entirely without conflict, but it contributed to breaking down the old divides.

LEFT: Humbled by history … the busts of apartheid-era leaders, including that of HF Verwoerd, on the left, were figuratively, but also literally in some cases, consigned to the basement.

to acknowledge South Africa's being in, and being of, Africa, and symbolically to promote 'transformation', the shift from a white-dominated republic to a constitutional democracy based on equality.

❖

The character of the government of national unity changed significantly in 1996 when FW de Klerk withdrew and went into opposition after failing to convince the ANC to go along with a proposal for a consultative council to operate within or alongside the government to give a voice to all parties. The NNP's idea was that, while the council would not have a veto, the cabinet should be obliged to refer issues of national importance to it. A few years later, De Klerk said:

> [The ANC] wanted a winner-takes-all model. I think they made an error of judgement. I still believe South Africa, with all its complexities, needs a consensus approach on key issues.

Some felt the withdrawal had troubling implications. Was it a sign of a fresh rupture in politics along race lines? If anything, most agreed, it was a token of confidence in the robustness of South African democracy.

Political debate was freer than it had ever been, and no less tough.

No sooner had the ANC government assumed control than Archbishop Tutu was launching into it for selling arms to Rwanda and the Sudan, and for approving salary increases for parliamentarians. His successor, Archbishop Ndungane, maintained a similarly independent mind on public affairs.

Former MK guerrillas marched in Pretoria to demand equal rights and pay in the new national army.

The liberal DP, intent on being a watchdog in parliament, maintained a beam of critical attention on the government. It was grudgingly respected, contributing to debate well beyond its numerical strength, though, being a watchdog on the small side, it earned some teasing as the 'chihuahua' of politics.

When De Klerk himself quit parliamentary politics in 1997, he remained actively engaged in the political debate, and optimistic. At the time of the launch of his autobiography, *The Last Trek – A New Beginning*, in 1998, he said that 'without doubt, warts and all, [the new South Africa] is better [than the old]'. Some among his former supporters were

From activist to keeper of the Treasury, Trevor Manuel rose rapidly and convincingly to the all-important cabinet portfolio of finance minister.

doubtful. But, he said,

> I urge people not to make the comparison with what they remembered liking in the old South Africa and what they now dislike, but to just imagine if we had not done what we did, what life would be like today. We would not have exported one ton of coal, one case of fruit, one case of wine; the whole world would have been united with the majority of South Africans [behind] overthrowing the regime.
>
> Unemployment would have been higher and we would have had a tremendous negative growth rate. Planes would not fly. That's where we would have been.

❖

Even with the changes, the task facing Mandela's cabinet was a tough one.

The challenges arose from the consequences of the apartheid decades, and the history of dispossession preceding them, but also from the costs, and the strategies, of the last decade of struggle. It proved difficult to reverse the culture of ungovernability, of non-payment of rents and service fees. These were important 'weapons' in the fight against apartheid. Now they were hampering reconstruction. Many activists ripe for key posts were afflicted by the trauma, or the breakdown in education, of the 1980s, and the deliberate deficiencies in education before then.

These factors were compounded by the ANC's inexperience in government, and the fact that it had to work with a civil service that was not universally imbued with the evangelical enthusiasm for reconstruction and development that the scale of the problems seemed to require. ANC administrations across the provinces also drew in politicians and officials from very different administrative and ideological cultures, such as the scores who had been part and parcel of a homeland system rife with corruption and abuse. The party 'redeployed' its no-nonsense Chief Whip Arnold Stofile to the Eastern Cape in 1997 to sort out a provincial administration that was near collapse, in part as a result of the homeland legacy. Everyone knew it was an unenviable task.

Difficulties arose from the very nature of the negotiated settlement in 1993, and the reality of a modern country locked into international economic relationships that often seemed to impose First World solutions on what were Third World problems.

So, delivery had to be balanced with fiscal discipline, liberal democracy with economic growth.

Within two years – coinciding with former Cape activist Trevor Manuel's shift from the Trade Ministry to Finance (replacing former banker Chris Liebenberg) – the Reconstruction and Development Programme made way for the Growth, Employment and Redistribution (GEAR) economic policy. It had become clear to the government that there was simply not enough money to sustain spending on reconstruction. Expanding the economy, attracting investment and empowering people through jobs became the new goal.

Within the ANC's alliance with the South African Communist Party and the union federation, Cosatu, the change was controversial, but while predictions of a split in the alliance came thick and fast, they proved unfounded.

As a party in government, the ANC remained in character a liberation movement whose constituency spanned the intellectual left, the rising black middle

Services such as electricity and water were finally expanded into deprived communities.

class, the rural poor, social democrats, and workers. The Communists knew very well they would get nowhere on their own, and the ANC and the unions had more to gain from each other by preserving the alliance. The bond of history was strong, but so was the bond of necessity.

The fact of being a 'broad church' – as the ANC has often been described – was acknowledged as its strength.

The shift in economic policy did not produce the gains many hoped it might, in part because the economy was hampered by unstable international economic conditions. But while Manuel was under fire from labour and left-wingers in his own party, he earned the respect of international business and institutions such as the World Bank and the International Monetary Fund by sticking to his growth-based policy and holding firm on conservative fiscal policies aimed at keeping inflation down, and limiting the size and spending of government.

Commentators generally felt the government promised too much in the detail of its assurances that democracy would mean a 'better life for all', and there was inevitably some disappointment that, with limited resources and an immense backlog, there were not more rapid everyday improvements.

Yet, as political scientist Tom Lodge summed it up in his survey of the first years of democracy, *South African Politics Since 1994* (1999), 'the statistics are quite impressive'. Highlighting improvements or advances in housing, electrification, provision of water, primary health care, and land resettlement, Lodge concluded:

Government programmes have attempted to address a range of concerns across a deeply divided society. The shortcomings of public policy in its conception and implementation have reflected these divisions but the limited achievements are all the more impressive because of them.

———— ❖ ————

In contrast to preceding centuries, women and their needs were recognised as they had never been before. This was true of new legislation and the provision of services as well as their political representation. In the second half of the Nineties, South Africa had one of the highest proportions of women political representatives in the world, with women making up a quarter of the National Assembly.

From June 1994, pregnant women and children under six were given free health care. The Commission on Gender Equality, led by the redoubtable Thenjiwe Mtintso, set about exposing gender discrimination in laws, policies and practices, promoting women's rights, advocating changes in sexist attitudes and challenging the stereotyping of women.

New legislation aimed at making practical improvements in the lives of women included the Prevention of Family Violence Act, the Sexual Offences Act, the Choice of Termination of Pregnancy Act and the Domestic Violence Act.

Even so, women at the turn of the century still found that their burden was disproportionate.

In her book on the lives of young people living in New Crossroads in the Cape in the Nineties, Mamphela Ramphele writes:

In almost every case it is a woman who has kept these young poeple's hopes alive. Women as single parents. Women as effective heads of households with husbands who are not able or willing to assume their responsibilities as partners. Women as grandmothers left to carry the burden of child rearing without the necesssary support except the social pension of R620 per month. Women as members of the extended family who pitch in when children are left with no available parent. It is even women as total strangers who establish supportive bonds to keep children safe and reasonably cared for. In some cases it is young women as siblings who provide each other with mutual support.

She adds:

Women who might be dirt poor and yet carry themselves with dignity defies logic. Women who can laugh through pain and anguish. Women who are able to lead even if they are not accorded the authority or recognition of leadership.

From *Steering by the Stars, Being young in South Africa* (2002) by Mamphela Ramphele

> Poor and overburdened though many women continued to be, Gcina Mhlophe's poem, 'A Brighter Dawn for African Women', suggests their resolve was emphatic:
>
> > *For hundreds of years hunger and disease*
> > *Have been her unwanted companions*
> > *Denied education and the dignity every woman deserves*
> > *As insults and humiliation were heaped on her*
> > *All too often made to feel like a refugee in her own home*
> > *She has been fighting the battles of colonialism*
> > *One after the other, without any recognition*
> > *But you would not say so by the smile she bears.*
>
> From *Love Child* (2002) by Gcina Mhlophe

South Africans had no doubt the ending of apartheid was a good thing. You couldn't ever hope, at the end of Mandela's presidency, to find anyone who would defend the old way. But South Africans were not at one on what had gone right, and what had gone wrong, in these extraordinary five years since 1994.

Reality Check, a representative national household survey of 3 000 adults in April 1999, made clear what all South Africans thought were the priorities for the next five years: jobs, crime and fixing the economy. Most were committed to democracy, were positive about race relations, and believed the country would eventually become more united.

But the survey also showed other things. It showed that while white citizens remained much better off than blacks, they didn't always recognise the fact. The well-off, not only among whites, were generally less happy with socio-economic changes since 1994 than the poor. The better-off tended to be pessimistic, and see themselves as the losers, while one in three optimists were from among the have-nots of society.

This schism in perception and reality between white and black South Africans would become one of the defining themes of Thabo Mbeki's presidency.

In June 1999, sooner than South Africans really wanted him to, Mandela stood down to make way for Thabo Mbeki.

In an interview shortly afterwards, Anthony Sampson said of it that 'while South Africans still feel slightly uncertain, the assumption of that succession [from Mandela to Mbeki], and the nation existing as an absolute, I thought seemed pretty emphatic'. There was no overt military presence, the authority was strictly civilian, the key attendants being judges.

'I suppose,' Sampson decided, '[Mandela's] greatest achievement is the manner of his departure.'

He had helped to change the country irrevocably, he had been a figurehead for all citizens, and he had instilled in them an assurance that, from 1999, he was not needed.

Mandela was uncommonly admired as a president, and he would be missed, but it was also a token of the lingering sentiments of the apartheid mindset that some people wondered, still, about majority rule.

Mandela was bowing out officially, but he would not be resting much. There was always something to do, or someone to help, or something important to say. His sense of having a continuing role in public life was prefigured in the closing passage of his autobiography, *Long Walk to Freedom*, in which he recognised, in 1994, that 'after climbing a great hill, one only finds that there are many more hills to climb'.

> *I have taken a moment here to rest, to steal a view of the glorious vista that surrounds me, to look back on the distance I have come. But I can rest only for a moment, for with freedom come responsibilities, and I dare not linger, for my long walk is not yet ended.*
>
> From *Long Walk to Freedom* (1994) by Nelson Mandela

It was, thoughtful South Africans knew, no less true for them.

By any
means

By any means

All she had was some of his hair – a fistful of it, but just hair. Joyce Mtimkulu had kept this human remnant for more than 20 years.

It was all that was left of her son, Siphiwo, in the physical sense. Everything else, the memory, the emotion, was intact.

What was hard for Joyce Mtimkulu was that after all these years, after all the pain and anguish and unanswered questions, the truth about her son's fate required her to confront, to be with, the man who had sealed it. And know that the truth would set him free.

It was a harrowing experience that was repeated for many thousands of other South Africans in the course of the months of hearings by the Truth and Reconciliation Commission (TRC) into the abuses – killings, torture, abductions, poisoning – of the last 33 years of the apartheid era.

It was hard. But, for Joyce Mtimkulu, never again would anyone be able to say that Gideon Nieuwoudt, policeman and killer, was justified in taking Siphiwo's life, and never again would anyone be able to say they didn't know.

The TRC story is a story of the extremes of humanness.

One set of extremes falls within the scope of the extraordinary capacity of men and women to be gentle, accommodating, caring, forgiving and selfless, and of their capacity to understand, to accept, to live with emotional and physical pain, and to confront, listen to, be in the same room with, tolerate and even forgive those who caused it.

The other set falls within the range of what is considered inhuman, barbarous, beyond forgiving; the extremes of brutality that are no less human, the product of the altogether human – if heartless and irrational – idea that sometimes it is justifiable to influence the world by any means.

For 20 years, Joyce Mtimkulu yearned to discover the facts of her son Siphiwo's murder, an awful truth brought to light by the Truth and Reconciliation Commission.

As the two sides – it was more complicated than that, but, broadly speaking, the two sides – of the South African conflict became more bitterly and violently engaged in the contest for power, the apartheid state and its increasingly desperate security agencies eventually believed that torture, abduction and death were justifiable measures to prevent defeat. And some among their enemy, across the wire, fighting what they believed was a just war, lapsed into thinking that torture or killing civilians or necklacing suspected informers were measures that could be justified in the name of securing liberation.

There would be lingering doubts, and disputes, about the difference between deaths in a just war and the deliberate extra-judicial killing of political opponents by the apartheid regime.

What is true about both categories of human cost is that they shared the same history.

———— ❖ ————

There was no doubt, back in the early Nineties that, having endured such a bitter and painful conflict, South Africa could not safely press on to the turn of the century without making time for a careful, collective and lingering backward look.

Justice demanded it. But there was a growing view that justice was only part of it. The courts could take care of justice. And some apartheid-era atrocities were dealt with in the conventional judicial way. The ANC, on its own, had also set up commissions to investigate claims of abuses at its camps in the Frontline states, particularly the notorious Quatro camp in Angola.

But the nature of the brutality spawned by apartheid, the way it had become ordinary and pervasive, and that it had for so long been part and parcel of the comforts and convenience of a minority of society, and of the deprivation of the majority, meant a different way of discovering the truth about the past had to be found.

And, most importantly, it had to occur within the limits of the settlement then taking shape in South Africa. It meant that, like the political talks, this taking stock of human rights abuses would have to serve the objective of reconciling opponents who would, afterwards, have to be able to live with one another.

—————— ❖ ——————

Towards the end of 1992, constitutional negotiators reached agreement on the principle that South Africa, then on the cusp of a political settlement, could not afford a punitive process imposed by the victors along the lines of the Nuremberg trials that, after the First World War, led to the conviction, and execution or imprisonment, of Nazi leaders who were held responsible for war atrocities and the Holocaust.

It was agreed there would be some form of amnesty for politically motivated crimes committed under apartheid, with the idea that 'divisions and strife of the past' would be dealt with in a conciliatory manner. As the postscript to the interim Constitution put it, the process would emphasise a 'need for understanding but not for vengeance, a need for reparation but not retaliation, a need for *ubuntu* [humanity] but not for victimisation'.

The aspect of truth-telling was slightly different. The idea of harnessing the 'cleansing power of truth' arose within the ANC, at a meeting of the National Executive Committee in 1993 on the report of the Motsuenyane Commission on human rights violations committed by ANC cadres in the movement's Angolan camps. There was vigorous discussion. The turning point was the setting out of a position by Kader Asmal – and recalled later by Albie Sachs – that

Senior ANC thinker and cabinet minister Kader Asmal insisted the search for truth about apartheid-era atrocities must be even-handed.

[a]ny torture or other violation has to be investigated on an even-handed basis across the board, not just by one political movement looking at itself, but at a national level with national resources and a national perspective.

A key figure in the formulation of the law that established the commission was then minister of justice Dullah Omar. There was much public anxiety about the prospect of an anti-Afrikaner witch-hunt. He allayed these fears:

I wish to stress that the objective … is not to conduct a witch-hunt or to haul violators of human rights before court to face charges. It is … to enable South Africans to come to terms with their past on a morally acceptable basis and to advance the cause of reconciliation.

Nor would the claims of abuses against the ANC be 'glossed over or swept under the carpet'.

Omar constantly emphasised the need to provide a forum for victims to speak the truth as they experienced it, and for perpetrators to reveal the truth as they knew it.

The TRC came into being early in 1996, under the joint leadership of Archbishop Desmond Tutu and former cleric and liberal politician Alex Boraine. Other commissioners spanned the racial and political spectrum.

Its task was to examine human rights abuses on all sides between 1960 and 1994, hear testimony from victims and perpetrators and, where there was full disclosure and political motivation was clearly present, grant perpetrators amnesty from prosecution or civil action. The objective was to encourage truth-telling. Separate amnesty hearings were held for this purpose. If perpetrators did not make use of this opportunity, it was made clear, they would be liable for prosecution. The TRC was also asked to suggest how victims could be compensated through reparations.

Throughout its tenure, the TRC endured much criticism, from every political quarter, but it was praised widely, too.

ABOVE: Alex Boraine and Archbishop Desmond Tutu, the two men who steered the Truth and Reconciliation Commission on its tragic but also exalting journey into the past.

BELOW: The poster was emphatic: nobody deserved to be freed from prosecution without coming clean.

BELOW RIGHT: Harrowing accounts by witnesses, victims and perpetrators often made TRC hearings difficult to bear, but offered the country a priceless opportunity to confront hard truths, and find a way to live beyond them.

It was attended by much controversy – this was perhaps especially true of the commission's taking the autonomous Amnesty Committee to court to overturn the collective granting of amnesty to 37 ANC leaders (because it was contrary to the TRC law), and also the plea from Archbishop Tutu to Winnie Madikizela-Mandela at the very least to say of her role in the circumstances surrounding the death of 14-year-old Mokhetsi 'Stompie' Seipei in the 1980s, 'things went horribly wrong'. (In 1991, Madikizela-Mandela had been found guilty for her role in the abduction of Stompie and three other teenagers, and sentenced to six years' imprisonment. Her sentence was later reduced to a R15 000 fine.)

But for the more than 21 000 victims the TRC was a priceless acknowledgement of their pain and suffering. Remarkably, in many cases, victims publicly or personally forgave perpetrators, sometimes embracing them in a kind of mutual redemption.

───── ❖ ─────

Looking back on the process, MP President Thabo Mbeki said in a speech in October 1999 that while

[s]ome might argue that [encouraging disclosure of the truth about gross violations of human rights in exchange for amnesty] … did grave injustice to our established jurisprudence … what cannot be questioned is that it brought our country and people the necessary stability. In turn, this made it possible for the ordinary law to apply and the Constitution to come into force, which would have been impossible if we had had to declare a state of emergency to contain the violence of those who would have resisted prosecution for the crimes they had committed in defence of the apartheid system.

The R70 million TRC process ended after seven years with the tabling in parliament of the last two volumes, a codicil, of its report in April 2003.

The more than 21 000 victim statements related to some 38 000 incidents, and the killing of 14 000 people.

The commission's main finding was that the 'predominant portion' of gross violations of human rights had been committed by the apartheid state and its security apparatus, including criminal activities and extra-judicial killings inside and outside the country. Those fighting apartheid were also found to

have committed gross violations of human rights in their campaigns, in the killing of innocent civilians, and the necklacing of suspected traitors. The tortures and executions in the ANC camps in southern Africa were found to be gross violations, too.

The bulk of the victims, 19 144 of whom were black people, had been subjected to apartheid atrocities and abuses. Later than the TRC had hoped, the government agreed in 2003 to give all victims a once-off reparation payment of R30 000.

The postscript to the TRC process is still being written: after the final reports had been tabled, the Scorpions investigating unit began probing evidence relating to cases in which perpetrators had not applied for amnesty. Forty-one such cases were being investigated by June 2003.

There were indications at the time that these, along with other 'unfinished business' (violations for which amnesty was not sought), might be settled by a new immunity mechanism, in exchange for the truth. In addition to the 14 000 deaths which the TRC collected evidence on, at least another 12 000 deaths known to other investigations remained unexplored.

The government remained opposed to the general or blanket amnesty favoured by a group of

former South African Defence Force (SADF) generals and some senior ANC members.

The Amnesty Committee received 7 127 applications for amnesty, of which only 1 146 were granted.

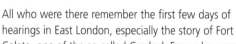

All who were there remember the first few days of hearings in East London, especially the story of Fort Calata, one of the so-called Cradock Four who were brutally murdered in the Eastern Cape in 1984. Fort Calata's widow, Nomonde, spoke on the second day.

Alex Boraine recalls it in his memoir of the TRC, *A Country Unmasked, Inside South Africa's Truth and Reconciliation Commission* (2000):

> In the middle of her evidence, she broke down and the primeval and spontaneous wail from the depths of her soul was carried live on radio and television, not only throughout South Africa but to many other parts of the world. It was that cry from the soul that transformed the hearings from a litany of suffering and pain to an even deeper level. It caught up in a single howl all the darkness and horror of the apartheid years.

Joyce Mtimkulu's story is about that darkness. Her son, Siphiwo, who was 21 and the father of two children, had been arrested and detained for six months in 1981. He was interrogated and tortured. The police wanted him dead, so, shortly before releasing him, they fed him rat poison, hoping he would die and it would look like a natural death. The poison didn't kill him – it confined him to a wheelchair. And he lost his hair. It alarmed his mother, who kept some of it, sensing it was evidence of some awful secret.

But Siphiwo's incapacity wasn't enough for the security police, who still saw the wheelchair-bound activist as a threat. So three of them, Gideon Nieuwoudt, Gerrit Erasmus and Nic van Rensburg, kidnapped Siphiwo and a friend, Topsy Madaka, took them to a disused police station at Post Chalmers

ABOVE LEFT: Her cry from the soul transformed the hearings ... Nomonde Calata, widow of murdered Cradock activist Fort Calata. She is comforted here by TRC commissioner Dr Wendy Orr moments before the start of a special service held to celebrate the first sitting of the TRC in Mdatsane, outside East London, on Sunday, 14 April, 1996.

LEFT: Police captain Dirk Coetzee, who had ordered the deaths of many activists, at Vlakplaas, the farm used by South Africa's murderous counter-insurgency unit in the 1980s.

Gideon Nieuwoudt, who, with two other policemen, interrogated, tortured and killed Siphiwo Mtimkulu, shooting him execution-style in the back of the head.

near Cradock and interrogated and tortured them. The policemen then drugged them – so they said (though Joyce Mtimkulu could not believe they had an ounce of compassion in them) – and shot them execution-style in the back of the head before burning their bodies and dumping the remains in the Fish River.

Another Eastern Cape activist and law graduate, Sizwe Kondile, met a similar fate in the same period. But he was drugged, shot and burned to ash outside Komatipoort on the Mozambique border.

One of the men involved in Kondile's killing was Dirk Coetzee, a man who had ordered the deaths of many ANC activists, including the human rights lawyer Griffiths Mxenge, who was stabbed 40 times by his killers at Umlazi Stadium in Durban.

Coetzee was the first commander of a special counter-insurgency unit based at a farm near Pretoria called Vlakplaas.

Vlakplaas is a dreaded name in the recent history of apartheid. From the late Seventies it was the base of a counter-insurgency unit that trained and deployed death squads made up of former liberation fighters who had been 'turned' and were now working for the apartheid state.

Between 1983 and 1993, Vlakplaas operatives were responsible for the abduction, torture and murder of thousands of activists. The bodies of their victims were buried secretly, or burned or dumped in the nearby Hennops River.

The man who epitomises Vlakplaas was named 'Prime Evil' by his colleagues. Colonel Eugene de Kock, commander at Vlakplaas between 1985 and 1993, was, with his group of askari killers, responsible for some of the worst atrocities of the apartheid years, including murders in Swaziland and Lesotho. He was also responsible for the bombing of the Congress of South African Trade Unions headquarters in Johannesburg in 1987, and the bombing of the South African Council of Churches headquarters, Khotso House, in Johannesburg a year later. At the time, the government blamed both attacks on

All the horror and complexity of apartheid crimes seemed to be bound up in the life of the man his colleagues called Prime Evil. Colonel Eugene de Kock, photographed in a thoughtful moment during a TRC hearing, cradling his chin in his right hand, was the subject of a remarkable book that sought, and found, this killer's humanity.

'enemies of the state'. (Former minister of law and order Adriaan Vlok applied for amnesty for the Khotso House bombing. He claimed PW Botha had ordered the attack.)

Just days after the elections in 1994, De Kock was arrested on 121 charges, nine of murder. He was convicted in late 1996 on 89 of the charges, six of them for murder, and sentenced to 212 years in prison, plus an additional two life sentences. In May 1997 he applied to the TRC for amnesty, which was granted for all except the charges for which he is serving a double life sentence. Not one of the commanding officers who gave De Kock his orders was charged.

—— ❖ ——

One of the most remarkable stories to emerge from the TRC is that of the encounter between Prime Evil and Pumla Gobodo-Madikizela, a clinical psychologist who served on the TRC's Human Rights Violations Committee.

Compelled to gain a deeper understanding of the killer, and the human, Gobodo-Madikizela decided to arrange a prison interview with him. She had intended to get all she needed out of the exchange in a single two-hour interview. She ended up spending more than 46 hours with De Kock, probing what was generally thought of as the heart of darkness of apartheid, but discovering, instead, a human being she could relate to.

Gobodo-Madikizela concludes her book on this journey, *A Human Being Died That Night, A Story of Forgiveness*, with a provocatively thoughtful and sympathetic sentiment:

Mercy should be granted cautiously. And yet society must embrace those who, like Eugene de Kock, see and even lead on the road of shared humanity ahead. Our capacity for such empathy is a profound gift in this brutal world we have created for one another as people of different races, creeds, and political persuasions.

Earlier in the book, she recounts a conversation with De Kock about the socio-political setting in which his murderous activities took place:

'White society had a good life,' De Kock said, sneering, as if there was something repulsive about the idea. 'They were quite happy with what they got, and now they are not so happy with who made it happen. I mean, how many whites really voted against the National Party? Whites say they didn't know, but did they really want to know? As long as they were now safe and they had their nice houses and their second cars and their third cars and swimming pools and kids at good government schools and university, they had no problem with cross-border raids and other counter-insurgency operations of security .... Why did they never question this?'

From *A Human Being Died That Night, A Story of Forgiveness* (2003) by Pumla Gobodo-Madikizela

'My experience,' writes TRC co-chairperson Alex Boraine, 'was that victims and survivors were in the main more than ready to forgive, but waited in vain for the apartheid leaders to say sorry.'

The TRC had hoped to hear from PW Botha, who had presided over the worst years of repression as minister of defence, prime minister and state president, from the 1970s to the end of the 1980s. An initial meeting between Archbishop Tutu and the cantankerous former president seemed a positive indication of his willingness to cooperate. But that soon soured. He dug in his heels and refused to work with the TRC, which, eventually, decided to subpoena him. A drawn-out legal battle ended, ironically, with Botha having his conviction and sentence (one year in jail or a R10 000 fine) for refusing to appear before the TRC overturned by the Appeal Court, on a technicality.

Botha's successor, FW de Klerk – who had backed the TRC in the hope that it would foster reconciliation through a sharing of truths about the past – did participate, but eventually felt aggrieved at what he thought was the TRC's keenness to 'humiliate' him.

He kept repeating that he had not at the time known of or authorised death squads or atrocities, yet was being expected to answer for them.

The TRC, on the other hand, hoped he would approach the matter in less juridical terms. And De Klerk's expressions of regret for the harm and suffering caused by apartheid fell short of what the TRC felt was required.

As for the sentiments of men such as Eugene de Kock, De Klerk argued that it was 'naturally ... in their interest to try to implicate those higher up the chain of command in their actions ... irrespective of the fact that the truth may have been carefully concealed' from higher authorities. And, anyway, most of the former security operatives were 'bitterly opposed to my reform policies' and would naturally be keen to damage his reputation.

Once again, the fault lines of South African history defined this new South African dispute.

The TRC undoubtedly succeeded in exposing the rot that had set in during, and because of, National Party rule, but the hearings and investigations left many unanswered questions about who knew what, and who gave the orders. Someone must have decided, someone must have known.

While the political leadership of the ANC and the command structure of Umkhonto we'Sizwe, as well as the leadership of the United Democratic Front, accepted full responsibility for all gross violations of human rights perpetrated by its members between 1960 and 1994, senior ANC leaders did not apply for amnesty.

In the end, both the ANC and the National Party, representing the former apartheid government, tried to block the final report, or sections of it that showed them in a critical light.

The ANC's court intervention came at the eleventh hour, and, given that it was now the government, was the source of much disquiet.

Archbishop Tutu reacted fiercely:

I have struggled against tyranny. I didn't do that in order to substitute another, and I believe if there is tyranny and an abuse of power then let them know that I will oppose it with every fibre of my being.

The hand-over of the final report to Nelson Mandela in Pretoria on 29 October, 1998, had to be delayed while the ANC presented its case in court. In the end, the court dismissed the application with costs, and the hand-over went ahead.

What the ANC objected to was that the struggle

Archbishop Desmond Tutu hands bound copies of the TRC's final report to Nelson Mandela. It would be years still before the TRC wrapped up the process.

and a consolidated democracy, it must be accompanied by an acknowledgement of mistakes made ... and a determination that these mistakes will never be repeated.

He felt it was 'nothing short of a tragedy' that the ANC had responded in the way that it had.

In our efforts to develop a culture of human rights, South Africa cannot afford double standards. It is correct to condemn violence and human rights violations when they come from the state. It is as important to condemn violations of human rights when they come from those who fought for the liberation of our country.

---------- ❖ ----------

Among those granted amnesty for acts committed in the name of liberation was Afrika Hlapo, who was one in a crowd that stoned two men to death in Cape Town's Klipfontein Road on 11 August, 1980. The two white motorists had fatefully stumbled into the cauldron of political anger on that day and paid with their lives.

One of the victims was 46-year-old building contractor Frederick Jansen, who often worked in the townships. As he drove down Klipfontein Road, he spotted the barricades ahead, but too late. As stones thrown by the crowd rained down, he tried to turn, but his bakkie stalled. The crowd set on him. Hlapo described what happened:

[He] refused to get out, and I and other members of the crowd pulled him from his vehicle and threw him to the ground. Mr Jansen sat on the road next to the driver's door. The crowd, including me, continued to stone him.

When the bakkie was torched moments later, Jansen, who could barely move, was severely burned.

The photograph that went round the world of a dazed Jansen sitting in a puddle of water, burned skin flaking off his face, arms and legs, his hands lightly, painfully, clasped across his knees, symbolised the horror of the South African conflict. He was dying.

Hlapo acknowledged at his amnesty hearing in 1999 that the mere fact of his being white made Jansen a target ... 'because we were sending a message to white people that even without guns we could make a difference'.

risked being 'deligitimised or criminalised'. It was 'erroneous' to regard the war of liberation, then deputy president Thabo Mbeki said in a TRC debate in parliament early in the next year, as being 'tantamount to a gross violation of human rights'. He added: 'We cannot accept such a conclusion, nor will the millions of people who joined in the struggle to end the system of apartheid.'

Reflecting on these tensions, Boraine writes:

It becomes clear that the expectations of some in the ANC were that the TRC would condemn the National Party and its many allies for their inhuman policies and that the ANC would emerge as the hero that had stopped the villain in its tracks and ushered in a new democracy with a human face.

Such expectations are understandable, and I have strong sympathy with them. But the goal of the TRC was to hold up a mirror to reflect the complete picture ... South Africans of all persuasions owe a huge debt of gratitude to those who fought for so long ... at such great cost against a tyrannical regime. ... But if the truly astonishing beginning is to flower into a human rights culture

Hlapo's application for amnesty was unique because he had already been tried and punished. He and 18 others, including the leading Cape activist Oscar Mpetha, were convicted in one of the major 'terror' trials of the Eighties. Hlapo had spent 11 years on Robben Island.

But his plea for forgiveness, he said, was to underline his belief that all South Africans must now come together and reconcile as best they could, for the future's sake.

❖

Going back into the past is a risk. But examining it is not the same as 'dwelling in the past', Alex Boraine believes.

We understandably spend a great deal of time remembering. But this too can be a powerful tool for the continuation of violence. There comes a time when forgiveness needs to take place in order to deal with the past.

But, on its own, he argues, forgiving is not enough, or is not convincing enough, not assuring enough. Some promise has to be made, a promise that forgiving is not permission to go back to the evil of the past, to allow the evil of the past to remain unchecked.

It is, he acknowledges, difficult to expect people to trust a promise from the powerful whose history perhaps contradicts what they say.

But we do not live in a perfect world, and if one can gain agreement on a new constitution for a society emerging from the horrors of the past, this is the contract, this is the promise, to which all parties can give their assent. This is the foundation on which the new society can be built. South Africa is a living example of this faculty to make and keep promises as enshrined in its new Constitution and carried forward by the Truth and Reconciliation Commission.

❖

There have been doubts about the TRC as a model for achieving good things.

Scholar Mahmood Mamdani argued in 1996 that the evil of apartheid should be thought of in social rather than in individual terms, and that it would be short-sighted to reduce human rights abuses to

Afrika Hlapo describes to the TRC how he and others in an incensed crowd stoned building contractor Frederick Jansen to death in August 1980.

relationships between perpetrators and victims of a 'fractured political elite'. The real relationship was between the mostly white beneficiaries and the mostly black victims of the system as a whole. That was the reality of the system, and reconciliation would depend on practical, material, measures really to undo the socio-economic and other effects of apartheid.

This was one of the themes of *Unfinished Business, South Africa, Apartheid and Truth* (2001) by Terry Bell and former senior staff member on the TRC, Dumisa Ntsebeza. They write that the TRC had hardly begun to probe the apartheid system when it wound up its 'unfinished business'. 'Even in terms of the narrow, personalised focus – which effectively treated a few symptomatic boils on a totally diseased body politic – it had fallen abysmally short.'

Bell writes that "no serious examination was made of the system that gave rise to some of the most horrific, racist social engineering of modern times. Instead there was a concentration on a proportion of the individual victims who came forward and on their immediate torturers, killers and persecutors".

Researcher Helen Macdonald wrote:

The TRC focus fell squarely on victims and perpetrators and therefore had the unfortunate and costly consequence of absolving most white South Africans who enjoyed social power without questioning its racist foundations. ... It would seem, therefore, that South Africa still requires a national initiative that will encourage accountability and responsibility amongst all South Africans for the past, but particularly amongst white South Africans who have, at most, paid a very small price for the benefits they enjoyed under the apartheid system.

In his assessment of post-1994 South Africa, *An Ordinary Country* (2002), academic Neville Alexander says he believes 'the contribution of the TRC to "reconciliation" ... is a very limited one ... [and that] the main impetus for "reconciliation" will come from the economic and educational sectors'. But he adds that the 'positive' significance of the TRC derives from its being 'one of the most high-profile indications of the existence of the desire of most South Africans to do away with racial prejudice and racial discrimination'.

One could say that the whole process had one irrefutable result. It narrowed the range of impermissible lies that one can tell in public.

So writes historian Michael Ignatieff in the introduction to *Truth and Lies* (2001), a book of stories and photographs from the TRC by photographer Jillian Edelstein. The TRC, Ignatieff argues, demonstrated that apartheid was not a benign system blighted by a few bad apples,

but a system, a culture, a way of life that was organised around contempt and violence for other human beings. Every South African was contaminated by that degradation, that deadness, that offence against the spirit.

In some future time,

when whites are emigrating and there is grumbling in the suburban gardens that the country is going to hell, when they are tempted to say: the old days weren't so bad, just maybe, the words will die in their throats. Because the Truth Commission had rendered some lies about the past simply impossible to repeat.

Equally, for the 'heirs of a just war of national liberation' of the victims of apartheid,

an essential taboo has been broken: the moral legitimacy of the liberation struggle has been subjected to scrutiny, and if the justice of the struggle has been reaffirmed, the crimes committed in the name of the struggle have been identified. It would be an impermissible lie to believe that all is permitted a people who have suffered ultimate injustice. The TRC may have made it impossible to give voice to this lie.

The Truth Commission was not plain sailing. There was, as Boraine acknowledges, 'suspicion, distrust and racism' at work even within the commission itself. Some might argue, he speculates, that if the commission itself 'found it difficult to be reconciled, how could it promote reconciliation in South Africa'? He offers an answer of his own:

This is to miss the point. South Africans, despite our differences and distrust of each other, despite incipient racism, can and often do rise above these problems in order to work together in our common pursuit for a new vision and a new society. The Commission was a microcosm of the country and in large measure achieved its goals. This surely is the pointer to the new South Africa. Despite the legacy of the past and the real divisions which still prevail, we can make it. It is therefore with a sense of hope rather than despair that I view the future of our country.

From *A Country Unmasked, Inside South Africa's Truth and Reconciliation Commission* (2000) by Alex Boraine

Constitutional Court judge Albie Sachs, who survived an assassination attempt by car bomb in Maputo, was convinced the TRC made an immeasurable contribution to 'humanising' South Africa.

———— ❖ ————

While the harrowing accounts that make up the TRC record do not claim to be comprehensive, they are presented as a 'living monument', stories that 'symbolise the greater experience and suffering of our people'.

The challenge was to remember, but transcend, the past.

'The names of the people in this volume,' the foreword to the Victim Findings, the seventh volume of the TRC report, concludes,

will remain as a memorial and testimony to the suffering endured during a time of conflict which must now be put behind the nation as a whole: not to be forgotten, but to be transcended in the building of a different and better society for all.

———— ❖ ————

Albie Sachs' first meeting with Henry was not an easy one. Henry, until then merely a disembodied voice on the telephone, was unknown to him, and unimaginable, but apparently a killer. Even so, as the Constitutional Court judge made his way from his chambers to the foyer where Henry was waiting, he was curiously excited. What could he expect of this exceptional encounter with one of the men who had tried to kill him, plotting the car bomb in Maputo that blew off his arm?

In this way, as it was reported in the *Cape Argus*, Justice Sachs reflected before a conference in 1999 on the post-TRC challenge, and the meaning of it all, the virtue of going back over difficult ground. At that first meeting with his intended killer, the judge decided he could not shake Henry's hand and make up in any meaningful way. First, he suggested, Henry should approach the TRC and try to be honest, 'and if we met later, we would see …'.

Meeting Henry, though, triggered some thinking about the TRC in the judge's mind: 'What was this TRC, an immersion in which was somehow going to humanise my relationship with my intended assassin?'

And he concluded eventually that, for all the misgivings about a narrow focus merely on a handful of perpetrators while all the rest of the beneficiary society got off scot-free, exposing individuals 'was a powerful counter-attack against the extreme forms of immorality rooted in apartheid's systematic, organised, banal injustice'. It meant 'people could see human beings were doing things to other human beings' and this 'wipes out the possibility of denial', creating 'some kind of shared understanding, not of the details and responsibilities, but that terrible things were done'.

In that, the TRC made an immeasurable contribution to 'humanising' the country.

It was true of the judge and Henry, too. Some time after their first meeting Justice Sachs was at a party when he heard a voice he recognised. Turning, he realised it was Henry's. It was deeply meaningful to Albie Sachs, the apartheid victim, to discover that his would-be killer had indeed approached the TRC and played his part in opening the door to truth. They shook hands, finally.

When that sunrise comes

chapter fifteen

When that sunrise comes

Life in the new South Africa often seemed little different from life under apartheid, a challenging factor in the ANC's second term in government.

**'So we shall have buried apartheid –
How shall we look at each other then
How shall we shake hands …
What shall we look like
When that sunrise comes.'**

Poet Mongane Wally Serote doesn't end his verse with a question mark, but it's a good question to ask.

It is authentic enough to answer it like this: after a long, dark night, the dawn was slow, and probably too slow for some, but the sun rose steadily nevertheless, shedding a brighter light that held the promise of renewal.

It's authentic, metaphorically: the new day, the sunrise, banishing the night that precedes it. But in the realness of South African life, the dawn and the dark are not so easily separated. After all, could it have been an unqualified truth – in 1995 or 1999 or 2003 – that South Africans had 'buried apartheid'?

———— ❖ ————

Ever since 1994, but especially since the second democratic election in 1999, a growing number of South Africans began to say that they had had enough of apartheid being blamed for everything that was wrong, deficient, in short supply, or for people who were corrupt, poorly educated or just plain self-interested.

Exasperated readers from the suburbs wrote to the newspapers saying it was time for South Africans to stop harping on the past and get on with building a better future.

And, without doubt, many failings were often pointlessly blamed on the events or mistaken choices of past decades and centuries.

But what was also – and remains – true is that the long history of dispossession had an inestimable impact on the resources and abilities, the wealth and education, the health and well-being, the thinking and the memory, of all South Africans.

Apartheid, though implemented systematically only from the late 1940s, drew on hundreds of years of ways of doing things. And though it was erased from the political slate on 27 April, 1994, it lingers in perhaps unseen but nevertheless deeply felt and deeply influential ways.

It was tellingly calculated in 1996 that, according to the United Nations Human Development Index, if the white 12 percent of South Africa were a separate country, it would have ranked 24th in the world, just behind Spain, whereas black South Africa would have ranked 123rd, just above Congo.

This observation underscored Thabo Mbeki's definition of South Africa as two nations, one white and wealthy, the other black and poor.

But the impact of the past goes well beyond material conditions, the state of poverty or inequity from which millions of people were discouraged from escaping by the elaborate structures of privilege spanning every feature of life from the cradle to the grave.

'The most devastating impact of apartheid on poor black South Africans,' medical doctor, scholar and administrator Mamphela Ramphele writes in her autobiography, *A Life* (1996),

> *has been the destruction of people's faith in themselves as agents of history. Their life experiences are scarred by strategies that destroy trust and faith in their fellow human beings. ... They have been taken advantage of for so long that they have stopped trying, and have become apathetic.*

The dawn metaphor, the sunrise theme of post-apartheid South Africa, was visited by Thabo Mbeki at his presidential inauguration at the Union Buildings in Pretoria on 16 June, 1999.

But he drew instead on the lyrically subtle seTswana conception of the 'dawning of the dawn', something different from the Western world's crisper image of the transition from dark to light:

> *Our country is in that period of time which the seTswana people ... graphically describe as 'mahube a naka tsa kgomo' ... when only the tips of the horns of the cattle can be seen etched against the morning sky.*

Thabo Mbeki, Nelson Mandela's successor, argued that liberation was more than freedom from oppression.

And it was doubtless this emergent dawn that characterised the second presidential term of the democratic era not only for the elected but also for the electors.

It was not a time of easily drawn conclusions or of clear definitions. Freedom from oppression was one thing, Mbeki argued, but liberation would be realised only once people were also freed 'from the dehumanising legacy of deprivation we inherited from our past'.

The reach of the past and the demands of the future muddled a present in which achievements and shortcomings could seldom be neatly matched to produce a balance sheet showing an obvious bottom-line success or failure.

The work-in-progress of the new South Africa was more complicated and more difficult than it might have seemed in 1994.

In his assessment of the post-apartheid period, *Beyond the Miracle, Inside the New South Africa* (2003), Allister Sparks quotes long-time ANC official

Global imperatives, and his own vision of a self-assured Africa, impelled Thabo Mbeki to assert South Africa's role as a member of the international community.

and, more recently, deputy governor of the Reserve Bank Gill Marcus reflecting on the tougher reality:

> There was a feeling that if you dealt with apartheid a lot of other things would automatically fall into place, but that has not been the case. It is much harder than we expected; a lot of problems are much more deep-seated.

Broadly, the emphasis in the second half of the democratic decade was twofold: transforming a deeply divided post-apartheid society and placing South Africa squarely in the context of a developing and renewing Africa.

With his African renaissance mission, President Mbeki sought to galvanise the energy of the rest of Africa to end its marginalisation in world affairs and to persuade the world to review the unquestioned Afro-pessimism – the expectation that Africa would forever yield war, famine and disease – that pervaded developed nations' thinking.

At the historic launch of the African Union in Durban in 2002, Mbeki set the scene for 'new forms of partnerships … to maximise our impact and change our continent for the better'.

It was time for Africa to 'end senseless conflicts … [and] work for a continent characterised by

democratic principles and institutions which guarantee popular participation and provide for good governance …'.

A key element of this was the South African-led New Partnership for Africa's Development (Nepad).

Addressing parliament on Nepad in 2001, the president emphasised that

> [o]ne of the most important challenges is to address the negative perception amongst investors who see Africa as a high-risk area. While we need to address the genuine concerns raised by potential investors, we have a responsibility to communicate better and correctly about the concrete improvements we continue to make.

At home, the transformation drive would focus on 'empowerment' in all its forms, corrective strategies aimed at empowering or enabling South Africans disadvantaged by decades of political, social and economic barriers based on race to overcome the effects, to secure better jobs, earn decent salaries, and have better chances and better choices. It included affirmative action – preference in the job market for people who were not white – and preference in awarding government tenders to black-owned or black-partnered companies.

ABOVE: An emerging black middle class was both a product of change and a necessary condition for the transformation of a divided society.

RIGHT: Affirmative action, not without controversy or shortcomings, transformed the racial complexion of the South African workplace.

Reducing poverty and building a more competitive, investor-attractive business environment had to go hand in hand with deracialising the economy.

Mbeki's vision, as he set it out at the 2002 ANC national conference in Stellenbosch, was one of simultaneously pursuing 'the two goals of social transformation and economic growth and development'.

It would be more than a government initiative, though. What he had in mind was a collaborative effort with the private sector, with incentives to draw 'the investment community, the private owners of capital' into the transformation process.

An essential element of the plan was that

our transformation programme does not merely focus on the redistribution of existing wealth. … To combine the objectives of both deracialising our economy and achieving its growth and development, we have to focus on the creation of new wealth and productive capacity.

It would depend on nurturing a substantial black middle class.

——— ❖ ———

The South Africa that defined Thabo Mbeki's first term was not one that emerged from bar graphs and statistics, or a chronology of international summits, diplomatic indabas and party conferences, important as these were. The consolidation of the transition, or the steps beyond freedom, the things that confirmed what it was that was vividly different about South Africa in the new millennium, were the everyday interactions in which people across society confronted and negotiated the 'deep-seated' problems highlighted by Gill Marcus.

Cape Town High pupils Dominique Reynecke and Olwethu Goni agreed that 'we're all humans'.

A journey starts with a single step. We're on our way to becoming a country that is united. Our parents obviously have that anger from the apartheid regime, but we're building our own foundations, our own attitudes, our own lives. We're just being ourselves.

These sentiments, expressed by 15-year-old Olwethu Goni, conveyed much about where South Africa was heading in 2003. Olwethu was one of six Cape Town High School pupils who took part in a Youth Day debate with five of her peers on everything from drugs, Aids and patriotism to emigration, affirmative action and apartheid. Cape Town High used to be an exclusively white school. In 2003, it was racially mixed – and uncomplicatedly so. The unselfconscious honesty the Youth Day debaters brought to their discussion of touchy topics said a lot about how the values of South Africa's constitutional democracy had permeated society and were being expressed, and being made part of everyday life. It was striking that the only white pupil among the six was at one with Olwethu on the virtue – or not – of affirmative action.

Olwethu Goni:

This is a topic I feel strongly about. This concept was introduced after apartheid, but it is time now to equalise all. Apartheid ended in 1994 and, yes, there are some people who are disadvantaged. But the time has come to end affirmative action. We always talk about equality, but is it really equality when you see people being given jobs because of skin colour?

Dominique Reynecke:

I agree. … We're all just people. Get over skin colour. We're all human beings. … When you want something in life, you have to go out and get it. If those children in rural villages really want to make something of themselves, believe me, they'll go out there and get it.

If the merits of their argument were open to question, their willingness to risk a controversial engagement on the topic remained an important sign of a lively national conversation in the making.

Mishka Khan, a Grade 2 pupil at Chapel Street Primary in Woodstock in Cape Town at the start of 2003, 'lived' in a toilet. Or so she said. She didn't actually live in it, but sometimes slept in one, or outside it. She was not quite a street child, but her parents, Dawid Williams and Nisa Khan, were homeless people who earned whatever they could by going through rubbish bins and salvaging goods such as paper and cardboard for recycling. They told their life story to *Cape Argus* assistant editor Andrea Weiss, who had befriended them while out walking her dog.

'Although this is a story of a poor family, with its roots in the diaspora of the Group Areas Act,' Weiss wrote, 'it is also a story of immense courage, because, poor as they are, Nisa and Dawid are making a conscious effort to send their little girl to school. It is their chief enterprise.'

Both parents grew up in District Six, though they weren't together then. When the Group Areas Act all but erased the suburb, Nisa and her family were packed off to the Cape Flats. Dawid was in prison at the time, for 'breaking into cars', but when he was released, he was shattered to find the area he regarded as his home had simply disappeared. In 2003, despite being homeless and having to rummage in bins for a living, their hopes were pinned on little Mishka, described by her teacher as 'one of my best readers ... and always eager to answer questions'.

Mishka's and her parents' hopes could not be said to have been the product solely of the political transition, nor were they guaranteed by it. But the essentially hopeful spirit of the time did grow from the ideas on which the transition was founded – the sense of equality, in education, in life. Throughout society, people who might otherwise have been left by the wayside were given the chance – or felt a chance was being given – to demonstrate their potential.

The scope of it was illustrated by the extraordinary achievements of 14-year-old Bongani Mvumvu in 2003.

Bongani was 11 when he made his way to a pig farm at Philippi on the Cape Flats to look for his missing mother some time after she had left him in the care of her husband and gone in search of work. Bongani did not find his mother at the farm where he remembered her sometimes going to look for food – and never did find her – but, in time, he found much else. When his father died soon after, the Mohr family, who owned the pig farm, took him in. Geoff and Linda Mohr enrolled him at school, and included him in all the family activities. One of these was horseriding.

Bongani displayed a natural flair for horsemanship and, within a year, had not only mastered riding skills but won trophies in virtually every event he entered. Often facing adult competitors, Bongani steadily worked his way to prominence in South African equestrian events. After winning the South African leg of the Federation Equestre Internationale Children's World Dressage Challenge in Franschhoek in October 2002, he was invited to the championship event in Germany. And it was in Hagen am Totenburger Wald in 2003 that 14-year-old Bongani Mvumvu, an equestrian of a mere three years' experience, became South Africa's youngest world champion when he beat 17 rivals from 15 countries.

Businessman Brett Kebble, who sponsored Bongani's trip to Europe, said of the teenager's triumph: 'It just shows what a depth of tremendous talent there is in South Africa.'

Inspiring young South Africans to develop their talents and prove their worth was the hallmark of Professor Kader Asmal's energetic leadership of transformation in education. Bongani's success

TOP: Mishka Khan, whose homeless parents pinned their hopes on putting her through school.

ABOVE: Champion horseman Bongani Mvumvu showed that 'everyone has potential'.

Restoring a truer sense of heritage was at the heart of the ceremony held at Settlers High School in Cape Town's northern suburbs in 2002 to rename one of the school quads Cochoqua Court in memory of the first Khoekhoe inhabitants of the area. At the renaming ceremony were, from left, Khoekhoe chief Basil-Mathys Coetzee, narrator Fran Booysen of the Cochoqua Cultural Council, headman Theo Carstens and headmaster Trevor Webster. An early Cochoqua settlement, based on a 1706 etching by Abraham Bogaert, is depicted on the mural on the wall behind them.

symbolised what he strove for. 'Every child has the potential to be the world dressage champion,' he told a gathering of young participants in the South African History Project's 'Our Roots are Speaking' programme in September 2003. Bongani Mvumvu, he said, had proved that 'you do not have to be rich or middle class. To have these things is an advantage, but everyone has the potential.'

Reaching back into the past, not just to interrogate it, to find truths or the lies laid to conceal them – as the Truth and Reconciliation Commission (TRC) had done – but to redeem heritage and acknowledge obscured identities became an important and powerful phenomenon in democratic South Africa.

It took various forms.

A vivid example of the awakening of pride and consciousness among young people was an initiative at a school in the Cape, the very naming of which expressed the ethos of the old South Africa.

Settlers High School in the northern suburbs of Cape Town had long been a whites-only school when it voluntarily opened its doors to learners who were not white in 1990. Within a decade, most of the learners were people previously classified as coloured. Against this reality, the words of the school song were out of key:

The Settlers came in days gone by to this our land so dear,
to live and die that you and I might work and prosper here.
The way was hard but they were brave, their purpose firm and sure.
Oh may the heritage they gave in Settlers High endure.

There was no doubting who these brave and purposeful forebears were, and what their legacy was, but, short of changing its name and expunging the tokens of its exclusive past, could the school acknowledge a broader, truer heritage?

The key to it was the school's geographical setting, its place in the historical landscape, as archaeologist Janette Deacon explained in a paper on heritage and African history at a history teachers' conference in 2002.

At the time of the first settler arrivals in the second half of the 1600s, the low hills between Table Bay and the mountains of Stellenbosch were occupied for a time by herders of the Cochoqua clan. They were among the first indigenous African people of the south to be dispossessed, to lose their land and, soon enough, their livelihood to the expanding settlement of new farmers from Europe.

In the Tygerberg, as this area came to be called, all traces of the pre-colonial Khoekhoe history were eventually erased.

But that changed in 2002 when the matriculation class at Settlers High were led to raise questions about identity and heritage.

They were, as Deacon put it, 'inspired by the efforts of some parents to raise awareness of their Khoekhoe heritage, and especially by the return to South Africa of the remains of Sarah Baartmann' and decided to donate to the school a ceramic mural depicting a herder encampment at the Cape in the late 1600s. At a special ceremony in September that year, the courtyard where the mural was installed was renamed the Cochoqua Court.

Redeeming a legacy of a different but no less significant form became the subject of complex legal negotiations after 2000.

In 1939, songwriter Solomon Linda recorded a catchy tune called 'Mbube' which, in the decades that followed, earned record companies between US$10 million and US$15 million worldwide. The song, better known today as 'The Lion Sleeps Tonight', didn't do much for Linda himself.

Through no fault of his own, he didn't understand his rights, and lost them. In a changed South Africa imbued with a spirit of fairness and a proper acknowledgement of wrongs and oversights, there was finally some hope that Linda's family might be compensated for his remarkable achievement.

Through a cooperative initiative that would have been rare in the past, the Ntsele family of Soweto began working with a team of specialists put together by Johnnic Entertainment, owners of Gallo Music, to attempt to gain fair compensation for the profits made from Linda's pre-Second World War tune.

Acknowledging the integrity of individuals who had been wrongly or falsely dishonoured in the past is a project that has restored the dignity of many who were ostracised or outlawed on the strength of their moral convictions.

One among them was a remarkable Afrikaner named Bram Fischer, whose prominence in the law, and in the struggle, is described in an earlier chapter.

His role as Nelson Mandela's advocate in the Rivonia Trial earned him the opprobrium of the establishment, but it was his courage in acting on his commitment to a democratic South Africa that his enemies used to try to rob him of a professional

---

ACT

To provide for the reinstatement of the enrolment of certain deceased legal practitioners who were struck off the roll of advocates or attorneys as a result of their opposition to the previous political dispensation of apartheid or their assistance to persons who were opposed to the said apartheid dispensation; and to provide for matters connected therewith.

PREAMBLE

WHEREAS it is appropriate to honour the memory of those legal practitioners who made a contribution to the opposition to the previous political dispensation of apartheid, or who assisted persons who were so opposed, and who were struck off the roll on account of such opposition or assistance;

AND IN ORDER TO redress the injustices of the past by restoring the professional status of those legal practitioners who were so removed during the apartheid dispensation,

BE IT ENACTED by the Parliament of the Republic of South Africa, as follows:—

Reinstatement on roll of advocates or attorneys

1. (1) Despite the provisions of the Admission of Advocates Act, 1964 (Act No. 74 of 1964), and the Attorneys Act, 1979 (Act No. 53 of 1979), the name of any deceased 5
person who was removed from the roll of advocates or attorneys prior to 27 April 1994, may, upon application brought by a member of such deceased person's family or, after consultation with the deceased person's family, by—
  (a) the General Council of the Bar of South Africa;
  (b) the Bar Council concerned;   10
  (c) the Society of Advocates concerned;
  (d) the Law Society of South Africa;
  (e) the law society concerned; or
  (f) any other interested person,
to any High court, be reinstated to the roll of advocates or attorneys, as the case may be, 15
if the court is satisfied that the conduct that led to that person's name being removed from the roll in question was directly related to that person's opposition to the previous political dispensation of apartheid and to bringing about political or constitutional change in the Republic, or to assisting persons who were likewise opposed to the said

---

integrity that was, in fact, beyond question.

Arrested in 1964 for being a Communist, he was put on trial under the notorious Suppression of Communism Act, but applied for – and was granted – bail to attend a Privy Council hearing in London, promising to return to face his accusers. He kept his word, but early in 1965, acting on what he saw was his duty to oppose the 'monstrous policy of apartheid with every means', he decided to jump bail and go underground.

Within two days, the Johannesburg Bar Council, of which Fischer had served as president, met to strike him from the roll, a gesture that devastated the senior advocate. He was rearrested in due course, tried and sentenced to life imprisonment. He died a prisoner.

After 38 years, and nearly 10 years of the democracy Fischer had sacrificed so much to achieve, his honour was formally restored. The determination of his daughters Ruth and Ilse – and a new law, the Reinstatement of Enrolment of Deceased Legal Practitioners Act – secured Fischer's posthumous reinstatement to the Bar in 2003.

'I think this is a chapter closing,' Ilse said in a *ThisDay* newspaper report. 'This is what reparation is all about. In this case, it's putting things right.'

Grounds for optimism … increasing integration went hand in hand with signs that South Africans were abandoning the racist attitudes of the past.

———— ❖ ————

Boeremag members were on trial in 2003 for allegedly plotting to overthrow the state. Their hare-brained scheme was the token of a right-wing threat that remained an ever-present factor in South Africa after 1994.

Yet right-wing sentiment of this kind belonged to a minority of diehard nationalist whites spurned by the bulk of the former beneficiaries of apartheid.

Even the once pernicious and influential secret society of Afrikaner men, the *Broederbond*, reinvented itself as the *Afrikanerbond*, and opened its doors to all races, and to women.

Race consciousness remained an often troubling feature of public debate and private talk, and racism was by no means a thing of the past.

This was confirmed in a telling and comprehensive survey of attitudes among adults in more than 2 000 households across all areas and types of residence in 2001. Yet the responses provided grounds for optimism.

Interpreting the results, researcher Professor Lawrence Schlemmer noted:

Institutional racism has to be combated. If,

however, it is defined so broadly that it has to cover the effects of history or the effects of legitimate rules that place some people at a disadvantage inadvertently and not because of their race, then one has defined problems in such a way that they are too large or complex to solve.

He went on:

Fortunately, this survey shows that most South Africans have defined the serious problems of racism and race discrimination in ways that relate to visible current social interaction, and that therefore can be solved. Even the more sophisticated and better-educated among them are no more inclined than others to have developed ideologies based on abstract institutional racism. This, coupled with the fact that they are more positive than negative about trends in race relations, are grounds for optimism.

Professor Schlemmer noted:

A major ground for optimism lies in the commitments to unity and racial cooperation among 80% or more respondents. Some of this commitment is merely fashionable, taking its cue from new South Africa rhetoric, but judging from the results in relation to each other, a great deal of it is genuine.

Intellectual Mamphela Ramphele urged people to speak up fearlessly, engage critically with one another and hold the powerful to account.

Being unapologetic in constructively criticising the new South Africa was possibly one of the most important indicators of the consolidation of democracy in its first decade. People within and outside politics showed that the national conversation was not at risk of becoming insipid.

World Bank executive and former University of Cape Town vice-chancellor Mamphela Ramphele warned in 2001 that achieving liberty through a long and bitter liberation struggle was no guarantee of lasting freedom. 'Liberation politics,' she said, 'is not an adequate preparation for democratic governance. An active process of institutional cultural change is called for to transform former liberation movements into political parties that are suited to serve a modern democratic state.' Critical self-reflection, and vigorous, fearless public debate, were vital.

African leaders, like their counterparts elsewhere, need to be made accountable to the people they represent. Intolerance of criticism should not be allowed to silence critics, even if the price of speaking up may be high.

She also warned white South Africans that 'it is likely to become more and more difficult … to justify demanding rights as citizens without being seen to be willing to participate in the civic duties beyond the minimalist liberal approach to citizenship.'

Prominent journalist and former newspaper editor Ken Owen noted in the mid-1990s that in the course of the apartheid years 'the idea that one should pursue the truth was replaced by the idea that one should pursue the enemy'.

Everybody knew what they were against rather than what they were for.

In the post-1994 environment, it became clear that the relatively quick removal of the 'enemy' (the system against which the critical debate and its participants were most readily and usefully defined) seemed to leave many individuals – activists, but also elements of institutions such as the Press – muddling along without a positive rationale, without fully understanding for themselves what they were for.

It was underscored by former director-general to Nelson Mandela, Jakes Gerwel, who focused critical attention on the fate of the political Left, and the erosion of the sense of 'human solidarity' that permeated the struggle, when people cared about people. In a lecture in 2002, he said that, in the light of crimes of senseless violence and abuse of children, it was important to raise questions about the apparent absence of debate on the basic decency of society.

Hard questions were raised elsewhere, too.

Outspoken *Sunday Times* editor Mathatha Tsedu wondered in a brave and forthright column in 2003 what it was that weakened African leadership. There was no doubting the impact of colonialism and racism, but he went further:

> Afrikaners built their own communities and businesses and, despite the loss of political power, are still a community – distinct and thriving. The African structures, on the other hand, are all gone, and those that are still around are being ridiculed each day, from circumcision and cultural practices to religion and the medicines of our forefathers. And yet Africans were not always like this. ... The leaders of the kingdoms of Monomotapa, Timbuktu and Mapungubwe were great leaders. They could never have succeeded in doing what they did if they were selfish. The reality today is that people in this country who are indigenous Africans are prone to irrational behaviour fed by greed and irresponsibility. The numerous corruption and fraud cases involving esteemed African leaders are worrying issues. Africans are not the only ones fingered for corruption, but the rate and level of occurrence is worrying.

Greed, irresponsibility, corruption and fraud had to be confronted and debated, he argued. 'This is a painful reality,' Tsedu wrote. 'We need to confront the legacy of colonialism and racism and its effects on African people in particular.'

Writing in 2002, veteran liberal Helen Suzman – never one to mince her words – summed up the transition by saying that while South Africa had 'shed the indignity of being a pariah state, been readmitted to the United Nations and plays a leading role in Africa ... expected foreign investment has been deterred by the introduction of rigid labour policy ... and the over-hasty implementation of affirmative action. While one can appreciate the need for affirmative action to redress the many hardships endured by blacks under the apartheid regime, not sufficient emphasis has been given to the training of the black population to take skilled jobs.'

Scholar Neville Alexander expanded on this in his book, *An Ordinary Country* (2002):

> In my view, given the capitalist realities of the transition, South Africa needs a large-scale, extended skills training programme rather than an affirmative action programme which is based, in too many cases, on tokenism, as unintended as this might be.

A provocatively controversial view of black economic empowerment (BEE) was taken by President Thabo Mbeki's younger brother, social and political analyst Moeletsi Mbeki. He caused a storm in 2003 by arguing that BEE amounted merely to a transfer of assets to individuals with good political connections:

> We are not creating entrepreneurs. We are taking political leaders and politically connected people and giving them assets which, in the first instance, they don't know how to manage. We are now seeing the Mining Charter and all sorts of other charters. But charters won't create entrepreneurs.

He charged that BEE was really supported by big business as a means to create a black elite buffer to protect them. Dali Mpofu, a member of the Black Business Council, hit back:

> Mbeki's views do nothing but pander to the most backward sensibilities of those who deny the economic effects of our apartheid past. I am referring to the latter-day preachers of equality, advocates of feigned colour-blindness and die-hard opponents of 'reverse racism'.

In a measured response to his brother's remarks, the president commented in parliament that if it were true that affirmative action was building 'only a small black elite, we would need to do something about it. ... It is incorrect. If it is being done, it must be stopped.'

Making sure national policies were achieving what they were meant to achieve became one of the biggest concerns of the woman who presided over the national legislature.

Described once by a headline writer as 'user-friendly, but no pushover', the Speaker of Parliament, Frene Ginwala, had a reputation for being fiercely intolerant of sloppiness. She famously castigated MPs in 2002 for being dozy because they had passed the wrong version of a Bill. It annoyed her, but she was more concerned towards the end of that year about redefining the role of parliament, making it a more vigorous, pro-active institution that, instead of merely passing legislation and exercising oversight on its implementation afterwards, would question the government more vigorously beforehand on whether a law really could be implemented, whether there was money for it, and sufficient staff to see that it actually benefited people. 'I'm talking chiefly of delivery-type legislation,' she explained at the time.

> We learned a tough lesson with the Maintenance Act ... we raised tremendous expectations among women, and only once it was passed we found the resources weren't there, people were not trained, there were no courts ... and women were queueing up. And all this because implementation was not thought through.

She added:

> If parliamentarians only become actors after the event, then we will not succeed in eradicating poverty for many decades. ... We may simply have to conduct oversight to establish the reasons for our failure. ... I do not buy into the argument of those who say simply that delivery is the business of government and not parliament. That's not what developing countries' parliaments should be about.

Right across the national debate, it was clear that by the end of 2003 South Africans had no difficulty matching the sentiments expressed a few years earlier by Mamphela Ramphele, that vigorous and fearless public debate was essential to the vitality of South African democracy.

❖

HIV/Aids, crime, the arms deal and Zimbabwe ... these were the most controversial aspects of President Mbeki's first term.

In 2003, about 4,7 million South Africans were HIV-positive, and of the 400 000 to 500 000 living with full-blown Aids, up to a thousand were dying each day. A long and bitter dispute over critics' deep concerns about the government's response to the

TOP RIGHT: Moeletsi Mbeki, the president's younger brother, cautioned that black economic empowerment would not on its own produce black entrepreneurs.

MIDDLE RIGHT: User-friendly, but no push-over ... Speaker of Parliament Frene Ginwala wanted MPs to look beyond their formal task of passing new laws.

RIGHT: Treatment Action Campaign leader Zackie Achmat was influential in refocusing the government's approach to Aids.

crisis began to subside with a decision in August 2003 to launch a national 'roll-out' of Aids drugs which the Health Department believed would dramatically improve the lives of millions of South Africans.

The high rate of violent crime drew much public criticism, and was blamed for a rise in vigilantism, which included the return of the 'necklace' in some cases where suspected criminals were apprehended and burned to death by members of communities frustrated by what they perceived to be the ineffectiveness of the criminal justice system.

Calls for the death penalty to be reinstated rose to a clamour. Redirecting the police service from one geared to combating the political threats of the Eighties to fighting crime and protecting citizens proved to be an immense challenge for the post-apartheid government. Innovations – such as the special Scorpions unit and an assets forfeiture unit, aimed at disabling multi-million rand organised crime syndicates – made significant gains. There were signs that better policing was paying off with a 17 percent drop in the murder rate between 1999 and 2003.

The Mbeki government's stance on Zimbabwe's tyrannical President Robert Mugabe was a source of much criticism, too, with detractors claiming its 'quiet diplomacy' was failing to achieve desired results in the neighbouring state, while also tarnishing South Africa's reputation as a defender of human rights.

On this particular issue, President Mbeki had an unexpected champion in former President FW de Klerk, who said in 2003 that, while travelling abroad, he always made a point of defending Mbeki's position 'because people don't realise there is a limit to what the leader of one country can do to influence events in another'.

The multi-billion rand deal for new ships, warplanes and other equipment for the South African National Defence Force was controversial in several respects: there was criticism of the huge spending on arms when other areas of government activity were more deserving of investment; of shortcomings in the approval of the deal in parliament, and of fraudulent dealings with some of the arms suppliers. Former ANC Chief Whip Tony Yengeni was found guilty in court of accepting payment towards a luxury vehicle from one of the arms suppliers. He was also publicly disciplined by his party.

Above all, though, there was a sense that the institutional fabric of the new South Africa was durable. In 2002, Paul Graham, director of the Institute for Democracy in South Africa (Idasa), noted:

Recent public controversies, such as the one concerning HIV/Aids policy, show how far we have come as a country, in such a relatively short period of time. While the intensity of the debate continues to provoke serious division both inside and outside of government, the democratic system has shown that it is robust and sophisticated enough to cope with the demands placed on it.

❖

Journalist Allister Sparks concludes in his book on the post-apartheid years that, while 'daunting problems' remain, South Africa had, by 2003, made significant progress in various ways:

We have made considerable progress along the rocky road from institutionalised racism to mutual tolerance. We have made progress in other ways, too. A decade ago we were not only racially divided and locked in social conflict, we were also in a fiscal mess. We were politically and economically, even psychologically, isolated in a globalising world, inflation and interest rates were sky high, our businesses were inefficient and uncompetitive, hiding behind high protective tariffs, and economic growth had been in decline for years.

Today all that has changed. Our apartheid society has become integrated across the board, from schools to workplaces to boardrooms and even bedrooms. We have a functioning multi-party democracy with regular free, fair and peaceful elections underpinned by the world's most progressive Constitution and protected by perhaps the world's finest panel of judges in the Constitutional Court. Economically, too, South Africa has transformed.

From *Beyond the Miracle* (2003) by Allister Sparks

❖

In an assessment of the results of the government's own 10-year review, minister of social development Zola Skweyiya highlighted trends in post-apartheid South Africa which helped explain why, as Gill Marcus pointed out, changing the country proved 'much harder than we expected'.

Between 1996 and 2001, Skweyiya revealed, the number of households in South Africa increased by 30 percent – almost three times as much as the rate of population increase.

Instead of having to provide housing and services for an expected one million new households, the government has found itself having to assist almost three million new households, let alone the apartheid backlog of unserviced households.

There was also a dramatic increase in the economically active population.

Despite employment loss through industrial restructuring as South Africa reintegrated into the world economy, the economy created 1,6 million new jobs between 1995 and 2002. However, the economically active population grew by about four percent per year, double the rate of population growth.

Change in the structure of the economy quickened: There was 'a shift from mining, construction and the public service to the services industry such as financial services and information technology'. The consequence was that there were two economies at work – the first being advanced and sophisticated, based on skilled labour and becoming more globally competitive, the second being mainly informal, marginalised and unskilled, and not likely to benefit from the flourishing of the first economy.

Another significant trend highlighted by Skweyiya was the extent of new migration.

In major metropolitan areas, and in some regional centres and small towns, over 20% of the population are new migrants. Thus, in rural areas, social capabilities are undermined by the loss of able-bodied and relatively skilled poeple, while in urban areas, the immigration of economically active people – though it might add to development potential – risks overwhelming service delivery and employment opportunities.

In a sense, the very success of the new South Africa was a factor in enlarging its developmental burden.

———— ❖ ————

South Africans, ever capable of defying the prophets of doom – and sometimes living a life of blithe optimism in the face of appalling odds – also have a grim affection for pessimism.

Often, when they look ahead, they see only the worst possible outcomes.

This is true of two intriguing attempts – at two very different junctures in the 20th century – to answer the question Serote poses: how will it be when apartheid ends?

Arthur Keppel-Jones's *When Smuts Goes* (1950) was first seen more as a satire than a prophetic book. It's an apocalyptic account of decline in South Africa, starting with the Nationalists coming to power. When the Nationalists did come to power in 1948, readers saw it more as a prophecy. And in several ways he was right about many things: worsening international relations, the declaration of a republic, repressive policy, revolt. And even, chillingly enough, in 2010, a plague that decimates the population. Earlier, in Keppel-Jones's 1970s, the Nationalist republic goes to war with Britain and its allies and, after being defeated, is supplanted by a military government. In time, this gives way to a black government, which is followed by a coup, and decline. The book ends, despairingly, in civil chaos with the plague of 2010.

The second book, by Tom Barnard, *South Africa 1994–2004*, was published just as the Nationalists were beginning to relinquish power, in 1991. In Barnard's narrower time frame, the story is much less dramatic than Keppel-Jones's, but it has Afrikaners, denied a homeland in constitutional negotiations, going off on their own and declaring their own territory. A brief civil war ends with the United Nations stepping in and partitioning the country. The state of South Africa is broken up, with the bitter secessionists in a fictional Orania living separately from a black-dominated Azania. Barnard concludes his book with the pregnant line: 'If only the right choices had been made at the right time.'

There is always, it seems, this fearful focus in South Africa on a future that doesn't work. And, in these two accounts from very different times, the idea that South Africans themselves are incapable of creating their own settlement, and that the resolution of the country's history would depend on foreign intervention, are fundamental assumptions. In the late 1990s, *The Economist* magazine suggested that '[i]f scare stories were an export-earner, South Africa would be a rich place these days'.

South Africa's 'second' economy, the informal sector, provided a livelihood to hundreds of thousands of people, yet remained marginalised and unlikely to benefit from gains in the mainstream economy.

In past decades, a unitary South Africa ruled by a democratic parliament under one of the most progressive constitutions in the world, a Constitutional Court to uphold it, institutions to protect human rights, freedom of speech, an independent judiciary, and an electoral commission to oversee free and fair elections, among other things, was inconceivable.

❖

People are usually not impressed by lists of relatively abstract achievements, which, implicitly, mainly look good on paper. There were many persuasive, concrete examples of the gains of the new South Africa. But one of the most telling was also ironic, a defining instance of what the country had become.

When the TRC failed to convince former President PW Botha to appear before it to answer claims made about his role in gross human-rights violations in the Seventies and Eighties, and he refused to respond to its subpoenas, the commission took him to court.

It was a highly symbolic moment when the man who embodied the securocratic rule of arrogant white nationalism was humbled by a conviction in a court presided over by a black magistrate.

But the consequences were unforeseen. When Botha appealed against his conviction and sentence – a year behind bars or R10 000 – he won, on a technicality.

Perhaps in that moment truth was defeated, and the ideals of the struggle for democracy eroded. Some thought so. But the plainest statement about the new South Africa, about the success of idealism, and the real meaning of freedom and democracy, lay in a brief passage of the Appeal Court's judgment:

This court is mindful of the fact that there will be many who may consider that it is unjust that [Botha] should succeed in his appeal upon … purely technical grounds.

But the judgment concluded:

The court is dutybound to uphold and protect the Constitution and to administer justice to all persons alike without fear, favour or prejudice. … Suffice to say that the same law, the same Constitution which obliges [Botha] to obey the law of the land like every other citizen, also affords him the same protections that it affords every other citizen.

In a nutshell, this was everything that generations of

Former president Botha's success – on a technicality – in appealing against his conviction and fine for refusing to appear before the Truth and Reconciliation Commission was an ironic token of democratic South Africa's triumph.

South Africans had fought for. It was everything that PW Botha's fortress apartheid had been conscientiously directed against.

But in the new setting, under the black rule he had refused to countenance, even Botha had his inalienable rights.

The great global shift of the 20th century towards equality and democratic governance founded on the idea of inalienable rights had long tormented South Africa's white voters, and Afrikaner nationalists especially.

Succeeding Nationalist administrations had tried to manipulate the tide and so put off what their opponents seemed to see as an inevitable outcome, or go with the current just a little but never so much that they would risk being swept away.

Writing in the mid-1950s, author Sheila Patterson concluded her study of Afrikaner nationalism:

The national-minded Afrikaner has no future in the world of today. His uncompromising values and attitudes are too directly in conflict with those of the outside world and with the conditions of survival. A future might perhaps be predicted for him in the event of atomic war and devastation leading to the resumption of isolated tribal life far from the main centres of urban civilisation.

Otherwise, the Afrikaner's future must lie in increased adaptability, in economic integration, and in a radical revision of his basic values so that they cease to be based on insecurity, fear and hatred. For national-minded Afrikaners, the next years represent the last trek – a trek into the twentieth century world, where no man nor nation can be an island, or a trek away from it into a barren and deadly wilderness which leads to no Promised Land.

From *The Last Trek, A Study of the Boer People and the Afrikaner Nation* (1957) by Sheila Patterson

There will always be argument about the degree to which Afrikanerdom was forced to change, and how much of the change was a voluntary, intelligent response to changing circumstances.

What is beyond doubt is that, when the change came, the bulk of Afrikaners did not, for all their reservations and anxieties, harbour an intrinsic, die-hard resistance to the democratic order.

Post-apartheid renewal was symbolised by the creation of a new national crest at the heart of which is a reminder of the long history of a contested, shared landscape. Here, a carving of the crest is held by President Thabo Mbeki and Frank Chikane, Director-General in the Presidency.

———— ❖ ————

On the other hand, there were, perhaps, in 1994, some delusions in all communities about what democracy could achieve.

It was a delusion that democracy somehow meant a problem-free society, an end to poverty, the arrival at the stroke of a pen of a fairer way of living, and a better-off, healthier, better-educated populace.

What perhaps dawned on South Africans in the clarifying light of the post-apartheid sunrise was that democracy was a means, not an end, a way of achieving results more than a result in itself. Rather than automatically delivering equality and equity, in health, schooling, money, jobs, security, welfare and prosperity, it made everyone a partner in seeking these things, and choosing how it was done.

It was not particularly comforting, and many South Africans felt disappointed. A petrol attendant, Maxwell Flekisi, a father of three and the sole breadwinner, earning just R193 a week, wondered in 1999 '... what does freedom mean if you have no money?'

Human rights commissioner Pansy Tlakula might have been speaking for Maxwell when she told a conference on culture, identity and citizenship:

If people are poor and their bellies are empty or half-empty, discussions of human rights make very little sense.

Yet it is also true that the absence of human rights, and the freedom to choose, was long an unbearable hunger.

A *Saturday Argus* editorial of 28 April, 2001, marking the 7th anniversary of the first democratic elections, noted:

The toughest lesson of these seven years is that being free to choose is not the same as being prosperous, being educated, employed and well-fed. But we probably need to remind ourselves that not having the choice is an intolerable poverty.

For more than 300 years, it was an immeasurable deprivation, for the poor of succeeding generations, but also for the rich.

The material advantage derived from exploitation could not be separated from the indignity and abuse of centuries of disadvantage. The moral bankruptcy, the rising anger, sapped all of South Africa.

'A man who takes away another man's freedom,' Nelson Mandela writes,

is a prisoner of hatred, he is locked behind the bars of prejudice and narrow-mindedness. I am not truly free if I am taking away someone else's freedom, just as surely as I am not free when my freedom is taken from me. The oppressed and the oppressor alike are robbed of their humanity.

In the remarkable decade since those liberating elections of 1994, the idealism and the reality of freedom converged to grant a society with a long history of conflict and chains the means and the desire to live up to its simple motto: !ke e: /xarra //ke (unity in diversity).

It was not the end of the road, and there was no magical Utopia in sight. But the sense of a shared destiny in a free, united country, however diverse and argumentative, was, in itself, at the heart of what it meant to have a better life.

Of course I still believe we are the rainbow people. Why not? I think we are doing remarkably well in learning to live together.

Archbishop Desmond Tutu

[endpiece]

Remembering
the future

Remembering the future

Yesterday is history. It's happened, it's in the past, and there's no getting away from it.

But if you think back to all the things you did from the moment you got up yesterday morning until you went to bed, you might recognise that whatever you do for the rest of today, or tomorrow, something would have been said or done in the past 24 hours that will in some way influence how you feel, where you go, what you say or do, what you think, and how others are towards you, what they say to you – or perhaps even say of you.

What happened or didn't happen, what was said or not said, all these things are fractions of your most recent past.

But recognising how they have influenced you, or those around you, requires a conscious effort. You actually have to think about it, weigh it up against other things. It's more difficult than merely calling it to mind. And while the conclusions you come to might not be accurate, but rather speculative, subjective or even selfish, recalling the past in this way is a means of understanding its continuous impact, even on things that haven't yet happened.

So while yesterday really is history, there is, not just in the obvious sense, no getting away from it.

To remember the past in this way is to confront its influences on the events and thoughts and plans of today, and tomorrow. It is, you could say, a matter of remembering the future.

—— ❖ ——

Many thinkers in years gone by have grappled with the power of the past, and the challenge of confronting it squarely in the present.

The German philosopher Georg Hegel's thinking on this was borrowed in the last century by playwright George Bernard Shaw, who suggested that 'the only thing that men learn from history is that men don't learn from history'. The record of human society often seems to bear out this perhaps cynical view.

Yet there is an argument that looking closely at the past is a way of giving careful consideration to the future. Archaeologist Patrick Mbunwe-Samba wrote in 1996:

> There is no greater treasure for the modern man than to know his past well as a basis for assessing and understanding the future.

In a lecture in 1995, novelist and essayist Nadine Gordimer said that 'the conclusion [to be drawn from "our century", the 20th century] is that humankind has not known how to control the marvels of its achievements'. She went on:

> Now that the deeds are done ... our last achievement could be in ... questioning honestly and reflecting upon the truth of what has been lived through, what has been done. There is no other base on which to found the 21st century with any chance of making it a better one.

It was what Alex Boraine, co-chairperson of the TRC of the 1990s was driving at when he said: 'Dealing with the past is not dwelling in the past – it is part of the promise of the future.'

The essence of all these insights is that what we choose to remember from our yesterdays is a way of recommending choices for our tomorrows.

———— ❖ ————

Remembering in South Africa is demanding. There is much to forget, or much that – out of pain or shame – most people would prefer to forget, to leave behind, to leave undisturbed. To dig up the bones buried in the past, this view suggests, is to risk being contaminated by them.

And it's no doubt true that the atrocities or abuses of years ago can rekindle anger and resentment which take us back to a world that is not the one we live in but one we re-enter through our bitter memory. And the temptation to relive the anger can be strong.

What is also true is that remembering in the usual or ordinary sense of personally or privately recollecting events and even feelings is limited and complicated. Memory plays tricks, as they say, and psychological studies suggest that what we say we remember is often an imperfect and sometimes even a false record of what actually happened.

But remembering in the sense of mulling over the evidence of the past, the records, statements, photographs, memoirs, videos – evidence which always throws up contradictions, the things that are unexpected or difficult to match – is the business of forming, and re-forming, historical memory, the creation of history.

Remembering occurs in the present.

The English historian Keith Jenkins has written in Re-Thinking History (1991) that, as a record of what has happened, 'history' is different from 'the past' and that at any given moment, while there remains just one past, there are many histories of it. The whole past can never be captured, he says, so there can never be a whole history, nor a 'correct' history.

Against this, an interesting and challenging way of considering the significance of the past is novelist George Orwell's argument that – as he set it down in his bleak story of totalitarianism, the novel 1984 (1949) – 'he who controls the present, controls the past, and he who controls the past controls the future'.

In the hands of the powerful, the unquestioned, this formula has literally far-reaching implications. For instance, when PW Botha told the House of Assembly in August 1953

> [w]e must accept that the non-European in South Africa in his level of civilisation is hundreds of years behind the European, and he can only insist on the same privileges and rights as those enjoyed by the European in South Africa today when he reaches that stage that the white man has reached.

he was brazenly – but, to many, quite believably – manipulating the past of southern Africa precisely to shape the future.

And the histories of the apartheid years that said southern Africa was an empty land when the Voortrekkers moved into the interior to make new lives for themselves were really seeking to justify one of the consequences: minority white rule in the 20th century.

In subtle and not-so-subtle ways the categorisation of racial importance by academic authorities – scientists, and historians such as George Theal – created for generations of South Africans the idea

that races were by nature different from one another physically and intellectually, and that it made sense to order them according to their differences, with the white man ranked first.

The power of this 'respectable' reasoning – prevalent throughout Europe, its colonial empires and North America – impelled often brutal discrimination, and justified it at the same time.

Assigning meaning to visible differences between people may not have been a deliberate manipulation of the record of the human past, but it served purposes in shaping the future. It is this making (or remaking) of history, the ongoing creation in the present of a record of the past, that illustrates the importance of Orwell's 'formula'.

History-making can be a risk. As the writer Es'kia Mphahlele warns: 'If used unwisely, [history] can reinforce a dangerously false image of ourselves.' But if it can be made a core part of society's conversation with itself, of the questions we ask of one another, it is an opportunity, and perhaps the primary source of hope in human life: the idea that the past can be acknowledged, judged, learned from, put in perspective, looked at from this or that angle, challenged, or even, in a sense, disowned. We can put things behind us. Or, if you like, we can remember them in order to forget them, to dispense with them. But it can't be done if we don't try to see what's there.

Historian Jeff Guy emphasises another element of this:

We have recently emerged from a past where every effort was made to turn history into propaganda. Values, where they existed, were always under threat and every attempt was made to silence those who held them and acted on them. A feature of liberation is the assertion of values in the present, our re-discovery of these values in the past, and bringing to light the stories of those who held, guarded, and nurtured them.

While 'bigotry and cruelty' form much of South Africa's history, he says, 'tolerance and understanding pursued with bravery' is part of it, too.

So, Guy urges,

I want to emphasise not only the role of the past in creating the present, but also our role as historians, researchers, and educators in creating a past of value for the present. We create our yesterdays, and we do this according to the values we hold today.

All these elements raise important questions about writing histories, creating records that claim to be 'the truth', 'our history'.

———— ❖ ————

The much-admired historian CW de Kiewiet cautions, in his 1940 *History of South Africa Social and Economic*, that the writing of history 'is always a process of simplification' and that '[t]he temptation which any historian must learn to resist is the desire to write two volumes instead of one'.

History is a bit like a movie script. A lot is left out because it seems unnecessary, the kind of extraneous detail that would only confuse the audience. Selected detail is often enough to contain and convey the plot, and describe the characters and what they did. But whose selection? And whose idea of the plot or the main characters? There is always a reason for selecting.

In the preface to his 1984 biography of Sol Plaatje, Brian Willan notes that in the decades after this remarkable South African's death, most people

were not even aware of his name, a failure that

> stems ... from South Africa's capacity to obscure
> and distort its own past, to neglect the lives of
> those whose ideals and aspirations have been in
> conflict with official orthodoxies, past and
> present.

Putting it another way, he went on, '[t]he South African historical memory ... has been highly selective in its recall'.

Such need-to-know history was satirised by Denis Hirson in his autobiography, *The House Next Door* (1986). Mimicking the shallow, rapid-fire style of much school-history teaching in the old days, he briskly summed up the Great Trek and the making of modern (white) South Africa in this way:

> When it is all over the rivers run red with blood
> and the Voortrekkers who are slowly becoming
> Boers, pick assegais out of their wagons. They
> make pledges and vows and covenants. Their
> leaders give their names to mountains and cities
> and swimming pools.

Selective recall is both the function and the weakness of history writing. In the preceding pages of this book there will be absences, untold stories, unacknowledged individuals, gaps. Perhaps the story itself, the way it has been told, will seem at times deceiving, 'untrue' even, or a story that within another five, 10 or 15 years will have to be rewritten to reflect a 'truth' of how things really were.

There might be new evidence. Unpublished letters, the discovery of documents long thought to have been lost, a video clip, an admission, a tape recording, a photograph – any of these could contradict the accepted version of an incident or a decision that changed South Africa's history.

By the same token, the given 'facts' – the data that are available to us today – are deceptive. Facts are not truths, and the more one examines any isolated 'fact' of history, the less certain one can be about the 'truth' it conveys.

This book is crammed with such 'facts', and will seem often enough to offer them as being truth. Even if the basic data are established, they are open to interpretation, or reinterpretation, to new ways of seeing. So it is clear the record is neither fixed nor beyond question.

'It is not necessary,' historian SB Spies once said,

> to choose a novel topic to present original ideas
> about the past. There is no topic in South African
> history that has been so thoroughly 'done' that
> there is nothing new to say about it.

So the curiosity of the unconvinced will continue to ensure that the inevitable simplification and the selective recall are tested, revisited, revised.

From this, at best, emerges the truer complexity of the past, the complicatedness that we know is as true of our own lives. It is the quality that historian Charles van Onselen described when he said of his expansive study of the life of black peasant share-cropper Kas Maine – *The Seed is Mine, The Life of Kas Maine, a South African Sharecropper 1894-1985* (1986) – and his decades-long dealings with white farmers:

> I want to convey that not everyone here is an
> oppressor or victim, that there's a whole middle
> terrain ... where our interactions are a lot more
> complicated, and our loves run a lot deeper than
> people think, as do our hates. ...

This is true of us, and true of our ancestors.

——— ❖ ———

Today, other aspects of history, of selecting, that were perhaps less obvious and less popular when racial and political conflict was the dominant and demanding 'story', have come to the fore.

History may sometimes be mistaken as a sequence of wars and peace treaties, of dates that fix people's lives in cycles of victories and defeats, of avoidable losses or unscrupulous gains. Such history overlooks the infinite detail of human lives, the family life, the leisure, the private goals, the setbacks and successes of ordinary people.

Yet if anything forms the past, it is the sum of these small things. 'It is the presence of the essential thing in a very small detail,' the Indian film-maker and writer Satyajit Ray once remarked, 'which one must catch in order to expose larger things.'

Today there is scope for new kinds of history-making, the histories of families, of sport or music, of banking or commerce or architecture, which are not, in fact, distinguishable from the 'national' history.

In the same way, events of the most recent past which will seem, on the face of it, the most obvious factors in shaping the next few decades might include the unbanning of the liberation movements, the freeing of Nelson Mandela, the advent of democracy in 1994, the new Constitution of 1996, the TRC, the shift to the Growth, Employment and Redistribution (GEAR) economic policy, the launching of the New Partnership for African Development (Nepad), and shifts in national policy on HIV/Aids.

But will this list account for the lives of individuals and their role in living the larger story, in bringing the big events into being?

Looking back over the longer narrative of southern Africa, perhaps the most testing discovery to be made is that there is a common humanity that binds us all to the conditions of living, the hardships, temptations, joys, weaknesses, achievements, mistakes, triumphs, certainties, fears. Reduced to an outline, South African history could be seen as the story of a developing convergence of interests that, by a succession of conflicts, created its own moment of crisis and resolution.

But how did it happen? Did South Africans suddenly change in 1990 or 1994?

Were there certain types of people – races or language groups or classes – who were naturally, by birth or inclination, exploiters or victims, inferior or superior, for decades, and who then miraculously changed?

Or are they still the same, living in a setting that obscures their truer natures? And how, then, did the setting change?

To ask these questions is to realise that there cannot be a convincing or authentic attempt at answering them without examining where we have come from and how we have made our way.

Among the pitfalls is to assume that we are better, or at least know better, than our forebears.

Educationist Jacqueline Dean of Leeds Metropolitan University in England told a history teaching conference in Cape Town in 2002 that

we will not help children to develop … a respect for diversity, and tolerance for others' attitudes and beliefs if they are not encouraged to under-stand and respect societies different in time as well as place.

She added:

To some extent we are all guilty of believing that our knowledge, values and civilisation are superior to those of earlier times. Such beliefs can be based on naïve and unexamined views of progress.

This is perhaps a special challenge in a country with a recent past of such deep shame and anger.

Historian Philip Bonner has argued that it is through individual experiences, decisions and reactions to moral dilemmas that a fuller understanding of apartheid can be reached, and an understanding of 'how so many people, both black and white, simply stood on the sidelines when apartheid was at its height, neither actively supporting nor opposing it'. Many were living in an atmosphere of 'disempowerment and helplessness … which so few people can comprehend now'.

It is no doubt true that 'law-abiding' – and not just white – South Africans did not need to know about the fate of Sizwe Kondile near the Mozambique border in the winter of 1981 to know in their hearts that something was very wrong in their society. Fear, uncertainty, self-interest – these are among the things that undoubtedly dissuade individuals from acting for the greater good, even when they can see quite clearly the negative consequences for others of not acting.

But if it's true that many white and black South Africans didn't do anything, or much, or enough, to right the wrongs, it is also true that, as they muddled along doing the best they could to survive or to succeed, many occupied that 'whole middle terrain', as Van Onselen saw it, where not everybody was 'an oppressor or victim'.

———— ❖ ————

Van Onselen writes in the introduction to his life of sharecropper Kas Maine:

Currents of anger, betrayal, hatred and humiliation surge through many accounts of modern South Africa's race relations, but what analysts sometimes fail to understand is that without prior compassion, dignity, love or a feeling of trust – no matter how small, poorly, or unevenly developed – there could have been no anger, betrayal, hatred or humiliation. The troubled relationship between black and white South Africans cannot be fully understood by focusing on what tore them apart and ignoring what held them together. The history of a marriage, even an unhappy one, is inscribed in the wedding banns as well as the divorce notice.

From *The Seed Is Mine, The Life of Kas Maine, a South African Sharecropper 1894–1985* (1986) by Charles van Onselen

———— ————

The real puzzle of our history probably lies in its apparent ordinariness, in the seemingly habitual, familiar ways of doing things.

It is not hard to recognise in the historical record, and in ourselves, just how habit and familiarity seem to make it 'permissible' to take the line of least resistance, to go with the flow, to join in with what everybody else is doing, to stick with what's convenient or ordinary. It's usually safer.

Yet limiting the past to humdrum, routine behaviour risks overlooking the gathering force of ideals, the foresight and sacrifices of individuals who were committed to them. These are often people whose reckless selflessness at one moment in their lives is later applauded as visionary wisdom, wisdom that everybody comes round to accepting eventually.

The most striking example is Nelson Mandela. He was jailed for life in 1964 for recommending what became the outwardly unremarkable reality of South Africa 30 years later in 1994.

There were many like him, people who believed – as William Schreiner had argued in 1909 – that the constitutional denial of human rights was 'a grave injustice'.

In the social and political spaces between the William Schreiners and the Nelson Mandelas, the John Philips, Lilian Ngoyis and Robert Sobukwes, lived the individuals who shaped the society of their time.

And it is recognising the unbreakable link between then and now – them and us – that is the key to that grand-sounding but difficult goal, the 'triumph of memory over forgetting'. It ought to be difficult, even unsettling.

———— ❖ ————

In the second half of the 19th century, German socialist and philosopher Friedrich Engels discussed the role of the individual in history in a letter to his long-time friend and socialist collaborator Karl Marx. 'History,' Engels wrote, 'makes itself in such a way that the final result always arises from conflicts between many individual wills, of which each again has been made what it is by a host of particular conditions of life. … What each individual wills is obstructed by everyone else, and what emerges is something that no one willed. … Yet each contributes to the result and is to that degree involved in it.'

One could pick a sample of 'South African' figures and assign each a role in shaping the past, present and future. The list might include Krotoa, Sheik Jusuf, Simon van der Stel, the map-maker John Barrow, Sarhili, Piet Retief, Nongqawuse, Shaka, Sir George Grey, Moshweshwe, Damon the cook, Cecil Rhodes, General Christiaan de Wet, Jan Smuts, Charlotte Maxeke, John Tengo Jabavu, Abdullah Abdurahman, Sol Plaatje, DF Malan, Albert Luthuli, HF Verwoerd, Steve Biko, Harry Oppenheimer, Archbishop Desmond Tutu, FW de Klerk, Cyril Ramaphosa, Nelson Mandela, Thabo Mbeki.

Each can be matched to events that have 'made history'. Or one could say they created the events that made history. Or did the history make them?

It might almost be comforting to think that there is a force of history – a power in successive events – that shapes our fate. It would make it possible to believe that there wasn't much that anyone could have done to change the course of events in 1659, 1856, 1899, 1910, 1948, 1964, 1976 or 1994.

But to say the past was ultimately beyond the willing of individuals, of the chiefs or thinkers or politicians of their time, of their parties, movements or clans, of ordinary people themselves, is also to say we are powerless today to influence, by our choices, what tomorrow could be.

And so, looking ahead, collectively as much as privately, we are drawn to what happened in the last decade, the last century, the last millennium. It is part and parcel of what it is to be human, to be conscious, to remember and, ultimately, to be hopeful.

History needs mobility and the ability to explore a large territory, that is the ability to move imaginatively beyond one's roots. True, the past remains another country. But its borders can be crossed by travellers.

From *Interesting Times* (2002) by Eric Hobsbawm

———— ❖ ————

There is an entirely unimaginable, and unthinkable, quality to the night-long fire that burned Sizwe Kondile to ash in 1981, as much as to the lives and thoughts of the policemen who perpetrated the atrocity. These seem to belong to another country – that *other* country – yet they are features of the historical landscape South Africans still occupy. To overlook them is to remain in the shadowed world of forgetting. Remembering them is an act of optimism, a letting in of light.

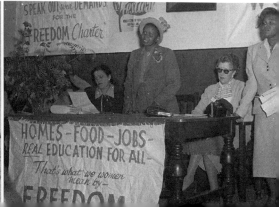

[readings]

Eric Hobsbawm's notion, at the close of the endpiece, that while 'the past remains another country ... its borders can be crossed by travellers ...' is a reminder of the scope for scholarly but also for imaginative exploration. This reading list is less a bibliography of the writings compassed in *Every Step of the Way* than a mapping of some routes and destinations in the historical landscape.

Many excellent histories – general histories of the region, and works on more narrowly focused topics and events – are available to the serious-minded explorer of the past who cannot travel without them, or without consulting the comprehensive bibliographies they contain. Of these, the following are among the references that were indispensable in making this book:

Beinart, William. *Twentieth-Century South Africa* (Second edition, Oxford University Press, 2001)

De Kiewiet, CW. *A History of South Africa Social and Economic* (Oxford University Press, 1941)

Ross, Robert. *A Concise History of South Africa* (Cambridge University Press, 1999)

Saunders, Christopher (consultant editor). *Reader's Digest Illustrated History of South Africa, The Real Story* (Third edition, Reader's Digest Association, 1994)

Saunders, Christopher. *Historical Dictionary of South Africa* (Second edition, Rowman & Littlefield, 1983)

Worden, Nigel. *The Making of Modern South Africa: Conquest, Segregation and Apartheid* (Juta & Co/Blackwell Publishers, 1994)

Other general surveys include:

Davenport, R. *South Africa: a modern history* (Fourth edition, Macmillan, 1991)

Shillington, K. *History of Southern Africa* (Longman, 1987)

Thompson, L. *A history of South Africa* (Yale University Press/Random Century, 1990)

Beyond these, writings that are engaging, revealing, provocative and sometimes even obscure – from archaeology, history and biography to reportage, fiction, poetry and even comics – form a significant record or impression of South African pasts. The following reading list is a sampling of this wider range of sources and narratives, grouped more or less chronologically.

Chapters One to Five

Axelson, Eric. *Vasco Da Gama, The Diary of his Travels through African Waters 1497-1499* (Stephan Phillips, 1998)

Bleek, WHI & Lloyd, LC. *Specimens of Bushman Folklore* (George Allen, 1911)

Burchell, William John. *Travels in the interior of Southern Africa* (Facsimile edition, C Struik, 1967)

Deacon, HJ & Deacon, Janette. *Human Beginnings in South Africa – Uncovering the Secrets of the Stone Age* (David Philip Publishers, 1999)

Huffman, Thomas. *Snakes and Crocodiles: Power and Symbolism in Ancient Zimbabwe* (Witwatersrand University Press, 1996)

Kirby, Percival. *A Source Book on the Wreck of the Grosvenor* (Van Riebeeck Society, 1953)

Kunene, Mazisi. *Emperor Shaka the Great: A Zulu Epic* (Heinemann, 1979)

Lenta, Margaret & Le Cordeur, Basil (eds). *The Cape Diaries of Lady Anne Barnard 1799-1800, Volumes 1 & 2* (Van Riebeeck Society, 1999)

Lewis-Williams, David & Dowson, Thomas. *Images of Power, Understanding Bushman Rock Art* (Southern Book Publishers, 1989)

Maclennan, Ben. *the wind makes dust* (Tafelberg, 2003)

Maggs, TMO'C. *Iron Age Communities of the Southern Highveld* (Natal Museum, 1976)

Mitchell, Peter. *The Archaeology of Southern Africa* (Cambridge University Press, 2002)

Mostert, Noel. *Frontiers* (Knopf, 1992)

Muller, CFJ. *A Pictorial History of the Great Trek, Visual documents illustrating the Great Trek* (Tafelberg, 1978)

Penn, Nigel. *Rogues, Rebels and Runaways, Eighteenth-Century Cape Characters* (David Philip Publishers, 1999)

Press, Karen. *Krotoa* (Centaur Publications, 1990)

Raven-Hart, R. *Before Van Riebeeck* (Struik, 1967)

Thom, HB. *Journal of Jan van Riebeeck Volumes I-III* (Van Riebeeck Society, 1952)

Wannenburgh, Alf. *Forgotten Frontiersmen* (Howard Timmins, 1978)

Worden, Nigel, with Versfeld, Ruth, Dyer, Dorothy, and Bickford-Smith, Claudia (eds). *The Chains That Bind Us, A history of slavery at the Cape* (Juta & Company, 1996)

Chapters Six to Eight

Churchill, Winston. *My Early Life* (T Butterworth, 1930)

Kruger, Rayne. *Goodbye, Dolly Grey* (Cassell, 1959)

Marks, Shula & Rathbone, Richard (eds). *Industrialisation and Social Change in South Africa* (Longman, 1982)

Nasson, Bill. *Abraham Esau's War, A Black South African War in the Cape, 1899-1902* (Second edition, Cambridge University Press, 2002)

Odendaal, André. *Vukani Bantu! The Beginnings of Black Protest Politics in South Africa to 1912* (David Philip Publishers, 1984)

Pakenham, Thomas. *The Boer War* (Weidenfeld & Nicolson, 1979)

Plaatje, Sol. *Native Life in South Africa* (Ravan Press, 1982)

Pretorius, Fransjohan. *Life on Commando during the Anglo-Boer War 1899-1902* (Human & Rousseau, 1999)

Raal, Sarah. *The Lady Who Fought, A young woman's account of the Anglo-Boer War* (First edition in English, Stormberg Publishers, 2000)

Reitz, Deneys. *Commando* (Second edition, Faber and Faber, 1931)

Roberts, Brian. *Kimberley: Turbulent City* (David Philip and Historical Society of Kimberley and the Northern Cape, 1976)

Schreiner, Olive. *The Story of an African Farm* (Ad Donker, 1975)

Schreiner, Olive. *Thoughts on South Africa* (Ad Donker, 1992)

Spies, SB. *Methods of Barbarism?* (Second edition, Jonathan Ball Publishers, 2001)

Trollope, Anthony. *South Africa* (Abridged edition, Longmans, 1938)

Van Reenen, Rykie. *Emily Hobhouse – Boer War Letters* (Second edition, Human & Rousseau, 1999)

Chapters Nine and Ten

Andrew, Rick. *Buried in the Sky* (Penguin Books, 2001)

Biko, Steve. *I write what I like* (Heinemann, 1978)

Brink, André. *Rumours of Rain* (Second edition, Mandarin Paperbacks, 1994)

Brink, Elsabé, Malungane, Gandhi, Lebelo, Steve, Ntshangase, Dumisani, & Krige, Sue (eds). *Recollected 25 years later: Soweto 16 June 1976* (Kwela Books, 2001)

Callinicos, Luli. *The world that made Mandela, A Heritage Trail, 70 sites of significance* (STE Publishers, 2000)

Coetzee, JM. *Waiting for the Barbarians* (Martin Secker & Warburg, 1980)

Gray, Stephen. *A World of Their Own, Southern African Poets of the Seventies* (Ad Donker, 1976)

Keppel-Jones, Arthur. *When Smuts Goes* (Second edition, Shuter & Shooter, 1950)

Daniels, Eddie. *There and Back, Robben Island 1964-1979* (Third edition, Eddie Daniels, 2002)

D'Oliviera, John. *Vorster – The Man* (Ernest Stanton Publishers, 1977)

Gordimer, Nadine & Goldblatt, David. *Lifetimes Under Apartheid* (Alfred A Knopf, 1986)

Huddleston, Trevor. *Naught For Your Comfort* (Collins, 1956)

Jenkin, Tim. *Inside Out, Escape from Pretoria Prison* (Second edition, Jacana, 2003)

Johnson, Jill. (ed) *South Africa Speaks* (Ad Donker, 1981)

Kuzwayo, Ellen. *Call Me Woman* (Ravan Press, 1985)

Lelyveld, Joseph. *Move Your Shadow, South Africa, Black and White* (Second edition, Sphere Books, 1987)

Lewin, Hugh. *Bandiet Out of Jail* (Random House, 2002)

Lewsen, Phyllis. (ed). *Helen Suzman's Solo Years* (Jonathan Ball/Ad Donker Publishers, 1991)

Maclennan, Ben. *Apartheid, The Lighter Side* (Chameleon Press, 1990)

Maharaj, Mac (ed). *Reflections in Prison* (Zebra/Robben Island Museum, 2001)

Meredith, Martin. *Fischer's Choice, A life of Bram Fischer* (Jonathan Ball Publishers, 2002)

Modisane, Bloke. *Blame me on History* (Ad Donker, 1986)

Moloi, Godfrey. *My Life, Volume One* (Ravan Press, 1987)

Mutloatse, Mothobi (comp). *Reconstruction, 90 years of black historical literature* (Ravan Press, 1981)

Ntantala, Phyllis. *A Life's Mosaic, The Autobiography of Phyllis Ntantala* (David Philip Publishers, 1992)

Paton, Alan. *Cry, The Beloved Country* (Jonathan Cape, 1948)

Rive, Richard. *'Buckingham Palace', District Six* (David Philip Publishers, 1986)

Royston, Robert. *To Whom It May Concern, An Anthology of Black South African Poetry* (Ad Donker, 1973)

Schadeberg, Jürgen. *voices from ROBBEN ISLAND* (Ravan Press, 1994)

Small, Adam. *Kanna hy kô hystoe, 'n drama* (Second edition, Tafelberg, 1980)

Suttner, Raymond. *Inside Apartheid's Prison* (Ocean Press/University of Natal Press, 2001)

Themba, Can. *The Will to Die* (Heinemann's African Writers Series, 1972)

Van Onselen, Charles. *The Seed is Mine, The Life of Kas Maine, A South African Sharecropper 1894-1985* (David Philip Publishers, 1986)

Van Woerden, Henk. *A Mouthful of Glass* (Second edition, Jonathan Ball Publishers, 2000)

Van Zyl Slabbert, Frederik. *The Last White Parliament* (Second edition, Sidgwick & Jackson, 1985)

Wilson, Monica (ed). *Freedom for My People, The Autobiography of ZK Matthews, Southern Africa 1901-1968* (Rowman & Littlefield, 1982)

Chapters Eleven and Twelve

Bernstein, Hilda. *The Rift, The Exile Experience of South Africans* (Jonathan Cape, 1994)

Coetzee, JM. *Life and Times of Michael K* (Second edition, Penguin Books, 1985)

De Klerk, FW. *The Last Trek – A New Beginning* (Macmillan, 1998)

Evans, Gavin. *Dancing Shoes is Dead, A tale of fighting men in South Africa* (Doubleday, 2002)

Hope, Christopher. *White Boy Running* (Martin, Secker & Warburg, 1988)

Gilbey, Emma. *The Lady, The Life and Times of Winnie Mandela* (Second edition, Vintage, 1994)

Gordimer, Nadine. *Something Out There* (Second edition, Penguin Books, 1985)

Johnson, Shaun. *Strange Days Indeed, Tales from the old, and the nearly new South Africa* (Bantam Press, 1993)

Lapping, Brian. *Apartheid, A History* (Grafton Books, 1986)

Mandela, Nelson. *Long Walk to Freedom* (Macdonald Purnell, 1994)

Marinovich, Greg & Silva, Joao. *The Bang-Bang Club* (Second edition, Arrow Books, 2001)

Mogoba, Mmutlanyane Stanley. *Stone, Steel, Sjambok* (Zwiningweni Communications, 2003)

Mphahlele, Letlapa. *Child of this Soil, My life as a freedom fighter* (Kwela Books, 2002)

Ramphele, Mamphela. *A Life* (Second edition, David Philip Publishers, 1996)

Oliphant, Andries & Vladislavić, Ivan. *Ten Years of Staffrider 1978-1988* (Ravan Press, 1988)

Chapters Thirteen to Fifteen

Bizzell, John. *Blueprints in Black and White, The Built Environment Professions in South Africa – an Outline History* (Solo Collective, 2002)

Boraine, Alex. *A Country Unmasked, Inside South Africa's Truth and Reconciliation Commission* (Oxford University Press, 2000)

Brink, André (comp). *South Africa 27 April 1994, an authors' diary* (Queillerie, 1994)

Dangor, Achmat. *Bitter Fruit* (Kwela Books, 2001)

Edelstein, Jillian. *Truth and Lies* (Second edition, M&G Books, 2001)

Gevisser, Mark. *Portraits of Power, Profiles in a Changing South Africa* (David Philip Publishers, 1996)

Gobodo-Madikizela, Pumla. *A Human Being Died That Night, A Story of Forgiveness* (David Philip Publishers, 2003)

Gordimer, Nadine. *The House Gun* (David Philip Publishers, 1998)

Hadland, Adrian & Rantao, Jovial. *The Life and Times of Thabo Mbeki* (New Holland/Struik, 2000)

Kannemeyer, A & Botes, C. *Bitterkomix*, No 4 (Bitterkomix, November 1994)

Krog, Antjie. *Country of My Skull* (Second edition, Random House, 2002)

Mbeki, Thabo. *Africa, Define Yourself* (Tafelberg/Mafube, 2002)

Ramphele, Mamphela. *Steering by the Stars, Being young in South Africa* (Tafelberg Publishers, 2002)

Nicol, Mike. *The Waiting Country, A South African Witness* (Victor Golancz, 1995)

Sparks, Allister. *Beyond the Miracle, Inside the New South Africa* (Jonathan Ball Publishers, 2003)

Steinberg, Jonny. *Midlands* (Jonathan Ball Publishers, 2002)

Endpiece

Jenkins, Keith. *Re-Thinking History* (Routledge, 1991)

Orwell, George. *1984* (Martin, Secker & Warburg, 1949)

Smith, K. *The changing past: trends in South African historical writing* (Southern Book Publishers, 1988)

[picture credits]

Associated Press/Greg English: page 247
Associated Press/Obed Zwila: page 299
Associated Press/*The World*/Sam Nzima: page 201
BAHA: pages 160, 167, 168, 170, 171, 172, 175, 181, 190, 210, 211
Cape Archives: pages 34, E4487; 35, M15; 48, E3301; 58 and 69, M3/333; 77, AG5812; 78, AG9789; 79, M928; 80, AC7380 and AC7380; 81, AC9917; 95 and 110, AG1433, 114 and 115, AG651; 117, AG6755; 119, E5276; 122–3, AC2191; 125, AG3034; 126, AG2214; 128, AG2192; 129, AG2285; 129 AG2235; 130, AG2243; 131, AG2517; 135, AG10483; 137, AG667; 141 AG7399; 142, J2265; 144, J6755; 144 and 146, AG7399
Cape Photo Library: Jeremy Jowell, prologue; Graeme Robinson, pages 120, 296; Alain Proust page 312
De Beers Consolidated Mines: page 116
Die Burger/Media 24: pages 156, 197, 220, 225, 234
Gideon Mendel/Corbis: pages 9, 24
Herman de Villiers: page 14
iAfrika Photos/Anna Zieminski: pages 300, 315
iAfrika Photos/Ellen Elmendorp: page 298
iAfrika Photos/Eric Miller: prologue, pages 228, 260, 276
iAfrika Photos/Per-Anders Pettersson: pages 228, 246, 301, 309, 319
iAfrika Photos/Rob White: page 289
iAfrika Photos/Rodger Bosch: pages 248, 254, 270
iAfrika Photos/Shaun Harris: pages 261, 279, 285
iAfrika Photos/Zaeem Adams: page 307
Independent Newspapers/*Argus*: pages 302, 303, 304, 314
Independent Newspapers/*The Star*: pages 203, 215
INPRA: prologue, pages 16, 22, 30, 74, 119, 130
Kimberley Museum: page 108
Local History Museum, Durban: page 65
Mayibuye Archives: prologue, pages 145, 163, 174, 175, 177, 182, 206, 211, 226, 228, 230, 232, 236, 295
Mapungubwe Museum/University of Pretoria: page 20
McGregor Museum: page 28
MuseumAfrika: page 203
National Library: pages 9, 19, 29, 31, 36, 42, 43, 44, 45, 46, 48, 49, 51, 54, 59, 60, 61, 67, 72, 76, 82, 83, 84, 85, 86, 87, 89, 91, 93, 94, 96, 97, 98, 99, 101, 102, 104, 112, 113, 114, 116, 117, 118, 125, 127, 132, 133, 137, 143, 144, 145, 148, 150, 151, 152, 153, 155, 157, 161, 162, 166, 175, 177, 178, 180, 181, 186, 189, 192, 213, 214
PictureNET Africa/Adil Bradlow: pages 286, 288, 292
PictureNET Africa/Benny Gool: pages 243
PictureNET Africa/Carin Matz: page 190
PictureNET Africa/Dennis Farrell: page 269
PictureNET Africa/Greg Marinovich: page 315
PictureNET Africa/João Silva: prologue
PictureNET Africa/Henner Frankenfeld: pages 121, 265, 266, 290, 315
PictureNET Africa/Don Boroughs: page 190
PictureNET Africa/Niel van Niekerk: page 22
PictureNET Africa/Nadine Hutton: pages 238, 287
PictureNET Africa/Paul Velasco: pages 121, 253, 271
PictureNET Africa/Petra Dammrose: page 38
PictureNET Africa/Sasa Kralj: pages 313, 315
PictureNET Africa/Shaun Harris: page 315
PictureNET Africa/Suzy Bernstein: prologue, page 268
PictureNET Africa/*Sunday Times*: pages 247, 261
Rapport: page 203
South Photographs: prologue, page 216
The Big Issue/James Garner: page 208
Times Media/*Sunday Times*: pages 194, 197
Touchline Photographs: page 270
Trace Images/Adil Bradlow: pages 256, 268
Trace Images/Benny Gool: pages 223, 246
Trace Images/Independent Newspapers: pages 221, 259
Trace Images/Louise Gubb: pages 239, 252, 256, 264, 270, 274, 315
Trace Images/Obed Zilwa: page 218
Trace Images/*Cape Argus*: pages 222, 240, 302, 303, 304, 314, 315
Transvaal Archives: pages 13, 134
University of Cape Town: pages 11, 85

In some instances, the publishers have been unable to trace copyright holders, but we will make appropriate arrangements at the first opportunity.

[index]

J

Jabavu, John Tengo 137, *137*, 143, 144, 147
Jacobs, Katie 82–83, *82*
Jameson, Leander Starr 124, 126
Jameson Raid 125–127, *126*
Java 39, 42, 54
Jordan, Pallo 238
Joseph, Helen *173*, 174, 210, *210*
Jusuf, Sheik 54, *54*, 67

K

Kaapmans *see* Goringhaiqua
//Kabbo 10–11, 28
Kadalie, Clements 152, *153*
Kasrils, Nathan 139
Kathrada, Ahmed 174, 181, 233, 239, 240
Kat River Settlement 104–105, 105
Kaunda, Kenneth 196, 197, *197*, 246
Keane, Susan 264, *264*
Khami 36
Khan, Mishka 303, *303*
Khoekhoe people *31*, *43*, 77
    recognition of heritage 304, *304*
    relationship with Dutch settlers 41–46, *42*, *43*, *45*
    views of early Dutch explorers 39–41, *40*
Kimberley 24, 25, 110–111, *112*, 113–116, 120
Kok, Adam 102–103, *102*
Kolben, Peter 40–41
Kondile, Sizwe 2, 7, 289, 321
Krotoa 42, 62–64, *62*
Kruger, JT 200, 206
Kruger, Paul 116, 118, 125, *125*, 127, 143
Kuzwayo, Ellen *211*, 212
Kwaaihoek 35

L

labour force 113, 114–115, *114–115*, 118–120, 212–213
Land Act (1913) 150–151, 255
language development 18
Lembede, Anton 154, *154*, 166
Lesotho *see* Basutoland
Le Vaillant, Francois 75
Liberal Party 177
Lichtenstein, Martin Karl Heinrich 75
Linda, Solomon 305
Lloyd, Lucy 10, 11, 23, 26, 83–84, *84*, 85, 88
London Missionary Society 68, 76, 77
Luthuli, Albert 6, 166, *166*, 167, 173, 174, 180, 193, 277

M

Macozoma, Saki 164
Madaka, Topsy 288
Madikizela-Mandela, Winnie *see* Mandela, Winnie
Majuba, battle of 125
Makanya, Nimrod 149
Makeba, Miriam 169

Malan, DF 152, 154, *155*, 164
    1948 elections 155, 158, *158*
Malan, Magnus *216*, 255
Mandela, Nelson 4, 8, 121, 136, *155*, *159*, *261*
    1948 elections 158
    1994 elections and inauguration 267, 269–270, *269*, *270*
    ANC Youth League 154, 166
    arrest (1962) 180
    on black consciousness 196
    Botha's offer *226*, 227, 229
    dialogue 233, 238–239
    meeting with Betsie Verwoerd 185, *185*, 272
    meeting with FW de Klerk 241
    meeting with PW Botha 240
    personality and stature 271
    release 244–249, *246*, *247*, *249*
    Rivonia Trial 181–182, *182*
    Robben Island 181–183
    Treason Trial 174
    underground 179–180
Mandela, Winnie 7, 236, 286
Mangena, Alfred 147
Manika of Bengal 52
Manuel, Trevor *278*, 279, 280
manumission 52
Mapote 21
Mapungubwe 20, 21, 36, 308
Maritz, Gerhardus 133
Marks, Sammy 120
Masekela, Hugh 169
Maseko, Job 6
Masemola, Jeff 240
Mass Democratic Movement 240
Masters and Servants Ordinance (1841) 56
Matthews, ZK 115, 166, 172–173, 174
Maxeke, Charlotte 145, *145*, 152
Mbeki, Govan 181
Mbeki, Moeletsi 308, *309*
Mbeki, Thabo 8, 87, 281, 286–287, *299*, *300*
    vision for future 299, 300–301
Mbulu, Letta 169
Meadowlands 169
Merriman, John X 110, 124, 145, 148
Meyer, Roelf 257–258, 261, 274, *274*
Mfecane 90, 92, 93
Mhlaba, Raymond 181, 233, 240
Milner, Sir Alfred *125*, 127, 136, 143
Mines and Works Act (1911) 148
Mines and Works Amendment Act (1926) 152
mining 20, 21, 109
    see also diamond mining; gold mining
Mining Charter 121
missionaries 67–68, 76–77
    see also Campbell, John; Philip, John; Read, James;
Vanderkemp, Johannes Theodorus